GENDER RECKONINGS

Gender Reckonings

New Social Theory and Research

Edited by
James W. Messerschmidt,
Patricia Yancey Martin,
Michael A. Messner, *and*
Raewyn Connell

NEW YORK UNIVERSITY PRESS
New York

NEW YORK UNIVERSITY PRESS
New York
www.nyupress.org

References to Internet websites (URLs) were accurate at the time of writing. Neither the author nor New York University Press is responsible for URLs that may have expired or changed since the manuscript was prepared.

ISBN: 978-1-4798-9714-8 (hardback)
ISBN: 978-1-4798-0934-9 (paperback)

For Library of Congress Cataloging-in-Publication data, please contact the Library of Congress.

New York University Press books are printed on acid-free paper, and their binding materials are chosen for strength and durability. We strive to use environmentally responsible suppliers and materials to the greatest extent possible in publishing our books.

Manufactured in the United States of America

10 9 8 7 6 5 4 3 2 1

Also available as an ebook

CONTENTS

ACKNOWLEDGMENTS

An edited volume such as this necessarily invites much appreciation and gratitude. First and foremost, we thank the contributors to this volume. They have all come together to both collectively celebrate the 30th anniversary of the publication of *Gender and Power*, and to offer insightful new social theory and research. We salute their wisdom and vision—this book would never have been written without them. Second, colleagues were kind enough to provide formal reviews of the entire manuscript and to impart valuable criticisms and recommend important changes. Their advice and guidance have certainly transformed this book into a higher quality publication than it otherwise would have been. Third, we wish to extend our appreciation to the entire staff at New York University Press, but especially to Ilene Kalish (Executive Editor), who was graciously and wholeheartedly supportive of this work from its inception, and to Caelyn Cobb (assistant editor), Dorothea Stillman Halliday (managing editor), and John Raymond (copy editor). Fourth, we are grateful to Madeleine Pape for her excellent preparation of the index. Finally, we extend warm hugs to each other. We have been treasured colleagues and valued friends for many years. Working on this volume together has been a stimulating, lovely, heartfelt, and collaboratively intellectual relationship from beginning to end.

Introduction

THE EDITORS

This book is about why gender matters, how gender relations work, and where the gender order is headed. We think the time has arrived for a fresh look at these questions, and a critical rethinking of current theory. The book is a celebration of history, a window on the present, and, we hope, an inspiration going forward.

The chapters of this book are written by social scientists. Questions about gender concern our bodies, but not bodies alone; identities, but not identities in a vacuum; and relationships, but not just face-to-face relationships. Powerful social processes are also involved. Corporations, markets, governments, the mass media, and social movements are actors on the gender scene. On a world scale, gender is woven into the history of empire and modernity, into the current neoliberal economy, and into the daily conflicts that make the shocking headlines in our news feed.

Understanding gender, its inequalities and violence, as well as its homeliness and pleasures, therefore requires a social perspective. Contemporary social science has resources for this. But a lot of what passes for social analysis of gender is conceptually weak. Hasty gestures toward "gender norms," "social construction," or "stereotypes" do not explain much. In this book we work with more powerful tools and hope to understand a great deal more. Our emphasis is twofold: celebrating one of the most significant books in the history of gender studies and advancing new social theory and research.

Celebrating *Gender and Power*

The publication of *Gender Reckonings* marks a prominent occasion: the thirtieth anniversary of Raewyn Connell's *Gender and Power: Society, the Person, and Sexual Politics*, which analyzed the social reality of gender with means available in the 1980s, in the immediate aftermath of the emerging women's liberation and gay liberation movements. A great deal has changed since then, and building on Connell's work, *Gender Reckonings* takes up the challenge of social analysis of gender in a new historical context.

As mainstream theory in the global North shifted from the concept of patriarchy to the concept of gender, and from structure to practice, *Gender and Power* found a receptive audience. Published in 1987, this book had its origins in the historical experience of the remote settler-colonial society of Australia, marked by dependence and cultural unease, a continuing indigenous presence, deep-seated race and gender hierarchies, state-centered class politics, and reformist optimism. In this environment Australian feminism became deeply involved in institutional struggles, especially in the labor movement, the school system, and the welfare state. Yet it was also deeply influenced by North American and European thought.

So *Gender and Power*, though it had a local subtext, was framed as an intervention in an international debate. Its first section set out to refute the popular models of gender that had led to an intellectual and political impasse: biological essentialism, sex role theory, and all categorical approaches—such as the theory of patriarchy—where women and men were seen as blocs sitting opposite each other. These models prevented an understanding of social process and historical change.

In their place, *Gender and Power* offered an account of gender as simultaneously social practice and social structure; as linked with, but not determined by, reproductive bodies. In place of single-cause explanations of gender inequality, the book treated gender relations as composed of three substructures—power, production, and cathexis. It tried to map the structure of gender relations in the whole society, the "gender order"; and in specific institutions and milieux, their "gender regimes." Structure and practice are not opposed; they are in a sense transformations of each other through time. *Gender and Power* adapted the existentialist idea of people encountering, and transforming, situations.

Structure was conceptualized as neither static nor fixed, although the label may imply that it is; we think of buildings, tables, and sidewalks as structures. In social life, structure is in continuous flux because practice—or the active constitution of social life—is in play. Gender was thus understood as fundamentally historical, made and remade through historical time. Each of the three substructures had its own tendencies toward crisis and change.

Picking up the concerns of feminist psychology and gay liberation, *Gender and Power* also offered an analysis of femininity and masculinity, which were seen as configurations of social practices in personal life, linked through the structure of gender relations. They too developed through time, as life projects and historical shifts in personality. This part of the argument produced the much-quoted concepts of "hegemonic masculinity" and "emphasized femininity." Much less quoted was the final section of the book, which tried to apply the approach to problems of ideology and political practice. It argued for recomposing gender relations, and multiplying gender patterns, the goal being to democratize rather than abolish gender.

In short, *Gender and Power* attended to how individual and collective practices are shaped, constrained, and enabled by the structures of gender relations and how those structures are changed by those very practices. Such a theoretical perspective allows us to assume that gender structures persist even as we take for granted the premise that they are constantly being altered through individual and collective practices.

Published simultaneously on three continents, *Gender and Power* was part of an internationalization of gender research. Powerful contributions to feminist thought had already come from the postcolonial world, with a strong social component. The International Women's Year in 1975 provided an occasion for official reports from national governments that in some cases (India and Australia among them) took a social view of gender, understood in terms of norms and roles. Activists and scholars from the Arabic-speaking world, from Latin America and Africa, as well as South Asia, made original contributions to understanding gender in colonialism, masculinities, and questions of race and violence, some of them before equivalent scholarship emerged in the global North.

Little of this work was immediately recognized in the North, except in specialized area studies or in development studies. A feminist presence in international aid grew from the 1970s under the rubric of "Women in Development," later reconceptualized as "Gender and Development." By the 1980s and 1990s this feminist presence was producing sophisticated economic analyses and ethnographic studies of rural communities and was reaching into questions of gender and environment in contexts of development.

New Social Theory and Research

There is a strand in activism that is impatient of theory, wanting action above all. Theoretical language, obscure and intimidating, can even be seen as oppressive in itself. The editors of this book take another view. We agree with the Mexican feminist leader Marta Lamas (2011, 128) that "[t]heory is not a luxury: it is a vital need."

Theory at its simplest is a way of crystallizing empirical research and information, summarizing a great many encounters with reality. Theoretical language communicates important experience, revealing what otherwise may remain hidden. It allows us to act in knowledge rather than ignorance.

But theory in the human sciences has more to do than classify and condense. Theory is needed to explain data, to express an understanding of how things work in social life, and how things change. This too is important for action; it allows practice based on reasoning about strategy.

Theory undertakes another vital task: critique. To change the world is not possible if we simply accept the accounts given by the powerful and privileged. We need concepts and methods to analyze and reveal, to unpack the immediately given.

Theory must be related to what we empirically know, but it always goes beyond the given. Theory extrapolates, builds hypotheses, and deploys imagination. It tells us about possibility. Theory allows us to formulate the purposes of action and identify conditions in the world that we seek to bring about. Theory shows us how to move forward.

Such ideas lie behind this book. We think new social theory and research are needed for contemporary gender politics, and we have brought together a group of writers who—using varied styles and conceptual languages—share an intention to make social research work for gender equality and social justice. The chapters in the volume, many of which are pathbreaking, represent a collective effort to encourage social scientists to move forward with theorizing gender, guided by what we have learned over the last 30 years.

And yet, an influential shift in Anglophone gender studies in the last 30 years came from another direction than the perspective outlined in *Gender and Power*: French poststructuralism and its merging with North American debates on sexuality and culture. This perspective gave theoretical form to critiques of the essentialism of mainstream feminism. At the same time the catastrophe of the HIV-AIDS epidemic disrupted the gay-liberation model of sexual community. In the harsher political environment of neoliberal power, struggle shifted increasingly to the terrain of identity and cultural definitions of gender. A performative understanding of gender became immensely influential, first in the United States and then globally.

The critique of heteronormativity became central to queer theory, which expressed the radicalism of many younger activists in the global metropole in the 1990s and 2000s. It gave rise to trans theory, offering a critique of cisgender dominance. A deconstructionist critique of identity proved hard to maintain, however. The main practical effect of this movement was to assert a multiplicity of sexual and gender identities and sometimes an unbounded "fluidity" of gender and sexuality. The acronym LGBT entered policy and media language, standing for plurality, with further initials added from time to time; in the 2000s, ironically, a singular "LGBT community" became the rhetorical subject of many human rights claims. In the academic world, the majority of women's studies programs were renamed as gender studies, adding courses about sexuality, lesbian and gay identities, men and masculinity, and trans issues.

The shift of so much gender scholarship to identity, sexuality, norms, and cultural contestation led attention away from questions of economic exploitation, inequality, domestic violence, and struggles over policy that 1970s feminism had highlighted. As creative as poststructuralist work has been, it has de-emphasized issues such as poverty and livelihood, policymaking, industrial struggle, housing and land, economic transformation, health, and institutional violence.

These latter issues are, however, core business for the social sciences. Research on them has continued and there now exists a formidable body of knowledge, international in scope and using all the techniques of sociological research, about the social realities of gender. This knowledge, embedding a generation's experience of struggles for gender equality, calls for a contemporary social theory of gender.

It is timely, then, to renew the *conceptual* contribution of social science and social activism for the understanding of gender. Our goal is not to reproduce the approach of *Gender and Power*. Rather, we use its anniversary to rethink the contribution of the 1980s and to bring together new theoretical ideas and new empirical work on the social analysis of gender.

* * *

The contributors to this book were invited to reflect on the past and present of feminist social theory; how we might theorize today the issues opened up by feminists in the 1970s and 1980s, especially the idea of gender as social structure. We asked them to consider the issues that have emerged over the last thirty years, and the limits of currently influential frameworks. Above all, we hoped to bring together *new* ideas and *new* theoretical work on the terrain that sociologists tried to map a generation ago—a distinctively *social* analysis of gender. We asked our contributors to give examples and ideas of what the social theory of gender might look like in the future, what audiences it should speak to, and where new thinking may come from.

We believe this book will stimulate new theorizations and analyses of gender. We challenge gender scholars to revisit existing work on gender and pose next-stage questions about the economic, political, cultural, and social dynamics that affect it. Tradition and the continuance of unequal gender relations, in the face of "modernization," are affecting women and men, boys and girls, in ways that we need to understand more. Dynamics related to sexual relations and identities are also changing, particularly as neoliberalism spreads and gains ground.

Gender Reckonings firmly asserts the centrality of the social dimensions of gender, and opens up new pathways for understanding them. Its chapters are written by accomplished social scientists from different continents, generations, and intellectual traditions. The authors are aware of the background sketched in this introduction and they too are trying to lay new foundations.

Thirty Years and Beyond

The sixteen chapters that constitute this book reflect the amazing array of changes that have occurred in gender theory and research in only three decades. Here we briefly review some of these changes and link them to the foci of the chapters that follow.

INTERSECTIONALITY. Of particular importance is the emergence of the concept of *intersectionality*. Since the early 1990s, gender scholars have argued that gender must be linked to other categorical distinctions—such as race/ethnicity, social class, sexuality, age, nation, religion—and not studied as if it "stands alone." Over three decades, social scientists have documented that gender does not exist in a universal form. Rather, gender is continuously shaped in relationship to other distinctions and in turn continuously affects those same—intersecting—distinctions. Intersectionality is a captivating concept whose applications have shown that inequalities are fashioned and orchestrated in complex, inconsistent, continuously changing, and historically varying ways. Chapters in this volume by Ferree, Misra, Viveros Vigoya, and Bridges and Pascoe place particular emphasis on this point.

MASCULINITIES. A second change has been a rapid development of *masculinities* theorizing and research. Taking its contemporary shape in the 1980s, this project changed and expanded rapidly into an international field in the 1990s onward. It was also linked to new forms of social activism. Studies of masculinities today form a significant part of what gender studies means, with scholars recognizing that the lives of women and girls, and especially boys and men, can be understood only if masculinities are examined. Social scientists have had a leading role in documenting the multiplicity of masculinities, their hierarchies, their connections with institutions, their complex histories, and their contemporary and future possibilities for change. Five chapters in this volume focus on this theme, those by Messerschmidt and Messner, Bridges and Pascoe, Ray, Ozyegin, and Ratele. Three of these chapters explore how masculinities (and femininities) are shifting in non-North/nonmetropole contexts.

ORGANIZATIONS AND WORK. Third, we note changes in research and theorizing about gender in relation to *organizations and (paid) work*. As the trend toward economic equality between women and men first progressed and then stalled, researchers tried to understand the reasons for gender hierarchy within organizations and their role in creating inequality—of class and race as well as gender—in the wider society. A rich library of workplace ethnographies, quantitative studies, and theories of gendered organizations now informs feminist thinking about the neoliberal economy and labor markets, science and technology, education, and new industries. Gender in the academy has received substantial attention over the past fifteen years, from the European Commission for the European Union member states and from the National Science Foundation for the United States. Chapters that address these issues include Williams and Neely, Poggio, and Benschop and van den Brink.

GLOBALIZATION/NEOLIBERALISM. A fourth development has been a deepening interest in the *global dimensions* of gender, including the influence of neoliberalism worldwide. During the 1990s, "globalization" became a buzzword in sociology and gender research became increasingly concerned with world-scale dynamics such as migration, economic (and cultural) neoliberalism, and anthropogenic climate change. There was an early tendency in globalization studies to homogenize the world in regard to gender, although postcolonial, decolonial, and Southern perspectives have contested this trend. However, research work from the global South has fostered the circulation of fresh ideas and research about gender. Especially since the 2000s, there has been growing interest internationally in postcolonial approaches that link gender analysis to the violent history of empire and contemporary forms of global power. Chapters in the volume that address such issues include Ray, Ratele, Ozyegin, Williams and Neely, and Poggio.

SEXUALITIES. A fifth development of note is the study of *sexualities* in relation to gender, a field of research that includes questions about heteronormativity, heterosexuality, homosexuality, and monogamy. Sex, gender, and sexuality are all related to the issue of reproduction, and sexual practices too are shaped by intersectional social processes. In the past three decades, gender scholars have studied the diversity of sexual practices, the cultural definitions of sexuality through norms and stereotypes, and the power relations reproduced—and challenged—among sexualities. Gender scholars have teased out the complex connection between gender and sexuality in identities and intimate relationships, in workplaces (including sex work), and in domestic and public violence. The advances in these areas can be seen in the chapters by Schilt, Ray, Jackson, and Schippers.

TRANSGENDER/DEGENDER. Sixth, gender studies has seen an upsurge in research and theory regarding *transgender* questions. The 1990s saw a marked expansion of scholarship about people who live outside the "gender binary" or who expressed their gender in ways contrary to their assigned sex at birth. Social scientists—some of whom are transgender or transsexual—have studied trans experiences in settings such as workplaces, schools, and prisons, and debated the significance of gender transition, or gender refusal, for an understanding of gender relations. Concepts such as "LGBT" and "cisgender," brought into use by social movements, now circulate in social science—though, as authors in this book suggest, these concepts are debatable. The idea of transgender seems to give new relevance to a long-established feminist idea that equality requires degendering society—but is this strategy right? These issues are explored in chapters including those by Schilt; Risman, Myers, and Sin; and Lorber.

We hope this book will speak to a broad audience across the social sciences, and beyond. We hope it will encourage imaginative thinking in new directions, and the exploration of gender relations in all facets of social life. This will only be possible, however, if gender scholars produce conceptual tools that both researchers and activists can use.

REFERENCES
Connell, R. W. 1987. *Gender and Power: Society, the Person and Sexual Politics*. Sydney: Allen and Unwin.
Lamas, Marta. 2011. *Feminism: Transmission and Retransmission*. New York: Palgrave.

PART I

Points of Departure

Gender and Power *and Its Sequels*

The chapters in part I address the structural theory of gender, the well-recognized consequences of structural theory for the study of masculinity, and the theory's unrecognized implications for understanding transsexuality.

Reviewing the historical and geopolitical contexts in which contemporary gender theorizing developed, Myra Marx Ferree notes a shift from an emphasis on gender's relation to social class to an emphasis on gender's relation to national context and global location. Ferree reviews Connell's conceptualization of gender as a social structure and spells out how the 1987 volume prompted others to employ and build upon it. Her assessment draws attention to multiple aspects of differentiation and evaluation, particularly as related to globalization, but more specifically in regard to race/ethnic structures, the influence of social class, and intersectionality. Ferree emphasizes the necessity of using an intersectional perspective to study gender at the local, societal, and global levels. She compares U.S. and German universities on their efforts to improve gender equality and shows how comparable global forces were reshaped by local conditions and thus produced different outcomes. She emphasizes gender as dynamic—involving situation and practice, as historically changing, and as geographically variable.

The chapter by James W. Messerschmidt and Michael A. Messner summarizes Raewyn Connell's well-known and popular framework on hegemonic and nonhegemonic masculinities, as well as the reformulation of the concept of hegemonic masculinity. They show how "new" masculinities can best be conceptualized by building on both Connell's original formulation and the reformulation by Connell and Messerschmidt. They review historical and recent scholarship on masculinities and show how this work expands upon Connell's ideas. In particular, they address confusions about the concept of hegemonic masculinity and contrast it with applications that misrepresent it. Finally, the authors discuss contemporary scholarly developments, including the variety of ways hegemonic masculinity is represented and practiced. They also identify numerous "new" masculinities—for example, dominant, dominating, positive, "female," and hybrid masculinities, among others.

Finally, Kristen Schilt explores issues related to transgender identities. Schilt considers how the term "transsexual" evolved in both life and scholarship, moving from the purview of medicine, biology, and psychiatry to an issue that sociology as a discipline first depicted as a social problem. She maps out Connell's initial work on this topic and contrasts it with predominant perspectives of the time. To show how Connell's approach suggested a "roadmap" for studying transgendered people as subjects in their own right rather than as problematic cultural objects to be explained, she examines the brief passages in the book that speak directly to what was then termed "transsexuality" and links this with Connell's wider approach to gender as practice. Schilt ends by showing how current work in transgender studies concentrates on people's understandings of their gender identities and lived experiences, and rejects the kind of categoricalism that depicts trans people as deviants who fall outside of the "normal" gender order.

1

"Theories Don't Grow on Trees"

Contextualizing Gender Knowledge

MYRA MARX FERREE

Raewyn Connell's *Gender and Power* profoundly influenced my thinking when it appeared in 1987, and I used it regularly in teaching until
the shorter volume, *Gender*, came out in 2002 (and a second edition in
2005).[1] Each book spoke to how gender appeared as a social structure of
practice in the particular moment of its publication, and varied importantly in emphasis as a result. As Connell recently said, although asked
by her publisher to write a second edition of *Gender and Power*, it was
really not possible to do that; *Gender* had to be a different book, coming
as it did in a different historical moment and speaking to different political and intellectual needs.

Each book speaks to the concerns both of their historical emergence
and those of the present moment through their distinctively structural
and historical approach to the now popular concept of intersectionality.
Both *Gender and Power* and *Gender* present gender as a relationship of
power and object of struggle that changes over time, but only indirectly
indicate how the historically shifting set of gender arrangements in the
decade and a half prior to the publication of each shape them. I argue
that Connell's dynamic, political, and historically specific understandings of intersectionality relate to the politics of class and the dynamics
of nationalism in the context of globalization in the period of each book.
To say that material conditions of history influenced Connell's theoretical claims does not disparage the claims' continued relevance, but rather
highlights the shifting terrain of political struggle that feminists face.

I draw my title from Connell's preface to *Gender and Power* (Connell 1987, xi): "theories don't grow on trees; theorizing is itself a social
practice with a politics." Indeed, like all feminist practice, theorizing is

a practical politics of "choice, doubt, strategy, planning, error and trans-formation" (61) that has to be done by situated thinkers, not all of whom are ever called theorists or hold academic positions. Theorizing is also to be understood as a form of embodied action that takes place in par-ticular historical moments; feminist theory is work aimed not only at understanding societies but intervening in them, guided by experience and directing strategic choices with a modesty that acknowledges the doubt and error as well as transformative aspirations. Looking back at past theory and rethinking it in present conditions is an essential ele-ment of the reflexive responsibility of feminist theoretical practice.

Bringing history more centrally into the work of feminist theoriz-ing also locates political struggles in the specific sites and circumstances that make intersectionality more than a merely academic exercise and offer insight into practices that can advance gender justice. I argue that the concept of intersectionality is weakened when it is treated primarily as operating at the meso or micro levels of group and identity forma-tions. Drawing on Connell's macro orientation to gender politics as his-torically grounded and continually contested, I present intersectionality as a matter of macro political dynamics (waves) that generate conflict (turbulence) of different sorts in different locations depending both on the history of the site (sediments) and the directions from which the "waves" come when political interventions happen (stones are thrown) from different positions.[2] I use my own social location as a student of gender politics in the United States and European Union (EU) today to illustrate this approach to intersectional analysis in a historical moment in which neoliberalism often appears as the preeminent challenge.

Locating *Gender and Power* in History

Gender and Power is revolutionary in the sense of being oriented pri-marily to overthrowing dominant paradigms and figures of theoretical authority. Its approach is to challenge the assumption of binary and ahis-torical gender "roles" based on the emergent practices of the feminist movements that had sprung into action in the late 1960s and early 1970s. In its time, the book offered a brilliant critique and reconceptualiza-tion of many classics of the social sciences from Karl Marx to Sigmund Freud and Jacques Lacan, and from these fragments built a new edifice, a critical theory of gender understood in structural and relational terms. To briefly recapitulate its core argument, gender is a social relation organizing action, a historically variable material framework in which collective consciousness and group coordination as well as individual performances and personalities take on their particular meanings at the micro level. However, it also defines structure and agency as recursively related, since out of the groups and identities formed by such structuring relations come the political activities that contribute to the making or unmaking of material social inequalities at a macro level.

The connections between the micro level of bodies, personalities, and emotional experience and the macro level of cultures, institutions, and societies are what Connell calls "practices," emphasizing their active, reflexive, and political nature (Connell 1987, 61). This middle (meso) level of practice is the site where structures—macro-level material contradictions and transformations—become visible as situated agents grapple with the situations they face, as they perceive them. As socially embedded agents, both individual and collective actors make choices constrained by their separate and joint histories and enabled and informed by their ethical and political judgments (95). These choices are *political*: they arise from power relations, give form to power, and generate specific conflicts (or turbulences). Seeing gender theorizing as a political practice is to emphasize its choices and consequences as constituting real social facts.

The gender theory Connell advanced in 1987 was drawn from experiences in challenging the powers of that time, including the intellectuals who provided what Connell judged to be justifications for inequality's resilience rather than a map for transforming it. *Gender and Power* was intended to be useful to the women's movement that had emerged over the previous decade and a half, and was struggling to understand the specific opportunities and resistances of that period. In addition to the predictable opposition from gender traditionalists, feminists faced two particular challenges from their "friends." One was the "sex roles" ideology of complementarity and pseudoequality with which most liberal theorists were still working. The other was the Marxist edifice of theory that defined class as the only fundamental structural contradiction, and class-based struggle as the only source from which true social equality could come (Sargent 1981). Both liberal and socialist theory informed the social sciences of the 1980s, placing gender relations into the role of being at best a "secondary" consideration.

"Radical" feminism in liberal societies (notably the US and UK) advanced an alternative view of "patriarchy" based on analysis of women and men as inherently and eternally oppositional categories. Thus, the boldest move that *Gender and Power* made was to translate the women's movement's self-understanding as a transformative social force into a theory of gender that recognized the movement's independent historical agency without making a claim for its autonomy from other oppressions or movements mobilizing with or against them.

To connect gender with other theories of injustice and social action, a theory of socialization was needed to connect macro injustice to transformative politics. To advance an intersectional view of injustice also called for severing the institutional anchors that tied gender to the institution of the family, race to community-level institutions like education, and class to impersonal-seeming macro models of the formal economy (capital formation, market relations, and national development). *Gender and Power* accomplishes both these tasks by building on Connell's research on educational institutions as sites of active stratification, an intersectional analysis in which gender and sexuality operate with and through social class to provide material and ideological resources for embedding the self in hierarchical social relations.

This empirical work on education and stratification (Connell et al. 1982; Connell 1985) was part of a larger, global theoretical project, most strongly represented by Raymond Williams (1976) in the UK and Pierre Bourdieu (1984) in France, that treated culture as a structuring force, not a mere superstructure to economics. Such class-critical theorists promoted ethnographic and historical methods as the means of capturing the cultural forces creating class relations in schools (e.g., Willis 1977) and actively producing meaningful and usable class categories (e.g., Thompson 1968). This context provided both a theoretical and methodological structure for *Gender and Power* to extend to gender relations.

The intersectionality of gender and class (not gender and race) that informed *Gender and Power* was prominent in the late 1970s and early 1980s. There was a vibrant discussion going on in the US, Australia, Canada and the UK, and in much of Europe and Latin America, about the proper relationship between Marxism and feminism, a line of empirical research and theorizing that engaged capitalist patriarchy (and patriarchal capitalism) in an intersectional way long before the term "intersectionality" itself was coined. The effort to understand patriarchy as a system of power that shaped how capitalism worked, and vice versa, focused largely on the macro level of analysis where class was theoretically situated. Gender relations were understood in historical material terms, especially among leading British Marxist feminists, such as Sheila Rowbotham (1974) and Juliet Mitchell (1971).

However, gender relations were still likely to be thought of in binary terms; studies focused only on women and their lives as sites where gender could be seen, not unlike the focus on studying Black experience as a way of understanding "race." Empirical research, including my own in the 1970s and early 1980s, focused on studying housework as reproductive labor and reflected a normative standard frame of families as the site of (re)production of gender inequalities; many feminist critics pointed out how women were excluded in studies of shop floors, class consciousness, union mobilization, social movements, and party politics, even in who was counted as a worker (e.g., Feldberg and Glenn 1979)

By the mid-1980s, however, the "separate spheres" approach that assigned women to home, family, and reproductive labor and men to formal employment and politics was being undermined by historical and sociological studies that connected home and work as institutions. Women of color such as Evelyn Nakano Glenn, Mary Romero, Bonnie Thornton Dill, and Judith Rollins used paid domestic labor as a theoretical wedge that not only introduced race into the consideration of women's lives and labor but also broke open the binary gendered boxes of home and work, love and money, and family and economy (Ferree 1990). But the reflexive theorizing that would specifically make use of the marginality of women of color in the US to construct "intersectionality" (Crenshaw 1989) or the "matrix of domination" (Hill Collins 1990) to bring race into macro-social models emphasizing gender and class was still to be done.

Gender and Power came at about the same time as Joan Scott's similarly brilliant and pathbreaking article, "Gender as a Useful Category for Historical Analysis" (1986), both addressing the historically specific material relations of power without either reducing them to class-economic relations or inscribing them into gendered binaries that stood outside history. Both Scott and Connell independently challenged the existence of universal symbolic meaning inherent in physical differences, making the discourse of difference itself visible as an object of politics. Both also came at a moment in which dissatisfaction was rising with the eternal sameness of depicting gender (or race or class) as simply a system of oppressors and oppressed. Reintroducing agency to the concern with structure was essential if theories of gender were to be *feminist* theories, that is, theories that contribute to the transformation of society toward being more inclusive, empowering, and egalitarian for women. This is why it is so important that Connell understood conflict not as a coincidental or temporary condition but as a fundamental principle of both social and psychic life.

As an intersectional argument of its time, *Gender and Power* borrowed tools from class-critical cultural analysis, introducing a theoretical structure that embedded a material, historical, gendered self in a macro-structural model of process that privileged conflict and contradiction as sources of transformation that outlived individuals. But *Gender and Power* did not devote as much attention to racializing social processes as would later feminist thought, including Connell's own.

Gender's Intersectional Moment

Gender is pragmatic, self-contained, and more future-oriented than *Gender and Power*; its practical politics strive to lay out a path forward for feminist engagements that would reflect the existing hard-won insights of the empirical and theoretical study of gender. Published in 2002, 15 years after *Gender and Power*, *Gender* entered an intellectual and political world that had experienced substantial transformations: the Cold War had abruptly ended in 1989 and the state socialist claim to have "emancipated" women was exposed as hollow; the Fourth World Conference on Women in 1995 in Beijing highlighted the ubiquity and strength of women's movements in the global South, spurred movement development into nongovernmental organizations (NGOs), and encouraged an unprecedented level of discursive recognition to women's rights as human rights; the integration of Europe dramatically accelerated, the European Union emerged as a political actor with global influence, and European feminists demonstrated the effectiveness of networking around a gender equality agenda.

Gender thus engages with a political climate in which the transnational dimensions of gender politics are more prominent. Moreover, the "women's movement" that seemed to be the main carrier of feminist thought in the 1970s and 1980s had left the streets to pursue a more institutional politics of gender transformation, a transformation that feminist activists in Australia had pioneered and for which they provided useful practical theory to feminists elsewhere (as in their coinage of the word "femocrat"; see Eisenstein 1996). South Asian and Latin American feminists such as Chandra Mohanty, Gloria Anzaldua, and Uma Narayan challenged those North American and European feminists who erased the visibility of colonialism and racism. The collapse of state socialism allowed sometimes-productive engagements between feminists from those countries and those from the now-triumphalist capitalist countries (Roth 2008). Feminist theory also began to make use of empirical insights arising from social locations outside of the more politically privileged parts of the world, drawing more explicitly and reflexively on understandings of gender grounded in the experience of African American women and women of the postcolonial countries of the global South.

The development of intersectionality as a concept is typically traced to the US-centered analysis of African American feminists from the Combahee River Collective through Patricia Hill Collins to Kimberlé Crenshaw. However, the real explosion of interest in the idea began with Crenshaw's presenting it to the UN Conference on Racial Discrimination and Racism in Durban, South Africa, in 2001. Thus, *Gender* enters into a debate founded on both the American analogy of *race* with gender (in which class appears often in the list but without any extended consideration of how it works similarly or differently) and on the international consideration of *racism* as an aspect of the macro social order. *Gender* engages with both, but stresses the latter, more global understanding of racism, carrying forward not only Connell's own position as an Australian (half-in and half-out of the metropole) but also *Gender and Power's* theoretical reflexivity and emphasis on political action as the purpose of feminist theory.

The global order that *Gender* theorizes is very different from the order that *Gender and Power* addressed where new grassroots women's movement activities had been sprouting up everywhere. As feminist political practice became less confined to the work of women with women, its political position was less obviously "outside, throwing rocks" at patriarchal institutions, as women were "moving in to occupy space" in political parties, international development agencies, NGOs, and social movements (Ferree and Martin 1995). A useful theory of gender politics had to account for this transformation, without accepting the media frame that saw this as the "death" of feminism (Ewig and Ferree 2013). On the one hand, theorizing pragmatically about gender politics in a world of increasing economic inequalities gave new life to theories that separated feminism from the macro-power relations of capitalism, suggesting gender and sexuality advocacy had failed to move beyond "recognition" to alter "redistribution" (e.g., Fraser 1997). On the other hand, in the newly postsocialist societies, gender theory had to contribute to making sense of the transformations of the present and future, rather than returning to the class-dominant theoretical legacy of the past (Gal and Kligman 2000).

The shift in historical conditions and thinking about these intersections is evident in the differences between the two books. Rather than *Gender and Power*'s effort to tell origin stories and make a case that gender is a "useful concept," *Gender* looks forward to offer a strategic analysis to deploy in a still uncertain and unstable future in which gender knowledge is now a highly contested resource. Indeed, a key tool of the feminist movement had become a politics of knowledge: socially situated collective labor that uses teaching, training, reporting, discussing, critiquing, and theorizing to advance a political agenda of equality. In addition to Connell's willingness to completely give up on the ideology-as-superstructure framing in Marxist theory, it is the gains feminists made in institutionalizing their discursive politics (however precariously) that helps to explain *Gender*'s otherwise surprising positioning of "discourse" as an institutional regime of its own, alongside labor, power, and cathexis (a term Connell deployed to refer to embodied emotions, sexuality, and interpersonal ties).

But the further challenge that *Gender* faced in the new millennium was to offer an understanding of macro politics that reflected the instability of categories like race, class, and gender, and framed the making and remaking of these categories as "real politics" in which power was central. Judith Butler's *Gender Trouble* (1990) moved feminist theory toward understanding bodies as sites of gender practices, but her framing emphasized their individual "performative" capacities as a dispersed politics of transformation. Connell uses *Gender* to offer ideas about more collective forms of politics. Rather than continuing to place systems of knowledge in the static category of "ideology," *Gender*'s strategic concerns included defining a range of discursive practices that can engage and change institutionalized meanings at both the macro and micro level. Discourse is now itself recognized as a structure, but not the only structure, that a politics of social justice must engage in order to be effective.

Gender (unlike *Gender and Power*) thus engages with postcolonialism and a global order in which women have been agents as well as victims of oppression. Race is much more explicitly identified as a form of intersectional gender politics, differentiating what gender can mean—not just as a multiplicative interaction that has effects on women and men assigned to different racial groups, but at the macro level of defining how nations define and treat other nations, "tribes," and ethnicities. By 2002, gender scholarship had responded to critiques of making white women of the global North the normative standard for feminism "in the abstract" and turned to increasingly sophisticated examinations of the gender politics informing concrete global transformations of political economies (e.g., Gal and Kligman 2000; Rosemblatt 2000). Debates had moved beyond framing gender transformation as a "Western import" to engage the more urgent business of bringing feminist theory into critical perspectives on colonialism and nationalism (Yuval Davis 1997).

This agenda comes to the book's surface in three main ways. First, *Gender* situates Connell self-consciously as Australian, and presents this as an ambiguous position: belonging physically to the geographic periphery, but accorded special status as a member of the British Commonwealth, being thus simultaneously in and not in the global South. Connell's political choice is to write as an advocate for the perspectives of the global South. Second, *Gender* is less engaged with works of theory (not just Freud and Marx but Butler and Bourdieu) than with empirical research findings. Not only are there many more studies to be drawn upon in 2002 than in 1987, but the studies Connell selects emphasize work not done in the US or Britain, but all over the globe. Third, intersectionality now frames the connection between "race" and "nation" as analogous types of extended kin-like structures (105). The "sphere of reproduction" where Connell situates gender is thus also inherently one that is racialized by colonialism and governed through race as well as by gender in defining citizenship and rights at the macro level. Ultimately, *Gender* presents globalization explicitly as a macro politics offering feminists both opportunities and threats.

The historical circumstances set in motion by the Beijing World Conference on Women constituted new structural conditions for theorizing feminist change at a global scale. The Beijing Platform for Action, signed by most of the world's national governments in 1995, demanded specific positive organizational efforts to incorporate awareness of gender inequality into all policy processes in the United Nations and its constitutive states. This "gender mainstreaming" mandate was adopted in the EU in 1997, and its own directives to member states demanded not only that gender discrimination be recognized and combatted, but that positive state action must be undertaken to increase gender equality in work-family outcomes, setting guidelines for minimum maternity and child-care leaves, equalizing part-time and full-time workers' benefits per hour, and setting goals for accessible state-funded child-care services. In 2002, there was still considerable enthusiasm for what the embrace of gender mainstreaming strategies could offer to deeply transform politics-as-usual (Beveridge, Nott, and Stephen 2000). Although a critique from femocrats and their allies was emerging that this new direction diminished power-holders' attention to women (Kantola and Nousiainen 2009), UN "gender and development" policies increasingly stressed protecting, supporting, and educating "the girl child" and offering economic opportunity to adult women in the form of microenterprise loans and training.

Another practical opportunity for feminist politics lay in the proliferation of transnational advocacy networks that deployed knowledge resources ("epistemic communities" with shared political values) to effect change (Keck and Sikkink 1998). "Gender experts" were increasingly called on to contribute advice to governments and organize programs of services to women as constituents of the state. The NGO sector exploded, triggering concerns about the extent to which "NGOized" politics could represent the interests of the marginalized (Lang 1997). Developing "gender expertise" began to run on a practitioner track separate from the theories and practices of academia. Gender analysis was not something that women's movements collectively produced; one part was now the intellectual product of formally accredited "gender and women's studies" departments and another was the discursive legitimation of policy change being produced by and for governments. Especially outside the US, gender theory found global resonance in agency white papers, national and international reports, state-mandated gender training, and transnational advocacy networks.

Gender could hardly fail to recognize the power relations among nations as an intersectional form of historical-material social organization that was gendered and that reproduced gender in various forms. Connell's theorizing of these connections didn't "grow on trees": it emerged from the transformational politics of governance in which feminists were now globally engaged. By displacing the Western/Northern metropole from the center of *Gender*, Connell presents global contestation over the shape of the future international order as a site of gender contradictions and specifically looks at the emergent discursive power of gender knowledge to take advantage of these opportunities to do feminist politics.

Gender Politics and Global Restructuring

In looking at the 15 years of change since *Gender* was published, I am struck by the extent to which the macro-level forces captured in the term "globalization" are operating in intersectional ways. Even the second edition of *Gender*, published only three years later, expands upon the account of the turbulence being produced by globalizing economic forces, producing not one wave of transformation but many, very specific sites of contested transformation, often called all-inclusively "neo-liberalism." I find most theories of intersectionality offer few strategic insights into the practical politics of contesting these changes and rarely improve upon the accounts of economic transformation that subordinate or ignore feminist, antiracist politics. *Gender* begins to offer such a "strong theory" of intersectionality, on which Connell's later work, as well as that of others, builds.

Connell's practical feminist politics of "choice, doubt, strategy, error and transformation" deploys an agentic understanding of class and nation as structural formations that intersect with gender at all levels from macro to micro. More categorical views of intersectionality that focus only on "giving voice" to marginalized people or on the multiplicatively distinctive experiences only of the less privileged, leaving privileged statuses invisible and looking away from the macro level of intersectional power relations, are not wrong, but they are incomplete (Choo and Ferree 2010). Labor, power, cathexis, and discourse are institutionalized in social formations like classes, nations, races, religions, and genders, but always intersectionally.

Walby's (2009) notion of intersecting positive and negative feedback loops is a way of operationalizing the recursivity in Connell's view of action and structure. This approach moves beyond unidirectional path-dependency models of the political economy. Tracing feedback suggests moving back and forth between action and reaction, with particular historical relations coming sometimes to the foreground of change, while sometimes establishing the institutional structures that enable and limit it. These institutionalized structures can at any point become the target of reconfiguring politics, with implications felt on all the others in varying ways.

These formations of inequality are and have always been produced through historically knowable interactions, processes that leave distinctive "shapes" behind. Thus, the US should be understood as a racialized state from its founding documents onward, and the embedding of racialization as a process in every other social relation is inescapable in this national context; politics directed at any element in the overall system will have feedback into structures governing "race." However, this process of racialization should not be casually generalized to other national contexts where the formation of their institutions and identities has not been so consistently and insistently done in and through privileged and disprivileged racial categorizations (Bose 2015). My own research on German feminism, for example, stresses the way in which class formations and conflicts intersected with gender historically to shape strategic opportunities for feminist mobilization over the previous century and a half (Ferree 2013). Most important, as Connell's empirical examples frequently illustrate, both racial politics and class politics in every setting have been and continue to be shaped by the specific gender relations that run through them.

If histories of struggle build up an emerging substructure of discursive opportunities, actual agents with particular agendas still need to survey the ground, draw conclusions, and mobilize action to transform not only themselves but the "facts on the ground" as they see them. As I have argued elsewhere, "Framing is a way of connecting beliefs about social actors and beliefs about social relations into more or less coherent packages that define what kinds of actions are possible and effective for particular actors. The point of frames is that they draw connections, identify relationships, and create perceptions of social order out of the variety of possible mental representations of reality swirling around social actors" (Ferree 2009, 87). The discursive approach that Connell brings into prominence in *Gender* offers additional ways of thinking about framing as a political process.

One broad framing project for feminist theory can be seen in the concentrated efforts directed at conceptually sorting out the meanings of "intersectionality" in classification schemes such as those of McCall (2005), Hancock (2007), and Choo and Ferree (2010). The number of feminist journals that have devoted special issues or symposia to the concept is enormous and still growing; intersectionality may be vague enough to be embraced by everyone, but where and how it could actually be useful is remarkably contentious. Some African American feminist scholars see its use in analyzing intersections that are not specifically concerned with Black experience as a form of intellectual misappropriation (e.g., Alexander-Floyd 2012), while others present it as a "heuristic" that can be deployed for various ends, including those inimical to social justice (Lindsay 2013). Some feminists in Europe see its application to policy debates there as fruitful (e.g., Lombardo, Maier, and Verloo 2009), while others are concerned that it is encouraging the transformation of gender mainstreaming into a shallow form of state "diversity" politics analogous to the "diversity management" that US corporations export (Prügl 2014).

The growth of feminist influence in governance projects has also drawn theorists' attention to the intersectional impacts of women's movement organizing. Concerns are increasingly expressed about the negative impacts of national or transnational gender equality projects on men of color in the US (Bumiller 2008) and on women, men, and families in the global South (Cornwall, Harrison, and Whitehead 2007). Orloff and Schiff (2014) note that this "governance feminism" is one that is facilitated by neoliberal economic transformations at the global level, but as Elizabeth Prügl (2014) argues, "Neoliberalism has become somewhat of a master variable, an explanatory hammer that fits all nails, used to account for a multiplicity of contemporary phenomena. . . . In order to make neoliberalism methodologically useful, it is necessary to transcend the reification of the concept, recall the indeterminate way in which doctrines circulate and are resisted, and [address] the process aspect of any class and governance project" (616). This "process aspect" includes the gender, race, and nationalist politics waged within and across specific sites (Bose 2015).

A more macro-level theory of intersectionality would help address the diversity of contested political changes currently tossed into the concept neoliberalism in a totalizing, often inherently condemnatory way that is just as problematic theoretically as the universalizing concept of patriarchy proved to be. Not only have defenders of patriarchy been able to cloak their agenda by presenting it as challenging a unidimensional gender division into dominant men and subordinate women, but defenders of neoliberalism adopt a discourse of "empowerment" that claims to resist universalizing claims of economic oppression. A more useful view of neoliberalism situates it intersectionally, as patriarchy has been, considering the specific nuances of class, nation, gender, race, and religious and sexual politics that shape it, and thus also the struggles against it (Collins 2017). As with all the other intersectional forces of inequality, neoliberalism is misunderstood if treated as one division between oppressed and oppressors. Institutions that follow intersectionally specific trajectories produce gender politics that are distinctive to their situations, both within and across national borders (see Bose and Kim 2009), but as Connell (1987) argues "the connection between structures of inequality is not a logical connection . . . [it] is empirical and practical" (292). Although some invoke neoliberalism as if it has co-opted and overwhelmed all feminist aspirations (e.g., Eisenstein 2009), Connell argues instead that how local feminisms relate to neoliberalism is not to be deduced logically but investigated empirically. Even such globally visible trends as empowering managerial authorities, preferring private rather than public investments, and framing economic costs and benefits as the most socially important outcomes—a standard definition of neoliberalism—take on quite remarkably different forms, which in particular cases may be empowering for individuals subordinated on other dimensions (Prügl 2014). Where and how these shifts generate turbulences (or contradictions) depends on what other forces they intersect with and what historical conditions provide a "seafloor" of normalized institutions, practices, and identities over which they move, shaping and being shaped by these "sediments." Effective understanding of neoliberal politics demands specific analysis of the politics of gender, race, and class in interaction with each other at a structural level, as Ewig's (2010) analysis of Peruvian health policies demonstrates can indeed be done.

Drawing on my own work, I illustrate the diversity this dynamic model of intersectional feminism brings to the analysis of institutional transformation by picking some particular sites (institutions of higher education in Germany and the US) where struggles over class and gender relations are currently highly visible. The university systems of both of these economically powerful and politically influential countries are being reconfigured, and feminist critics in both countries strongly identify these transformations with neoliberalism (Tuchman 2009; Kahlert 2003). But in each national context, the path being taken is so remarkably different that the common label is misleading.

In the US, the restructuring takes the form of intensified competition at the bottom from exploitative for-profit institutions that particularly take advantage of Black women's desires for economic security and a less-stigmatized identity. These organizations, which McMillan Cottom (2016) calls "lower-ed," reflect the intersections of gender, race, and class in US educational policy as much as do the immense endowments of the exclusive private universities. State disinvestments, tuition increases, and reliance on highly competitive research funding and on alumni donations are fiscal characteristics that shape the entire hierarchy of US higher education, making most jobs more precarious and decreasing institutional reliance on professorships just at the historical moment in which women are claiming a larger share of these jobs (Ferree and Zippel 2015). University administrators use "globalization" to troll for affluent tuition-paying students from all over the world and brag about the "diversity" this form of internationalization produces.

In Germany, by contrast, the neoliberal intensification of competition has given rise to increased federal and state investments in universities and research allocated in the form of grants, and political efforts to add differentiation in status among its research universities (Zippel, Ferree, and Zimmermann 2016). EU directives on gender equality, specifying that measures must to be taken to increase the share of women in science and technology, have been used quite effectively to prod the German government to fund extra professorships for women and to demand regular audits of success in meeting goals for gender inclusivity (Zippel, Ferree, and Zimmermann 2016). Competitive pressure and political mobilization lie behind these gender politics, but also explain the decision to abolish tuition at all German public universities. EU pressure for "mobility," especially among its member states, has also increased pressure for standardization of curricula, English-language instruction across many subject areas, and more regular formal grading of student progress along with time limits on funding degree completion.

In other words, both German and US universities are going through restructurings called neoliberal that are not merely economic in either case. Given that there are transnational gender politics, geopolitical national interests, and racialized beliefs about academic success entwined in specific ways with the neoliberal impulse, one can see very different trajectories of restructuring and radically different types of opportunities for feminist engagement. While the shared label neoliberal creates an illusion that such change is driven by class relations alone, any closer look reveals a variety of specific struggles going on simultaneously in each site, ones that are shaped by gender, in the United States also by race and in Germany also by nationality.

Conclusions Also Don't Grow on Trees

While current concerns about neoliberalism—as it shapes governments and globalization as well as universities—are wholly appropriate, I believe theories of neoliberalism will benefit greatly from Connell's macro-level understanding of intersectionality. This conviction grows from my own engagement in feminist politics, comparative research on gender relations, and personal experiences of universities in different countries. I see the current changes hitting universities—and other knowledge-producing institutions—as a tangle of feedback among diverse forces, not one disembodied economic transformation.

More generally, like Connell, I am convinced that not neoliberalism alone, but intersecting macro forces today are reorganizing social systems globally. These upheavals are being felt in the specific institutions we inhabit, are linked across space and time with those of all other people, can be framed as being about gender or race or class or sexuality or nation, and are being contested by diverse social justice movements arising around the world. What gender means to movement activists, and what they plan to do with it in the future is the "choice, doubt, strategy, planning, error and transformation" Connell has argued is inherent in historical agency.

In addition to neoliberalism, other struggles that are global—the racialization of Muslims, the pressures of migration on affluent countries, the gendering of technological expertise—also are better understood, I argue, by attending specifically to the sites where multiple forces intersect to generate "turbulences" that actors can use to generate energy for transformation. Neoliberalism alone is not the explanation for social change, nor is a new class politics alone the solution to new or persistent inequalities. Rather than "taking a break from feminism," as Halley (2008) has suggested might be necessary to confront neoliberal globalization, I suggest that a macro-oriented and dynamic gender theory should inspire a greater range of feminist strategic thinking. Taking intersectionality into account would suggest that governance feminism, as mobilized from the inside of state, NGO, and corporate organizations, offers just one of a number of options for hydra-headed feminist activism. This implies a discourse about feminism less deeply ambivalent about power and more willing to act with conviction. Looking at politics from the standpoint of 2016, new forms of feminist collective action seem to be emergent in social media and cultural politics throughout the world (Ewig and Ferree 2013), including high-risk activism challenging gender relations in nondemocratic sites like China (Wang and Ferree 2015), Russia (Sperling 2014), and the Middle East (Al-Ali 2012).

An intersectional feminist theory of politics worthy of the name can find a powerful foundation in Connell's evolving understanding of gender and power at the global scale. The macro intersections that neoliberalism, fundamentalism, nationalism, environmentalism, and neocolonialism have with patriarchy and feminism were already visible in *Gender*. Connell's newest work (2015) stresses the need that feminists everywhere have for feminist theory from the global South about imperialism, postcolonialism and collective identities or states, violence, and human rights (see also Tripp, Ferree, and Ewig 2014). Such historically specific, intersectional accounts of struggle are essential, Connell suggests, particularly for those of us whose perspective is easily mistaken for being universal—the white, privileged, highly educated theorists of the metropole.

Nonetheless, Connell is hardly alone in advocating a more thoroughly intersectional account of the struggles of our own era. Gender politics in this macro-intersectional sense have been persuasively studied in the way civil war in El Salvador was fought and settled (Viterna 2013), the framing of work and workers in the antiausterity protests in Wisconsin (Collins 2017), and the roots and spread of the global financial crisis of 2008 (Walby 2015). The global resonance of Connell's work suggests that macro-intersectional analyses will continue to illuminate the contradictions in the many interacting forces shaking contemporary institutions in many locations, and reveal how these turbulent times are perceived and experienced, resisted, and changed through the practices of both men and women around the world. This is a global feminist knowledge project not restricted to the academy but one in which all who have a desire for social justice have a stake.

NOTES

1 Acknowledgments: Many thanks are due to Raewyn Connell and the editors of this book for shaping this chapter by raising wonderful questions on an earlier draft; also to Lisa D. Brush, Christina Ewig, Sarah Kaiksow, Silke Roth, and Aili Tripp for helping me refine this one.

2 Thanks to Mieke Verloo for providing the core of this imagery.

REFERENCES

Al-Ali, Nadje. 2012. "Gendering the Arab Spring." *Middle East Journal of Culture and Communication* 5 (2012): 26–31.

Alexander-Floyd, Nikol. 2012. "Disappearing Acts: Reclaiming Intersectionality in the Social Sciences in a Post-Black Feminist Era." *Feminist Formations* 24 (1): 1–25.

Anzaldua, Gloria. 1987. *Borderlands/La Frontera*. San Francisco: Aunt Lute.

Beal, Frances. 1970. "Double Jeopardy: To Be Black and Female." In *The Black Woman: An Anthology*, edited by Toni Cade Bambara. New York: New American Library.

Beveridge, Fiona, Sue Nott, and Kylie Stephen. 2000. "Mainstreaming and Engendering of Policy-Making: A Means to an End?" *Journal of European Public Policy* 7 (3): 385–405.

Bose, Christine E. 2015. "Patterns of Global Gender Inequalities and Regional Gender Regimes." *Gender & Society* 29 (6): 767–791.

Bose, Christine, and Minjeong Kim. 2009. *Global Gender Research: Transnational Perspectives*. New York: Routledge.

Bourdieu, Pierre. 1984. *Distinction: A Social Critique of the Judgment of Taste*. New York: Routledge.

Bumiller, Kristen. 2008. *In an Abusive State: How Neoliberalism Appropriated the Feminist Movement against Sexual Violence*. Durham, NC: Duke University Press.

Butler, Judith. 1990. *Gender Trouble*. New York: Routledge.

Choo, Hae Yeon, and Myra Marx Ferree. 2010. "Practicing Intersectionality in Sociological Research: A Critical Analysis of Inclusions, Interactions and Institutions in the Study of Inequalities." *Sociological Theory* 28 (2): 29–49.

Collins, Jane. 2017. *The Politics of Value*. Chicago: University of Chicago Press.

Connell, R. W. 1985. *Teachers' Work*. Sydney: Allen and Unwin.

———. 1987. *Gender and Power: Society, the Person and Sexual Politics*. Sydney: Allen and Unwin.

———. 2002. *Gender*. Oxford: Polity.

———. 2015. "Meeting at the Edge of Fear: Theory on a World Scale." *Feminist Theory* 16 (1): 49–66.

Connell, R. W., D. J. Ascherton, S. Kessler, and G. W. Dowsett. 1982. *Making the Difference: Schools, Families and Social Division*. Sydney: Allen and Unwin.

Cornwall, Andrea, Elizabeth Harrison, and Ann Whitehead. 2007. "Gender Myths and Feminist Fables: The Struggle for Interpretive Power in Gender and Development." *Development and Change* 38 (1): 1–20.

Crenshaw, Kimberlé. 1989. "Demarginalizing the Intersection of Race and Sex: A Black Feminist Critique of Anti-discrimination Doctrine, Feminist Theory, and Anti-racist Politics." *University of Chicago Legal Forum* 19: 139–168.

Dill, Bonnie Thornton. 1986. "Our Mothers' Grief: Racial-Ethnic Women and the Maintenance of Families." Memphis, TN: Center for Research on Women.

Eisenstein, Hester. 1996. *Inside Agitators: Australian Femocrats and the State*. Philadelphia: Temple University Press.

Eisenstein, Hester. 2009. *Feminism Seduced: How Global Elites Use Women's Labor and Ideas to Exploit the World*. Boulder, CO: Paradigm.

Ewig, Christina. 2010. *Second-Wave Neoliberalism: Gender, Race, and Health Sector Reform in Peru*. University Park: Penn State University Press.

Ewig, Christina, and Myra Marx Ferree. 2013. "Feminist Organizing: What's Old, What's New? History, Trends and Issues." In *Oxford Handbook of Gender and Politics*, edited by Georgina Waylen, Karen Celis, Johanna Kantola, and Laurel Weldon, 437–461. Oxford: Oxford University Press.

Feldberg, Roslyn, and Evelyn Nakano Glenn. 1979. "Male and Female: Job versus Gender Models in the Sociology of Work." *Social Problems* 26 (5): 524–538.

Ferree, Myra Marx. 1990. "Beyond Separate Spheres: Feminism and Family Research." *Journal of Marriage and the Family* 52 (4): 866–884.

———. 2009. "Inequality, Intersectionality and the Politics of Discourse: Framing Feminist Alliances." In *The Discursive Politics of Gender Equality: Stretching, Bending and Policy-Making*, edited by Emanuela Lombardo, Petra Meier, and Mieke Verloo, chapter 6. New York: Routledge.

———. 2013. *Varieties of Feminism: German Gender Politics in Global Perspective*. Palo Alto: Stanford University Press.

Ferree, Myra Marx, and Beth B. Hess. 2000. *Controversy and Coalition: The New Feminist Movement*. 3rd ed. New York: Routledge.

Ferree, Myra Marx, and Patricia Yancey Martin. 1995. *Feminist Organizations: Harvest of the New Women's Movement*. Philadelphia: Temple University Press.

Ferree, Myra Marx, and Silke Roth. 1998. "Gender, Class and the Interaction among Social Movements: A Strike of West Berlin Daycare Workers." *Gender & Society* 12 (6): 626–648.

Ferree, Myra Marx, and Kathrin S. Zippel. 2015. "Gender Equality in the Age of Academic Capitalism: Cassandra and Pollyanna Interpret University Restructuring." *Social Politics* 22 (4): 561–584.

Fraser, Nancy, 1997. "From Redistribution to Recognition? Dilemmas of Justice in a 'Post-Socialist' Age." In *Justice Interruptus: Critical Reflections on the "Postsocialist" Condition*. New York: Routledge.

———. 2009. "Feminism, Capitalism and the Cunning of History." *New Left Review* 56: 97–117.

Gal, Susan, and Gail Kligman. 2000. *The Politics of Gender after Socialism*. Princeton: Princeton University Press.

Glenn, Evelyn Nakano. 1986. *Issei, Nisei, Warbride: Three Generations of Japanese American Women in Domestic Service*. Philadelphia: Temple University Press.

Halley, Janet. 2008. *Split Decisions: How and Why to Take a Break from Feminism*. Princeton: Princeton University Press.

Hancock, Ange-Marie. 2007. "When Multiplication Doesn't Equal Quick Addition: Examining Intersectionality as a Research Paradigm." *Perspectives on Politics* 5 (1): 63–79.

Hill Collins, Patricia. 1990. *Black Feminist Thought*. New York: Routledge.

Kahlert, Heike. 2003. *Gender Mainstreaming an Hochschulen Anleitung zum qualitätsbewussten Handeln*. Opladen: Leske + Budrich.

Kantola, Johanna, and Kevat Nousiainen. 2009. "Institutionalizing Intersectionality in Europe." *International Feminist Journal of Politics* 11 (4): 459–477.

Keck, Margaret E., and Kathryn Sikkink. 1998. *Activists beyond Borders: Advocacy Networks in International Politics*. Ithaca: Cornell University Press.

Lang, Sabine. 1997. "The NGOization of Feminism." In *Transitions, Environments, Translations: Feminisms in International Politics*, edited by J. W. Scott, C. Kaplan, and D. Keates. New York: Routledge.

Lindsay, Keisha. 2013. "God, Gays, and Progressive Politics: Reconceptualizing Inter-sectionality as a Normatively Malleable Analytical Framework." *Perspectives on Politics* 11 (2): 447–460.

Lombardo, Emanuela, Petra Maier, and Mieke Verloo, eds. 2009. *The Discursive Politics of Gender Equality: Stretching, Bending and Policy-making*. New York: Routledge.

McCall, Leslie. 2005. "The Complexity of Intersectionality." *Signs: Journal of Women in Culture and Society* 30 (3): 1771–1800.

McMillan Cottom, Tressie. 2016. *Lower Ed: The Troubling Rise of For-Profit Colleges in the New Economy*. New York: New Press.

Mitchell, Juliet. 1971. *Women's Estate*. New York: Pantheon.

Mohanty, Chandra Talpade. 1997. "Under Western Eyes: Feminist Scholarship and Colonial Discourses." *Feminist Review* 30: 61–88.

Orloff, Ann Shona, and Talia Schiff. 2014. "Feminists in Power: Rethinking Gender Equality after the Second Wave." In *Emerging Trends in the Social and Behavioral Sciences: Interdisciplinary Directions*, edited by Robert A. Scott and Stephen M. Kosslyn. New York: John Wiley.

Prügl, Elizabeth. 2014. "Neoliberalising Feminism." *New Political Economy* 20 (4): 614–631.

Rollins, Judith. 1985. *Between Women: Domestics and Their Employers*. Philadelphia: Temple University Press.

Romero, Mary. 1992. *Maid in the U.S.A.* New York: Routledge.

Rosemblatt, Karin. 2000. *Gendered Compromises: Political Cultures, Socialist Politics, and the State in Chile, 1920–1950*. Chapel Hill: University of North Carolina Press.

Roth, Silke, ed. 2008. *Gender Politics in the Expanding European Union: Mobilization, Inclusion, Exclusion*. New York: Berghahn Books.

Rowbotham, Sheila. 1974. *Women, Resistance, and Revolution: A History of Women and Revolution in the Modern World*. New York: Vintage.

Sargent, Lydia, ed. 1981. *Women and Revolution: A Discussion of the Unhappy Marriage of Marxism and Feminism*. Boston: South End Press.

Scott, Joan W. 1986. "Gender: A Useful Category for Historical Analysis." *American Historical Review, 91(5)*: 1053–1076.

Sperling, Valerie. 2014. *Sex, Politics and Putin: Political Legitimacy in Russia*. New York: Oxford University Press.

Thompson, E. P. (1963) 1968. *The Making of the English Working Class*. Rev. 2nd ed. London: Victor Gollancz.

Tripp, Aili Mari, Myra Marx Ferree, and Christina Ewig. 2014. *Gender, Violence, and Human Security: Feminist Perspectives*. New York: New York University Press.

Tuchman, Gaye. 2009. *Wannabe U: Inside the Corporate University*. Chicago: University of Chicago Press.

Viterna, Jocelyn. 2013. *Women in War: The Micro-Processes of Mobilization in El Salvador*. Oxford: Oxford University Press.

Walby, Sylvia. 2009. *Globalization and Inequalities: Complexity and Contested Modernities*. Thousand Oaks, CA: Sage.

Walby, Sylvia. 2015. *Crisis*. New York: Polity.

Wang, Di, and Myra Marx Ferree. 2015. "Radical Feminist Activism in China." Working paper. Department of Sociology, University of Wisconsin.

Williams, Raymond. 1976. *Keywords: A Vocabulary of Culture and Society*.London: Croom Helm/Routledge.

Willis, Paul E. 1977. *Learning to Labor: How Working-Class Kids Get Working Class Jobs*. New York: Columbia University Press.

Yuval-Davis, Nira. 1997. *Gender and Nation*. Thousand Oaks, CA: Sage.

Zippel, Kathrin S., Myra Marx Ferree, and Karin Zimmermann. 2016. "Gender Equality in German Universities: Vernacularizing the Battle for the Best Brains." *Gender and Education* 28 (7): 867–885.

2

Hegemonic, Nonhegemonic, and "New" Masculinities

JAMES W. MESSERSCHMIDT AND MICHAEL A. MESSNER

The most frequently cited passages in Raewyn Connell's 1987 book, *Gender and Power*, are found in the final section of chapter 8. In these six pages (183–88), Connell introduces the concept of "hegemonic masculinity" and its relation to "emphasized femininity" and nonhegemonic masculinities. The subsequent canonization of these concepts, however, has created new problems—not because Connell was "wrong," but rather because too often gender scholars deploy the concepts in structurally and historically decontextualized ways.

Nearly two decades ago, Pat Martin (1998) raised the issue of inconsistent applications of the concept of hegemonic masculinity, insightfully observing that some scholars equated the concept with a fixed type of masculinity or with whatever type of masculinity happened to be dominant at a particular time and place. More recently, Christine Beasley (2008) and Elias and Beasley (2009) labeled such inconsistent applications "slippage," arguing that "dominant" forms of masculinity— such as the most culturally celebrated or the most common in particular settings—may actually do little to legitimate men's power over women and, therefore, should not be labeled hegemonic masculinities, and that some masculinities that legitimate men's power actually may be culturally marginalized. And Mimi Schippers (2007) argued that it is essential to distinguish masculinities that legitimate men's power from those that do not.

Martin's, Beasley's, and Schipper's insights continue to ring true as there remains a tendency among some scholars to read hegemonic masculinity as a static character type and to ignore the whole question of gender relations and thus the legitimation of gender inequality. And some scholars continue to equate hegemonic masculinity with (1) particular masculinities that simply are dominant—that is, the most culturally celebrated or the most common in particular settings—but do *not* legitimate gender inequality, or (2) those masculinities that are practiced by certain men—such as politicians, corporate heads, and celebrities—simply because they are in positions of power, ignoring once again questions of structured gender relations and the legitimation of gender inequality (see Messerschmidt 2012).

The potential of Connell's concepts can only be realized when coupled with what we see as the theoretical heart of *Gender and Power*: chapter 6, the centerpiece of three chapters in which Connell elaborates a structural theory of "the gender order" (the state of play of gender relations in a society) and "gender regimes" (the state of play of gender relations in an institution). As the phrase "state of play" implies, Connell's view of social structure is dynamic, emphasizing a dialectical relationship between structural constraint and human agency, foregrounding the mechanisms and processes of historical change and continuity in gender relations. If a reader of *Gender and Power* fails to grasp this structural foundation of Connell's theory, then what follows—particularly in the deployment of concepts like hegemonic masculinity—can too easily descend into decontextualized, ahistorical, and individualized descriptors disguised as "theory."

Grounded in Connell's structural analysis, gender is revealed not merely as individual attributes or styles, but as collective agency, constrained and enabled by social structures. Historical crisis tendencies in the gender order, as well as within and across gender regimes, create both constraints on and opportunities for action. Examining *Gender and Power* alongside Connell's *Masculinities* (1995) illustrates the method we seek to underline in this chapter. In *Gender and Power*, Connell introduces a richly theorized framework for understanding gender as social structure, with a particular focus on how historical crisis tendencies create both constraints on and opportunities for action. And in *Masculinities*, she engages empirically with men at carefully chosen social locations where crisis tendencies in gender relations come to the surface—young working class men in a declining labor market; gay men; men in the environmental movement who are working closely with feminist women—with the aim of understanding the collective construction of masculinities in these dynamic social locations. Connell then uses these observations to understand the possibilities for both progressive and regressive social change in gender relations. In other words, Connell shows how a close-up empirical engagement with the "trees" of concrete gender relations is constituted by, and in turn constitutes, the historical and structural context, the "forest," so to speak. The key challenge is how to think about different collective configurations of gender—including constructions of masculinities and femininities—within this larger structural and historical framework.

In this chapter we first discuss the initial formulation of Connell's framework and outline some of its early applications as well as some of the criticisms leveled against it. Second, we discuss the reformulation of Connell's perspective that was sketched out by Connell and Messerschmidt (2005) and we summarize some recent scholarly publications supporting that reformulation. Finally, in the last two sections we outline ways in which hegemonic, nonhegemonic, and "new" masculinities can be productively viewed in structural contexts, with a particular focus on research that illuminates new directions in masculinities studies as well as prospects for how masculinities change.

Formulation

Connell's initial conceptual formulation concentrated on how hegemonic masculinity in a given historical and society-wide setting legitimates unequal gender relations between men and women, masculinity and femininity, and among masculinities. As Connell (1987, 183; emphasis added) points out in *Gender and Power*: "Hegemonic masculinity is always constructed in *relation* to various subordinated masculinities as well as in *relation* to women." And in *Masculinities* Connell (1995, 77; emphasis added) defines hegemonic masculinity "as the configuration of gender practice which embodies the currently accepted answer to the problem of the *legitimacy* of patriarchy, which guarantees (or is taken to guarantee) the dominant position of men and the subordination of women." Both the *relational* and *legitimation* features were central to her argument, involving a particular form of masculinity in unequal relation to a certain form of femininity—that is, "emphasized femininity," which is practiced in a complementary, compliant, and accommodating subordinate relationship with hegemonic masculinity—and to certain forms of nonhegemonic masculinities. And the achievement of hegemonic masculinity occurs largely through discursive legitimation (or justification), encouraging all to consent to, unite around, and embody such unequal gender relations.

For Connell, then, gender relations are structured through power inequalities between and among men and women. Accordingly, the concept of emphasized femininity is essential to Connell's framework, underlining how this feminized form adapts to masculine power through compliance, nurturance, and empathy as "womanly virtues" (188). But Connell (183–84) identifies additional femininities, such as those defined "by strategies of resistance or forms of compliance" and "by complex strategic combinations of compliance, resistance and cooperation."

Hegemonic masculinity is also constructed in relation to what Connell identifies as four specific nonhegemonic masculinities: first, *complicit* masculinities do not actually embody hegemonic masculinity yet through practice realize some of the benefits of patriarchal relations; second, *subordinate* masculinities are constructed as lesser than or aberrant from and deviant to hegemonic masculinity; third, *marginalized* masculinities are trivialized or discriminated against, or both, because of unequal relations, such as class, race, ethnicity, and age; and finally, *protest* masculinities are constructed as compensatory hypermasculinities that are formed in reaction to social positions lacking economic and political power.

Connell emphasized that hegemonic and nonhegemonic masculinities are all subject to change because they come into existence in specific settings and under particular situations. And for the former, there often exists a struggle for hegemony whereby older versions may be replaced by newer ones. The notion of hegemonic masculinity and nonhegemonic masculinities then opened up the possibility of change toward the abolition of gender inequalities and the creation of more egalitarian gender relations.

Connell's perspective found significant and enthusiastic application from the late 1980s to the early 2000s, being utilized in a variety of academic areas. For example, the conceptualization of hegemonic and nonhegemonic masculinities was used to understand educational processes; the social construction of crime; media representations of and men's involvement in sport; determinants of men's health; and organizational structures. The perspective also was used in psychotherapy with men, youth violence prevention programs, and educational programs for boys, as well as in discussions of art, geography, law, and feminist politics. Eventually the perspective was fleshed out further by documenting the costs of hegemony, by uncovering the mechanism of hegemony, by showing even greater diversity in nonhegemonic masculinities, and by discovering changes in hegemonic masculinities (see Connell and Messerschmidt 2005).

Despite considerable favorable reception of Connell's concepts, her perspective nevertheless attracted criticism that concentrated almost exclusively on the concept of hegemonic masculinity. For example, some scholars raised concerns about the underlying concept of masculinity itself, arguing that it may be flawed in various ways (Collinson and Hearn 1994; Hearn 1996, 2004; Petersen 1998, 2003). Critics of hegemonic masculinity also raised questions regarding who actually represents hegemonic masculinity (Donaldson 1993; Martin 1998; Wetherell and Edley 1999; Whitehead 1998, 2002). Some critics additionally argued that hegemonic masculinity simply reduces in practice to a reification of power or toxicity (Holter 1997, 2003; Collier 1998; McMahon 1993), while others have suggested that the concept maintains an alleged unsatisfactory theory of the masculine subject (Wetherell and Edley 1999; Whitehead 2002; Collier 1998; Jefferson 1994, 2002). Finally, some commentators claimed that the pattern of gender relations outlined by Connell is unsound (Demetriou 2001).

Reformulation

In a paper published in 2005, Connell and Messerschmidt responded to the above criticisms and reformulated the concept of hegemonic masculinity in numerous ways. That reformulation first included certain aspects of the original formulation that empirical evidence over almost two decades indicated should be retained, in particular the relational nature of the concept (among hegemonic masculinity, emphasized femininity, and nonhegemonic masculinities) and the idea that this relationship is a pattern of hegemony—not a pattern of simple domination. Also well-supported historically are the foundational ideas that hegemonic masculinity need not be the most powerful or the most common pattern of masculinity, or both, in a particular setting, and that any formulation of the concept as simply constituting an assemblage of fixed "masculine" character traits should be thoroughly transcended. Second, Connell and Messerschmidt suggested that a reformulated understanding of hegemonic masculinity must incorporate a more holistic grasp of gender inequality that recognizes the agency of subordinated groups as much as the power of hegemonic groups and that includes the mutual conditioning (or intersectionality) of gender with other social inequalities such as class, race, age, sexuality, and nation. Third, Connell and Messerschmidt asserted that a more sophisticated treatment of embodiment in hegemonic and nonhegemonic masculinities was necessary, as well as conceptualizations of how hegemonic masculinity may be challenged, contested, and thus changed. Finally, Connell and Messerschmidt argued that instead of simply recognizing hegemonic masculinity at only the society-wide level, scholars should analyze empirically existing hegemonic masculinit*ies* at three levels: first, the *local* (meaning constructed in gender regimes involving the face-to-face interaction of families, organizations, and immediate communities); second, the *regional* (meaning constructed at the level of a society-wide gender order); and, third, the *global* (meaning constructed in the global gender order involving transnational world politics, business, and media). Obviously, within any level multiple and often conflicting hegemonic masculinities will be at play. For example, Michela Musto's (2014) research on a coed children's swim team reveals more egalitarian gender relations in the formally controlled context of the swimming pool, yet a binary gender divide was constructed when the kids moved to more informal interactions and relations, such as on the pool deck. And links among the three levels exist: global hegemonic masculinities pressure regional and local hegemonic masculinities, and regional hegemonic masculinities provide cultural materials adopted or reworked in global arenas and utilized in local gender dynamics.

Scholars have applied this reformulated concept of hegemonic masculinity in a number of ways. First, gender researchers increasingly are specifically examining hegemonic masculinities at the local, regional, and global levels as well as how each level may affect the other levels (Morris 2008; Weitzer and Kubrin 2009; Hatfield 2010; Messner 2014). Second, research demonstrates how women and subordinated men under certain situations may actually contribute to the cultivation of hegemonic masculinity (Talbot and Quayle 2010; Irvine and Vermilya 2010). Third, studies have appeared that demonstrate how hegemonic masculinities may be open to challenge and possibly reproduced in new form, resulting in new strategies of patriarchal relations and re-definitions of hegemonic masculinities (Duncanson 2009; Light 2007). Finally, scholarly work is now analyzing how neoliberal globalization affects the construction of hegemonic masculinities in several countries in Asia, Africa, and Central and Latin America, as well as how new nonhegemonic masculinities may arise under such conditions in these countries (Groes-Green 2009; Broughton 2008).

New Directions

Recent work on hegemonic and nonhegemonic masculinities takes gendered knowledge in promising new directions. We identify four recent developments in the conceptualization of hegemonic and nonhegemonic masculinities.

Dominant, Dominating, and Positive Masculinities

As mentioned above, to elucidate the significance and salience of hegemonic masculinities, gender scholars must distinguish masculinities that legitimate gender inequality from those that do not, and some researchers have now begun to accomplish this. For example, Messerschmidt (2016) recently distinguished "hegemonic masculinities" from "dominant," "dominating," and "positive" forms of masculinities. For Messerschmidt, *hegemonic masculinities* are those masculinities constructed locally, regionally, and globally that legitimate an unequal relationship between men and women, masculinity and femininity, and among masculinities. *Dominant masculinities* are not always associated with and linked to gender hegemony but refer to (locally, regionally, and globally) the most celebrated, common, or current form of masculinity in a particular social setting. As an example of dominant masculinities, Messerschmidt (2016) interviewed teenage boys who all identified certain boys in school who were structurally dominant: they were popular, were often tough and athletic, attended parties, participated in heterosexuality, and had many friends. In other words, these dominant boys represented the most *celebrated* form of masculinity in the "clique" structure within schools, yet they did not in and of themselves legitimate gender inequality. *Dominating masculinities* refer to those masculinities (locally, regionally, and globally) that also do not necessarily legitimate unequal relationships between men and women, masculinities and femininities, but rather involve commanding and controlling particular interactions, exercising power and control over people and events: "calling the shots" and "running the show." For example, in Messerschmidt's (2016) discussion of former president George W. Bush's involvement in the Iraq War, he demonstrates how Bush refused to engage in peaceful geopolitical diplomatic negotiations with foreign leaders, choosing instead to practice "hard diplomacy" and thus control worldwide geopolitical diplomatic negotiations through a global dominating masculinity. Dominant and dominating masculinities at times may also be hegemonic, but neither is hegemonic if they fail culturally to legitimate unequal gender relations. *Positive masculinities* are those masculinities (locally, regionally, and globally) that contribute to legitimating egalitarian relations between men and women, masculinity and femininity, and among masculinities. Messerschmidt (2016) found such masculinities constructed by nonviolent boys, who frequently reported, for example, hanging out with the "laid back" crowd at school (or some other unpopular groups) that included both boys and girls who were inclusive and nonviolent, did not emphasize heterosexuality and accepted celibacy, embraced diversity in bodies and sexuality, were nonhierarchical, had no desire to be popular, and the boys were not misogynist. Indeed, members of such groups viewed themselves as different from, rather than inferior to, the dominant boys and girls. Consequently, such positive masculinities were not constructed in a structural relationship of gender and sexual inequality, they did not legitimate unequal gender and sexual relations, and they were practiced in settings situated outside stable unequal gender relations.

Research on such dominant, dominating, and positive masculinities is significant because it enables a more distinct conceptualization of how hegemonic masculinities are unique among the diversity of masculinities, and making a clear distinction between hegemonic and dominant and dominating masculinities will enable scholars to recognize and research various nonhegemonic yet powerful masculinities and how they differ from hegemonic masculinities as well as how they differ among themselves. Moreover, such research will be considered valuable in the sense of recognizing and pinpointing possible positive masculinities and thus gender practices that challenge gender hegemony and consequently have crucial implications for social policy.

Hegemonic Masculinities

The concept of hegemonic masculinity continues to be used by scholars in diverse ways throughout the world. Consider the examples of South Africa and Sweden. In the former, many researchers have followed Connell and Messerschmidt's (2005) reformulation of hegemonic masculinity by using the concept in the plural; however, in some instances this has resulted in a fixed understanding of hegemonic masculinity. Therefore, South African scholars have argued that for the concept to be fully realized "the realms (in relation to race, class, and age) and levels (i.e., global, national, or local) of its use need to be specified and observed" (Morrell, Jewkes, and Lindegger 2012, 25). In the latter, scholars use the concept of hegemonic masculinity in a variety of ways: as part of a typology; by linking it to how unequal gender relations are maintained; through the application of Connell's initial formulation; relating the concept to poststructuralist theory; and attempting to reconceptualize hegemonic masculinity through queer theory and postcolonialism (Hearn et al., 2012).

Recent research from the United States suggests that hegemonic masculinities—at the local, regional, and global levels—are constructed differently. For example, Messerschmidt (2016) found that hegemonic masculinities vary in the significance and scope of their legitimating influence—the justifying of unequal gender relations by *localized* hegemonic masculinities is limited to the confines of the gender regimes in particular institutions, such as schools, whereas *regional* and *global* hegemonic masculinities have, respectively, a society-wide regional gender order and worldwide global gender order legitimating impact. Messerschmidt (2016) also distinguished between "dominating" and "protective" forms of hegemonic masculinities and accordingly between different constructions of gendered power relations. He found different ways hegemonic masculinities were constructed: localized hegemonic masculinities were fashioned through relational *material* practices that had a discursive legitimating influence, whereas regional and global hegemonic masculinities were constructed through *discursive* practices— such as speeches and rap albums—that concurrently constituted unequal gender relations linguistically, metaphorically, and thus symbolically.

Finally, Messerschmidt (2016) noted the significance of *reflexivity* in the construction of both hegemonic and nonhegemonic masculinities. Reflexivity refers to exercising our conscious mental ability to consider ourselves in relation to the particular social context and circumstances we experience by engaging in internal conversations about particular social experiences and then deciding how to respond appropriately. However, masculinities may also be constructed nonreflexively through the practicing of gender that is emergent, directional, temporal, rapid, immediate, and indeterminate (Martin 2003, 2006; see also Bird and Sokolofski 2005).

"Female" Masculinities

Certain individuals in specific times and places transcend their assigned "female" sex at birth and construct masculinities. For example, in many traditional Native American societies—such as the Klamath, Mohave, Maricopa, and Ciocopa—girls who practice masculinities were recognized as "two-spirits" through specific formal ceremonies (Blackwood 1994). As adults, two-spirit women engaged in exclusively masculine practices and wore "male" clothing; that is, they were defined socially as constituting "social man with a vagina" (Bolin 1994). And in his book *Female Masculinity*, Jack Halberstam (1998) catalogs the diversity of gender expressions among masculine women, uncovering the hidden history of female masculinities (see also the pioneering work of Devor 1989, 1997; Rubin 2003).

More recently, Messerschmidt (2016) carried on this tradition by showing that masculinity is not exclusively coupled with people assigned "male" at birth. For example, he found that under particular social situations masculinity by specific individuals assigned "female" at birth becomes the primary foundation of their identity while "sex" is then transformed into the qualifier. The coherence of one's initial fundamental sex and gender project may be altered whereby masculinity becomes primary and "real" and "sex" is transmuted to epiphenomenon. Additionally, Messerschmidt found that individuals assigned female at birth who practiced masculinity may experience specific contradictions between their bodies and masculinity, and through the discursively sexed meanings of certain bodily developments (such as breasts and menstruation) and the fact that culturally their bodies were expected to be congruent with femininity, not masculinity. Indeed, people assigned female at birth often experience a degree of bodily anxiety in constructing masculinities, especially when embedded in cultural conceptions of two and only two sexes and its accompanying discursive assertion that men have penises and women do not. For such individuals, masculinity can be experienced in certain situations—such as sexual situations (see, further, Schilt and Windsor 2014; Westbrook and Schilt 2014)—as a *disembodied* phenomenon that affects future practice. Finally, Messerschmidt's data on individuals assigned female at birth shows that eventual genderqueer constructions represent examples of what Haywood and Mac an Ghaill (2012, 2013) recently labeled "post-masculinities," in the sense of not being exclusively masculine but rather that masculinity is merely a specific part of their overall gender construction and not its sole defining characteristic.

Globalization

From the 1950s to the 1980s numerous writers in the global South raised important questions and inspired significant debate on the relationship among globalization, colonialism, and masculinity (Mernissi 1975; Paz 1950; Nandy 1983). A surge of social research and debate on masculinity followed within different parts of the global South in the 1990s, at much the same time as in the global North (though less noticed in Anglophone sociological literature), and as usual in the global economy of knowledge the work in the global South often used concepts and methods circulating in the global North. For example, Robert Morrell (1994, 1998, 2001), in an early series of studies, identified three distinct localized hegemonic masculinities in South Africa: a *white* hegemonic masculinity constructed by the politically dominant white ruling class men; an *African* hegemonic masculinity fashioned by indigenous male chiefs;

and a *black* hegemonic masculinity that existed in the various South African townships (see also Cornwall and Lindisfarne 1994; Pease and Pringle 2001). And in the early 2000s, the empirical base of research and theoretical development on globalization and masculinities was greatly diversified to include, for example, studies on Japan (Roberson and Suzuki 2003), Australia (Tomsen and Donaldson 2003), Latin America (Viveros Vigoya 2001; Gutmann 1996), the Middle East (Ghoussoub and Sinclair-Webb 2000), and China (Louie 2002).

Connell (1998, 2005) developed a theoretical framework for under-standing the relationship among hegemonic masculinity, globalization, and a global gender order. First, Connell (2005, 72) defines globalization as "the current pattern of world integration via global markets, transna-tional corporations, and electronic media under the political hegemony of the United States." Second, Connell illuminates how a global gender order is articulated as part of this larger operation of globalization, tar-geting two basic links currently constituting a global gender order. The first link involves the interaction, interconnection, and interdependence of nation-states and their regional gender orders. As Connell (2005, 73) puts it, "The gender patterns resulting from these interactions are the first level of a global gender order. They are [regional] patterns but carry the impress of the forces that make a global society." The second link creates new "spaces" beyond individual nation-states: transnational and multinational corporations (that maintain strong gender divisions of labor and strong masculinist management cultures); the international state (centered on a masculinized approach to diplomacy and war); the international media (consisting of multinational firms that circu-late gendered meanings through film, video, music, and news world-wide); and global markets (the increasing reach of capital, commodity, service, and labor markets into individual nation-state economies). The combination of these forms of linkage is "a partially integrated, highly unequal, and turbulent set of gender relations, with global reach but uneven impact," which now structures the context for considering the construction of local, regional, and global hegemonic masculinities (74). Messerschmidt's (2016) examination of the speeches by two recent US presidents—George W. Bush and Barack Obama—are relevant examples of global hegemonic masculinities that accord with the "second link" identified above, and are therefore salient components of the "global gender order."

More recently, Connell (2014) has outlined a strategy for conceptualizing global masculinities based on North/South relations. In examining masculinities scholarship in both the global North and the global South, Connell notes how scholars in the latter often rely on theories and research developed in the former because of the structure of knowledge production in the global economy of knowledge, which has made it difficult to fully comprehend masculinities constructed in the global South. Connell chronicles a rich archive of examinations of masculinities from around the global South that provide a foundation for understanding the relationship among masculine constructions in the North and South. Connell concludes that the global formation of masculinities must be conceptualized through an understanding of worldwide processes of colonial conquest and social disruption, the building of colonial societies and the global capitalist economy, and postindependent globalization (see, also, Connell 2016).

In various recent publications, Jeff Hearn and colleagues (2015; Hearn, Blagojevic, and Harrison 2015; Ruspini et al. 2011) have likewise noted that most studies of men and masculinities have concentrated their research efforts within the boundaries of individual national contexts, leaving men and masculinities in globalization and transnational situations unexamined. Following Connell's (1998) suggestion that masculinities scholars move beyond the "ethnographic moment," Hearn similarly suggests the development of international, transnational, and global perspectives. Hearn (2015) argues that various forms of "transnationalization" have created new and changing material and representational gender hierarchies—or what Hearn refers to as "transnational patriarchies"—that structure men's transnational gender domination. For Hearn, some contemporary arenas involving transnational gender inequalities include transnational corporations and government organizations with men in almost exclusive positions of power; international trade, global finance, and the masculinization of capital; militarism and the arms trade; international sports; migrations and refugees; information and communication technologies; and the sex trade.

"New" Masculinities

In this final section we underline the importance of understanding the development of "new" masculinities within a structural theory of gender relations and power. Hondagneu-Sotelo and Messner (1994) argued, for instance, that the often celebrated shifting "styles" of the class-privileged white "New Man" of the 1990s were often constructed in relation to the supposedly atavistic and "macho" masculine gender displays projected onto subordinated men, such as Mexican immigrant men. When an intersectional (race-class-gender-citizenship status) structural analysis was foregrounded, however, it was revealed that these men's common "styles" of masculinity were linked to their social locations. The Mexican immigrant man's supposedly "macho" gender displays were actually revealed to be public responses to low levels of public power, privilege, and status, but research showed that Mexican immigrant men contributed more to housework and child care than did white, middle-class men. The "New Man," by contrast, displayed "softer" styles of masculinity that helped to cement their public power and privilege over women, and over class- and race-subordinated groups of men.

Recent work on hybrid masculinities by Bridges (2014) and by Bridges and Pascoe (2014; chapter 13, this volume) reveals such "New Man" constructions of masculinity as collective (and culturally creative) intersectional responses to strains and tensions experienced at structural sites of crisis tendencies. Hybrid masculinities involve the incorporation of subordinated styles and displays (masculine or feminine, or both) into privileged men's identities, in the process simultaneously securing and obscuring their access to power and privilege. For instance, Kristen Barber (2016) shows how class-privileged men's embrace of previously feminine-typed consumption of personal grooming styles actually serves to enhance their positions of privilege in relation to women and to class-subordinated men. When widespread consent congeals around such a hybrid masculinity formation—particularly when it is grounded in a multibillion-dollar men's grooming industry replete with a continual barrage of celebratory media and advertising—a situationally hegemonic masculinity emerges, seeming on the surface to signal the emergence of a "new," less rigid masculinity while simultaneously concealing and reproducing gender, race, and class inequalities.

As Bridges and Pascoe (chapter 13, this volume) put it, "The appropriation of elements of subordinated and marginalized 'Others' into configurations of hegemonic masculinities works to recuperate existing systems of power and inequality," and thereby must be understood as expressions of, rather than challenges to, gender hegemony. Paraphrasing Bridges and Pascoe's argument, hybrid hegemonic masculinities illustrate some of the changes taking place in reproducing gender hegemony, demonstrating how the experiences and views of privilege have been transformed, thus making a host of new identity projects available, which in turn is enabling different groups of men to navigate social change in different ways.

Structurally contextualized analyses of "new" masculinities can also help us to understand the engagements of men in feminist and other progressive social movements (Messner 1993). Messner, Greenberg, and Peretz (2015) examine how, from the 1970s to the present, the shifting state of play of feminist movement politics, higher education, the state, nonprofit organizations, and other institutions shaped U.S. men's engagements with progressive gender politics—particularly efforts to stop sexual and domestic violence against women. Their analysis emphasizes how intersectional (especially race, class, and gender) structural contexts shaped *which* men engage in political action with feminist women at particular historical moments, and also *how* these men and women strategize to stop gender-based violence. Activists of the 1970s and 1980s, for instance, were disproportionately white (often Jewish) college-educated men who were drawn to antirape and anti–domestic violence work by their immersion in feminist and other radical social movements of the era. Today's younger male activists come to gender-based violence prevention via different paths: white middle class men commonly find their way to the work via campus-based activism, women's studies courses, and volunteer or paid work in feminist community nonprofits. A growing number of younger men of color have taken on gender-based violence prevention through work with boys and young men in poor communities around youth gang violence, substance abuse programs, and prison reform.

In thinking about "new" masculinities, global perspectives are important in deploying emergent concepts like hybrid masculinities. Bridges and Pascoe's work concentrates on the global North, yet hybrid hegemonic masculinities also seem to be taking place in some parts of the global South. For example, Christian Groes-Green's (2012) notion of "philogynous masculinities" in Mozambique illustrates this. Groes-Green discusses what he labels the *bom pico* (meaning, a good lover) heterosexual form of masculinity, which prioritizes women's sexual pleasure and emphasizes caring and attentiveness toward women. However, in prioritizing women's sexual pleasure, *bom pico* men reproduce hegemonic notions of virility, potency, and strength and subordinate men who are seen as being "sexually weak" (that is, unable to perform). Men who practice *bom pico* masculinity then are aligning themselves with hegemonic masculinity even as their practices might seem to distance themselves from it, and, therefore, they reproduce masculine power over women and "Other" men in a novel way. Moreover, the work of Ratele (2013; chapter 11, this volume) demonstrates how past traditions remain significant among men living in South Africa in their constructions of masculinities under both colonization and postcolonization.

Shari Dworkin and her colleagues have drawn from theories of multiple masculinities as foundations for developing structural interventions for change, thus building an important dimension to HIV prevention in South Africa and other parts of the global South, where the focus has thus far been primarily on empowering women (Dworkin 2015; Dworkin, Fleming, and Colvin 2015). The researchers critically examine different approaches to health interventions in the global South, ranging from "gender-neutral" to "gender-sensitive" to "gender-empowering" to "gender-transformative" approaches (Dworkin 2015, 29–30). They argue that the keys to maximizing the potential success of "gender-transformative" efforts—that is, programs that aim to create more egalitarian local gender regimes—are (a) introducing programs that are not isolated health interventions, but are connected with other issues like reducing gender-based violence and increasing economic independence; (b) as much as possible, creating interventions with men that operate from an understanding of gender as *relational*—that is, from an understanding of the state of play of men's structural relations of labor, power, and sexuality with women; and (c) that this relational theory is also *intersectional*, addressing not just gender inequalities but also race and class hierarchies among men. As the researchers note,

> it is important in programme content not only to consider the democratisation of the gender order in terms of women and men, but also how hierarchies of masculinities can be taken into account. It is therefore critical to highlight that men's disempowerment contributes to their increased likelihood of being victims of violence at the hands of other men, perpetrating violence against other men and perpetrating violence against women. (Dworkin, Fleming, and Colvin 2015, 9)

Fundamentally this means linking HIV and violence prevention programs with men in an effort to address men's and women's economic, colonial, and racial marginality in broader structural contexts. Understood this way, "hegemonic masculinity" is deployed by the researchers not as a way to describe a type of man, but rather as "an ideal that collectively structures a field of gender relations" (Dworkin 2015, 13). And, in this high-stakes effort, "changing masculinities" means far more than shifting styles of gender display; it means addressing deep issues of poverty, health, and violence by attempting to alter the social structure that generates these problems.

Conclusion

In this chapter we reviewed the initial formulation of Connell's framework and outlined some of its early applications as well as some of the criticisms leveled against it. We then discussed the reformulation of Connell's perspective by Connell and Messerschmidt (2005) and summarized some recent scholarly publications supporting that reformulation. Finally, in the last two sections we outlined contemporary scholarly directions on hegemonic and nonhegemonic masculinities as well as research examining the emergence of "new" masculinities. It is clear from the studies we have chronicled in this chapter that scholars are now engaged in impressive research on masculinities and their relationship to unequal gender relationships around the globe, and this research documents the continued significance of the concept of hegemonic masculinity and simultaneously inspires additional gender research that further extends our knowledge in similar and previously unexplored areas.

REFERENCES

Barber, K. 2016. *Styling Masculinity: Gender, Class, and Inequality in the Men's Grooming Industry*. New Brunswick, NJ: Rutgers University Press.

Beasley, C. 2008. "Re-thinking Hegemonic Masculinity in a Globalizing World." *Men and Masculinities* 11 (1): 86–103.

Bird, S., and L. Sokolofski. 2005. "Gendered Socio-Spatial Practices in Public Eating and Drinking Establishments in the Midwest United States." *Gender, Place & Culture* 12 (2): 213–30.

Blackwood, E. 1994. "Sexuality and Gender in Certain Native American Tribes: The Case of Cross-Gender Females." In *Theorizing Feminism*, edited by A. C. Hermann and A. J. Stewart, 301–15. Boulder, CO: Westview Press.

Bolin, A. 1994. "Transcending and Transgendering: Male-to-Female Transsexuals, Dichotomy, and Diversity." In *Third Sex, Third Gender: Beyond Sexual Dimorphism in Culture and History*, edited by G. Herdt, 447–86. New York: Zone Books.

Bridges, Tristan. 2014. "A Very 'Gay' Straight? Hybrid Masculinities, Sexual Aesthetics, and the Changing Relationship between Masculinity and Homophobia." *Gender & Society* 28 (1): 58–82.

Bridges, T., and C. J. Pascoe. 2014. "Hybrid Masculinities: New Directions in the Sociology of Men and Masculinities." *Sociology Compass* 8:246–58.

Broughton, C. 2008. "Migration as Engendered Practice: Mexican Men, Masculinity, and Northward Migration." *Gender & Society* 22:568–89.

Collier, R. 1998. *Masculinities, Crime and Criminology: Men, Heterosexuality and the Criminal(ised) Other*. London: Sage.

Collinson, D., and J. Hearn. 1994. "Naming Men as Men: Implications for Work, Organization and Management." *Gender, Work and Organization* 1 (1): 2–22.

Connell, R. 1987. *Gender and Power*. Sydney: Allen and Unwin.

———. (1995) 2005. *Masculinities*. 2nd ed. Cambridge: Polity Press.

———.1998. "Masculinities and Globalization." *Men and Masculinities* 1:3–23.

———.2005. "Globalization, Imperialism, and Masculinities." In *Handbook of Studies on Men and Masculinities*, edited by M. S. Kimmel, J. Hearn, and R. Connell. Thousand Oaks, CA: Sage.

———. 2014. "Margin Becoming Center: For a World-Centered Rethinking of Masculinities." *Norma: International Journal for Masculinities Studies* 9:217–31.

———. 2016. "100 Million Kalashnikovs: Gendered Power on a World Scale." *Debate Feminista*, http://dx.doi.org/10.1016/j.df.2016.03.001.

Connell, R., and J. W. Messerschmidt. 2005. "Hegemonic Masculinity: Rethinking the Concept." *Gender & Society* 19:829–59.

Connell, R., and R. Pease. 2014. *Gender: In World Perspective*. 3rd ed. Cambridge: Polity Press.

Cornwall, A., and N. Lindisfarne, eds. 1994. *Dislocating Masculinity: Comparative Ethnographies*. New York: Routledge.

Demetriou, D. Z. 2001. "Connell's Concept of Hegemonic Masculinity: A Critique." *Theory and Society* 30 (3): 337–61.

Devor, A. 1989. *Gender Blending: Confronting the Limits of Duality*. Bloomington: Indiana University Press.

———. 1997. *FTM: Female-to-Male Transsexuals in Society*. Bloomington: Indiana University Press.

Donaldson, M. 1993. "What Is Hegemonic Masculinity?" *Theory and Society* 22:643–57.

Duncanson, C. 2009. "Forces for Good? Narratives of Military Masculinity as Peacekeeping Operations." *International Feminist Journal of Politics* 11:63–80.

Dworkin, S. L. 2015. *Men at Risk: Masculinity, Heterosexuality, and HIV Prevention*. New York: NYU Press.

Dworkin, S. L., P. J. Fleming, and C. J. Colvin. 2015. "The Promises and Limitations of Gender-Transformative Health Programming with Men: Critical Reflections from the Field." *Culture, Health and Sexuality* 17: 128–143.

Elias, J., and C. Beasley. 2009. "Hegemonic Masculinity and Globalization: 'Transnational Business Masculinities' and Beyond." *Globalization* 6:281–96.

Ghoussoub, M., and E. Sinclair-Webb, eds. 2000. *Imagined Masculinities: Male Identity and Culture in the Modern Middle East*. London: Saqi Books.

Groes-Green, C. 2009. "Hegemonic and Subordinated Masculinities: Class, Violence and Sexual Performance among Young Mozambican Men." *Nordic Journal of African Studies* 18:286–304.

———. 2012. "Philogynous Masculinities: Contextualizing Alternative Manhood in Mozambique." *Men and Masculinities* 15:91–111.

Gutmann, M. 1996. *The Meaning of Macho: Being a Man in Mexico City*. Berkeley: University of California Press.

Halberstam, J. 1998. *Female Masculinity*. Durham, NC: Duke University Press.

Hatfield, E. F. 2010. "'What It Means to Be a Man': Examining Hegemonic Masculinity in *Two and Half Men*." *Communication, Culture & Critique* 3:526–48.

Haywood, C., and M. Mac an Ghaill. 2012. "'What's Next for Masculinity?' Reflexive Directions for Theory and Research on Masculinity and Education." *Gender and Education* 24:577–92.

———. 2013. *Education and Masculinities: Social, Cultural and Global Transformations*. New York: Routledge.

Hearn, J. 1996. "Is Masculinity Dead? A Critique of the Concept of Masculinity/Masculinities." In *Understanding Masculinities: Social Relations and Cultural Arenas*, edited by M. Mac an Ghaill. Buckingham, UK: Open University Press.

———. 2004. "From Hegemonic Masculinity to the Hegemony of Men." *Feminist Theory* 5 (1): 49–72.

———. 2015. *Men of the World: Genders, Globalizations, Transnational Times*. Thousand Oaks, CA: Sage.

Hearn, J., M. Blagojevic, and K. Harrison, eds. 2015. *Rethinking Transnational Men: Beyond, between and within Nations.* New York: Routledge.

Hearn, J., M. Nordberg, K. Andersson, D. Balkmar, L. Gottzen, R. Klinth, K. Pringle, and L. Sandberg. 2012. "Hegemonic Masculinity and Beyond: 40 Years of Research in Sweden." *Men and Masculinities* 15 (1): 31–55.

Holter, Ø. G. 1997. *Gender, Patriarchy and Capitalism: A Social Forms Analysis.* Oslo: University of Oslo.

———. 2003. *Can Men Do It? Men and Gender Equality—the Nordic Experience.* Copenhagen: Nordic Council of Ministers.

Hondagneu-Sotelo, Pierrette, and Michael A. Messner. 1994. "Gender Displays and Men's Power: The 'New Man' and the Mexican Immigrant Man." In *Theorizing Masculinities*, edited by Harry Brod and Michael Kaufman. Thousand Oaks, CA: Sage.

Irvine, L., and J. Vermilya. 2010. "Gender Work in a Feminized Profession: The Case of Veterinary Medicine." *Gender & Society* 24:56–82.

Jefferson, T. 1994. "Theorizing Masculine Subjectivity." In *Just Boys Doing Business? Men, Masculinities and Crime*, edited by T. Newburn and E. A. Stanko. London: Routledge.

———. 2002. "Subordinating Hegemonic Masculinity." *Theoretical Criminology* 6 (1): 63–88.

Light, R. 2007. "Re-Examining Hegemonic Masculinity in High School Rugby: The Body, Compliance and Resistance." *Quest* 59:323–38.

Louie, K. 2002. *Theorizing Chinese Masculinity: Society and Gender in China.* Cambridge: Cambridge University Press.

Martin, P. 1998. "Why Can't a Man Be More Like a Woman? Reflections on Connell's *Masculinities*." *Gender & Society* 12 (4): 472–74.

———. 2003. "'Said and Done' versus 'Saying and Doing': Gendering Practices and Practicing Gender at Work." *Gender & Society* 17 (3): 342–66.

———. 2006. "Practicing Gender at Work: Further Thoughts on Reflexivity." *Gender, Work and Organization* 13 (3): 254–76.

McMahon, A. 1993. "Male Readings of Feminist Theory: The Psychologization of Sexual Politics in the Masculinity Literature." *Theory and Society* 22 (5): 675–95.

Mernissi, F. 1975. *Beyond the Veil: Male-Female Dynamics in Modern Muslim Society.* London: Saqi Books.

Messerschmidt, J. W. 2012. "Engendering Gendered Knowledge: Assessing the Academic Appropriation of Hegemonic Masculinity." *Men and Masculinities* 15:56–76.

———. 2016. *Masculinities in the Making: From the Local to the Global.* Lanham, MD: Rowman and Littlefield.

Messner, M. A. 1993. "'Changing Men' and Feminist Politics in the United States." *Theory and Society* 22 (5): 723–37.

———. 2014. "Gender Relations and Sport: Local, National, Transnational." In *Playfields: Power, Practice, and Passion in Sport*, edited by Mariann Vaczi, 17–35. Reno, NV: Center for Basque Studies Press.

Messner, M. A., M. Greenberg, and T. Peretz. 2015. *Some Men: Feminist Allies and the Movement to End Violence against Women.* Oxford: Oxford University Press.

Morrell, R. 1994. "Masculinity and the White Boys' Boarding Schools of Natal, 1880–1930." *Perspectives in Education* 15:27–52.

———. 1998. "Of Boys and Men: Masculinity and Gender in Southern African Studies." *Journal of Southern African Studies* 24:605–30.

———, ed. 2001. *Changing Men in Southern Africa*. London: Zed Books.

Morrell, R., R. Jewkes, and G. Lindegger. 2012. "Hegemonic Masculinity/Masculinities in South Africa: Culture, Power, and Gender Politics." *Men and Masculinities* 15 (1): 11–30.

Morris, E. W. 2008. "'Rednecks,' 'Rutters,' and 'Rithmetic': Social Class, Masculinity, and Schooling in a Rural Context." *Gender & Society* 22:728–51.

Musto, M. 2014. "Athletes in the Pool, Girls and Boys on the Deck: The Contextual Construction of Gender in Co-ed Youth Swimming." *Gender & Society* 28:359–80.

Nandy, A. 1983. *The Intimate Enemy: Loss and Recovery of Self under Colonialism*. New York: Oxford University Press.

Paz, O. 1950. *The Labyrinth of Solitude*. New York: Penguin.

Pease, B., and K. Pringle. 2001. *A Man's World? Changing Men's Practices in a Globalized World*. London: Zed Books.

Petersen, A. 1998. *Unmasking the Masculine: "Men" and "Identity" in a Sceptical Age*. London: Sage.

———. 2003. "Research on Men and Masculinities: Some Implications of Recent Theory for Future Work." *Men and Masculinities* 6 (1): 54–69.

Ratele, K. 2013. "Masculinities without Tradition." *Politikon: South African Journal of Political Studies* 40:133–56.

Roberson, J. E., and N. Suzuki, eds. 2003. *Men and Masculinities in Contemporary Japan*. New York: Routledge.

Rubin, H. 2003. *Self-Made Men: Identity and Embodiment among Transsexual Men*. Nashville, TN: Vanderbilt University Press.

Ruspini, E., J. Hearn, B. Pease, and K. Pringle, eds. 2011. *Men and Masculinities around the World: Transforming Men's Practices*. London: Palgrave.

Schilt, K., and E. Windsor. 2014. "The Sexual Habitus of Transgender Men: Negotiating Sexuality through Gender." *Journal of Homosexuality* 61:732–48.

Schippers, M. 2007. "Recovering the Feminine Other: Masculinity, Femininity, and Gender Hegemony." *Theory & Society* 36 (1): 85–102.

Talbot, K., and M. Quayle. 2010. "The Perils of Being a Nice Guy: Contextual Variation in Five Young Women's Constructions of Acceptable Hegemonic and Alternative Masculinities." *Men and Masculinities* 13:255–78.

Tomsen, S., and M. Donaldson, eds. 2003. *Male Trouble: Looking at Australian Masculinities*. London: Pluto Press.

Viveros Vigoya, M. 2001. "Contemporary Latin American Perspectives on Masculinity." *Men and Masculinities* 3:237–60.

Weitzer, R., and C. E. Kubrin. 2009. "Misogyny in Rap Music: A Content Analysis of Prevalence and Meanings." *Men and Masculinities* 12:3–29.

Westbrook, L., and K. Schilt. 2014. "Doing Gender, Determining Gender: Transgender People, Gender Panics, and the Maintenance of the Sex/Gender/Sexuality System." *Gender & Society* 28:32–57.

Wetherell, M., and N. Edley. 1999. "Negotiating Hegemonic Masculinity: Imaginary Positions and Psycho-Discursive Practices." *Feminism and Psychology* 9 (3): 335–56.

Whitehead, S. M. 1998. "Hegemonic Masculinity Revisited." *Gender, Work and Organization* 6 (1): 58–62.

———. 2002. *Men and Masculinities: Key Themes and New Directions*. Cambridge: Polity.

3

From Object to Subject

Situating Transgender Lives in Sociology

KRISTEN SCHILT

Raewyn Connell's *Gender and Power* sets out a social theory of gender and embodiment that simultaneously strikes down biological determinism and the then-dominant sociological theories of sex roles. Drawing insights from feminist theory and gay liberation activism, Connell charts the work that beliefs in natural differences (male/female, hetero/homo) do at a societal level to naturalize gender and sexual hierarchies. She goes on to outline the institutional forms, such as the family and the workplace, that often reproduce structural inequality. To this "top-down" theory, she brings in the necessity of addressing people's agency within systems of constraints—an inclusion that sets the stage for a structural theory of gender inequality that accounts for the ways in which social change can and does happen in the face of institutional and interactional mechanisms of cultural reproduction. As she argues, such a structural theory of gender must recognize the "interweaving of personal life and social structure without collapsing towards voluntarism and pluralism on one side, or categoricalism and biological determinism on the other" (1987, 67).

While the value of Connell's work to the sociology of gender has been widely recognized, there has been less attention to the seeds of a particularly nuanced sociological perspective on the lives of transgender people planted across the pages of the book. Drawing upon the work of ethnomethodologists (Garfinkel 1967; Kessler and McKenna 1978), Connell argues that social science research on what was then termed "transsexualism" provides "exceptional insight into the social construction of gender in everyday life" (1987, 76).[1] Yet she goes beyond this theoretical point by offering a sociohistorical analysis that takes into account broader societal change in cultural ideas about gender and sexuality alongside the impact and possibilities such changes bring for people's sense of identities and embodiment. As I show in this chapter, such a theory—which Connell continues to develop in her later works (1995, 2002, 2012)—stands in stark contrast to the then-dominant approaches to theorizing about transgender people in sociology. I argue that this nascent discussion provides an early roadmap for a sociological perspective that takes transgender people's lived experiences as a starting point of analysis (see also Rubin 2003; Namaste 2000/2005). I conclude with a look at how these ideas have evolved in the field of transgender studies within sociology.

Categorizing "the Transsexual" as a Social Problem

That Raewyn Connell included even a small discussion of transgender people in *Gender and Power*—a manuscript she wrote in 1984[2]—is notable. In the 1960s and 1970s, a great deal of media attention had been dedicated to spectacular accounts of people undergoing "sex change" operations (see Meyerowitz 2002). In the fields of psychology and medicine, doctors and researchers were engaged in fierce debates about the appropriate treatment for patients diagnosed with what was then termed "gender dysphoria" (Meyerowitz 2002). While a small group of sociologists were developing critical gay and feminist studies in the 1970s and 1980s (see, for example, Altman 1971; Huber 1973), very few researchers were conducting empirical research on the lives and experiences of transgender people. The few studies that did emerge in this time period typically did not link activism around gender identity by transgender and gender nonconforming people to other liberation movements, such as women's liberation and gay liberation (see Perkins 1983 for an exception; see Stryker 2008 for the history of such activism). Rather, within these works,[3] transgender people were taken up as cultural objects useful for theorizing the concept of "passing" (Kando 1973), stigma management (Feinbloom 1976), the social impact of homophobia (Altman 1971), the social pathology of the gender binary (Raymond 1979), the social construction of medical knowledge (Billings and Urban 1982), and the social construction of gender (Garfinkel 1967; Kessler and McKenna 1978; see King 1987 and Namaste 2000 for a more detailed overview and critique of these studies).

Thomas Kando's *Sex Change* (1973) and Deborah Feinbloom's *Transsexuals and Transvestites: Mixed Views* (1976), which draw on participant observation and interview data in a university-sponsored gender clinic and at community support groups, respectively, highlight one strand of sociological research that investigated the experiences of transgender people in the 1970s. Influenced by the naturalistic works of the "second Chicago school" (Matza 1969), namely Howard Becker and Erving Goffman, that sought to document how social "outsiders" deemed to be deviant by mainstream society navigated social control and stigma, Kando and Feinbloom use empirical data to detail what they position as an emerging marginalized subculture. Through these studies, they grapple with providing a career model of "transsexuality," a focus much in line with sociological work of the time on "becoming deviant" (Matza 1969) and the construction of social problems. In a departure from most of the clinical studies of the time in psychiatry and medicine, these works contain a wealth of information about the challenges that transgender people faced in accessing medical care, within family relationships, and in seeking employment. While both researchers include interview excerpts from transgender respondents in their analysis, however, they often undermine their respondents' own understandings of their gender identities by maintaining a distinction between "natural" (e.g., chromosomal) men and women and "constructed" transgender people. Highlighting one such example, Kando writes of his interviewees, "while feminized transsexuals [trans women] may sometimes pass quite successfully as natural females, we know that they are not, and so do they" (1973, 5). Within these analyses, the authors focus predominantly on the stages of physical and identity transformation that can accompany a person's gender transition—which, in the early 1970s, appeared to these researchers as a new social phenomenon in need of empirical investigation—rather than on the subjectivity and social embeddedness of transgender people.

A second strand of research in the 1970s and 1980s positioned "transsexuality" as an effect of the social pathology created within a society that only legitimated a gender and sexual dimorphic model of attraction between female/feminine and male/masculine people. In the feminist and gay variant of this research, authors expressed a deep suspicion of the diagnosis of gender dysphoria and the emphasis in the medical and psychiatric community on surgical and hormonal modifications as a form of treatment. In Dennis Altman's *Homosexual Oppression and Liberation* (1971), he acknowledges the connections between early trans and gender nonconforming activism and gay liberation, but worries that people who seek to physically transition are motivated by an internalized homophobia.[4] Janice Raymond's *The Transsexual Empire* (1979) offers a more detailed critique. Drawing on a lesbian feminist perspective, she argues that genital reassignment surgeries are commodities that advertise an impossible dream: to change one's sex in order to embody a pathological social construction of femininity or masculinity. Emphasizing this point, she refers to transgender people as "female-to-constructed male" and "male-to-constructed female" throughout the book. The social pathology frame presents transgender people as agents of conservatism who seek to reify the gender status quo. Such an idea is echoed in other sociological work of the time, with transgender people described as "Uncle Toms of the sexual revolution" (Kando 1973, 145) who "do not challenge the social institution of gender. In many ways, they reinforce it" (Billings and Urban 1982, 269; see also Bem 1993).

Sociologists Dwight Billings and Thomas Urban (1982) build on this social pathology critique in their ethnographic study of a university-sponsored gender clinic. Their article presents one of the only empirical studies of such clinics in the 1970s and 1980s. Yet, while they document the ways in which doctors' views of who makes a "good candidate" for medically supervised transitions are infused with their preconceived notions about class, race, and gender, they fail to bring this critique forward in a way that considers the impact of such procedures on transgender people's lives (see Spade 2006 for a more detailed critique). Dropping Raymond's lesbian feminist framework for a Marxist lens, Billings and Urban argue that "the legitimation, rationalization, and commodification of sex-change operations have produced an identity category— transsexual—for a diverse group of sexual deviants and victims of severe gender role distress" (1982, 266). Here, they position people seeking genital reassignment surgery as cultural dupes buying into the medical establishment's offerings of empty, high-price commodities. Thus, in this frame, "the transsexual" is pathologically attempting to embody what the researchers set out as a socially constructed norm—the ultimate example of a person who has been "brainwashed" by gender ideologies.

The final strand of this early sociological research on transgender people—and the strand that has had the most "staying power" in the discipline—uses transgender people's interactional experiences with "gender crossing" to bolster a theoretical argument that gender is a social, rather than a biological, category. In this body of work, feminist ethnomethodologists Suzanne Kessler and Wendy McKenna (1978) build upon the first sociological case study of a person who might identify today as transgender: Harold Garfinkel's 1967 case study of "Agnes," a young woman assigned male at birth who was seeking medical treatment in the 1950s at the UCLA gender clinic. During over 35 hours of interviews, Garfinkel sought to determine how Agnes was able to live and work as any other young woman in Los Angeles without having the so-called biological and biographical credentials that other people assumed her to have on the basis of her appearance and behavior. This case study—and its conceptual argument that all people must interactionally achieve their gender in social settings—became the cornerstone for the now-canonical theory of "doing gender" (West and Zimmerman 1987). Yet, while this body of work formed a strong sociological critique of biological essentialism that was key to the development of feminist sociology, the theoretical frame paid little attention to the actual lives and experiences of transgender people (for a more in-depth critique of these studies, see Rogers 1992; Rubin 1999; Namaste 2000).

If sociologists in the 1970s and 1980s largely took "transsexuality" as *an object* of theoretical investigation, I suggest that Raewyn Connell's theoretical framework set out in *Gender and Power* and developed in her later works locates transgender people as historically and culturally *situated subjects*. The few passages in *Gender and Power* in which she engages in an explicit discussion of "transsexualism" are located alongside her advocacy for a structural approach to theorizing gender and sexual relations that emphasizes historical and cultural change in the development and meaning of social categories, such as "woman" and "homosexual." Connell further makes a case for the necessity of shifting the understanding of bodies as passive receivers of culture norms to historically located agents of practice—a concept she would later term "social embodiment" (2002, 47). It is through "seeing the historicity of gender" (1987, 77) and the ways in which "the body is never outside of history, and history never free of bodily presence and effects on the body" (1987,

87) that Connell is able to set the stage for a sociological theory that accounts both for the cultural and historical emergence of "the transsexual" as a new social category and the subjectivity and agency of transgender people.

From the Categorical to the Sociohistorical

To set out what I see as Connell's intervention into sociological theorizing about transgender people, I begin with a short overview of her critique of the "categorical" thinking she identifies as prevalent in much academic feminist, Marxist feminist, and structuralist/psychoanalytic feminist work that grapples with the historical and persistent devaluation of women *vis-à-vis* men. For Connell, the features of a categorical theory are, first, a "close identification of opposed interests in sexual politics with specific categories of people" (1987, 54), such as men versus women. Second, categorical theorizing focuses the argument on "the category as a unit, rather than on the processes by which the category is constituted, or on its elements or constituents" (1987, 54). Finally, such accounts conceive of the social order as constructed of only a few categories—opposing categories that are related to each other hierarchically. This approach often elides the ways in which intersecting identities, such as race and class, might foster unity rather than conflict between groups imagined to be oppositional, such as men and women, and neglects the importance of historical change, cultural context, and experiential practice. For her, such theories stay "within the big picture and pain[t] it with a broad brush" (1987, 54), operating, in effect, as if "the person and personal practice can be eliminated from the equation altogether" (1987, 56). While Connell does not discuss research on transgender people in this section, her critique could easily be extended to the work that I detailed in the previous section that theorizes the social category of "the transsexual" while ignoring or glossing over the experiences and practices of transgender people.

In Connell's reading, while proponents of categorical approaches to gender and sexual inequality generally are in opposition to biological determinists, both sets of theorists take binaries of male/female, masculine/feminine, or straight/gay as unproblematic, static categories—though they link this stasis to social structures and cultural stereotypes or to chromosomes and reproductive capacities, respectively. Further, for Connell, categorical thinking is imbued with a "bland optimism about progress" (1987, 77) that imagines social change only in the form of making existing binaries more equal or eradicating categories altogether. Connell tempers this "progress" focus, arguing instead that such a utopian project is always destined for failure because gender and sexuality are structural, embodied, and "a fundamental feature of the way we have knowledge of human beings" (1987, 76). She proposes instead a theoretical approach that understands the current sex/gender system as a social process that varies historically and across cultures, creating space for shifting power dynamics and the possibility for the emergence of new identity categories and forms of activism. Such a theory emphasizes change but not progress. Shifts in the sex/gender system, in other words, could bring more freedom and opportunity to socially marginalized groups, could result in unforeseen new barriers, constraints, and forms of discrimination, or, perhaps more likely, could do both simultaneously.

Connell illustrates how such a sociohistorical and structural analysis of the sex/gender system could work in practice by drawing on the then-emerging research on the social construction of homosexuality (see, for example, McIntosh 1968; Foucault 1978; D'Emilio 1983). While same-sex acts long had been documented in many historical eras and across a wide variety of cultures, this body of work posited, based on historical and archival research, that the concept of the homosexual as a category of person did not develop in the Western world until the late 19th century. Emergent discourses surrounding "normal" and "pathological" sexual practices in medicine and religion, and the rise of scientific measurements of sexual behavior, generated a shift toward defining those who engaged in same-sex acts as sick or deviant *people* rather than as people engaging in bad or sinful *acts*. Yet, while the creation of "the homosexual" as a medicalized and socially pathological category of person generated an increase in social control and policing around same-sex behaviors and acts, it also made possible a "reverse discourse" (Foucault 1978, 101) that would make space for the emergence of homosexual subcultures, and, later, homosexual political movements, such as gay liberation, that were aimed at dismantling societal stigma around homosexuality.

Connell then considers what it might mean for sociologists to take seriously "the transsexual" as a new gender category—one that would be in addition to "women" and "men," rather than a problematic imitation of these "natural" categories. In thinking through how the social recognition of this category might be possible, she gives examples of the radical shifts that the idea of "women" and "men" have undergone in the last hundred years—including the idea that women have shared, common interests with one another that are opposing and unique from the shared, common interests of men. She notes:

> This social solidarity is a *new* fact, in no way implied by the biological category. It can therefore be constructed, historically, in a variety of ways. Thus, it is possible for a new type of solidarity, a new organization of gender, to emerge. Masculinities and femininities can be re-constructed historically, new forms can become dominant. It is even possible for a whole new gender category to be constructed, as with the emergence of "the homosexual" in the late nineteenth century, and perhaps "the transsexual" now. (1987, 81; italics in the original)

She acknowledges that historical research and cross-cultural comparisons show that what could be categorized as cross-gender desires and practices existed long before the term "transsexual" was coined in the late 1940s (for more on this point, see Meyerowitz 2002). Yet, within the 1960s, a cultural shift occurred that provided a historical context for "the transsexual" to coalesce as first a social problem and then later as an embodied identity—much in the same way the late 19th century saw the creation of "the homosexual."

Transgender People as Situated Subjects

Connell's argument could remain distanced from people and practice—similar to Foucault's theoretical work, which is marked by an absence of social actors. Yet she makes an important departure from a purely theoretical argument that opens up new sociological approaches to understanding the lives of transgender people. Discussing the possible emergence of "the transsexual" as a new gender category, she notes that "practical transformations open up new possibilities which are the tissue of human life. But they do this by creating new social pressures and risks" (1987, 77). To make this point concrete, Connell draws on an ethnographic study, *The "Drag Queen" Scene: Transsexuals in Kings Cross* (1983), by Australian sociologist Roberta Perkins. The use of this particular work by Connell is notable, as it is a rare exception to the strands of sociological work about transgender people that I detailed in the previous section. First, Perkins focuses explicitly on how trans women negotiate their everyday lives across a variety of social contexts. Her sociological project, in other words, takes the subjectivity and specific social practices of trans women as its central focus. Second, Perkins begins her book by locating herself as both a sociologist and a trans woman. She acknowledges that her motivations for the work came from her personal hope that empirical research could alleviate the stigma many trans women faced, such as "being told that we were disgusting, deviant, weird, insane, immoral" (1983, 17).

Perkins notes that the majority of existing empirical research on transgender people falls within the fields of medicine and psychology. Within sociological work, there was a "dearth of material dealing with the social structure of a community of transsexuals and its interactions with a wider society" (1983, 18). To address this gap, she conducts participant observation with a cohort of trans women working in what she terms "drag queen" bars—the only locations where many of them can find employment in the 1980s due to widespread economic discrimination against transgender and gender nonconforming people. To locate her respondents within their larger social worlds, she also conducts interviews with patrons of their clubs, the social workers they interact with, and their coworkers. Prioritizing how the women she interviews talk about their experiences at work, in relationships, with family, and with doctors, Perkins challenges prior sociological and feminist claims that transgender people are pathologically invested in gender conformity. Instead, she highlights the expectations of doctors and social workers that pushed trans women into performing traditional femininity in order to gain access to medical services. Connell uses Perkins's findings in *Gender and Power* to argue for the need for a more complex understanding of transgender lives that encompasses history, social structures, and individual choices and agency within a system of constraints—or, as I am suggesting, a roadmap for what an empirical sociology of transgender studies might look like.

After briefly bringing Perkins's empirical work into her theoretical scaffolding, Connell adds a nuanced analysis of the link between bodies and social structure. While bodies are made of "natural" materials, she argues that chromosomes, genitals, and reproductive capacities are not determinative of identity or practices. She argues instead that bodies are shaped by their social and historical locations, as a person's sense of identity that "grows through a personal history of social practice, a life-history-in-society" (1987, 84). In other words, social categories such as "transgender" emerge in particular historical moments and become incorporated into people's social practices and embodiment. Through the cultural solidifying of such a category, people can come to see themselves as transgender and, as such, can begin to organize around this identity in an effort to get structural and cultural change. Thus, bodies incorporate and are shaped by social categories and exert pressure on such categories to shift, transform, and change. These "circuits"—to draw on a concept she develops in her later works—linking bodily processes and social structures "add up to the historical process by which society is embodied, and bodies are drawn into history" (2002, 47). For Connell, such a historical look at the varied and complex social processes that bring a new social category into existence—and with it, new possibilities for embodiment and identity—is what makes the difference between broad, ahistorical categoricalism and a social analysis that accounts for sociohistorical change, cultural context, and the embodied practices of people.

In light of Raewyn Connell's growing body of work that contributes directly to transgender studies (see, for example, 2012), it may seem strange to focus an analysis on two short passages in *Gender and Power* that reference the now outdated concept of "transsexuality." But, considering this inclusion from a historical standpoint, Connell's references—and, in particular, her use of Roberta Perkins's ethnography—stand in stark contrast to the dominant theorization of transgender people in sociology at the time. Perkins highlighted the importance of examining how transgender people's lived experiences were embedded in larger social structures, such as the workplace, the family, and the medical establishment, and how these experiences shifted across historical moments. In the introduction to *The "Drag Queen" Scene*, Perkins argued explicitly "that the position of transsexuals in our society will only improve once they are studied as a group, the emphasis being placed on the social processes involved in transsexualism rather than on the psychological processes of the individual" (1983, 18). She added her hope that "this relatively untouched area will come under serious study by social researchers and fieldworkers" (ibid.). Through using Perkins's empirical work to ground her theoretical discussion of the historical emergence of transsexuality, Connell takes up this challenge and introduces a sociostructural theory of gender that locates transgender people as situated subjects in their own right rather than as cultural objects to be explained.

Toward a Sociology of Transgender Studies

It is interesting to look back at Connell's emergent ideas about transgender identities in 1984 from the vantage point of the late 2010s. Over the more than three decades between the publication of *Gender and Power* and this edited volume, the category of "the transsexual" has largely been subsumed by the term "transgender," an umbrella term that encapsulates many different embodied identities and practices (see Valentine 2007; Stryker and Aizura 2013). The interdisciplinary field of transgender studies has gained prominence in academia, generating new areas of specialty, academic departments, pedagogy, and journals (see, for an overview, Stryker and Whittle 2006; Stryker and Aizura 2013). Within the growing field of the sociology of transgender studies, sociologists are examining the diversity of transgender people's identities and social locations (see, for example, Rubin 2003; Dozier 2005; Namaste 2005; Lombardi 2009; Abelson 2014), as well as the ways in which transgender and gender nonconforming people navigate institutional contexts such as the medical establishment (Windsor 2011; Nordmarken and Kelly 2012; Miller and Grollman 2015); the family (Pfeffer 2012); legal institutions (Meadow 2010); and the workplace (David 2015). In a notable and important shift from previous eras, much more of this research is being conducted by transgender, genderqueer, and nonbinary identified sociologists.

Further, social scientists are interrogating how the increasing visibility of transgender people and transgender rights movements in the United States is reshaping cultural ideas about gender and sexuality (Westbrook and Schilt 2014; Sumerau, Cragun, and Mathers 2016), and opening up new questions around issues such as how transgender and gender nonconforming children should be raised (Meadow 2011). This cultural shift in transgender visibility signals a new sociohistorical context that, following a Connellian model, will likely bring new forms of constraints and calcification of categories but also open up new possibilities for social embodiment and meanings of gender. Such changes necessitate new theoretical models for understanding identity and embodiment but also require an empirical focus on the structural constraints, the emerging possibilities, and the situated, contextual lives of transgender, gender nonconforming, and nonbinary people. It is in this intersection of structural theories and empirical analysis that a trans-centered sociology that builds on the legacy of Roberta Perkins has much to contribute to the emerging interdisciplinary field of transgender studies.

NOTES

1 Prior to the late 1990s, social science research on transgender people used the term "transsexual" and "transsexualism." The terms "transgender" and "trans" reflect more current terminology.

2 I thank the editors for providing me with this timeline.

3 I restrict this overview to sociological works that Connell could have referenced in her 1984 manuscript. While Janice Raymond is not a sociologist, her book *The Transsexual Empire* was often cited in feminist sociological work on gender in the 1980s, so I include it in this discussion.

4 Altman's view—which shifted in his later works—was shared by some gay men in the early homophile movement in the 1950s. The media attention to Christine Jorgensen spurred a fear among some gay men that "sex changes" would become mandated by medical and psychiatric professionals as the appropriate treatment for homosexuality (still, then, an official mental illness) (see Meyerowitz 2002). Such a normalizing project did not develop in the United States, as homosexuality was taken out of the *DSM* in 1978.

REFERENCES

Abelson, Miriam. 2014. "Dangerous Privilege: Trans Men, Masculinity, and Changing Perceptions of Safety." *Sociological Forum* 29 (3): 549–570.

Altman, Dennis. 1971. *Homosexual Oppression and Liberation*. New York: New York University Press.

Bem, Sandra. 1993. *The Lenses of Gender: Transforming Debate about Sexuality Inequality*. New Haven: Yale University Press.

Billings, Dwight, and Thomas Urban. 1982. "The Socio-Medical Construction of Transsexualism: An Interpretation and Critique." *Social Problems* 29: 266–282.

Connell, R. W. 1987. *Gender and Power*. Palo Alto, CA: Stanford University Press.

———. 1995. *Masculinities*. Berkeley: University of California Press.

———. 2002. *Gender*. Malden, MA: Polity Press.

———. 2012. "Transsexual Women and Feminist Thought: Toward New Understanding and New Politics." *Signs* 37 (4): 857–881.

David, Emmanuel. 2015. "Purple-Collar Labor: Transgender Workers and Queer Value at Global Call Centers in the Philippines." *Gender & Society* 29 (2): 169–194.

D'Emilio, John. 1983. *Sexual Politics, Sexual Communities*. Chicago: University of Chicago Press.

Dozier, Raine. 2005. "Beards, Breasts, and Bodies: Doing Sex in a Gendered World." *Gender & Society* 19 (3): 297–316.

Feinbloom, Deborah. 1976. *Transvestites and Transsexuals: Mixed Views*. New York: Delta.

Foucault, Michel. 1978. *The History of Sexuality, Vol. One*. New York: Vintage Books.

Garfinkel, Harold. 1967. *Studies in Ethnomethodology*. Englewood Cliffs, NJ: Prentice-Hall.

Huber, Joan, ed. 1973. *Changing Women in a Changing Society*. Chicago: University of Chicago Press.

Kando, Thomas. 1973. *Sex Change: The Achievement of Gender Identity among Female Transsexuals*. Springfield, IL: Charles C. Thomas Publisher.

Kessler, Suzanne, and Wendy McKenna. 1978. *Gender: An Ethnomethodological Approach*. New York: Wiley.

King, Dave. 1987. "Social Constructionism and Medical Knowledge: The Case of Transsexualism." *Sociology of Health and Illness* 9 (4): 351–377.

Lombardi, Emilia. 2009. "Varieties of Transgender/Transsexual Lives and Their Relationship with Transphobia." *Journal of Homosexuality* 56 (8): 977–92.

Matza, David. 1969. *Becoming Deviant*. Englewood Cliffs, NJ: Prentice-Hall.

McIntosh, Mary. 1968. "The Homosexual Role." *Social Problems* 16 (2): 182–192.

Meadow, Tey. 2010. "A Rose Is a Rose: On Producing Legal Gender Classifications." *Gender & Society* 24 (6): 814–837.

———. 2011. "'Deep Down Where the Music Plays': How Parents Account for Childhood Gender Variance." *Sexualities* 14 (6): 724–747.

Meyerowitz, Joanne. 2002. *How Sex Changed: A History of Transsexualism in the United States*. Cambridge: Harvard University Press.

Miller, Lisa R., and Eric Anthony Grollman. 2015. "The Social Costs of Gender Nonconformity for Transgender Adults: Implications for Discrimination and Health." *Sociological Forum* 30 (3): 809–831.

Namaste, Viviane. 2000. *Invisible Lives: The Erasure of Transsexual and Transgendered People*. Chicago: University of Chicago Press.

———. 2005. *Sex Change, Social Change: Reflections on Identity, Institutions, and Imperialism*. Toronto: Canada School Press.

Nordmarken, Sonny, and Reese Kelly. 2014. "Limiting Transgender Health: Administrative Violence and Microaggressions in Health Care Systems." In *Health Care Disparities and the LGBT Population*, edited by V. L. Harvey and T. Heinz, 143–169. New York: Lexington Books.

Perkins, Roberta. 1983. *The "Drag Queen" Scene: Transsexuals in Kings Cross*. Sydney: George Allen and Unwin.

Pfeffer, Carla. 2012. "Normative Resistance and Inventive Pragmatism: Negotiating Structure and Agency in Transgender Families." *Gender & Society* 26 (4): 574–602.

Raymond, Janice. 1979. *The Transsexual Empire*. Boston: Beacon Press.

Rogers, Mary. 1992. "They Were All Passing: Agnes, Garfinkel, and Company." *Gender & Society* 6 (2): 169–191.

Rubin, Henry. 1999. "Trans Studies: Between a Metaphysics of Presence and Absence." In *Reclaiming Genders: Transsexual Grammars at the Fin de Siècle*, edited by K. More and S. Whittle, 173–192. New York: Cassell.

———. 2003. *Self-Made Men: Identity and Embodiment among Transsexual Men*. Nashville, TN: Vanderbilt University Press.

Spade, Dean. 2006. "Mutilating Gender." In *Transgender Studies Reader*, edited by Susan Stryker and Stephen Whittle, 315–334. New York: Routledge.

Stryker, Susan. 2008. *Transgender History*. Seattle, WA: Seal Press.

Stryker, Susan, and Aren Z. Aizura, eds. 2013. *The Transgender Studies Reader 2*. New York: Routledge.

Stryker, Susan, and Stephen Whittle, eds. 2006. *The Transgender Studies Reader*. New York: Routledge.

Sumerau, J. E., Ryan Cragun, and Lain A. B. Mathers. 2016. "Contemporary Religion and the Cisgendering of Reality." *Sociological Currents* 3 (3): 293–311.

Valentine, David. 2007. *Imagining Transgender: An Ethnography of a Category*. Durham, NC: Duke University Press.

West, Candace, and Don Zimmerman. 1987. "Doing Gender." *Gender & Society* 1 (1): 125–151.

Westbrook, Laurel, and Kristen Schilt. 2014. "Doing Gender, Determining Gender." *Gender & Society* 28 (1): 32–57.

Windsor, Elroi. 2011. "Regulating Healthy Gender: Surgical Body Modification among Transgender and Cisgender Consumers." PhD diss., Georgia State University.

PART II

The Larger Scope of Gender Analysis

The chapters in this section examine two of the ways—postcoloniality and intersectionality—in which the episteme of gender studies has developed and expanded in the last thirty years.

Raka Ray begins this section by broadening the discussion of gender and social structure using a transnational theoretical framework. She combines structural analyses of gender with more recently emerging postcolonial perspectives to explore connections and contradictions in the global gender order. Ray reviews the practices and cultural/ideological justifications that shaped gender relations in colonial and postcolonial India. Using case studies of two nonaffluent Indian young people—a man and a woman—she shows how each struggled to escape the "bounded" situations of their gendered lives in order to find affirmation in the wider world. Ray demonstrates how global economic forces, including neoliberalism, are affecting them and also shaping gender relations in a postcolonial nation that is the second most populated on earth. Ray concludes that the most fruitful theoretical foundation for understanding the workings of gender in an interconnected world is to link critical gender theory with postcolonial theory, while simultaneously remaining cognizant of how the neoliberal global economy has affected the global South.

Mara Viveros Vigoya discusses the history of feminism in Colombia from the 1970s to now, reviewing its struggles with Marxism and, later, with various feminisms that were imported from the global North but failed to fit the Colombian context. A legacy of isolation, impoverishment, and exclusion from state political processes culminated in recent feminist mobilizations among indigenous and Black Colombian women who sought to protect their communities and cultural heritage. Viveros Vigoya explores the impact of globalization, neoliberalism, and colonialism on feminism in Colombia. Employing historical data, she shows how gender perspectives come out of social struggle and how the struggles of indigenous and Black Colombian women have different contours from those of women of the privileged Spanish-descendant classes who embraced feminisms from the global North. Her chapter illustrates the need for multiple perspectives on the social dimensions of gender and rejects a one-size-fits-all theoretical model; the need to recognize the different macro-social situations in the global North and global South (and across the South); and the need for solid social-scientific knowledge of those situations in order to make sense of gender dynamics. Viveros Vigoya concludes that feminists from the global North can learn from Colombia's distinctive forms of feminist mobilization.

Joya Misra's analysis of intersectionality contrasts its utility for a structural analysis with a poststructural analysis of gender. She argues that the former is more effective at conceptualizing historical developments, social change, and power and inequality, yet she affirms the value of both structural and poststructural applications, acknowledging that discourse theories can produce insights about gender. Misra maintains that an intersectional approach to the study of gender avoids reducing complex realities to either discourse or a few categories. Her contrast of structural and poststructural perspectives emphasizes how discourse can be used as part of structural analysis without assuming that discourse is "unlinked" to structural conditions. She critiques the use of a single category (e.g., of gender or race) for studying the social world, urging instead a multiple categorical method or the avoidance of categories altogether in favor of a focus on intersectional processes.

4

Postcoloniality and the Sociology of Gender

RAKA RAY

Gauri from Ferozabad, a small town in India, was a badminton champion at 14, whose parents (who had a small bangle selling business) refused to let her play anymore when she won a scholarship to go away to badminton school. From that moment on she plotted her escape. She hated school because she was ostracized after her sister chose her own husband. Eventually, she managed to persuade her family that she had won a scholarship for an information technology course in Agra, which she had not, but they did permit her to leave. Far away from home she kept herself going with one job after another, selling scooters, and working as a guidance counselor and a tutor: "All I knew was that I could not go back, my small town would just shut everything down inside me." After she graduated she moved from Agra to Delhi where she worked in a call center. While working there, she took a course on film editing. She finally managed to come to Bombay and started making a living editing news, while auditioning for roles at the same time. So far Gauri has made a couple of regional language films, and has bought a car. For her, Bombay is a city where people work all the time. If you work hard you will be fine. And you are free to go where you are, within limits, but "no boundation" as she put it.

Jagdish comes from a district in the state of Uttar Pradesh where almost half the population lives below the poverty line. His father worked in a sugar factory; and his family circumstances were too inconsistent for anyone to either pay attention to him or to train him for anything. Jagdish failed to pass the 10th grade examinations, but then bribed someone to take the examinations for him the following year. He took a videography class in 11th grade and then started work as a wedding videographer since his father could no longer support him. Because he loved to dance and sing, he started participating in Hindu nationalist religious festivals, for which he was paid a little. After four years there, he moved to a nearby town because it had a theater company. He worked backstage for the company, until he got a break; he had memorized the whole play and was able to step in for someone who was sick. Jagdish managed to get a BA in English from the town of Bisalpur, then found and lost a series of jobs, tried to get into the police but failed the high jump. He prayed that he could get into a theater academy—he had been on two pilgrimages, so surely he should be rewarded. He finally got in, borrowed money with interest from his grandmother (the only one with any money in his extended family), and went to Bombay to seek his fortune.

I begin with these two vignettes of young lower middle-class people from small towns who have migrated to Bombay in the hope of making it in Bombay's entertainment industry with the same aim as Raewyn Connell in *Gender and Power*—to lay out the interconnectedness of labor, power, and cathexis in the creation of young people's lives. For Connell, the protagonist was Delia Prince, a young Australian teenager. The year was 1978. Through Delia Prince's life, and those of her parents, the reader is made aware that (1) gender patterns are structured and not random and (2) the personal and the collective are fundamentally linked. This "normal" Australian teenager's aspirations and trajectories are put in the context of the state of gendered labor, education, and violence against women worldwide, and in Australia. This is fully fledged structural analysis, but with a Connellian twist. It is also about practice, for Delia Prince's life reconstitutes social structure even as it constitutes her life. Can we use Connell's concepts to understand gender in the lives of young men and women in small town India today, against the backdrop of a rising nation and a neoliberal[1] and global economy? In what follows I argue that we can do so by combining insights from Connell's four major works—*Gender and Power, Gender, Masculinities*, and *Southern Theory*.

The importance of *Gender and Power* lay in Connell's attempt to produce a theory of gender formation and power that was comprehensive, but not monolithic. She understood the task that implicitly lay before us as the identification of the historically and culturally specific structures of labor, power, and cathexis that obtained at any one time and place, in order to understand the gender order of that place or institution. Thus, in describing the configuration of the power of men in *advanced industrialized societies*, Connell suggested that it was concentrated in four sites: (a) the forces of institutionalized violence, (b) heavy industry and high technology, (c) the planning and control machinery of the central state, and (d) a working class milieu. This precise configuration, Connell implies, would not necessarily hold for countries of the Global South. This implication is significant, since it enables us to ask what the power of men would look like in the Global South at different historical moments. What Connell herself did not do in *Gender and Power*, however, was to pay enough attention to intersectionality either within nations or across nations. In other words, while she was well aware that countries are differently placed in terms of global economic power, and that this differential placement has consequences for their gendered relations, she did not, at the moment of writing *Gender and Power*, pay attention to the interconnectedness either of their economies and histories, or of ideas, and thus to the interconnectedness of their gender orders.

In her next major book, *Masculinities* (1995), Connell brought masculinity into the study of the sociology of gender, changing, once and for all, our analytic repertoire with the introduction of the concept of hegemonic and other masculinities. With this, we were enabled to think of masculinity as a practice that can only be understood in conjunction with other factors such as race, class, and sexuality. While much more needs to be done in this field, this chapter derives as much of its motivation from Connell's work on nonhegemonic masculinities as from *Gender and Power*.

In *Southern Theory* (2007) and *Gender* (2009), Connell expands her definition of power to include colonial power, acknowledging colonialism as "the most sweeping exercise of power of the last 500 years" and referring to the "creation of global empires, the invasion of indigenous lands by the imperial powers . . . and the domination of the postcolonial world by economic and military superpowers" (Connell 2009, 78). In her analysis of labor, there is a greater recognition of women as a globally flexible, cheap labor force. And most important, she initiates a long overdue conversation between postcolonial theory, which considers seriously the continuing impact of colonialism on the social, cultural, and economic development of both colonial powers and the colonies, and American sociology. *Southern Theory* is a critique of the parochial nature of sociology in America. It promotes a sociology that takes the interconnected history of the world more seriously than it does now, and argues that, in order to do so, we must be more open to theoretical ideas from a wider range of places than we are today.

Drawing on these concepts, in the remainder of this chapter I argue that our best approach to understanding gender (for both men and women) in today's neoliberal world must lead us to the nexus of colonial power, production, and discourse.[2] In thinking about colonial power I elaborate on the issue of the interconnected world with the help of one body of theory that Connell discusses in *Southern Theory*—postcolonial theory. In my discussion of production I pay attention to the effects of the neoliberal economy on the Global South. I use the term "discourse" as shorthand for the tools we are given to interpret our world because it bypasses the structure versus culture binary. This version of discourse analysis is perfectly compatible with nonmonolithic structural analyses, as it suggests that structures and experiences themselves become legible only through discourse. I end with an analysis of the vignettes with which I began this chapter and suggest that to understand gender relations today we must inhabit a flexible structural analysis that pays attention to history and to the effects of discourse on subject formation. But first I turn to why we need to understand colonialism in order to understand gender.

Why Colonialism Should Matter to Sociology

Theorists of postcolonialism remind us that colonialism was simultaneously a system of rule and of knowledge production (Hall 1996). The economic effects of colonialism are well known; in terms of cultural shifts, it is worth paying attention to the way in which colonial powers represented the colonized so as to draw attention not to the interconnectedness of the world but to the unequal difference between them. As British sociologist Gurminder Bhambra writes, "The western experience has been taken both as the basis for the construction of modernity and, at the same time, that concept is argued to have a validity that transcends the western experience" (2007a, 4). The construction of binaries such as tradition and modernity, which lies at the very heart of sociological exploration, is an outcome of colonial systems of knowledge production. Yet until recently there has been little critique of the colonially constructed categories upon which sociologists rely (Connell 1997)—in other words, there has not been a postcolonial critique.

Over 30 years ago, Judith Stacey and Barrie Thorne (1985) wrote, in their now legendary article, that the feminist revolution had touched anthropology, history, and literature far more deeply than it had sociology. Thus, in teaching courses on feminism in sociology, they found themselves having to rely more on theorists in those disciplines than on sociologists. They suggested that feminism had made more headway in disciplines more comfortable with interpretive rather than positivist methodologies. Today, these same arguments could be made for the absence from American sociology of postcolonial theory, which considers seriously the continuing impact of colonialism on the social, cultural, and economic development of both colonial powers and the colonies (see Go 2013; Bhambra 2007a, 2007b). In addition to sociology's allegiance to positivism (I say this despite my awareness of and participation in the healthy interpretive minority tradition), the discipline's attachment to its own modernist foundations and to universalism heightens its discomfort with postcolonial theory.

The attachment to modernity, as Connell (2007) has shown, cuts across most sociological theorizing, whether mainstream or radical. Of central concern to the "founding fathers," the analytic stories of the unfolding of modernity they narrated assumed a self-contained Europe that formed the empirical crux from which they generated their theories. While the European countries on which they based their theories (France, Germany, and England) were fully in imperial mode when they wrote, this did not seem to have affected Karl Marx's, Max Weber's, or Durkheim's understanding of the transformation of those societies. Elided was the possibility that imperial adventures were a constitutive force of European modernity, and thus that the history of the world was irreducibly connected rather than divided into two worlds—one with history (that moves into capitalism and modernity) and one without (the traditional world). This division between tradition and modernity marks not only the founding of sociology but is reproduced by sociologists as varied at James Coleman and Pierre Bourdieu (Connell 2007), and holds particularly true for the way gender is understood.

Sociology also centers the experience of the West in its scholarship, in an approach Julian Go refers to as metrocentrism (Go 2013). In contemporary American sociology, even within the field of comparative work, the US is the norm against which other countries are compared. The feminist version of this challenge is, of course, the understanding of men as the norm and women as the difference. The field of sociology, as Dorothy Smith (1987) pointed out so many years ago, was founded on questions that are of concern to men. It was also founded on questions of concern to Europe and the US, but rather than assuming that Europe and the US were places with particular histories, and thus particular social formations, the questions that concerned them became the big questions for the entire discipline of sociology. For contemporary American sociology, the norm to which all societies are compared is, by and large, the US. The rest of the world, then, is the difference.

While some sociologists have recently put forward the case for postcolonial theory within sociology, calling for understanding European experiences as particular and not universal (Connell 2007; Bhambra 2007b), attention to the formative experiences and effects of colonialism (Steinmetz 2008; Go 2011), and the decentering of the European experience (Ray 2013), little attention has been paid to the importance of the colonial in the field of sociology of gender. Yet it is imperative that we understand relationships between nations both historically and today if we are to truly understand how gender works.

Through both its economic and cultural power, British, French, Dutch, and German colonialism fundamentally (though not uniformly) transformed gender in the countries they colonized. By the mid-20th century it had redrawn women's legal status around property; introduced the concept of family law, which divided women's rights by religion (Mahmood 2015); abolished matrilineal descent where it could (Nair 1996); made women legal minors (through the hut tax in South Africa, for example); weakened women's property rights in Nigeria (Oyewumi 1997); made globally normative the idea of the male breadwinner and female homemaker (Lindsay 2003); cast existing sexual practices in the colonies as inferior and immoral; and even created new patterns of masculinity—for example, demarcating some groups of men in India as masculine and others (often those who resisted them) as effete (Nandy 2009; Sinha 1995). Amina Mama (1997) argues that patterns of gendered violence in the Global South today can be traced to the gendered violence of imperialism, as can, as we will see shortly, resistance to ideas of gender reform that emanate from formerly colonial powers.

Colonialism also affected gender relations within the colonizing powers. It provided certain classes of men from colonizing countries with job opportunities, while for women imperial adventures offered a chance to move from being seen as an inferior group, to being part of a superior one, to being able to flourish abroad as wives of colonists, travelers, or missionaries, in a way they could not at home (McClintock 2002). Of signal importance is that colonialism enabled an understanding of gender relations on the part of men and women of the metropole (i.e., from the center of empire as opposed to the colonies) that has had lasting consequences.

By the end of colonialism, the gender orders of societies had been transformed. Three additional legacies most relevant for understanding gender in the world today remain. First, while most countries in the world are today neither colonizers nor colonized, we have in its place a radically unequal world that approximates the colonial world. Second, anticolonial struggles produced forms of nationalism in which gender came to play a central, and resistant, role. Third, in the struggle over the demise of colonial rule, women colonizers were on one side while colonized women were on the other (of course there were exceptions), locked in a battle over land, over ways of life, and over freedom. As a result of these three legacies, we have a world in which memories of colonialism trouble questions of global sisterhood, where postcolonial nations are both dependent on and resentful of the Global North, and where these resentments may take the form of masculine aggression or the policing of the gender order.

While the radical restructuring of gendered power relations as a result of colonialism has been brought to the fore by postcolonial historians and anthropologists, and indeed was first brought to our attention in Fanon's (1967) searing work, within sociology we have been slow to incorporate colonialism into our analyses, and to thus fold colonialism into our understanding of gender.

Postcoloniality and Discourse

Postcolonial theorists of gender have shown us that while colonial adventures put into place a new set of understandings about gender and race, creating what we have come to accept as the master narratives of global patriarchy (McClintock 2002), global inequities in power mean that these narratives continue to get created and re-created in the contemporary world (Sangari 1999). These discourses exert their own, often distorted, effects on our understanding of gender relations in the world.

In this context, Chandra Mohanty's (1988) now classic critique bears repeating in its essence. In an influential article, Mohanty argued that even in feminist writing Northern women erased the diversity of third world women, by producing the figure of an "average Third World woman" who was uneducated, constrained by tradition and religion, and victimized, in contrast to sexually liberated, educated middle-class white feminists from the Global North. Mohanty argued that these accounts not only silenced women in the Global South, and were a reconstitution of colonial relations between North and South, but they also helped constitute the way Northern feminists understood themselves—as more liberal, modern, and better off than third world women, and thus in a position to be their saviors (Mahmood 1995; Abu-Lughod 2002).

These representations have not faded away. For instance, in *Voice and Agency: Empowering Women and Girls for Shared Prosperity*, the World Bank's 2014 Report on Gender, there is a map of the world that shows the share of women who have faced physical or sexual intimate partner violence at least once in their lives. The map shows that 21 percent of women in North America, 33 percent in Latin America, and 43 percent in South Asia have faced intimate partner violence. In short, violence against women is high, even in North America. Yet the report does not include a single photograph of a woman from North America. Rather, all the photographs show black and brown women from the Global South, pictorially reinforcing the colonially created idea about oppression of women in "traditional" as opposed to "modern" societies.

These discursive constructions matter because the Global North has economic power over the Global South. What the Global North thinks filters into policies that then affect women elsewhere. It is this representational power that Connell begins to acknowledge in *Gender*, and elaborates more fully in *Southern Theory*. A classic example of the interweaving of politics, stereotypes of "third world" women and men, and its consequences is the US war in Afghanistan (Russo 2006).

Much before the attacks of September 11, 2001, and the US war on Afghanistan, and even before the Taliban came to power in 1996, feminists in the US began getting worried about the Taliban because of its terrible reputation around gender. In 2000–2001, an urgent e-mail was circulated throughout progressive circles in the US, cataloguing the oppressive and untenable situation of women in Afghanistan, and urging US military intervention on behalf of Afghan women, even as women's organizations in Afghanistan such as the Revolutionary Association of the Women of Afghanistan protested the intervention.[3] But these discussions of Afghanistan have a history—going back to the colonial era—in which writing about barbaric gendered treatment has been used to justify military intervention. About 75 years before this e-mail, American journalist Katherine Mayo's famous *Mother India* (1927) adopted a similar tone in describing the treatment of Indian women by Indian men. Her over 200-page scathing critique of India and particularly the condition of Indian women fit in beautifully with British arguments against Indian independence.[4] During the period when the Indian independence movement against the British was escalating, *Mother India* galvanized the American and English public around "victimized" Indian womanhood. In colonial India, just as in Afghanistan, women's "oppression" provided a justification for both ongoing colonial intervention and war. Such writing set into motion the idea that brown women must be saved from brown men. The saviors were thus to be white men—and, later, white women.[5]

Postcolonial feminists point to the complications that inhere in attempts to create a transnational or global feminism based on an awareness of such gendered colonial interventions in the past (Shohat 2001). Feminists from the Global South have argued that Northern accounts frequently ignore the diversity of feminist movements that exist outside the North. They argue further that Northern feminists often do not see that the sources of women's oppression in countries of the Global South may not be men from their own cultures, but may in fact be linked to the disadvantaged economic and political position of the Global South in relation to the Global North. Like feminists of color in the United States, who argued that it was impossible to separate "gender" from "race" and "class" in their political struggles, feminists from the Global South have argued that their "gender" interests could not be addressed without also addressing imbalances in the global political economy and the legacies of colonialism. Finally, they critique the unequal relations between feminists of the North and South, pointing to the ways in which inequalities of resources have allowed Northern women to become authors and theorists of the global agenda on women, leaving Southern women to be its object and beneficiaries (Basu 1995), with a few positive models of solidarity that are able to work with, and through, these inequalities (Basu 1995; Alexander 1994; Mohanty 2003; Otto 2010).

The Postcolonial Neoliberal Economy and Subject Formation

The neoliberal economy ushered in a heightened regime of deregulation, privatization, insecure labor, predatory extraction, "trickle down" personal responsibility, and, of course, the infamous "structural adjustment" that required countries of the South to withdraw subsidies to the poor. Globally, men and women have been incorporated differentially into this economy. Some well-established practices of the global economy continue, shaped as they were by the drastic differences between rich and poor nations and colonial histories, such as women from Mexico and the Philippines seeking work as domestics in the US, Italy, and Saudi Arabia. Newer economic relationships have emerged with call centers and other "business processing outsourcing" situated in India and Mexico serving customers in the US and Europe, global medical tourism, and women in the US and Europe "renting" wombs in India so they can have a surrogate baby cheaply.

While the global assembly line was one of the first ways in which we learned about the interdependence between North and South, in today's economy the loss of male working-class jobs worldwide, and the service sector availability of women's jobs, has somewhat changed the relationship between male domination and the economy. In this new "romance of capitalism" (Fraser 2013, 220), women's labor force participation has increased worldwide, though it is still below 50 percent in many regions, while global labor force participation rates for men have steadily declined. Women are increasingly active participants in the professional world as well as in the world of call centers, hospitality, temp jobs, migrant workers, and microcredit borrowers. In addition, they are now often preferred by global development agencies as more responsible subjects of intervention (see the NIKE film on "the girl effect").

Colonial constructions about docile brown women have morphed and yet persist in the neoliberal economy. The economy's welcoming of women workers is accompanied by the discursive embrace of women as those who live self-managed lives through self-application and self-transformation (Brown 2003; McRobbie 2009). Nancy Fraser (2003, 219) argues that second wave feminism and neoliberalism found an affinity as the emancipatory aspirations aroused by second wave feminism were channeled into entrepreneurial models both within the advanced industrialized world and the third world. The much touted microfinance model, for example, inevitably assumes a female entrepreneur (Roy 2010). In the meantime, globally, young men who do not have a class advantage are not only being left behind, they are increasingly seen as the losers in the new global order. This development changes substantially the picture of the gendered order of the global economy.

The consequences of neoliberal globalization for men are much less studied than the consequences for women (Connell 2014). With the disappearance of work from many parts of the world, in particular work formerly performed by working-class men, the numbers of men considered surplus or irrelevant to the economy keeps growing. The power of men can no longer be easily found in a working-class milieu. An analysis of gender therefore must take into consideration the different ways in which men seek to establish their masculinity if they cannot do it through production. Within the United States, Jennifer Sherman's (2009) work in areas formerly dominated by the logging industry illustrates how white rural men who can no longer work use moral capital to distinguish themselves from poor men or women of other races, putting them down as dependent and weak even as they collect their disability checks from the state. Jennifer Carlson's (2015) work shows how men increasingly turn to carrying guns as the possibilities of protecting their families and futures rapidly disappears. And Jordanna Matlon's (2014) work shows us how men in precarious work in Cote D'Ivoire try desperately to hang on to style or to political patronage in order to remain men. Anxieties about poor disaffected men have begun to circulate globally, with the US Agency for International Development now contemplating giving loans to young men in the Middle East so that they can start their own falafel businesses instead of becoming suicide bombers (Roy 2010, 147).

In considering the role of labor in today's economy, therefore, we must be mindful both of the actual changes in jobs worldwide—the decline of male and manufacturing jobs and the rise of less well-paid and even more precarious female and service sector jobs—and of the anxieties elicited by these changes. While the capacity to aspire, as anthropologist Arjun Appadurai (2004) reminds us, has traditionally belonged to the affluent (and, I would add, men), global discourses about women, which result both from the effects of the global women's movement and consumerist capitalism, have resulted in an increase in middle-class women's aspirations. This combination of new discourses about men and women and the changes in the economy have begun to create their own, often violent, backlash.[6]

Conclusion

The two anecdotes with which I began this story illustrate what happens if we wed *Southern Theory* and an understanding of global relationships with *Gender and Power* and the attention to men from *Masculinities*. It involves women, who are increasingly seen as the acting aspirational subject, particularly in the Global South, and men, who are seen as having little going for them, men who would once have held public sector lower middle class jobs, or upper working class jobs, but who have less space in the new economy.

For Gauri, work offered her a way out of the boundation of her home and life in a small town. Her story was similar to that of many other girls in lower middle class or solidly middle class families in small town India. Their mothers do not usually work, but their fathers are school teachers or principals, small-business owners, doctors, or government employees. The girls are talented and notice discrimination in their families between them and their brothers. When Gauri left Ferozabad, it was an individual decision to migrate, and she did not rely on her family or a husband. She believed in her own talent. Girls like Gauri would not have left home in the past; few middle class girls in India did. We cannot understand this point if we ignore colonial history, for part of the ideological struggle of an India trying to free itself from the British lay in the production of a middle class womanhood that did not work out-side the home: middle class women were to be culturally refined and re-sponsible for the inner life of the family, and protected by their menfolk (Chatterjee 1990). Educated middle- and upper-middle-class women were relegated to the domestic sphere, materially and ritually, and had the overall responsibility for managing typically joint family households while deferring to their husbands' ultimate authority (Sangari 1999, 307). That Gauri leaves home therefore indicates a major shift. But her move was enabled by the idea that the economy had opened up, that there were in the world out there opportunities for women that did not previ-ously exist, accompanied by the idea that girls should, and could, aspire. Yet it is not clear that the economy has actually opened enough to ac-commodate the thousands of aspiring Gauris. In this slippage between aspiration and economic opportunity lies a story that is yet to unfold.

If the women who leave home are ambitious and aspirational, the men reveal a startlingly different story. Jagdish has not been successful growing up. In fact, he has failed in almost everything he has tried. He epitomizes the narrative of the new male loser, unable to become a man because he cannot stand on his own two feet. His story reveals a certain abjectness, a sense of consistent failure, a desperation. He comes from a class that no longer has the possibility of participating in a stable work-ing class job. Yet he has a college degree (a BA in English, a subject that to a postcolonial subject like Jagdish implies prestige) that is of little value in today's economy. Men like Jagdish are one step away from the educated unemployed, given the minimal value of their degrees, and must therefore seek jobs in more precarious sectors than they did before. They have been told they are losers and, while they search for a way to survive, their lives are suffused with anxiety and tension, unlike Gauri, whose life seems filled with hope. It is telling that Jagdish joined a Hindu nationalist organization, for they are one of the last spaces where men like him may get to reclaim their masculinity.

Rethinking the configuration of gendered power in the Global South today then requires us to think about men who (1) lose their ability to be breadwinners as the economy loses its manufacturing, and (2) are less desirable workers of the global service economy, but (3) who still have access to the forces of institutionalized violence, and (4) whose mascu-linity may increasingly rely on ideologies of nationalism, born out of the anticolonial struggle, and now emanating from the state. In the face of this, women face both new possibilities and new dangers.

Connell makes evident in all her work that gender has a history. Colonialism brought about huge changes in the gender order, as did anticolonial and nationalist struggles. So, too, now, with the neoliberal global economy and its discursive exhortations, is the gendered order being shaken. As the process unfolds before our eyes we can keep our theories relevant by being open to the sort of layered analysis Connell first encouraged in *Gender and Power*. Our task is still the identification of the historically and culturally specific structures that obtain at any one time and place. In this essay I have suggested that the way to do so is to develop a flexible structural analysis that pays attention both to colonial history and to subject formation.

NOTES

1 By neoliberalism I refer to the heightened privatization, lower government regulation, and reduced public expenditure for social services that has increasingly marked the global economy over the past 30 years.

2 While there are hegemonic and nonhegemonic discourses, structures and experiences themselves become legible only through discourse. This version of discourse analysis is perfectly compatible with structural analyses. In the words of Laclau and Mouffe (2001, 108): "The fact that every object is constituted as an object of discourse has *nothing to do* with whether there is a world external to thought, or with the realism/idealism opposition. An earthquake or the falling of a brick is an event that certainly exists, in the sense that it occurs here and now, independently of my will. But whether their specificity as objects is constructed in terms of 'natural phenomena' or 'expressions of the wrath of God' depends upon the structuring of a discursive field. What is denied is not that such objects exist externally to thought, but the rather different assertion that they could constitute themselves as objects outside any discursive conditions of emergence."

3 "The government of Afghanistan is waging a war upon women. Since the Taliban took power in 1996, women have had to wear *burqua* [full veils] and have been beaten and stoned in public for not having the proper attire. . . . Women are not allowed to work or even go out in public without a male relative; professional women such as professors, translators, doctors, lawyers, artists and writers have been forced from their jobs and restricted to their homes. . . . At one of the rare hospitals for women, a reporter found still, nearly lifeless bodies lying motionless on top of beds, wrapped in their burqua, unwilling to speak, eat, or do anything, but slowly wasting away. Others have gone mad and were seen crouched in corners, perpetually rocking or crying, most of them in fear. . . . If we can threaten military force in Kosovo in the name of human rights for the sake of ethnic

Albanians, citizens of the world can certainly express peaceful outrage at the oppression, murder and injustice committed against women by the Taliban." This is an excerpt taken from a petition circulated to support Afghan women; see Rahel Nardos, Mary K. Radpour, William S. Hatcher, and Michael L. Penn, *Overcoming Violence against Women and Girls: The International Campaign to Eradicate a Worldwide Problem* (Lanham, MD: Rowman and Littlefield, 2003).

4   In this context, Mayo (1927) described India as follows:

> We stop at the bedside of a young girl who looks at us with the eyes of a hungry animal . . . married as a baby, sent to her husband at ten, the shock of her incessant use was too much for her brain. . . . All she could do was crouch in a corner, a little twisted heap, panting . . . her husband, in despair and rage . . . cast her among the scrub thicket at the edge of the jungle to die. But there she was found and saved by an English lady under whose proper care she has at last "begun to blossom into normal intelligence." (55)

5   Historian Mrinalini Sinha tells us that far from traveling alone without any assistance from a government agency, Katherine Mayo was in direct contact with the British administration who had "encouraged her to write a book critical of Indian habits and traditional Indian practices, partly as a rejoinder to Gandhi, who was making major strides in building a mass-movement to end British rule" (2000, 627).

6   For an excellent analysis of the terrible rape of a young woman in New Delhi, often read in these terms of aspirational women and loser men, see "Delhi Rape: How the Other Half Lives," by Jason Burke, *Guardian*, September 10, 2013.

REFERENCES

Abu-Lughod, Lila. 2002. "Do Muslim Women Really Need Saving? Anthropological Reflections on Cultural Relativism and Its Others." *American Anthropologist* 104 (3): 783–790.

Alexander, M. Jacqui. 1994. "Not Just (Any) Body Can Be a Citizen: The Politics of Law, Sexuality and Postcoloniality in Trinidad and Tobago and the Bahamas." *Feminist Review* 48 (1): 5–23.

Appadurai, Arjun. 2004. "The Capacity to Aspire: Culture and the Terms of Recognition." In *Culture and Public Action*, edited by V. Rao and M. Walton, 59–84. Palo Alto, CA: Stanford University Press.

Basu, Amrita. 1995. *Challenge of Local Feminisms*. Boulder, CO: Westview Press.

Bhambra, Gurminder. 2007a. *Rethinking Modernity: Postcolonialism and the Sociological Imagination*. Basingstoke: Palgrave Macmillan.

———.2007b. "Sociology and Postcolonialism: Another 'Missing' Revolution?" *Sociology* 41 (5): 871–884.

Brown, Wendy. 2003. "Neo-liberalism and the End of Liberal Democracy." *Theory & Event* 7: 1. doi:10.1353/tae.2003.0020.

Burke, Jason. 2013. "Delhi Rape: How the Other Half Lives." *Guardian*, September 10.

Carlson, Jennifer. 2015. *Citizen-Protectors: The Everyday Politics of Gun Carry in an Age of Decline*. Oxford: Oxford University Press.

Chakrabarty, Dipesh. 2000. *Provincializing Europe: Postcolonial Thought and Historical Difference*. New Delhi: Oxford University Press.

Chatterjee, Partha. 1990. "The Nationalist Resolution of the Woman Question." In *Recasting Women: Essays in Indian Colonial History*, edited by Kumkum Sangari and Sudesh Vaid, 233–253. New Brunswick, NJ: Rutgers University Press.

Connell, Raewyn. 1987. *Gender and Power*. Stanford: Stanford University Press.

———. 1995. *Masculinities*. Berkeley: University of California Press.

———. 2007. *Southern Theory: The Global Dynamics of Knowledge in Social Science*. Malden, MA: Polity.

———. 2009. *Gender: A World Perspective*. 2nd ed. Malden, MA: Polity.

———. 2014. "Margin Becoming Centre: For a World-Centred Rethinking of Masculinities. *NORMA: International Journal for Masculinity Studies* 9 (4): 217–231.

Fanon, Frantz. 1967. *Black Skin, White Masks*. New York: Grove Press.

Fraser, Nancy. 2013. *Fortunes of Feminism: From State-Managed Capitalism to Neoliberal Crisis*. London: Verso.

Go, Julian. 2011. *Patterns of Empire: The British and American Empires, 1688 to the Present*. Cambridge: Cambridge University Press.

———. 2013. "For a Postcolonial Sociology." *Theory and Society* 42 (1): 25–55.

Hall, Stuart. 1996. "When Was the 'Postcolonial'? Thinking at the Limit." In *The Postcolonial Question: Common Skies, Divided Horizons*, edited by Iain Chambers and Lidia Curti, 242–258. London: Routledge.

Kristof, Nicholas, and Shirley WuDunn. 2009. *Half the Sky: Turning Oppression into Opportunity for Women Worldwide*. New York: Vintage.

Laclau, Ernesto, and Chantal Mouffe. (1985) 2001. *Hegemony and Socialist Strategy: Towards a Radical Democratic Politics*. London: Verso.

Lindsay, Lisa. 2003. *Working with Gender: Wage Labor and Social Change in Southwestern Nigeria*. Portsmouth, NH: Heinemann.

Mahmood, Saba. 2005. *Politics of Piety: The Islamic Revival and the Feminist Subject*. Princeton: Princeton University Press.

———. 2015. *Religious Difference in a Secular Age: A Minority Report*. Princeton: Princeton University Press.

Mama, Amina. 1997. "Sheroes and Villains: Conceptualizing Colonial and Contemporary Violence against Women in Africa." In *Feminist Genealogies, Colonial Legacies, Democratic Futures*, edited by M. Jacqui Alexander and Chandra Talpade Mohanty, 46–62. New York: Routledge.

Matlon, Jordanna. 2014. "Narratives of Modernity, Masculinity and Citizenship amid Crisis in Abidjan's *Sorbonne*." *Antipode* 46 (3): 717–735.

Mayo, Katherine. 1927. *Mother India*. New York: Harcourt, Brace & Co.

McClintock, Anne. 2002. *Carnal Knowledge and Imperial Power: Race and the Intimate in Colonial Rule*. Berkeley: University of California Press.

McRobbie, Angela. 2009. *The Aftermath of Feminism: Gender, Culture, and Social Change*. Thousand Oaks, CA: Sage.

Mohanty, Chandra Talpade. 1988. "Under Western Eyes: Feminist Scholarship and Colonial Discourses." *Feminist Review* 30:61–88.

———. 2003. *Feminism without Borders: Decolonizing Theory, Practicing Solidarity.* Durham, NC: Duke University Press.

Nair, Janaki. 1996. *Women and Law in Colonial India.* Delhi: Kali for Women.

Nandy, Ashis. 2009. *The Intimate Enemy: Loss and Recovery of Self under Colonialism.* Delhi: Oxford University Press.

Otto, Diane. 2010. "Power and Danger: Feminist Engagement with International Law through the UN Security Council." *Australian Feminist Law Journal* 32:97–121.

Oyewumi, Oyeronke. 1997. *The Invention of Women: Making an African Sense of Western Gender Discourses.* Minneapolis: University of Minnesota Press.

Ray, Raka. 2013. "Connell and Postcolonial Sociology." *Political Power and Social Theory* 25: 147–156.

Roy, Ananya. 2010. *Poverty Capital: Microfinance and the Making of Development.* New York: Routledge.

Rubin, Gayle. 1975. "The Traffic in Women: Notes on the 'Political Economy' of Sex." In *Toward an Anthropology of Women,* edited by Rayna R. Reiter, 157–210. New York: Monthly Review Press.

Russo, Ann. 2006. "The Feminist Majority Foundation's Campaign to Stop Gender Apartheid: The Intersections of Feminism and Imperialism in the United States." *Feminist International Journal of Politics* 8:557–580.

Sangari, Kumkum. 1999. *Politics of the Possible: Essays on Gender, History, Narrative, Colonial English.* New Delhi: Tulika.

Sherman, Jennifer. 2009. *Those Who Work, Those Who Don't: Poverty, Morality, and Family in Rural America.* Minneapolis: University of Minnesota Press.

Shohat, Ella, 2001. "Area Studies, Transnationalism, and the Feminist Production of Knowledge." Special issue on "Globalization and Gender," *Signs* 26 (4): 1269–1272.

Sinha, Mrinalini. 1995. *Colonial Masculinity: The 'Manly Englishman' and the 'Effeminate Bengali' in the Late Nineteenth Century.* Manchester: Manchester University Press.

———. 2000. "Refashioning Mother India: Feminism and Nationalism in Late-Colonial India." *Feminist Studies* 26 (3): 623–644.

Smith, Dorothy E. 1987. *The Everyday World as Problematic: A Feminist Sociology.* Boston: Northeastern University Press.

Stacey, Judith, and Barrie Thorne. 1985. "The Missing Feminist Revolution in Sociology." *Social Problems* 32 (4): 301–316.

Steinmetz, George. 2008. "The Colonial State as a Social Field: Ethnographic Capital and Native Policy in the German Overseas Empire before 1914." *American Sociological Review* 73:589–612.

World Bank. 2014. *Voice and Agency: Empowering Women and Girls for Shared Prosperity.* Washington, DC: World Bank.

5

Race, Indigeneity, and Gender

Lessons for Global Feminism

MARA VIVEROS VIGOYA

In this chapter I consider the dilemmas about race and indigeneity faced by Colombian feminisms and their implications for feminist concepts of gender. These dilemmas arise from a tension between social movements' search for a "general subject" and a political project that not only recognizes the idea of difference but also holds it as a central tenet. This tension has deep roots in the Latin American region, going back to the postcolonial building of national identities. All the contemporary societies that have tried to adopt liberal principles to create social pacts have faced an evident contradiction between legal equality and persistent inequalities of class, race, gender, and sexuality (Wade 2009, 158).

This chapter also seeks, from a perspective of feminist solidarity, to build a bridge between Colombian experience and thought and feminist debates in the global North. Such dialogue takes place too rarely. Globalization and neoliberalism have had a great impact on the possibilities of resistance against oppression both in the center and the periphery of the world capitalist system. We cannot avoid considering feminist movements from a transnational viewpoint. Yet we need to see global feminism not as an expression of fixed universal principles, but as an open process combining the thoughts and demands of different movements, both national and transnational (Millán 2012, 37).

Within feminism, the idea of difference has developed in opposition to the idea of universality. Difference has been presented either as a demand for a specific identity or as a principle of radical pluralism (Fraser 1997). In both cases "difference" emerges as a counterpoint to the project of modernity and its use of universal categories. This opposition has profoundly marked the strategies used by different feminist groups, and has defined their positions toward the state, the nation, and social intervention.

In Colombia, and more widely in Latin America, the development of feminism over the last thirty years has been marked by debates about differences among women and the multiple differences that "intersect" or "co-construct" each other. Feminist practice in this period—one of profound social and political change across the region—has reworked the global debates about gender in the light of what we now call "feminist epistemologies of the South" (Mendoza 2010; Viveros Vigoya 2016).

In common with other epistemologies of the South, feminist epistemologies—which involve not just one perspective but a range of perspectives—call for new processes of producing and validating feminist knowledges, academic and nonacademic, and new relations between forms of knowledge. This is based on the practices of the social groups that have suffered most from the consequences of colonialism and neoliberal capitalism (Santos 2011). The reflections and experiences of a significant part of Latin American feminism are anchored in a South that is less a geographical concept than a metaphor of struggles and resistance against oppressions and discriminations based on gender, class, ethnicity, race, and sexuality. This constitutes an important input to the construction of a "feminism without borders," and to the understanding of the dynamics of gender on a global scale.

In what follows, we will first examine the process that Colombian feminism has gone through since the 1970s, in developing its paradigms of action and reflection, which have become increasingly diverse. Second, we will examine the position currently occupied by social movements of indigenous and Afro-descendant women in Colombian feminist debates about the dilemmas and new perspectives that globalization has imposed upon social movements.

Colombian Feminism, from the Marxist Paradigm to Policy Activism

During the 1960s and 1970s, in Colombia as in the rest of Latin America, civil and military groups emerged with demands based on Marxist ideology. The leading social movements assumed that the proletariat was the key political actor, with both the capacity and the duty to transform the social order. Colombian women were slow in joining electoral political action, and their representation in political bodies was minimal for a long time (Villarreal Méndez 1995). However, from 1970 onwards, and to the astonishment and fear of some political parties, feminist groups emerged. These were mainly made up—as in the US—of "white" women (or their Colombian equivalent, *mestiza* [mixed race] women with fair skin) from the middle classes; many had had feminist experience in Europe or North America.

Mostly these were small consciousness-raising groups, seeking to make political what used to be seen as personal, such as sexuality and contraception (Sánchez Gómez 2005). They widened the definition of politics and the traditional way of doing politics. These collectives did not necessarily aspire to state power. They worked in favor of cultural transformations in society, at risk of being overshadowed by the demands of the "general" Marxist-oriented movement, which recognized no specific oppression other than class. Feminist groups engaged in debates on "double militancy"—feminist and political—and autonomy, abortion and sexuality, women's health, and the life of the marital couple.

A key event, the First Latin American and Caribbean Feminist Encounter, was held in Bogotá, Colombia, in July 1981. Systematic discussions took place about the agenda just mentioned (Sánchez Gómez 2005, 384). But from that moment, voices were raised to express concern about "the small attendance of working women, peasant women and women from low-income classes" (Restrepo and Bustamante 2009, 15) at the event. It was not until the meeting in 1987 in Taxco, Mexico, that the Feminist Encounters managed to attract "large numbers of women from various sectors of the grassroots movement, women not necessarily identified with feminism" (ibid., 15). Since the first meeting in Bogotá in 1981, these encounters have encouraged transnational debates and interchanges among feminist activists from different countries, with undeniable effects on feminist agendas, such as the production of new identity discourses and new feminist practices (Álvarez 2000).

During the 1980s, Latin American feminist currents became more diverse, and tendencies such as "radical," "moderate," and "political" began to be defined. At the same time a wide social movement emerged at the grassroots level, made up of women who sought to work with women from low-income sectors and create alliances with left-wing parties and organizations of the armed struggle (Fischer 2005). At this time the first women's centers were formed in Cali, Medellin, and Bogotá. They produced information, provided legal and medical services, documentation centers, publications, and so forth. More solid links were formed across Latin America and the Caribbean. Regional and continental events multiplied around the commemoration of significant dates: among others, March 8, International Women's Day; May 28, Day of Action for Women's Health; and November 25, International Day against Violence against Women (Páez et al. 1989).

The collapse of many left-wing projects, in Colombia and across Latin America, and the advent of neoliberal globalization, affected all social movements including feminism (Vargas 2008, 155). Feminism in the 1990s went through a radical change in its organizational strategies and its theoretical-political agenda. The movement went from proposing maximalist demands to specific projects with real social impact. But what was won in specificity was lost in creativity, as the utopian search was subordinated to achieving efficacy and policy reform (Gargallo 2007).

The Institutionalization of "Gender" and the Advent of Multiculturalism

In the 1990s a process of institutionalization of the gender concept and gender perspective began. This occurred through state programs aimed specifically at women and through gender studies programs in the universities. The process was reinforced by events like the UN Conference on Population and Development in Cairo in 1994 and the Beijing World Conference on Women in 1995. Amid the turbulence that brought constitutional reform in 1991 and the implementation of a neoliberal economic model, new gender-specific institutions were created. They included at the national level the Presidential Council for Youth, Women and Family; at the regional or local level, secretariats and offices of women, aimed at promoting women's participation in economic and social development. In 1996, after the Beijing conference, a National Equity Directorate was created, and the Equality and Participation Policy for Women was promulgated (Peláez Mejía 2001).

This process meant increased knowledge, dissemination, and visibility of gender issues throughout society. But a greater use of the concept of gender sometimes stripped the idea of the feminist political dimension from which it arose. Many feminists left the social movements to join government bodies or NGOs (Millán 2012). Financing from international sources was often received uncritically, and this became another cause of fragmentation (Fischer 2005). The neoliberal emphasis on efficacy and modernization of the social affected feminism, too. The *professional* displaced the *militant*, and the *operative* became more important than the *discursive* (Richard 2001, 230). Gender equality was incorporated into the instruments of neoliberal governance—but did not achieve the transformation of reality for Latin American women (Millán 2012).

In the 1990s a crisis arose between "institutional" feminists and "autonomous" feminists. The category of institutional feminism included women working in a great variety of organizations. They ranged from development-oriented centers with only a weak feminist profile, to collectives with a perspective of strong countercultural feminism (Vargas 2008, 151). Autonomous feminism, too, had a heterogeneous range of groups. Their common stance was to operate without international finance, to maintain a distance from the state and political parties, and generally to seek self-determination and independence from any institution. The depth and intensity of conflict between these two tendencies were openly expressed in the Seventh Latin American and Caribbean Feminist Encounter held in Chile in 1996. Since then the polarization between the two feminisms has lessened, without losing its importance as a reference point in political and theoretical debates (Vargas 2008, 156).

During the 1990s the academic institutionalization of feminism gained ground in many Latin America countries (Arango and Puyana 2007). This meant an undeniable recognition of the gender issue in the university world. Academic feminism supported a greater commitment to gender equity in government agencies and public policies. It provided technical expertise, both in interventions and in research in this new field. Paradoxically, however, the institutionalization of feminism in universities was accompanied by the isolation of feminist academics, and discrimination against gender programs from the faculties and discipline-based programs. Universities, too, could make rhetorical use of the theme of gender, separated from its rebellious origins.

One cornerstone of autonomy was the independence of feminist struggles from left-wing parties and the ideology of class struggle. Defense of that autonomy relied on a political premise: the real or potential existence of a common identity shared by all women, as a social group dominated by men. This was the implicit gender theory of canonical feminism. In presupposing that masculine domination overrides any other power relationship, canonical feminism ignored the interplay between gender differences and inequalities, and the differences and inequalities of race, ethnic group, and sexual orientation. By avoiding criticism of the hegemony of whiteness, denying ambivalences around the ideology of *mestizaje*, and ignoring the heteronormativity of social institutions, many Latin American feminists unwittingly reproduced racial hierarchies, a Eurocentric orientation, and heterosexism.

In the 1990s a new era began where "the right to be different" replaced the search for an undifferentiated national identity based on one language, one race, and one religion. The new Constitution of 1991 played a part: its multicultural ideology and emphasis on human dignity threw into relief ethno-racial hierarchies and ingrained heteronormativity in the nation (Curiel 2013).

Though racism and sexuality were mentioned in the First Latin American and Caribbean Feminist Encounter, self-critical discussion did not immediately take place. It was only in the Second Encounter, held in Lima in 1983, that the topic of racism was thematized. The fight against racism and heterosexism was part of the political agenda of Latin American feminism. But it was very difficult to get the movement to accept that racism and homophobia might exist within the movement, and even more difficult to give everyone access to the privileges enjoyed by white heterosexual feminists.

From the 1990s, the number of women's groups forming around the defense and consolidation of a specific ethnicity began to grow. These became movements of indigenous and Afro-descendant women. These movements have questioned theoretically certain key concepts of feminism, such as gender and patriarchy. At the same time, they have strengthened their links with women's social movements and with feminism.

What are the theoretical and political challenges posed by these movements and their links with feminism? To answer this question one must examine the path followed by the movements of indigenous and Black Colombian women.

Indigenous Women's Movements

Ever since colonization in the 16th century, women have been involved in the struggles of indigenous peoples and organizations for survival and full recognition of their rights (Sánchez Gutiérrez and Molina Echeverri 2010). According to the National Planning Department, there are currently 84 indigenous communities, with a combined population of around 1.4 million, representing 3.4 percent of the total population (DANE 2005). Their struggles, from the colonial period to the present, to maintain their social organization and to occupy a place in social life, have had three main directions: the defense of the land and the communal regime, the defense of self-government, and the defense of their own cultures (Sánchez Gutiérrez and Molina Echeverri 2010).

Indigenous organization was reshaped between 1910 and 1946, amid a series of struggles in areas where indigenous communities were predominant (Jimeno 2006). However, during the period called "The Violence" in Colombia and the subsequent political repression, between 1946 and 1958, a great part of the indigenous population was killed and the remaining population could only merge into peasant organizations. In the 1960s, for the first time, a wide public debate on the living conditions of indigenous peoples took place (Gómez 1998). In the 1970s, autonomous organisations of indigenous peoples were founded that gave rise to the first "modern" indigenous movement, with a program and a regional organization linking different ethnic groups.

From that moment on, the associations of indigenous peoples were transformed into political actors. They aimed not only to gain legal recognition but also to engage in debates and wider social processes concerning forms of government, the education that indigenous communities needed, and protection of the natural resources in indigenous territories (Villa and Houghton 2005; Sánchez Gutiérrez and Molina Echeverri 2010).

However, the importance of indigenous women's contributions on this political stage has been recognized only recently (Méndez Torres 2006). Since the 1991 national Constitution, the formation of grassroots organizations by indigenous women has become more common (Ulloa 2007, 20). Organized indigenous women who advocate for collective processes are beginning to be respected and recognized as leaders (Méndez Torres 2006, 2007).

Their organizations vary greatly; what they have in common is a search for justice and respect for their peoples and their way of life (Méndez Torres 2007). Colombian indigenous women have held leadership positions from which they have questioned the customs and traditions of their peoples that affect the dignity of women, as well as questioning the effects of neoliberal policies and the armed conflict in their regions.

Gender and feminism—as categories and political projects that came from the development projects of international organizations and from the women's movement—have been taken up in these indigenous organizations in very different ways. For instance, Julieta Paredes, a well-known indigenous leader in the Bolivian feminist collective Mujeres Creando, suggests that gender, as a concept and a category, holds possibilities for transforming the conditions of women's oppression. However, the revolutionary potential of gender was undermined by those technocrats who reduced this term to a mere pursuit of gender equity, an objective very different from transcending gender as a system of oppression (Paredes 2010).

In the case of Colombia, women such as Avelina Pancho—an indigenous leader from the Nasa people, an advocate for the indigenous university project and indigenous peoples' right to higher education in Colombia—suggests that "the category of gender has no equivalent term, at least with the same meaning and nuance, in the indigenous languages originating on the American continent." In their conception of the world, the relations between men and women are historical products of ancestral laws and values, which "have changed gradually due to influences of the broadest environment." What is important, for her, is to take advantage of indigenous women's potential, though often invisible, to generate harmonious and balanced relations between the communities (Pancho 2007, 60).

Florina López, an indigenous leader from the Kuna people and coordinator of the Indigenous Women's Network on Biodiversity in Latin America, introduces other perspectives to the discussion of gender. In her community, the topic of gender is taboo because it is linked, especially for men, with the rupture of the indigenous communities' cultural unity. Therefore, one of the most important tasks is to sensitize men to the topic of gender, to make them understand that the issue of gender is "as much a problem for them [men] as for us women," "because the joint involvement of both men and women is necessary" (López 2007, 81–82).

Other groups have begun to redefine the concept of gender on the basis of their own experiences. They advocate *complementarity* as an alternative perspective about relationships between people, and between humans and nature. An emphasis on harmony with the environment, inherent in the traditional cosmo-vision of indigenous peoples, assists their recognition "as ecological actors in national and international representations, discourses and policies, where it is assumed that spirituality and feminine sensitivity can be found in their traditions" (Ulloa 2004; Ulloa 2007, 22). The discourse of cosmic harmony provides a critique of the discrimination and exclusion experienced daily by women— illiteracy, the weight of domestic duties, devaluation of their work and products, ignorance of indigenous issues, and exclusion from decision making. These are seen to fracture the harmony, which must be reestablished by combatting the inequalities.

The resulting struggles emphasize collective action, since the defense of collective rights is seen as key to guaranteeing their survival as a people (Méndez Torres 2007; Pancho 2007). New dynamics of migration and urbanization have modified older organizational patterns, giving women a newly important role. Female leaderships have emerged, with positive repercussions for the community. But this has involved huge personal costs for the women leaders themselves (López 2007).

Indigenous women's collectives have taken different views of demands for gender equality, whether positioning themselves in cultural specificities or vindicating their political and social role in their communities. However, the current tendency is to seek alliances between indigenous and nonindigenous women. In such alliances, indigenous women demand that the common struggle incorporate their voices and their experiences of "otherness" and that the shared agenda be sensitive to their questioning of canonical feminism. This was expressed clearly in a document from an international meeting in Bangkok in 2005:

> From the indigenous women's organizations we consider that the feminist movement must review its paradigm, to incorporate cultural, linguistic,

spiritual dimensions and the cosmo-vision of the indigenous woman, as part of the enrichment and integration of the struggle of women of all peoples. Another important aspect is the formation of alliances between organizations of indigenous and non-indigenous women, as a united front of the women's struggle. (Cited in Millán 2012, 46)

Feminist academics and women intellectuals have also taken part in this process of building alliances. The decolonization of feminism has meant the recuperation of indigenous women's organizational experiences, stories, and strategies of resistance in different parts of the continent. It has also destabilized both the Eurocentric vision prevailing in the academic world, and the racial and class hierarchies that maintain patriarchy in indigenous communities and in mixed-race societies (Hernández Castillo 2013).

Black Women's Social Movements

To understand current social movements of Black women in Colombia it is necessary to place them in the history of the country's Black population. Colombia has the second largest African-descendant population in Latin America, after Brazil. African-descendant people represent 19.2 percent of the total Colombian population (Urrea, Viáfara, and Viveros 2014, 96). Africans arrived in the territory that would become Colombia in the 16th century, and worked as slaves in mining, agriculture, cattle raising, commerce, fishing, domestic work, and craft production.

From the start of the slave trade, multiple forms of resistance to enslavement developed. They included rebellions, abortions and infanticide, escapes, and the creation of *palenques*—fortified communities created by slaves who escaped and established autonomous spaces for social life, organization, and even economic production (Viveros Vigoya and Cifuentes 2010). After the official abolition of slavery in 1851, the former slaves, escapees (*cimarrones*), and their descendents were gradually absorbed into the nation-building project. However, their inclusion was marginal, as they were ignored by the republican legal system and the "rights-based state" (*Estado de Derecho*). From then on, they fought continuously through the 20th century for the extension of their citizenship, full participation in politics, and their economic and social advancement (Andrews 2007).

Between the 1930s and 1950s, claims by Black people were principally made through mainstream political channels, especially the Liberal Party (Urrea, Viáfara, and Viveros 2004, 91). A modern Black movement began in 1976, leading in 1982 to the first national organization, the Cimarron National Movement. It was influenced by the U.S. civil rights movement and the anticolonization and antiapartheid movements (Agudelo 2005). After the 1991 Constitution, a second wave of modern Afro-Colombian organizations formed around ethnic-territorial and environmental issues. The Black movement by then had adopted an ethnic-based discourse, raising tensions between those advancing ethnic and racial claims inside its ranks (Urrea, Viáfara, and Viveros 2014, 91).

Afro-Colombian women have faced obstacles within both the Black movement and Colombian feminism in expressing their racial, ethnic, and gender demands together (Lozano Lerma 1996, 2010; Rojas 1996; Flórez 2004; Lamus Canavate 2012). A first difficulty is the state's and social scientists' ignorance of the particularities of Black women, who belong to a historically racialized group. A second difficulty is a hidden "Andino-centrism" in feminist demands put forward as universal or necessary for all women, invalidating or making invisible the particular contributions of Black women (Lozano Lerma 2010). Andino-centrism is a legacy of racial and regional hegemony. The Colombian elite of the 19th century articulated a model of nationhood in which the sphere of civilization belonged to the temperate zones of the Andes upland region, as opposed to the torrid lowland region where most of the Black population was located. The hot coastal lowland and the savage inland frontiers were associated, in this imaginary, with barbarism and ignorance (Arocha and Moreno 2007).

One of difficulties in making the demands of the Black women's social movement comprehensible comes precisely from the singularity of their experiences. Their movement is not defined from a separatist perspective, because "black/Afro-Colombian women, before thinking of themselves as women, saw themselves as black people, as black communities" (Lozano Lerma 2010, 21). Nor does their movement consider the gender conditions of men and women as a dichotomy. But there is, de facto, recognition of female subordination. Grueso and Arroyo (2007) are correct in saying that there is complementarity in gender roles in the productive space of the building of territory, but inequality in political and family environments. In this sense, the complementarity of gender roles is "complementarity lacking fluidity that ends up making the women subordinate" (Lozano Lerma 2010, 18).

Black women's demands have particularly concerned recognition of their land rights and the protection of their cultural traditions. Given the predatory occupation of their lands by forces in the armed conflict, and by national and international capital, Black women have had to adjust their mobilization plans to the general demands of the Black or Afro-Colombian social movement. The way their gender demands are shaped by social circumstances is shown by Flórez (2004), discussing the Process of Black Communities (PCN) network in the Colombian Pacific region. The PCN began in 1993 and gained strength by demanding government recognition of the multiethnic and multicultural character of the nation, respect for Black people's cultural differences, and acknowledgement of their territorial rights under Law 70, which recognized collective land rights (Castillo 2007).

According to Flórez (2004), in the early 1990s the PCN made the radical defense of Black identity a priority, before any other identity. At the same time, it promoted activities for women in rural areas, in the context of widely criticized "development" practices (Rojas 1996). In this contradictory context, the Network of Black Women of the Pacific emerged in 1992 to create solidarity between different women's organizations and to strengthen their ethnic identity. In the second half of the 1990s the PCN accepted the importance of gender issues, but resisted pressure to include them in their political agenda. In a third phase, beginning in the 2000s, the PCN opened up to gender questions. A search began for conceptual tools adequate to express the specificity of gender oppressions in those contexts, and to produce "a perspective of localized gender"—for example, linking the issue of gender with the defense of place or territory (Grueso and Arroyo 2007).

When the armed conflict arrived, this strategy was indispensable for the survival of the communities (Flórez 2004, 240). One of the main challenges concerns land rights. Illegal mining, often linked to multinational corporations, tries to displace Afro-Colombians from their ancestral lands, rich in minerals and natural resources. Forced relocation of Afro-Colombians often involves intimidation and violence, including sexual violence, by the armed groups: principally the paramilitaries, but also the guerrillas and the national army. Consequently the Afro-Colombian community has had to close ranks.

The need for Black women to create nonseparatist agendas for mobilization partly obscured gender demands. But it also aided recognition of Black women's participation and leadership in social organizations whose actions gained recognition by the state. As Lozano Lerma (2010, 22) says:

> Although at that time [the women] were not proposing specific rights, the existence of patriarchy in their communities and organizations led them not so much to a discourse in defense of their rights as [such], but to actions that obliged the men to take them into account, to listen to them and respect them, given the important leadership roles they had begun to develop.

Flórez (2004) notes the progressive "implosion" of gender identities and demands within the two main strands of the Black social movement—the PCN and the Cimarron movement—among activists and intellectuals and also in the grassroots movements. Increasingly, the women included in their agenda feminist themes such as the struggles for the rights of women, for political visibility, and against violence against women (Lamus Canavate 2012). However, neoliberal policies and the new capitalist extractivism imposed the need to include the defense of territory, biodiversity, cultural rights, and ancestral knowledge in these partially autonomous initiatives.

The armed conflict and capitalist depredation have undoubtedly affected all Colombian women. Black women have paid heavier costs, in terms of displacement, sexual violence, selective assassinations, and political persecution, because of their active participation in the defense of their ancestral lands. This is true especially in the Colombian Pacific region. Only recently this biodiverse and pluri-ethnic territory ceased being a peripheral zone exempt from violence; indeed, it became the strategic theater of the armed conflict, with grave consequences for its inhabitants (Agudelo 2001, 7). The impact of armed conflict and capitalist intrusion dramatizes the importance of considering the specificities of Black women's experiences.

Finally, we should note the changes that have occurred in the Afro-Colombian social movement, changes made evident during the last

National Autonomous Congress of the Black, Palenquero and Raizal Peoples, held in the city of Quibdo in August 2013. Women participated actively, putting forward precise demands to transform their gender status within the Afro-Colombian movement. In an open declaration released through a delegate to the discussion group on national authority, they demanded not only recognition of the LGBTI community but also the opening of participatory and decision-making spaces on equal terms to the women of the movement:

> Black, Afro-Colombian, Palenquero and Raizal women are advancing in the defense of our strategic gender interests. . . . We are not content with improvements that enable us to fulfill our traditional roles, but we dare to question the relations of masculine domination as a social and cultural imposition and we are no longer prepared to accept it. The voice of women in this sense was unanimous, demanding a participation of 50% in all the organizational spaces of the social Afro movement, both at a grassroots level and at the level of interaction with the State. (Otras Negras . . . ¡Y Feministas! 2013, 1)

By Way of Conclusion: Lessons for Global Feminism

Organizations of both indigenous and Black women have questioned Colombian feminism, beginning with reclaiming their own stories and particular experiences of sexism. Both groups have shown reserve toward what they see as interference by external agents, be they institutions, NGOs, or individual researchers of either sex (Ulloa 2007, 23). The two groups have related differently, however, to feminist discourse and its gender theory. This follows from the different positions held by Afro-Colombian women and indigenous women in the political and symbolic space of the Colombian nation from its beginnings.

These differences have become less absolute due to the effects of multiculturalism, as a social and political practice, on all the social movements. To be recognized by the state, movements have had to "fit the images of cultural difference expressed in the unique paradigmatic ethnic subject" (Bocarejo and Restrepo 2011, 9). Thus, the demands and self-representations of Black communities have been ethnicized, with all the internal tensions that this implies. Many of their political strategies and their relations with experts, state officials, and NGOs have been made comparable with those of the indigenous movement (Restrepo 2013).

Not all the indigenous or Afro-descendant women's organizations have made antisexist demands. Some years ago Yuderkys Espinosa (1999) and Ochy Curiel (2009) pointed out that the aim of defending the specificity of a collective historical, political, and cultural experience does not necessarily entail challenging patriarchal practices.

Those who have done so have developed a culturally situated political discourse and practice on gender and have strongly questioned academic feminist theory (Hernández Castillo 2013). As indigenous and Black movements developed, a promising convergence can be seen between feminist policy agendas and the field of "decoloniality studies," which focuses on understanding the "colonial matrix of power" (Bidaseca and Vásquez Laba 2011). One example is the search for understanding of the historic links between colonialism and the widespread discrimination and violence to which indigenous and Afro-descendant women have been subjected in the Colombian armed conflict.

The emphasis given by indigenous and Afro-descendant women to the fact that their struggles are collective, not individual, points to a distinctive form of politics: the totality of their social relations is expressed in a single struggle. For many of these women, it is not a matter of choosing between their rights as women and their loyalties to their ethnic-racial groups. Rather, it is a matter of anchoring respect for their rights as women *in* their collective struggles, so that both men and women defend them. It is also seen as important to link the defense of these rights to more general struggles in society, such as resistance against neoliberal development and its megaprojects.

Global feminist theory has much to learn from the lived experiences, epistemological proposals, and political projects described above. Colombian indigenous women's defense of their lands implies protecting a way of life not focused on the individual but on the collectivity; shielding "the continuity of life" and passing on an ancestral knowledge that involves other forms of relations between human and nonhuman; and food self-sufficiency (Ulloa 2016). The struggles that black women have undertaken in defense of their life and ancestral lands allow us to imagine "a future option that does not only address our own needs" (Kuagro 2014), and alternative economic dynamics that respect the rule that says "don't take more that what the Earth allows" (Proceso de Comunidades Negras 2015; Mina et al. 2015). All these projects are currently threatened by a context of global capitalism and by policies in favor of extractive multinational companies.

Recognizing these lessons is the first step in the development of a transnational feminist project of solidarity, which is willing to listen to, and to draw lessons from, the political practices and worldviews of indigenous women and Afro-descendent women. The struggles undertaken by indigenous and Afro-descendent women demonstrate the connections that exist between a global economic model that facilitates the accumulation of private and foreign capital and the privatization of soil and subsoil, the militarization of mining regions, the increase of political and sexual violence, and the forced displacement of ethnic communities from those territories.

While their social experiences are irreducibly different, the weave of life for women in the Global North is nevertheless closely connected with the lives of women in the Global South. It is, therefore, necessary to connect the knowledges that arise from political movements led by indigenous women and Afro-descendent women to the struggles undertaken by feminist women in other geographical areas, who may stand in solidarity with their struggles and share responsibility for their problems. To think feminisms from a transnational perspective means to open intercultural dialogues and create "feminist solidarities capable of crossing the divisions of place, identity, class, work and faiths" (Mohanty 2003), based on a continuous review of our own commitments and political assumptions.

This does not guarantee that we will eliminate the existing tensions between different feminisms. However, it does enable us to overcome the many ethnocentric errors that have been committed vis-à-vis this imagined community of the Other Women (Hernández Castillo 2013), whose lives and struggles have been subjected to a discursive colonization. It is a matter of annulling any privilege of canonical academic feminism, yet at the same time avoiding any cultural essentialism that attributes homogeneity or a decisive role to the social movements of Black or indigenous women. Feminist epistemologies of the South (Mendoza 2010), based on the varied theorizing and experience of women of the Global South, can thus enrich our understanding of the functioning of global gendered power and, at the same time, the means to resist this power.

REFERENCES

Agudelo, Carlos. 2001. El Pacífico colombiano: De "remanso de paz" a escenario estratégico del conflicto armado: Las transformaciones de la región y algunas respuestas de sus poblaciones frente a la violencia. *Cuadernos de Desarrollo Rural* 46: 7–37.

———. 2005. Movimiento social de comunidades negras: La construcción de un nuevo sujeto político. In *Retos del multiculturalismo en Colombia: Política y poblaciones negras*, 171–193. Medellín: Editorial IEPRI—IRD—ICANH—La Carreta.

Álvarez, Sonia. 2000. Translating the global effects of transnational organizing on local feminist discourses and practices in Latin America. *Meridians* 1 (1): 29–67.

Andrews, George Reid. 2007. *Afro-Latinoamerica 1800–2000*. Spanish ed. Madrid: Iberoamericana Editorial.

Arango, Luz Gabriela, and Yolanda Puyana, comp. 2007. *Género, mujeres y saberes en América Latina: Entre el movimiento social, la academia y el Estado*. Bogotá: Universidad Nacional de Colombia.

Arocha, Jaime, and Lina del Mar Moreno. 2007. Andinocentrismo, salvajismo y Afro-reparaciones. In *Afro-reparaciones: Memorias de la Esclavitud y Justicia Reparativa para negros, afrocolombianos y raizal*, edited by Claudia Mosquera Rosero-Labbé and Luiz Claudio Barcelós, 587–603. Bogotá: FCH, Universidad Nacional de Colombia.

Bastidas, Edith. 2007. Conocimiento tradicional indígena: Normatividad, propuestas de protección y retos de los pueblos y sus organizaciones. In *Mujeres indígenas, territorialidad y biodiversidad en el contexto latinoamericano*, edited by Astrid Ulloa, Georgina Méndez, Lucrecia Pisquiy, Avelina Pancho Aquite, Eliana Huitraqueo Mena, M. López, Anny Gutiérrez, et al., 3231–3253. Bogotá: Universidad Nacional de Colombia.

Bidaseca, Karina, and Vanesa Vázquez Laba, comp. 2011. *Feminismos y Poscolonialidad: Descolonizando el feminismo desde y en América Latina*. Buenos Aires: Godot.

Bocarejo, Diana, and Eduardo Restrepo. 2011. Introducción: Hacia una crítica del multiculturalismo en Colombia. *Revista Colombiana de Antropología* 47 (2): 7–13.

Carneiro, Sueli. 2005. Ennegrecer al feminismo. *Nouvelles Questions Féministes* 24 (2): 21–26.

Castillo, Luis Carlos. 2007. *Etnicidad y nación: El desafío de la diversidad en Colombia*. Cali: Universidad del Valle.

Curiel, Ochy. 2009. Identidades esencialistas o construcción de identidades políticas: El dilema de las feministas afrodescendientes. *Construyendo nuestra interculturalidad* 5 (November). www.interculturalidad.org.

———. 2013. *La nación heterosexual*. Bogotá, Buenos Aires: Grupo Latinoamericano de Estudios, Formación y Acción Feminista, Brecha Lésbica.

Departamento Administrativo Nacional de Estadísticas (DANE). 2005 Datos Preliminares, Censo Nacional de Población de 2005. Bogotá: DANE.

Dietz, Mary. 2005. Las discusiones actuales de la teoría feminista. *Debate Feminista* 32 (16): 179–224.

Dorlin, Elsa. 2008. Introduction: La Révolution du féminisme noir! In *Black feminism: Anthologie du féminisme africain-américain, 1975–2000*, edited by Hazel Carby, Beverly Guy-Sheftall, Laura Alexandra Harris, Patricia Hill Collins, bell hooks, Audre Lorde, and Michelle Wallace, 9–42. Paris: Editions L'Harmattan.

Espinosa, Yuderkys. 1999. ¿Para qué nos sirven las identidades? Por un milenio plural y diverso. In *Feminismos plurales*, Serie Aportes para el Debate de ALAI, 7. www.alainet.org.

Fischer, Amalia. 2005. Los complejos caminos de la autonomía. *Nouvelles questions féministes* 24 (2): 54–74.

Flórez-Flórez, Juliana. 2004. Implosión identitaria y movimientos sociales: Desafíos y logros del Proceso de Comunidades Negras ante las relaciones de género. In *Conflicto e (in) visibilidad: Retos en los estudios de la gente negra en Colombia*, edited by Eduardo Restrepo, 219–246. Popayán: Editorial Universidad del Cauca.

Fraser, Nancy. 1997. *Iustitia interrupta: Reflexiones críticas desde la posición "postsocialista"*. Bogotá: Siglo de Hombres Editores.

Gargallo, Francesca. 2007. *Ideas feministas latinoamericanas*. México, D. F.: Universidad Autónoma de la Ciudad de México.

Gómez, Augusto. 1998. La guerra de exterminio contra los grupos indígenas cazadores-recolectores de los llanos orientales (siglo XIX y XX). *Anuario Colombiano de Historia Social y de la Cultura* (25): 351–376.

Grueso, Libia, and Leyla Andrea Arroyo. 2007. Mujeres y la defensa del lugar en las luchas del movimiento negro colombiano. In *Las mujeres y la política del lugar*, edited by Wendy Harcourt and Arturo Escobar, 113–130. México, D. F.: UNAM/PUEG.

Hellebrandová, Klara. 2014. El proceso de etno-racialización y resistencia en la era multicultural: Ser *negro* en Bogotá. *Universitas Humanística* 77 (1): 145–168.

Hernández Castillo, Rosalva Aída. 2013. Comentarios a Mujeres Mayas-Kichwas en la apuesta por la descolonización de los pensamientos y corazones. In *Senti-pensar el género: Perspectiva de los pueblos originarios*, coordinated by Georgina Méndez, Juan López Intzín Sylvia Marcos, and Carmen Osorio Hernández, 63–72. Guadalajara: Red-IINPIM, Red de Feminismos Descoloniales, La casa del Mago.

Jimeno, Myriam. 2006. Juan Gregorio Palechor: Historia de mi vida. Bogotá: ICANH.

Kuagro. 2014. Comunicado de solidaridad con la Marcha de las Mujeres del Norte sel Cauca a la Opinión pública. Cali, Colombia

Lamus Canavate, Doris. 2012. *El color negro de la (sin) razón blanca: El lugar de las mujeres afrodescendientes en los procesos organizativos en Colombia*. Bucaramanga: Publicaciones Universidad Autónoma de Bucaramanga.

Livingstone, Grace. 2004. *Inside Colombia: Drugs, democracy, and war*. New Brunswick, NJ: Rutgers University Press.

López M., Florina. 2007. Los nuevos roles de las mujeres kuna en las organizaciones de base en Panamá. In *Mujeres indígenas, territorialidad y biodiversidad en el contexto latinoamericano*, edited by Astrid Ulloa, Georgina Méndez, Lucrecia Pisquiy, Avelina Pancho Aquite, Eliana Huitraqueo Mena, M. López, Anny Gutiérrez, et al., 79–82. Bogotá: Universidad Nacional de Colombia.

Lozano Lerma, Betty Ruth. 1996. Mujer y desarrollo. In *¿Pacífico: Desarrollo o biodiversidad? Estado, capital y movimientos sociales en el Pacífico colombiano*, edited by Escobar Arturo y Álvaro Pedroza, 176–204. Bogotá: Cerec.

———. 2010. El feminismo no puede ser uno porque las mujeres somos diversas: Aportes a un feminismo negro decolonial desde la experiencia de las mujeres negras del pacífico colombiano. *La manzana de la discordia* 5 (2): 7–24.

Méndez Torres, Georgina. 2006. Participación y demandas de las mujeres indígenas en la ciudad de Bogotá: La pregunta por la inclusión Tesis. Master's thesis, Gender Studies, Universidad Nacional de Colombia.

———. 2007. Nuevos escenarios de participación: Experiencias de mujeres indígenas en México y Colombia. In *Mujeres indígenas, territorialidad y biodiversidad en el contexto latinoamericano*, edited by Astrid Ulloa, Astrid, Georgina Méndez, Lucrecia Pisquiy, Avelina Pancho Aquite, Eliana Huitraqueo Mena, M. López, Anny Gutiérrez, et al., 34–46. Bogotá: Universidad Nacional de Colombia.

Mendoza, Brenny. 2010: La epistemología del sur, la colonialidad del género y el feminismo latinoamericano. In *Aproximaciones críticas a las prácticas teórico-políticas del feminismo latinoamericano*, compiled by Yuderkys Espinosa Miñoso. Buenos Aires: En la frontera.

Millán, Márgara. 2012. De la périphérie vers le centre: Origines et héritages des féminismes latino-américains. *Revue Tiers Monde* 209 (1): 37–52.

Mina, Charo, Marilyn Machado, Patricia Botero, and Arturo Escobar. 2015. Luchas del buen vivir por las mujeres negras del Alto Cauca. *Nómadas* 43 (1): 167–185.

Mohanty, Chandra Talpade. 2003. *Feminism without borders*. Durham: Duke University Press.

Otras Negras . . . ¡Y Feministas! 2003. *¡Sí hubo congreso! Reflexiones post Congreso Nacional Autónomo del Pueblo Negro, Afrocolombiano, Palenkero y Raizal*. www.afrodescendientes.com.

Páez de Tavera, Helena, María Cristina Ocampo de Herrán, and Norma Villarreal Méndez. 1989. *Protagonismo de mujer: Organización y liderazgo femenino en Bogotá*. Bogotá: PRODEMOCRACIA, Fundación Friedrich Naumann.

Pancho, Avelina. 2007. Participación de las mujeres nasa en los procesos de autonomía territorial y educación propia en el Cauca, Colombia. In *Mujeres indígenas, territorialidad y biodiversidad en el contexto latinoamericano*, edited by Astrid Ulloa, Georgina Méndez, Lucrecia Pisquiy, Avelina Pancho Aquite, Eliana Huitraqueo Mena, M. López, Anny Gutiérrez, et al., 53–62. Bogotá: Universidad Nacional de Colombia.

Paredes, Julieta. 2010. *Hilando fino: Desde el feminismo comunitario*. La Paz: Comunidad Mujeres Creando Comunidad.

Peláez Mejía, Margarita. 2001. La política de género en el estado Colombiano: Un camino de conquistas sociales. PhD thesis in public health, Escuela Nacional de Salud Pública, Fundación Osvaldo Cruz-Fiocruz, Rio de Janeiro.

Proceso de Comunidades Negras. 2014. *Construyendo buen vivir en las comunidades del rio Yurumanguí y en Pílamo, Cauca*. Cali: PCN-Solsticio.

Restrepo, Alejandra, and Ximena Bustamante. 2009. *Encuentros feministas latino-americanos y del Caribe: Apuntes para una historia en movimiento*. México, D. F.: Monarca Impresoras.

Restrepo, Eduardo. 2013. *Etnización de la negridad: La invención de las 'comunidades negras' como grupo étnico en Colombia*. Popayán: Editorial: Universidad del Cauca.

Richard, Nelly. 2001. La problemática del feminismo en los años de la transición en Chile. In *Estudios Latinoamericanos sobre cultura y transformaciones sociales en tiempos de globalización 2*, compiled by Daniel Matos, 227–239. Buenos Aires: CLACSO.

Rojas, Jeannette. 1996. Las mujeres en movimiento: Crónicas de otras miradas. In *¿Pacífico: Desarrollo o biodiversidad? Estado, capital y movimientos sociales en el Pacífico colombiano*, edited by Escobar Arturo y Álvaro Pedroza, 205–219. Bogotá: Cerec.

Sánchez Gómez, Olga Amparo. 2005. El movimiento social de mujeres. In *Las Mujeres en la historia de Colombia: Tomo i Mujeres, historia y política*, directed by Magdala Velásquez Toro, 379–402. Bogotá: Consejería Presidencial para la Política Social/ Editorial Norma.

Sánchez Gutiérrez, Enrique, and Hernán Molina Echeverri, comp. 2010. *Documentos para la historia del movimiento indígena colombiano contemporáneo*. Bogotá: Ministerio de Cultura.

Santos, Boaventura de Sousa. 2011. Introducción: Las epistemologías del Sur. In "Formas-Otras. Saber, nombrar, narrar, hacer," IV Training Seminar de Jóvenes investigadores en Dinámicas interculturales, 9–22. Barcelona: CIDOB.

Ulloa, Astrid. 2004. *La construcción del nativo ecológico: Complejidades, paradojas y dilemas de la relación entre los movimientos indígenas y el ambientalismo en Colombia*. Bogotá: Instituto Colombiano de Antropología e Historia (ICANH)/ Colciencias.

———. 2007. Introducción: Mujeres indígenas: Dilemas de género y etnicidad en los escenarios latinoamericanos. In *Mujeres indígenas, territorialidad y biodiversidad en el contexto latinoamericano*, edited by Astrid Ulloa, Georgina Méndez, Lucrecia Pisquiy, Avelina Pancho Aquite, Eliana Huitraqueo Mena, M. López, Anny Gutiérrez, et al., 17–33. Bogotá: Universidad Nacional de Colombia.

———. 2016. Feminismos, géneros y mujeres indígenas en América Latina. Unpublished document.

Uribe, María Tila. 1994. *Los años escondidos: Sueños y rebeldía en la década del 20*. Bogotá: Cestra, Cerec.

Urrea, Fernando, Carlos Viáfara, and Mara Viveros. 2014. From whitened miscegenation to tri-ethnic multiculturalism: Race and ethnicity in Colombia. In *Pigmentocracies: Ethnicity, race, and color in Latin America*, edited by Edward Telles and the PERLA Project, 81–125. Chapel Hill: University of North Carolina Press.

Vargas, Virginia. 2008. *Feminismos en América Latina: Su aporte a la política y a la democracia*. Lima: Universidad Nacional Mayor de San Marcos, Fondo Editorial de la Facultad de Ciencias Sociales.

Villa, William, and Juan Houghton. 2005. *Violencia política contra los pueblos indígenas en Colombia, 1974–2004*. Bogotá: Iwgia/Cecoin/Oia.

Villarreal Méndez, Norma. 1995. Mujeres y espacios políticos. In *Las Mujeres en la historia de Colombia: Tomo I Mujeres, historia y política*, directed by Magdala Velásquez Toro, 319–347. Bogotá: Consejería Presidencial para la Política Social/Editorial Norma.

Viveros Vigoya, Mara. 2004. El gobierno de la sexualidad juvenil y la gestión de las diferencias: Reflexiones a partir de un estudio de caso colombiano. *Revista Colombiana de Antropología* 40: 155–184.

———. 2016. Sex/gender. In *The Oxford handbook of feminist theory*, edited by Lisa Disch and Mary Hawkesworth, 852–873. New York: Oxford University Press.

Viveros Vigoya, Mara, and Alexander Cifuentes. 2010. Une rébellion inachevée: Le projet politique des Afrocolombien. *Multitudes* n.s., 1 (40): 194–201.

Wade, Peter. 1997. *Race and ethnicity in Latin America*. London: Pluto Press.

———. 2009. *Race and sex in Latin America*. London: Pluto Press.

Werneck, Jurema. 2005. Ialodês et féministes: Réflexions sur l'action politique des femmes noires en Amérique latine et aux Caraïbes. *Nouvelles Questions Féministes* 24 (2): 27–40.

6

Categories, Structures, and Intersectional Theory

JOYA MISRA

The importance of feminist theory endures in the 21st century, as scholars increasingly recognize the centrality of gender to all facets of social life. Structural feminist theories of the 20th century played a crucial role in identifying gendered inequalities in a wide array of institutions—including politics, economics, religions, legal systems, the media, families, schools, and workplaces—highlighting strategies for social change. While socialist feminist theory analyzed the relations between class and gender, intersectional theory first emerged as Black, Latina, and postcolonial feminist scholars further considered how race, ethnicity, nationality, citizenship, sexuality, and the other characteristics intersect with gender and class to form more multifaceted patterns of inequalities (Beale 1970; Anzaldúa 1987; Collins 1986; Zinn et al. 1986). Intersectional theory then complicates the notion of gender as a stable category, building on insights from poststructural theory, but remains focused on structural inequalities and social change. This makes understanding *how* categories figure into intersectional analyses particularly important.

Structural analyses of gender remain dominant in sociology. Sociologists refer to gender as an order (Connell 1987), a social institution (Martin 2004), or a social structure (Risman 2004; Lorber 1994), calling attention to the enduring yet dynamic nature of gender, and how power and inequality are embedded in gendered social relations (Connell 2009). Analyzing gender as a structure identifies the gendered ideologies, practices, and power conflicts embedded in all parts of society, as well as how these serve as potential sites for social change (Connell 1987, 2009; Lorber 1994; Risman 2004; Martin 2004; Acker 2006).

Because much intersectional theory was aimed at correcting a troublingly universal depiction of women's experiences (Beale 1970;

King 1988; Zinn et al. 1986; Collins 2000; Anzaldúa 1987; Morgan and Anzaldúa 1981), most intersectional scholarship in sociology remains structural, even as it insists that gender is complicated by other structures, such as race, class, sexuality, age, nationality, and citizenship. Sociological intersectional theory primarily analyzes inequalities with an aim to social change. Yet intersectional theory also breaks down artificially neat categorical distinctions between "men" and "women," drawing insights from poststructural theory that undermine simple categorizations. Intersectional theory refines structural understandings of inequality, recognizing gender, race, class, and other characteristics as structures reflecting power and inequality, providing new blueprints for social change.

Intersectional theory thus challenges universal understandings of gendered social relations. Yet this complex and dynamic understanding of gender does not negate the idea that gender is a structure that leads to unequal outcomes based on power differentials. While influenced by poststructural theory, much intersectional theory in sociology remains deeply committed to understanding structural inequalities, including economic, political, and social power differences. By specifying how gender is structured differently over time, place, and across groups, intersectional theory identifies important variations in gendered structures and outcomes, creating more accurate understanding of how these processes work, and how they can be altered.

For example, consider different theoretical approaches to neoliberalism, defined as strategies aimed at reducing public sector intervention and regulation in favor of promoting private sector development and growth. Neoliberalism is deeply implicated in growing inequality, as it tends to lead to fewer protections for the vulnerable and more opportunities for the wealthy to accumulate resources. A feminist structural analysis focuses on how neoliberal strategies reconfigure gender inequalities, while a poststructural feminist analysis considers what kind of gendered subject is constituted by a neoliberal discourse, calling attention to the contingent and relational nature of identity. A structural intersectional analysis considers how an array of social relations are reflected in neoliberal discourse, and how neoliberal strategies lead to inequalities being reconfigured not only around gender but also around race, nation, class, age, and so forth. I argue that an intersectional approach provides the greatest insight into how neoliberalism operates, and therefore provides better traction to resist neoliberal strategies.

In this chapter, I specify the meaning of intersectional theory in sociology and its emphasis on understanding how different elements of social identity intersect within particular geographic and historical contexts to create both opportunities and constraints, with these identities further intertwined so that privileges and disadvantages are connected. Central to my argument is the role of categories in intersectional theory. I argue that intersectional theory bridges poststructural theory's emphasis on disrupting categories with structural theory's emphasis on analyzing power and inequality through examining differences by or across categories. I illustrate how intersectional researchers actually use, complicate, and undermine categories as they carry out their research—sometimes all at the same time—and what this means for gender theory. I end by arguing that the tools intersectional theory gives us are critical to creating truly progressive social change.

Structural Theory, Intersectional Theory

Change is central to structural theories of gender, which is unsurprising given that these theories emerged during a time of enormous change (Connell 1987, 2009; Martin 2004; Risman 2004). Drawing on Giddens's (1984) theory of structuration, Risman (2004, 433) argues that "structure shapes individual choice and social interaction and . . . human agency creates, sustains, and modifies current structure." Therefore, structural theory recognizes change and dynamism, both in terms of how shifting structures may affect peoples' opportunities and how agency may change the very structures they inhabit. Structural theory has had to understand both change and why, although change has occurred, gendered inequalities in media representations, employment, wages, poverty, violence, political power, to name only a few, remain troubling—in other words, why inequality remains durable (Tilly 1999; Lorber 1994, 2005).

Intersectional theory explores how gender intersects with multiple other structures to affect opportunities and experiences (Browne and Misra 2003; Baca Zinn and Thornton Dill 1996; Glenn 2009; Collins 2000; Crenshaw 1991). Intersectional theory is often read as identifying differences among women by race. For example, the theory suggests that a Black woman has different experiences than a White woman. Yet intersectional theory makes a broader intervention. For example, a White, straight, upper-class woman will have different experiences than a White, straight, poor woman. Similarly, an African American middle-class gay man will have different experiences in Detroit and in Seattle, while an Asian American working-class straight trans woman will have different experiences in 1990 and 2015. Race and gender intersect, and depend on many factors, including class location, sexuality, gender identity, parenthood status, and age—as well as time and place (Baca Zinn and Thornton Dill 1996). Intersectional theory requires us to understand *how* gender combines with race, class, sexuality, gender identity, and other statuses, in specific geographic and historical contexts, to create a very particular set of opportunities and constraints. This does not mean that scholars must design research to include attention to all possible statuses—yet it does mean that scholars must be attentive to the conditions their research addresses.

While some critics suggest that intersectionality is most useful for redressing the harms inflicted on and experienced by Black women specifically (Howard Frederick 2010; Nash 2008, 2011), most intersectional scholars in sociology make a more relational argument, theorizing statuses as relational and interconnected (Collins 2000; Glenn 2009; Ken 2010; Baca Zinn and Thornton Dill 1996). In developing the concept of the "matrix of domination" Collins (2000, 222) notes that the goal is to understand how these systems of oppression interconnect. Glenn (1992, 34) further clarifies, "Thus, to represent race and gender as relationally constructed is to assert that the experiences of white women and women of color are not just different but connected in systematic ways." Therefore, an intersectional approach does not mean simply recognizing the similarities between different types of oppression (e.g., class oppression, gender oppression, racial oppression), but analyzing how these systems of oppression are intertwined.

All people are located in a relational "matrix of domination," in that disadvantage for some leads to privilege for others, while almost all experience both disadvantage and privilege relative to others (Baca Zinn and Thornton Dill 1996; Collins 2000; Glenn 2009). While intersectional theory can be used to focus specifically on Black women (Nash 2008, 2011), sociological intersectional theory theorizes the experience of all people as relationally situated in positions of privilege and disadvantage. For example, White women's entrance to the workplace displaced both Black women and White and Black men (Browne 1999). As argued by Baca Zinn and Thornton Dill (1996), each person's experiences are shaped by the experiences of those in differing groups around them, with these relationships defined and enforced through institutions and interactions, and contributing to the construction of group identities. Intersectional theory gives us the tools to analyze how privilege and disadvantage are connected and intertwined.

By recognizing the dynamic and specifically localized nature of particular inequalities, intersectional scholars emphasize context. Intersectional scholarship has developed over complex historical terrain, where progress has varied by location, and been complicated, halting, and sometimes lost. As a result, intersectional research highlights dynamics and change. Raced, gendered, and classed inequalities shift and change, and differ from place to place. Rather than having absolute consequences, race, class, and gender consequences differ by context (King 1988), which allows for change, such as Barack Obama's election to the U.S. presidency. Such a perspective "demands that scholars ground their work historically in the production of the dynamics of oppression" (Ken 2008, 171). Yet, because this approach suggests that it is not enough to analyze categorical differences between men and women, intersectional research has sometimes been viewed as poststructural rather than structural.

Poststructural Theory, Intersectional Theory

Poststructural theory argues that categories come into being through discourse—rather than existing "naturally," they are made through language (Weedon 1996; Cixous 1976). This leads to a focus on discourse, and understanding how discourse—for example "welfare queen"—creates certain subjects. Analyzing the discourse can help uncover the production of the subject, and ultimately the subject's experience. Yet this approach may lead to a focus on identity unmoored from analyses of power and inequality.

Intersectional theory also emphasizes the socially constructed nature of categories. The meaning of race, for example, changes with historical circumstance; in one U.S. era, Blackness was defined by the "one drop rule" (Omi and Winant 2004), while Jews in the U.S. came to be defined as White (Brodkin 1998); in both cases, there are important social consequences to these changing definitions. Gender, class, sexuality, gender identity, and other statuses also undergo changing definitions and understandings, which are interdependent (Glenn 2009; Ken 2008). While these categories and intersections are not stable, they have weighty effects. Intersectional theories in sociology focus less on identity than much poststructural theory does, and assume that these social constructions contain inherent power differentials that deeply suffuse all identities, interactions, and institutions (Collins 2000; Glenn 2009; Weber 2001; Browne and Misra 2003).

Feminist analyses of knowledge have long argued against the notion of objectivity, and for situated knowledge (Haraway 1988; Harding 1992; Hartsock 1989; Fonow and Cook 1991). Both poststructural theory and intersectional theory also build from a notion of situated knowledge, with intersectional theory drawing attention to how standpoint affects knowledge production (Collins 1986, 2000; Glenn 2009; Yuval-Davis 2012; Mann 2013).[1] While sociological knowledge has at times aspired to be "objective" or "neutral," intersectional researchers show that understanding inequality requires knowledge from multiple standpoints. Those in dominant groups are less likely to see inequality, so even as White middle-class women articulate gendered inequalities based on their experience, they may miss gendered inequalities faced by other groups of women (Acker 2006; Hartsock 1989). Following W. E. B. DuBois's (1903) notion of "double consciousness," intersectional researchers suggest that those in the most marginalized positions may better understand social relations than those in privileged positions, because they need to understand both perspectives to navigate a world in which they are marginalized (Baca Zinn and Thornton Dill 1996).

Following from these critiques, intersectional research has worked to uncover the biases in feminist theory that saw women as occupying a "universal" category (Truth 1998; Cooper 1990; Collins 2000; Morgan and Anzaldúa 1981). Although women differ from men, women also differ from one another. Rather than viewing one group of women as the norm, with all other women deviating from that position, intersectional scholars argue for recognizing the multiplicity of women's experiences, based on their structural locations not simply in gender but also in class, race, sexuality, gender identity, nationality, and other statuses. For example, experiences and expectations regarding caregiving and paid employment have long differed for women by class and race/ethnicity (Branch 2011; Glenn 2009; Amott and Matthaei 1991); in recognizing this differentiation, intersectional researchers posit more nuanced, varied, and complex understandings of gender, caregiving, and paid work. Standpoint epistemology helps create new understandings and knowledge, as scholars from marginalized groups identify what is missing in existing theory.

This emphasis on the socially constructed nature of categories, standpoint epistemologies, and destabilizing categories all share common ground with poststructural approaches (Butler 1999). There are resonances that might help explain why intersectional theory may be viewed as part of the poststructural feminist project. Yet there are multiple strains within poststructural theory—some distinct and some allied with the political project of intersectional theory (Scott 1988; Butler and Scott 1992). As Kimberlé Crenshaw (1991, 1296) describes, "One version of antiessentialism, embodying what might be called the vulgarized social construction thesis, is that since all categories are socially constructed, there is no such thing as, say, Blacks or women, and thus it makes no sense to continue reproducing those categories by organizing around them." This may be further read as arguing that all knowledge is contested, and therefore that all viewpoints are equally valid.

Intersectional theory draws from a more structural analysis to correct an overriding focus on discourse and identity, while working with the problematization of categories noted by poststructuralists. Intersectional theory argues, in consonance with structural theory, that understanding the socially constructed nature of categories like race, gender, and sexuality allows us to challenge them (Glenn 1992; Collins 2012). Power is certainly embedded in how categories are made, and organizing around categories may shore up existing categorizations. Yet challenging the consequences and meanings of these categories also has potential for social change (Crenshaw 1991). As Joan Scott (1988) argued, critiquing and disrupting categories can have profound consequences for political practice. This analytic move places intersectional theorists strongly in consonance with theorists who argue that while structure shapes agency, agency, in turn, has the potential to modify (always dynamic) structure (Giddens 1984; Risman 2004; Sewell 1992).

Therefore, most intersectional research in sociology remains structural, even as it pushes against natural or simple categories or a unified, objective scientific perspective. Engaging with poststructural theory can thus help clarify this position and recognize what the convergences suggest. From a poststructural position, Butler (1997, 269–70) argues against the rubric of a universal, noting the universal become possible only when abstracted from locations in power. Yet an intersectional structural analysis argues instead for historicization that specifies, differentiates, and grounds understanding of gendered processes and the creation of gendered categories (Fraser 1997; Connell 1987, 2014; Connell and Messerschmidt 2005). While both intersectional and poststructural perspectives see important reasons to deny universalities, in that they tend to conceal power differentials, a structural intersectional perspective further historicizes and contextualizes inequalities, and, from this, identifies ruptures and opportunities for action (Glenn 2009; Baca Zinn and Thornton Dill 1996; Connell 2014).

The Use of Categories in Intersectional Research

Most structural feminist research is predicated on categories, even when those categories can be broken down: gender categories may be further delineated in terms of race, ethnicity, class, education, sexuality, trans or cis gender identity, intersex, nationality, citizenship, and the like. Yet if the intersectional critique does not simply mean that categories need to be specified, but also that the categories themselves are unstable and problematic—this has ramifications for both theory and method. If categories—such as gender—are not clearly differentiated, but partial, dependent on context, and unstable, how do intersectional researchers carry out research? If scholars see categories as partial, should they always incorporate a dizzying array of categories to ensure that they reflect the complexity of social life? If scholars cannot rely on categories as fixed, does this mean that scholars should not use categories, or that they should emphasize gendered processes, rather than gendered outcomes? In this section, I provide illustrations of how intersectional researchers complicate, use, and unmake categories in their research, and the utility of their doing so.

Much intersectional research in sociology relies upon categories, but queries the meaning of the categories and their effects (McCall 2001, 2005; Crenshaw 1991). McCall's (2005) influential model suggests three different orientations toward categories in intersectional research: intracategorical research, intercategorical research, and anticategorical research. Intracategorical work focuses on examining the experience of a particular group—such as working-class Latina women; intercategorical research compares the experiences across groups—such as comparing middle-class and working-class Latina women; while anticategorical work undermines and questions the notion of distinct categories based on "Latina," "working class," "middle class," and "women." I argue that while these three orientations may appear mutually exclusive, there is considerable overlap. Table 6.1 summarizes McCall's (2005) argument as well as the prevalence of these methods in top sociology journals (Jones et al. 2013). Among these approaches, intercategorical research is more prevalent, followed by intracategorical and anticategorical research (Jones, Misra, and McCurley 2013).

TABLE 6.1. Analysis of Intersectional Research

	Intracategorical	Intercategorical	Anticategorical
Approach to Categories	Interrogates	Uses relationally	Rejects
Frequency in Sociology Journals	6%	9%	3%
Example	Harvey Wingfield on Black male nurses facing glass barriers	Flippen on Latina migrants in the New South	Penner and Saperstein on racial categorization in surveys

"Intracategorical" research has focused on a single social category, often one that has been understudied (McCall 2005, 1780). For example, Stone (2007) discusses how professional women leave high-paying jobs not because they "opt out," but because they are "pushed out" of workplaces that are inhospitable to working mothers. Yet Barnes (2015) further identifies that married Black professional mothers are met with substantial disapproval from their families and communities if they do not maintain full-time jobs. Black women are judged based on assumptions that they should be financially independent and represent their race as professional women rather than provide care for their children.

Barnes's intracategorical research helps point to differences in how Black professional women's "opting out" is met relative to White professional women, even though both face largely unwelcoming working conditions.

Another example of intracategorical intersectional research is Adia Harvey Wingfield's (2009) research on Black male nurses. Here, Harvey Wingfield (2009) builds on the insight developed by Christine Williams (1995) that men in jobs dominated by women may ride a "glass escalator" to promotions, rather than hitting the glass ceiling that women experience in jobs dominated by men. Harvey Wingfield (2009) notes that Black men nurses do not ride the glass escalator, and instead face "glass barriers" in the form of challenges from coworkers, supervisors, and patients. While Harvey Wingfield (24) focuses on the category of Black men, her analysis has important implications for the intersection of gender and race for both men and women in workplaces. Although Harvey Wingfield's research relies on categories of race and gender, her intersectional analysis shows that Black men's masculinity does not benefit them in women-dominated jobs as White men's masculinity does, undermining a simplistic notion of "masculinity."

McCall (2005) identifies "intercategorical" research as intersectional research that also focuses on categories, yet in this case with an aim of identifying patterns of relations *between* them. Rather than focusing on one social category, this research considers the relationships between two or more categories. Yet at times the boundaries between intracategorical and intercategorical research are unclear. For example, Mignon Moore (2006) compares middle-class and working-class Black lesbians, describing how middle-class Black lesbians who enact feminine gendered presentations are more integrated into their families and communities than working-class lesbians who enact more masculine gender identities. Moore's work calls attentions to variations *among* Black lesbians by class, rather than assuming that all Black lesbians have similar experiences; yet Moore (2012) herself identifies her research as intracategorical, given her focus on Black lesbians.

Intercategorical intersectional research also argues for close attention to context in shaping inequality. For example, Miliann Kang (2010) shows that Korean immigrant women who give manicures provide "pampering body labor" to White upper-class customers in spas, "expressive body labor" to Black working-class customers in nail art salons, and "routinized body labor" to racially diverse middle-class customers in discount salons. Context matters in understanding the classed, racialized, and gendered experience of Korean immigrant nail salon workers. In another example, McCall (2001, 2005) shows how gender wage gaps differ not only by race and class but also by region, leading to complex patterns: wage gaps by race, class, and gender differ depending on whether manufacturing jobs are exiting (Detroit), high-tech manufacturing is occurring (St. Louis), high-tech industries are developing (Dallas), or immigrant workers are increasing (Miami). As McCall argues (2001), without attending to multiple dimensions of inequality and context, policy attempts to reduce inequality may exacerbate other forms of inequality.

Intercategorical research also helps identify new intersections and considers which intersections may be particularly salient for group outcomes. Chenoa Flippen's (2013) survey research on Latina immigrants in the New South shows how employment, occupation, and work hours reflect intersecting disadvantages including nationality, immigration status, marital status, parenthood, and location of children. For example, while married women are less likely to work than single women, undocumented married women are much less likely to work. Similarly, mothers whose children accompany them have different work opportunities than those whose children are "back home." Flippen shows how migrant women are differentiated in a multitude of ways, offering new understandings of the gendered inequalities they face. In another example, C. J. Pascoe's (2011) analysis of masculinity in a high school shows how achieving masculinity differs by race. Unlike White teenage boys, Black teenage boys can dance and dress well without threatening their masculinity (also see Craig 2013). Yet Pascoe also points out how White students enacting masculinity in school are less likely to be disciplined by teachers and staff, illustrating how contextualized analyses of masculinities allow new insights (Connell and Messerschmidt 2005). Pascoe's insights identify how intersectional approaches shed light not only on marginalized groups but also on dominant groups, such as White boys. If masculinities are performed differently by race among teenage boys in the same school (Pascoe 2011), or femininities are performed differently among working-class and middle-class Black lesbians (Moore 2006), this means race and class condition masculinities and femininities. While the intercategorical approach may subvert broad categories by arguing for finer categories, these finer categories create more accurate understandings of gender inequalities.

McCall (2005) also identifies "anticategorical" intersectional research as work that challenges the very notion of categories as artificial and reductionist. As she argues, "Social life is considered too irreducibly complex—overflowing with multiple and fluid determinations of both subjects and structures—to make fixed categories anything but simplifying social fictions that produce inequalities in the process of producing differences" (McCall 2005, 1773). Such research, as described by Hae Yeon Choo and Myra Marx Ferree (2010, 134), analyzes the dynamic production of social identities—racialization, economic exploitation, and gendering as opposed to race, class, and gender—to identify how power operates.

For example, Nikki Jones (2009a, 2009b) considers the experiences of inner city Black girls and how they negotiate their identities as they navigate challenging terrain. She argues that the same women strategically choose among performances of gender, race, and class, depending on context and situation. By choosing among different displays, even just as a woman walks down the street, Jones (2009a, 2009b) shows how gender, race, and class are accomplished through situated interactions even as they are simultaneously affected by structural factors. Categories are unstable and mean different things from moment to moment.

Penner and Saperstein's (2013) research also illustrates a more complex reading of categories. They show that interviewers for the National Longitudinal Survey of Youth identify race differently over time, in relation to class markers; these identifications also show gendered effects. For example, men and women living in the suburbs are more likely to be seen as White. For women, welfare receipt makes them more likely to be seen as non-White, although this does not occur for men. For men, incarceration makes them more likely to be categorized as non-White, although this does not occur for women. Knowing that survey researchers are more likely to read a woman as "non-White" if she has received welfare makes clear how race, gender, and welfare are tied together discursively. Their research illustrates that categories are dynamic and unstable, and that understandings of race, gender, and class intersect in consequential ways (Penner and Saperstein 2013).

Yet, again, it can be difficult to identify the dividing line between different kinds of research. Kristen Schilt's (2006, 2010) research on how trans men experience the workplace before and after their transition calls attention to the dynamic nature of categories. Some trans men experience gender privilege in the workplace after they transition, showing how gendering is dynamic, and reflects a set of workplace assumptions that benefit those who enact masculinity. This suggests an anticategorical approach. But in comparing the experiences of trans men before and after transition, the work illustrates intercategorical research. And by examining variations among trans men, for example by showing how trans men of color must learn to navigate the stereotypes assigned to men of color, or trans men who are short or slight identify fewer advantages in the workplace posttransition, the work is also intracategorical. Intersectional researchers are not, then, choosing to either interrogate, use, or undermine categories, but may be doing all of the above, in any given research.

Anticategorical intersectional approaches may be influenced by poststructural theory, but primarily rely on understandings of the socially constructed nature of many categories. These intersectional scholars emphasize the fluidity of gender and sexuality, as well as how these intersect with one another, and with class, race/ethnicity, nationality, and so forth, dynamically and contextually. Yet this allows theorizing and analyzing change in the organization of gender; it can be used to point to how structural inequalities shape changing interactions and shifting identities (Jones 2009a, 2009b; Schilt 2006, 2010), and well as how identities may be understood differently based on structural cues (Penner and Saperstein 2013).

All three approaches to using categories can be beneficial for structural analyses of power and inequality. Barnes's (2015) and Harvey Wingfield's (2009) analyses of how both race and gender affect "opting out" or career opportunities for nurses draw attention to how femininity and masculinity are not societally supported and rewarded for Black women and men, shining light on how cultural scripts and organizational practices limit these groups. McCall's (2005) analyses of the effects of race, gender, and class in shaping wages in Dallas and Detroit opens the window to analyzing different historically and regionally specific intersections, which help devise more contextually specific approaches to addressing inequality in these locations. Flippen's (2013) analysis of how national origin, legal status, family structure, and location of children matter to unpacking gender inequalities among immigrant Latinas gives needed information to organizations focused on labor and migration. Penner and Saperstein's (2013) findings on how survey researchers read men and women's races differently based on their experiences provide important empirical weight to claims of racial bias. The studies described here use categories, even as they complicate them, to identify complex inequalities and suggest strategies to redress them.

Conclusions

I have traced how intersectional theory in sociology relates to both structural and poststructural theory, and considered how categories are complicated, used, and undermined by intersectional researchers. Intersectional theory in sociology shares an emphasis on inequality and power, as well as on change and dynamism, with structural theory. By highlighting the intertwining of oppressions, the relationality of privilege and disadvantage, and the importance of spatial and historical context, intersectional theory in sociology analyzes inequality to develop tools for effective social change. Intersectional theory in sociology also shares certain insights with poststructural theory, including its identification of the socially constructed nature of categories such as gender and race, its aims to challenge universal notions of "womanhood," and its recognition of the importance of standpoint. Yet intersectional theory as practiced in the field of sociology rejects relativism, and instead analyzes the power and inequality embedded in these categories (Mann 2013).

Gender theory profits by building from these insights to develop more consistently intersectional understandings of power, inequality, and change. Research on social movements and activist organizations, for example, identifies how intersectional theory has helped register variations in power, and helped to envision and sometimes enact new social relations (Chun, Lipsitz, and Shin 2013; Lepinard 2014; Kuumba 2002; Bose 2012; Yuval-Davis 2006). Yet, at times, attempts to recognize difference simply reify stereotypes, or miss the way privilege and disadvantage are tied together (Lepinard 2014). Avoiding these challenges requires a more relational approach to inequality. Much of the progress on the gender gap in wages, for example, does not simply reflect women's earning more—but also men's decreasing wages in the postindustrial economy

(Bernhardt, Morris, and Hancock 1995; Misra and Murray-Close 2014). A relational lens leads us, then, to strategize to create an economy that provides more equitable jobs that pay wages and have work hours that allow both single and partnered people, whatever their identity statuses, to provide economically and care for themselves and their families (England and Folbre 1999; Jacobs and Gerson 2004). Theory is most useful if it reflects multiple perspectives—as the perspectives of the marginalized often recognize vulnerabilities that remain hidden to those in more dominant groups. During the shift from an agrarian to an industrial society, enormous dislocations led to class mobilization, which was successful in ameliorating some of the worst outcomes of unfettered capitalism, though in ways that reinforced many gender and racial inequalities. Theory was crucial to guiding those mobilizations. During the shift from an industrial to a postindustrial economy, theory can again play a key role. Yet, in the 21st century, intersectional theorizing has the best hope for identifying strategies that do not sacrifice particular groups, such as less educated men of color or migrant women workers.

Intersectional theory should be at the center of sociologists' analyses of inequality. Attending to how different groups experience particular struggles allows for analyzing gender, race, and class not only from different perspectives but also relationally. For example, intersectional theory can identify assumptions of racialized and classed masculinities that are embedded in policing, and require undoing (Messerschmidt 1997; Brunson and Miller 2006; Rios 2011). Sociologists have been building the tools to recognize the relational and complex nature of inequality, and must use these tools for structural and cultural change (Connell 2014). As Glenn (1992) argues, the relational nature of intersectional theory shows us that any political agenda must recognize not only differences in priorities between groups, but how gains for some groups may lead to loss of privilege for others. Yet, as she articulates, "This does not mean we give up the goal of concerted struggle. It means we give up trying falsely to harmonize women's interests" (37).

NOTE

1 Indeed, more than a century ago, Anna Julia Cooper (1990 [1892], II) argued in *A Voice from the South* that "I feel it essential to a perfect understanding and an equitable verdict that truth from *each* standpoint be presented. . . . And not

many can more sensibly realize and more accurately tell the weight and the fret of the 'long dull pain' than the open-eyed but hitherto voiceless Black Woman of America."

REFERENCES

Acker, Joan. 2006. "Inequality Regimes: Gender, Class, and Race in Organizations." *Gender & Society* 20 (4): 441–464.

Amott, Teresa, and Julie A. Matthaei. 1991. *Race, Gender, and Work: A Multicultural Economic History of Women in the United States.* Montreal: Black Rose Books.

Anzaldúa, Gloria. 1987. *Borderlands/La Frontera.* San Francisco: Aunt Lute.

Baca Zinn, Maxine, and Bonnie Thornton Dill. 1996. "Theorizing Difference from Multiracial Feminism." *Feminist Studies* 22 (2): 321–332.

Barnes, Riché J. Daniel. 2015. *Raising the Race: Black Career Women Redefine Marriage, Motherhood, and Community.* New Brunswick, NJ: Rutgers University Press.

Beale, Frances. 1970. "Double Jeopardy: To Be Black and Female." In *The Black Woman: An Anthology,* edited by Toni Cade Bambara, 109–122. New York: Washington Square Press.

Bernhardt, Annette, Martina Morris, and Mark S. Hancock. 1995. "Women's Gains or Men's Losses? A Closer Look at the Shrinking Gender Gap in Earnings." *American Journal of Sociology* 101 (2): 302–328.

Bose, Christine E. 2012. "Intersectionality and Global Gender Inequality." *Gender & Society* 26 (1): 67–72.

Branch, Enobong. 2011. *Opportunity Denied: Limiting Black Women to Devalued Work.* New Brunswick, NJ: Rutgers University Press.

Brodkin, Karen. 1998. *How Jews Became White People and What That Says about Race in America.* New Brunswick, NJ: Rutgers University Press.

Browne, Irene. 1999. *Latinas and African American Women at Work.* New York: Russell Sage Foundation.

Browne, Irene, and Joya Misra. 2003. "The Intersection of Gender and Race in the Labor Market." *Annual Review of Sociology* 29 (1): 487–513.

Brunson, Rod K., and Jody Miller. 2006. "Gender, Race, and Urban Policing: The Experience of African American Youths." *Gender & Society* 20 (4): 531–552.

Butler, Judith. 1997. "Merely Cultural." *Social Text* 52–53: 265–277.

———. 1999. *Gender Trouble.* New York: Routledge.

Butler, Judith, and Joan W. Scott. 1992. *Feminists Theorize the Political.* New York: Routledge.

Choo, Hae Yeon, and Myra Marx Ferree. 2010. "Practicing Intersectionality in Sociological Research: A Critical Analysis of Inclusions, Interactions, and Institutions in the Study of Inequalities." *Sociological Theory* 28 (2): 129–149.

Chun, Jennifer Jihye, George Lipsitz, and Young Shin. 2013. "Intersectionality as a Social Movement Strategy: Asian Immigrant Women Advocates." *Signs: Journal of Women in Culture and Society* 38 (4): 917–940.

Cixous, Helene. 1976. "The Laugh of the Medusa." *Signs: Journal of Women in Culture and Society* 1 (4): 875–893.

Collins, Patricia Hill. 1986. "Learning from the Outsider Within: The Sociological Significance of Black Feminist Thought." *Social Problems* 33 (6): S14–S32.

———. 2000. *Black Feminist Thought*. New York: Routledge.

———. 2012. "Looking Back, Moving Ahead: Scholarship in Service to Social Justice." *Gender & Society* 26 (1): 14–22.

Connell, Raewyn. 1987. *Gender and Power*. Cambridge: Polity.

———. 2009. *Gender*. Cambridge: Polity.

———. 2014. "Global Tides: Market and Gender Dynamics on a World Scale." *Social Currents* 1 (1): 5–12.

Connell, Raewyn, and James W. Messerschmidt. 2005. "Hegemonic Masculinity: Rethinking the Concept." *Gender & Society* 19 (6): 829–859.

Cooper, Anna Julia. (1892) 1990. *A Voice from the South*. Edited by Mary Helen Washington. New York: Oxford University Press.

Craig, Maxine Leeds. 2013. *Sorry, I Don't Dance: Why Men Refuse to Move*. Berkeley: University of California Press.

Crenshaw, Kimberlé. 1991. "Mapping the Margins: Intersectionality, Identity Politics, and Violence against Women of Color." *Stanford Law Review* 43 (6): 1241–1299.

DuBois, William Edward Burghardt. 1903. *The Souls of Black Folk: Essays and Sketches*. Chicago: A. C. McClurg.

England, Paula, and Nancy Folbre. 1999. "The Cost of Caring." *Annals of the American Academy of Political and Social Science* 561: 39–51.

Flippen, Chenoa A. 2013. "Intersectionality at Work: Determinants of Labor Supply among Immigrant Latinas." *Gender & Society* 28 (3): 404–434.

Fonow, Mary Margaret, and Judith A. Cook. 1991. *Beyond Methodology: Feminist Scholarship as Lived Research*. Bloomington: Indiana University Press.

Fraser, Nancy. 1997. "Heterosexism, Misrecognition, and Capitalism: A Response to Judith Butler." *Social Text* 52–53: 279–289.

Giddens, Anthony. 1984. *The Constitution of Society: Outline of the Theory of Structuration*. Berkeley: University of California Press.

Glenn, Evelyn Nakano. 1992. "From Servitude to Service Work: Historical Continuities in the Racial Division of Paid Reproductive Labor." *Signs: Journal of Women in Culture and Society* 18 (1): 1–43.

———. 2009. *Unequal Freedoms: How Race and Gender Shaped American Citizenship and Labor*. Cambridge: Harvard University Press.

Haraway, Donna. 1988. "Situated Knowledges: The Science Question in Feminism and the Privilege of Partial Perspective." *Feminist Studies* 14 (3): 575–599.

Harding, Sandra. 1992. "Rethinking Standpoint Theory: What Is 'Strong Objectivity'?" *Centennial Review* 36 (3): 437–470.

Hartsock, Nancy. 1989. "Postmodernism and Political Change: Issues for Feminist Theory." *Cultural Critique* 14: 15–33.

Harvey Wingfield, Adia. 2009. "Racializing the Glass Escalator: Reconsidering Men's Experiences with Women's Work." *Gender & Society* 23 (1): 5–26.

Howard Frederick, Angela. 2010. "'Practicing Electoral Politics in the Cracks': Intersectional Consciousness in a Latina Candidate's City Council Campaign." *Gender & Society* 24 (4): 475–498.

Jacobs, Jerry A., and Kathleen Gerson. 2004. *The Time Divide*. Cambridge: Harvard University Press.

Jones, Katherine Castiello, Joya Misra, and K. McCurley. 2013. "Intersectionality in Sociology." Sociologists for Women in Society Fact Sheet. Accessed July 24, 2017. http://socwomen.org.

Jones, Nikki. 2009a. "'I Was Aggressive for the Streets, Pretty for the Pictures': Gender, Difference, and the Inner-City Girl." *Gender & Society* 23 (1): 89–93.

———. 2009b. *Between Good and Ghetto: African American Girls and Inner-City Violence*. New Brunswick, NJ: Rutgers University Press.

Kang, Miliann. 2010. *The Managed Hand: Race, Gender, and the Body in Beauty Service Work*. Berkeley: University of California Press.

Ken, Ivy. 2008. "Beyond the Intersection: A New Culinary Metaphor for Race-Class-Gender Studies." *Sociological Theory* 26 (2): 152–172.

———. 2010. *Digesting Race, Class, and Gender: Sugar as a Metaphor*. New York: Palgrave Macmillan.

King, Deborah K. 1988. "Multiple Jeopardy, Multiple Consciousness: The Context of a Black Feminist Ideology." *Signs: Journal of Women in Culture and Society* 14 (1): 42–72.

Kuumba, M. Bahati. 2002. "'You've Struck a Rock': Comparing Gender, Social Movements, and Transformation in the United States and South Africa." *Gender & Society* 16 (4): 504–523.

Lepinard, Eleonore. 2014. "Doing Intersectionality: Repertoires of Feminist Practices in France and Canada." *Gender & Society* 28 (6): 877–903.

Lorber, Judith. 1994. *Paradoxes of Gender*. New Haven: Yale University Press.

———. 2005. *Breaking the Bowls: Degendering and Feminist Change*. New York: W. W. Norton.

Mann, Susan. 2013. "Third Wave Feminism's Unhappy Marriage of Poststructuralism and Intersectionality Theory." *Journal of Feminist Scholarship* 4 (Spring): 54–73.

Martin, Patricia Yancey. 2004. "Gender as Social Institution." *Social Forces* 82 (4): 1249–1273.

McCall, Leslie. 2001. *Complex Inequalities: Gender, Race, and Class in the New Economy*. New York: Routledge.

———. 2005. "The Complexity of Intersectionality." *Signs* 30 (3): 1771–1800.

Messerschmidt, James. 1997. *Crime as Structured Action: Gender, Race, Class, and Crime in the Making*. Thousand Oaks, CA: Sage.

Misra, Joya, and Marta Murray-Close. 2014. "The Gender Wage Gap in the United States and Cross-Nationally." *Sociology Compass* 8 (11): 1281–1295.

Moore, Mignon R. 2006. "Lipstick or Timberlands? Meanings of Gender Presentation in Black Lesbian Communities." *Signs: Journal of Women in Culture and Society* 32 (1): 113–139.

———. 2011. *Invisible Families: Gay Identities, Relationships, and Families among Black Women.* Berkeley: University of California Press.

———. 2012. "Intersectionality and the Study of Black, Sexual Minority Women." *Gender & Society* 26 (1): 33–39. doi:10.1177/0891243211427031.

Morgan, Cherríe, and Gloria Anzaldúa. 1981. *This Bridge Called My Back: Writings by Radical Women of Color.* New York: Kitchen Table/Women of Color Press.

Nash, Jennifer C. 2008. "Rethinking Intersectionality." *Feminist Review* 89: 1–15.

———. 2011. "Practicing Love: Black Feminism, Love-Politics, and Post-Intersectionality." *Meridians* 11 (2): 1–24.

Omi, Michael, and Howard Winant. 2004. *Racial Formation in the United States.* New York: Routledge.

Pascoe, C. J. 2011. *Dude, You're a Fag.* Berkeley: University of California Press.

Penner, Andrew M., and Aliya Saperstein. 2013. "Engendering Racial Perceptions: An Intersectional Analysis of How Social Status Shapes Race." *Gender & Society* 27 (3): 319–344.

Rios, Victor M. 2011. *Punished: Policing the Lives of Black and Latino Boys.* New York: New York University Press.

Risman, Barbara J. 2004. "Gender as a Social Structure: Theory Wrestling with Activism." *Gender & Society* 18 (4): 429–450.

Schilt, Kristen. 2006. "Just One of the Guys? How Transmen Make Gender Visible at Work." *Gender & Society* 20 (4): 465–490.

———. 2010. *Just One of the Guys? Transgender Men and the Persistence of Gender Inequality.* Chicago: University of Chicago Press.

Scott, Joan W. 1988. "Deconstructing Equality-versus-Difference: Or, the Uses of Poststructuralist Theory for Feminism." *Feminist Studies* 14 (1): 32–50.

Sewell, William H., Jr. 1992. "A Theory of Structure: Duality, Agency, and Transformation." *American Journal of Sociology* 98 (1): 1–29.

Stone, Pamela. 2007. *Opting Out? Why Women Really Quit Careers and Head Home.* Berkeley: University of California Press.

Tilly, Charles. 1999. *Durable Inequality.* Berkeley: University of California Press.

Truth, Sojourner. 1998. *Narrative of Sojourner Truth.* New York: Penguin.

Weber, Lynn. 2001. *Understanding Race, Class, Gender, and Sexuality: A Conceptual Framework.* Boston: McGraw-Hill.

Weedon, Chris. 1996. *Feminist Practice and Poststructural Theory.* New York: Wiley Blackwell.

Williams, Christine L. 1995. *Still a Man's World: Men Who Do Women's Work.* Berkeley: University of California Press.

Yuval-Davis, N. 2006. "Intersectionality and Feminist Politics." *European Journal of Women's Studies* 13 (September): 193–209.

————. 2012. "Dialogical Epistemology—an Intersectional Resistance to the 'Oppression Olympics.'" *Gender & Society* 26 (1): 46–54.

Zinn, Maxine Baca, Lynn Weber Cannon, Elizabeth Higginbotham, and Bonnie Thornton Dill. 1986. "The Costs of Exclusionary Practices in Women's Studies." *Signs: Journal of Women in Culture and Society* 11 (2): 290–303.

PART III

Four Dimensions of Relationship, Struggle, and Change

The chapters in this section cover four dimensions of gender according to what Raewyn Connell terms "structural theory": emotional and sexual relations, economic and production relations, symbolic and cultural relations, and organizational and power relations.

The first chapter, by Stevi Jackson, is on emotional and sexual relations, and summarizes critical feminist thinking on heterosexuality. She questions this work raises regarding structure and action. Jackson critiques the concept of heteronormativity and argues for a simultaneous structural analysis of gender and sexuality. Just because heterosexuality is normatively required in a society does not account for either gender or sexual practices. She argues that practices, structures, and cultural understandings must be taken into account in order to explain gender and sexuality in a particular context. To make her case, she compares young women in Hong Kong and the United Kingdom in relation to how their mothers view and treat their daughters' sexuality. UK mothers are far more accepting of their daughters' premarital sexual activities, a finding she attributes to cultural patterns as well as to economics and history. Knowing that a society favors (or enforces) the institution of heterosexuality does not explain the variations in sexual practices and emotions that characterize it.

In the second chapter, which covers economic relations, Christine L. Williams and Megan Tobias Neely bring neoliberalism to account by documenting how labor markets in the developed world have changed over time. Williams and Neely show how, compared to thirty years ago, an intersectional feminist approach helps to explain current labor market dynamics, and provides insight into how one might change the status quo. They argue that a form of intersectional feminism should drive future demands for change in the gender order. In reviewing changes over the period, they explore how globalization, outsourcing, and the subsequent demise of the standard employment contract in the United States have affected working class men's labor market experiences (and thus have affected the women in their lives). Williams and Tobias Neely conclude that changes touted as promoting diversity and fairness have undermined job security and rewards for both men and women.

Focusing on European universities, Barbara Poggio analyzes education as a cultural institution that creates gender privilege and disadvantage. Exploring neoliberal influences on what is valued and done, she finds that the influence of markets and market logic on educational processes is ever more prevalent, displacing knowledge in an increasingly "rationalized and commodified" context. Poggio reviews the gender equality projects that the European Union and the European Commission have supported, yet despite these projects, at a cost of millions of euros, scant evidence exists regarding their effectiveness. Whereas some gender-related changes have occurred, it is unclear whether they were produced by such projects or if they will last. Poggio surmises that although universities have proportionally more women as students and faculty than previously, minimal change has occurred in women academics' power, rank, and status.

Finally, Yvonne Benschop and Marieke van den Brink examine power relations by comparing gender inequality among organizational consultants and academics, concluding that the latter focus on the effects of change efforts with little attention to change initiatives while the former provide strategies for producing change without appreciating the complexities of implementation. Producing a robust theory of organizational change toward gender equality requires these two groups to "work together," with attention to organizational dynamics that produce inequality, the invisibility of power inequalities, the multiple versions of masculinity and femininity at work, and leadership. Benschop and van den Brink analyze why academics and organizational consultants talk past each other while proclaiming a common goal: improved gender equity at work. Using research on gender equity published between 1995 and 2015, they found three issues of concern to both academics and consultants: explicit change efforts toward gender equality; the commitment of top management to gender-based change; and the engagement of men in gender equality. They allege that neoliberal values that have spread around the globe emphasize competition, winning, and publishing in top-tier international journals and discourage a gender equity priority. They conclude by urging that academics become less theoretical and consultants more attentive to the "how's" rather than only the "what's" of positive change, although they hold out little hope that the two groups will work together anytime soon.

7

Why "Heteronormativity" Is Not Enough

A Feminist Sociological Perspective on Heterosexuality

STEVI JACKSON

Critical approaches to heterosexuality are often assumed to have origi-
nated with queer theory, but the concept of "queer," which has only been
prominent since the 1990s, was a relative latecomer to sexuality studies.
Sociological challenges to the "naturalness" of sexuality date back to the
late 1960s and early 1970s (Simon and Gagnon 1969; Gagnon and Simon
1974), while the conceptualization of heterosexuality as a compulsory
imposition began with the rise of the gay and women's liberation movements in the same period. The idea that sexuality was socially constructed
derived from interpretive sociologies, with the emphasis on everyday
meaning-making and practices, but most feminists and gay liberationists
highlighted structural constraints and the links between gender division and the institution of heterosexuality (Seidman 2009); only a small
minority concerned themselves with everyday gendered and sexual practices (e.g., Plummer 1975; Kessler and McKenna 1978; Stanley and Wise
1983). When, in the late 1980s and early 1990s, structural approaches were
found wanting for their inability to deal with the complexity and diversity
of gendered and sexual relations many scholars looked to poststructuralism and postmodernism for alternatives. The resultant shift in focus from
social structures to culture and representation, or the "cultural turn," was
the context in which queer theory emerged.

Raewyn Connell's *Gender and Power* (1987), published at the cusp of
the cultural turn, made a highly significant and distinctively sociological intervention in arguing for the importance of structure *and* practice
in the analysis of gender, in taking account of the subjective, emotional,
and embodied aspects of gender, and in addressing both the persistence
of gender inequality and variations within gender relations. Her advo-

cacy of "a form of theory that gives some grip on the interweaving of personal life and social structure" (1987, 61) is very much in keeping with the aim of this chapter: to outline a feminist and sociological approach to heterosexuality. Before explaining further, I will chart the development of critical thinking on heterosexuality and the questions it raises about structure and practice. I will then discuss my own approach, partly in dialogue with Connell's, before going on to apply it to a recent cross-cultural and collaborative study I conducted with Petula Sik Ying Ho (see Jackson, Ho, and Na 2013; Jackson and Ho 2014).

The Feminist and Sociological Critique of Heterosexuality

In the early years of second wave feminism, it was, unsurprisingly, lesbian feminists who made the connection between "compulsory heterosexuality" (Rich 1980) and other manifestations of male domination. Monique Wittig arguably took this argument furthest, tying heterosexuality to the very existence of "women" and "men" as social categories and arguing that "the category of sex is the product of a heterosexual society in which men appropriate for themselves the reproduction and production of women and also their persons by means of . . . the marriage contract" (Wittig [1982] 1992, 7). In locating heterosexuality within wider gender relations, these analyses made it clear that heterosexuality involves far more than (erotic) sexuality. Subsequently, however, some radical lesbians accused heterosexual feminists of colluding in women's subordination (see, e.g., Leeds Revolutionary Feminists 1981). What had initially been a strength of lesbian feminist analyses, highlighting the institutional character of heterosexuality, became a weakness because of the failure to distinguish structure from practice, the critique of heterosexuality from criticism of heterosexual women. The effect of this divisive move was to close off debate for nearly a decade. However, the revival of feminist interest in heterosexuality in the 1990s, which occurred alongside the rise of queer theory, created space for a reworking of structural analysis that avoided structural determinism and attended to other aspects of sociality.

In order to argue for a feminist sociology of sexuality, it is first necessary to establish how it might both converge with and diverge from queer theory. Briefly, and at the risk of oversimplifying a complex body of work, queer theory is concerned with destabilizing the binaries of gender and heterosexuality/homosexuality, with revealing them to be "regulatory fictions" (Butler 1990). Influenced by Foucault's (1981) analysis of the discursive constitution of diverse sexualities, queer theory represented a challenge to the older gay affirmative politics seen as resting on essentialist categories (as gay, lesbian, straight); to be queer was to "assume a de-essentialized identity that is purely positional in character" (Halperin 1995, 62). While oriented to the destabilization of gendered and sexual binaries, queer theory is also associated with analyzing how they are sustained. The main object of critique, therefore, is what has come to be called "heteronormativity."[1]

Neither everyday social interaction nor social structural arrangements fall within the scope of queer theory. Moreover, in queer critique of normative binaries, heterosexuality appears simply as the norm against which other sexualities are defined, thus working against exploration of heterosexuality itself. The same could be said of the concept of heteronormativity, though I would not wish to deny its analytic utility; it does serve as a convenient shorthand for the multitude of ways in which heterosexuality is sustained as the default form of sexual and personal life. My point, however, is that this is not enough. Focusing only or primarily on heteronormativity can lead to the neglect of what was central to the early lesbian feminist critiques: the link between institutionalized heterosexuality and gender hierarchy. It also leaves us without a means of exploring how gender hierarchy might be modified, negotiated, or challenged within everyday heterosexual lives. Paying attention to hierarchies suggests the need to return to issues of social structure and to broader definitions of heterosexuality as involving more than simply (erotic) sexuality, more than the identities built around the gendered objects of our desires and/or their destabilization.

While queer can be identified with the critique of heteronormativity and feminism with a focus on gender hierarchy, neither is a singular perspective. There are both differences within and overlaps between them. Feminists draw on queer theory and some queer theorists are also feminists; queer theorists are not entirely unconcerned with questions of social regulation and injustice, any more than feminists are indifferent to the privileging of heterosexuality (McLaughlin 2008). The differences are more a matter of emphasis and modes of theorizing. Nonetheless, given the influence of queer and poststructuralist analysis in the 1990s, it was necessary to reassert the importance of material, structural inequalities (Ingraham 1996; Hennessy 2000). It is equally important, however, to recognize that heterosexuality is sustained not only structurally but also through the ways in which it is lived—the practices, meanings, and desires that are part and parcel of everyday heterosexual existence and that can also serve to perpetuate (and sometimes challenge) heteronormativity and gender hierarchy.

The necessity of taking account of the everyday was central to Connell's original argument on gender (1987), allowing for varied masculinities and femininities, for human agency and social change. Like gender, heterosexuality is not monolithic: there is considerable diversity in how it is practiced (Beasley et al. 2011). Heteronormativity, too, is not rigid and appears to accommodate to change; arguably the recent advances in rights granted to lesbian, gay, and transgendered individuals in many countries, mostly those of the "global North," have not deinstitutionalized heterosexuality but have merely shifted the boundaries of good sexual citizenship, assimilating those who live according to "responsible" neoliberal "family values," but excluding others (Seidman 2005; Richardson 2005). Moreover, changes in the state regulation of personal life (e.g., partnership and parenting rights) may reflect changing social attitudes, but have not effected a total social and cultural transformation. In the UK, for example, hostility and violence toward LGBT individuals is still widely reported, and among British schoolchildren the word "gay" has become a term of abuse. A sharper disjunction is evident in South Africa, where constitutional rights for sexual minorities coexist with the widespread practice of "corrective rape" of lesbians, reflecting complex issues of cultural beliefs and practices along with the legacies of colonialism and apartheid (Mkhize et al. 2010; Gunkel 2011).

Heterosexuality can be institutionalized in the presence and absence of laws against same-sex practices and relationships, in the presence and absence of rights to diverse sexual lifestyles. Among societies in which heterosexuality remains strongly institutionalized there is considerable variation in both its structural underpinnings and the social and cultural practices through which it is perpetuated, as well as the beliefs that sustain them. A critical sociological approach should, therefore, be able to take account of both differing structural arrangements and other elements of the social.

The Multidimensional Social

These arguments are congruent with Connell's work. She has argued consistently against mono-causal, one-dimensional accounts of gender that do not take account of its complexity, of disjunctions and contradictions within the gender order (Connell 1987, 2002). In *Gender and Power* (1987) and in later work Connell has argued for a multidimensional approach to gender. In the most recent articulation of this argument, Connell and Pearse (2015) identify four dimensions of gender relations: power; "production, consumption and gendered accumulation"; emotions; and "symbolism, culture, discourse" (Connell and Pearse 2015). Just as there are "multiple dimensions in gender relations" (Connell 2002, 56), so, I would argue, there are in the ordering of heterosexuality.

Heterosexuality is multifaceted. It can be seen as a sexual preference or practice—an expression of desire and a set of sexual acts. As a social practice it involves far more than sexuality, including, for example, gendered divisions of labor in both domestic and market spheres. As an institution, it is structurally intertwined with gender hierarchy; bound up with marriage, family formation, and kinship ties; and subject to state regulation. It is also endowed with symbolic significance, with the meaning that heterosexual relations have for those living both within and outside them, with the binary cultural distinctions routinely made between women and men, between heterosexual and homosexual. It has subjective dimensions encompassing emotions and desires, feelings for and about others, which can range from love to loathing—including that manifested as homophobia. These various facets of heterosexuality could be accommodated within Connell's dimensions of gender relations. While I share her aim of allowing for complexity, variability, agency, and change, I have developed a slightly different approach.

Rather than thinking of heterosexuality or gender relations as being multidimensional, I see the social itself as multidimensional and the ordering of gender, sexuality and heterosexuality as reflecting this. This approach facilitates analysis of the intersections between gender and institutionalized heterosexuality and other social institutions, practices, divisions, and differences. I have previously identified four dimensions of the social: social structure, practice (including interaction), meaning, and subjectivity/selfhood (Jackson 1999, 2006). These multiple dimensions of the social do not constitute an integrated unified whole. They cut across each other, sometimes reinforcing each other, sometimes producing disjunctions. Moreover, as I have previously argued (Jackson 2006), it is difficult, if not impossible, to "see" all dimensions at once—while we focus on one, others slip from view. So, for example, in analyzing the mechanisms whereby global capitalism produces huge gulfs between rich and poor we are not able to attend simultaneously to what cultural practices are meaningful to those living at any specific location within it. A perspective that illuminates one dimension may obscure another, suggesting the need for a degree of theoretical and methodological eclecticism in order to appreciate all aspects of the social. It is therefore necessary to bring together both structural and interpretive sociologies. While these have often been seen as incompatible, I suggest they enable us to attend to different, but equally verifiable, aspects of the social: the powerfully constraining effects of structures that preexist us, on the one hand, and, on the other, the meaningful interactions and practices of reflexive social actors through which everyday sociality goes on.

A multidimensional approach should enable us to take account of potential or actual variability and change and, just as important, of continuity, stability, and resistance to change—for example, the persistence of the gender divide despite diversity and change in what it means to be male or female, which is closely connected with the maintenance of the heterosexual/homosexual binary. Institutionalized heterosexuality is a key point of articulation between gender and sexuality. Gender and sexuality are not, however, phenomena of the same order. "Gender," as I use the term, denotes the social division and cultural distinction between male and female, women and men. "Sexuality" encompasses all erotically significant aspects of social life including desires, practices, relationships, and identities. It is therefore more fluid and less objectively identifiable than gender since what is erotically significant is a matter of definition and shifts contextually as well as historically and cross-culturally. Gender is binary (the existence of third genders or gender-bending practices inevitably refer back to the binary); sexuality is not, except in terms of the object of desire, as homo or hetero attraction. But sexuality is not reducible to this binary; it is not ordered only by the gender of the desired other but by numerous other potential preferences and practices that exist across the divides of gender and heterosexuality/ homosexuality (see, e.g., Whittier and Simon 2001). While there can, therefore, be many "sexualities," I use the singular term, "sexuality," to refer to the sphere of social life within which diverse forms of sexual life (sexualities) are pursued (just as there are varieties of jobs and tasks that take place within the sphere of work).

Sexuality as a sphere of life and gender as a social division are empirically interconnected in the institutionalization and practice of heterosexuality and the maintenance of heteronormativity. These interconnections are complex. Heterosexuality is implicated in the ordering of far more than sexuality, but it is, by definition, gendered; gender cannot be reduced to sexuality as it involves much wider social relations; sexuality cannot be reduced to gender or to the heterosexual/homosexual binary because it is about more than gendered desires or the gender of the object of desire. These interconnections are further complicated by the varied ways they operate within different dimensions of the social.

Heterosexuality within the Multidimensional Social

Structure, practice, meaning, and subjectivity/selfhood are all aspects of the social that interrelate in constituting heterosexuality and perpetuating heterosexual privilege. Social structure provides the constraining parameters within which we exist. Social reality, however, does not reside only in structures, but also in the everyday actions and interactions of individuals. These local and particular practices and the meanings associated with them are the stuff of everyday social life. It is in the space and context of the everyday that reflexive selfhood is both constituted and deployed, making sociality possible.

Structure

From a structural viewpoint gender is a hierarchical social division and heterosexuality is a social institution. Like Connell I see social structure in terms of "enduring or extensive patterns" of social relations and as constraining on individuals (Connell 1987, 92; Connell and Pearse 2015, 73). This constraining effect is crucial; without it, social patterns cannot be considered structural. For example, eating is a social practice (Warde 2015) and is extensively patterned: there are particular, culturally specific ideas about what should be eaten, when, and how. I would not, however, see them as constraining in the same way as the inequalities that determine who has enough to eat. Similarly, sexual practices are patterned in specific and often predictable ways, but these are not structural in the same way as inequalities produced by gender and institutionalized heterosexuality. Social structure has a material facticity that exists independently of each of us—but since it is the product of a history of human relations and practices, it requires the continued compliance and reaffirmation of most of us to persist. Social-structural analyses give us purchase on the material inequalities and injustices that characterize our world.

I also concur with Connell's view of social structures as differentiated and subject to historical change and cross-national variability. The most pervasive structure of all, global capitalism, does not take identical forms even within the wealthy countries from which transnational capital is controlled. For example, Chang Kyung-Sup's (2010) analysis of South Korean modernity reveals how familialism remains exceptionally strong in the organization of Korea's capitalist economy and state institutions, resulting in a far less individualistic and far more male dominated society than in Europe or North America. It is also a society where heterosexuality is strongly institutionalized, despite the lack of laws against same-sex relations. Cross-national studies in capitalist East Asia highlight the differing ways in which gender relations can be ordered in societies with similar (post)industrial economies and a degree of shared cultural heritage and history (see, e.g., Sechiyama 2013). Patriarchal heterosexuality can coexist in diverse forms with a variety of local economic and social arrangements, and in both rich and poor countries within global divisions of labor and resources.

Structural factors order life within heterosexual relations and the options open to those who seek to live lesbian, gay, or queer lives. Most obviously choices are enabled and constrained by the regulative and coercive power of the state, which globally varies from jurisdictions that prescribe the death penalty for same-sex acts to those legislating for near equality with heterosexuals (Itaborahy and Zhu 2015). The degree to which individuals can escape the constraints of institutionalized heterosexuality are also affected by other inequalities that intersect with those of gender and sexuality in relation to the wider capitalist order. Even before rights began to be extended to sexual minorities, consumer capitalism accommodated queer lifestyle choices within Western cultures (Evans 1993), but such choices are themselves the product of global and local inequalities. The queer lifestyles of the materially privileged rest upon the exploited labor of the underprivileged, often in poorer countries, who produce the commodities on which that lifestyle depends (Hennessy 2000). Within any given country lifestyle choices are not equally available to all. Throughout the world, for example, the constraints on working class lesbians, a consequence of both class and gender inequality, can limit access to everything from queer spaces to housing (Taylor 2004; Chao 2002).

Economic inequality also affects heterosexual lives in a variety of ways, influencing patterns of marriage and cohabitation and domestic divisions of labor (Irwin 2005). Innovations in heterosexual lifestyles often reflect class locations and their associated constraints and opportunities. To take one example, some of those heterosexual couples maintaining "distance" relationships or "living apart together" (Holmes 2004; Beasley, Brook, and Holmes 2011) find themselves in that situation because of the difficulties of pursuing two individual professional careers in the same geographic location, but who are also privileged by having the economic resources to maintain two households. Living apart together can, for others, be a result of financial constraint or care responsibilities (Duncan et al. 2013).

Personal and sexual life, then, is shaped by wider structural inequalities as well as being ordered by the intersection of heterosexuality and gender. While institutionalized heterosexuality and thus the heterosexual/homosexual binary can be considered structural, sexuality in general (including individual erotic desires, relationships, and practices) cannot. Nonetheless, since sexual relationships and practices are always embedded within wider, nonsexual relations, they are constrained and enabled by wider structural arrangements and individuals' locations within them, both locally and globally. Commercial sex illustrates this well. It has globalized along with other aspects of the capitalist economy, resulting in the growth of sex tourism as well as the migration of sex workers, patterned in ways that often reflect inequalities between rich and poor nations and rich and poor within nations, as well as the intersections of these inequalities with gender and racialized hierarchies (Agustín 2007; Aoyama 2009; Kempadoo, Sanghera and Pattaniak 2012). Commercial sexual transactions, however, are also enacted within and through the localized practices of both sex workers and their clients and the meanings associated with them (see, e.g., O'Connell Davidson 2001; Ding and Ho 2008; Hoang 2015). Thus dimensions of the social other than the structural are in play here.

Practices

Gendered and sexual practices are both shaped by structures and can help to sustain them, but are also negotiated in everyday situations and can therefore sometimes contribute to challenge or change. Practices are closely connected with interaction—they are frequently effected in interaction with others, and, conversely, interaction involves locating ourselves within ongoing social activities. Through everyday interaction and practice we "do" gender, sexuality, and heterosexuality in two senses. First, in the ethnomethodological sense, this "doing" produces a socially intelligible "reality" as a "practical accomplishment" through everyday interpretive interaction, for example through the way we talk about men, women, and relationships. The second sense of "doing" is through actual practical activities, or "practices of intimacy" (Jamieson 2011), such as having sex, negotiating domestic chores, or organizing family parties.

The doing of heterosexuality is not just about its normativity but also, very centrally, about gender division and hierarchy. Heterosexual couples "do" heterosexuality and simultaneously do gender through divisions of labor and distributions of household resources—and often these practices become habitual and taken for granted. There are certainly normative ideas about who should do what in heterosexual households, and there is copious evidence internationally that women still do the bulk of domestic work, though to what degree varies from one country to another. To the extent that these gender-defined practices persist they contribute to upholding a male dominated heterosexual order, but they are subject to change, negotiation, and, indeed, argument as each heterosexual couple goes on with their daily routines.

The practice of heterosexual sex is also patterned in particular ways. There are defining features (albeit historically and culturally variable) that determine what counts as (hetero) sex and the expected order of embodied procedures. There are notions of when and where it should occur and standards of both good and bad sex, elaborated in self-help manuals instructing couples in how to do it better (Jackson and Scott 2010). Gendered patterns of heterosexual sex are, in some ways and some places, changing. Active engagement in heterosex has become normalized among young women in many wealthier countries and there is evidence that, in the UK at least, they are becoming more sexually adventurous (Mercer et al. 2013). Yet double standards persist, as do sexual objectification, coercive sex, and sexual violence—all of which are global issues, occurring in societies where young women's sexual conduct is strictly controlled as well as those where it is not.

In some societies heteronormativity is less absolute than it was in the past, but even in the most liberal places much of everyday life still proceeds on the assumption that everyone is heterosexual unless known to be otherwise. Heteronormativity is mobilized and reproduced in everyday life through routine activities in which gender, sexuality, and heterosexuality interconnect. In daily interaction women's location within heterosexual relations, as wives and mothers, is often assumed. In Britain (still) adult women are routinely (much to my irritation) addressed as "Mrs.," a practice that positions them in terms of marital status, but to which men are not subjected. Women are still frequently evaluated in terms of their (hetero)sexual attractiveness. It has been suggested that "erotic capital" can aid women's career advancement (Hakim 2011), but if so it reinforces both gender division and heteronormativity—as well as being unequally available and dependant on age-related and culturally specific standards of beauty. Hence gendered assumptions are often informed by heterosexual ones. But this does not apply in the same way to heterosexual men. While womanliness is almost always equated with (hetero)sexual attractiveness and (heterosexual) domesticity, manliness can be validated in numerous nonsexual ways (Connell 1987, 2002). Where a man's or boy's heterosexuality is unquestioned, his gender is less bound to and defined by (hetero)sexuality than that of a woman, but

if his embodied practices are read as effeminate this can lead to imputa-
tions of homosexuality and undermine his claims to masculinity.

Embodied practices such as dress, posture, and demeanor are central
to the performance of masculinity and femininity and are historically
and culturally variable. These practices are sometimes conscious, as in
choosing what to wear, albeit constrained by standards of what is acceptable in a given social setting and appropriate to our gender. Some are
unconscious, not in a psychoanalytic sense, but as habitually embodied
in our everyday doing of gender. These performances are available to be
read by others and thus associated with the meanings of femininity and
masculinity and their relationship with heterosexuality.

Heteronormative Gendered and Sexual Meanings

Meanings and practices often interlock so that it is often hard to tease
them apart. Social practices are sustained by wider cultural mores, but
also by the "sense-making" that goes on in everyday social interaction.
Like practices, meanings can support the status quo—when they are
normative or ideological—or they can be neutral or oppositional. The
realm of meaning is close to Connell and Pearse's (2015) "symbolism,
culture, discourse." It includes discourses, those meanings circulating
within the wider culture, as well as those emergent from and enmeshed
with everyday interaction—which can be very specific to a given setting
and its participants. Meaning thus cuts across macro and micro aspects
of social relations, although the two can intersect. For example, a couple
might be influenced by cultural discourses of romantic love but might
have their own idiosyncratic understanding of what, for them, is romantic. Some meanings, especially in the form of discourses, can be seen as
both deriving from and helping to sustain given social structures, such
as ideas about innate differences between men and women. These wider
discourses also then operate within and guide routine social practices in
the form of commonsense knowledge.

From a macro-social perspective, gender, sexuality, and heterosexuality are constituted as objects of discourse. The discourses in circulation at any historical moment within a given society serve to distinguish
male from female, to define what is sexual and what is "normal." Such
discourses can and do change: in many countries same-sex attraction

is no longer as deviant as it once was. Yet where there have been advances in the social inclusion of lesbians and gay men, these have been paralleled by the increasing acceptance of the idea that "sexual orientation" is innate; thus the normalization of gay and lesbian lifestyles does not appear to have unsettled the understanding of heterosexuality as a "natural" proclivity of the majority. The rights gained by transgendered people have made it possible to think of gender as mutable for some, but has not dislodged the assumption that we should all, by our natures, belong to one category or the other or that any observable or imagined differences in the aptitudes and temperament of women and men are "natural." In large swathes of the world heteronormative condemnation of sexual "others" remains entrenched. Ironically, there are numerous nations where taboos against same-sex practices derive from British colonial rule but where gay and lesbian sex is now understood as "un-Asian" or "un-African" (Johnson 2006; Gunkel 2011.

The shifts in and contestations of the meanings of normative and nonnormative sexualities in many parts of the world are inexplicable if norms are conceived simply as properties of a cultural order external to us. Any norm, Judith Butler contends, "renders the social field intelligible" (2004, 42). Such intelligibility, however, does not simply derive from external norms but is also negotiated in, and emergent from, the mundane social interaction through which each of us makes sense of our own and others' gendered and sexual lives. Creating a sense of an intelligibly gendered, heterosexually ordered world involves a variety of cultural competences and complex interpretational processes, evident even in the simple act of attributing gender to another person (Kessler and McKenna 1978; West and Zimmerman 1987). The interpretive work this involves goes unnoticed because it is so habitual that it is assumed that we are simply recognizing a natural fact. Thus, insofar as heteronormativity persists in everyday meaning-making, it is contingent upon being constantly reaffirmed; it can also, potentially at least, be unsettled or renegotiated.

The Social Self

To be active meaning-making subjects able to interact with others requires a self that is reflexive and relational. Selfhood is social: it originates not inside ourselves, but through interactions with others and, through such interactions, is continually modified over time. These ideas derive from the work of George Herbert Mead (1934) for whom the self is not a fixed inner essence of the individual, but is always in process by virtue of its reflexivity. It is this reflexivity that makes the self part of the social rather than in some way outside or opposed to it. Reflexive selfhood is based on the human capacity to see ourselves as both subject and object, as "I" and "Me," and therefore to reflect back on ourselves and locate ourselves in relation to others. It makes sociality, and the interpretive processes on which it rests, possible. This conceptualization of the self allows for agency through the emphasis on interpretive processes, but agency here is not envisaged as existing in opposition to the social but as embedded *in* the social. Agency can exist even in conformity: we all reflexively understand our social worlds and act in accordance with that understanding even when we behave wholly conventionally.

This idea of the self fits with Gagnon and Simon's (1974, 2004) interactionist account of the social origins of sexuality. Gagnon and Simon argued for an analytical separation between the gendered and sexual aspects of the self, seeing them as empirically and contingently, rather than necessarily, interrelated. The forms that gendered and sexual selfhood take are culturally and historically specific; particular modes of self-construction become available at different historical moments in specific social locations. Moreover, gendered and sexual selves are reflexively renegotiated or reconfirmed throughout our lives, allowing for some fluidity. This does not mean that we are free to make and remake our sexual selves just as we please—we are constrained by the cultural and interpersonal resources available to us within the social milieu we inhabit, but because these are resources rather than determinants, variability and change are possible. We are not all sexually alike, nor are our sexualities fixed over our life span.

In most societies gender attribution is foundational to the self; the moment we are born, or even before, we are ascribed a gender. This significant act of social categorization profoundly affects our earliest and ongoing sense of who we are and our place in the world (both for those who accept their initial gender attribution and those who seek to change or transcend it). From this perspective, a gendered sense of self precedes our awareness of ourselves as sexual. This does not mean that children are intrinsically asexual (or intrinsically sexual); rather, because access to crucial elements of adult sexual knowledge is restricted, children cannot make sense of themselves as sexual until they gain access to the relevant sexual scripts (Gagnon and Simon 2004). While children in Western societies now become sexually knowing earlier than in the recent past, the pattern of gendered self-awareness preceding sexual self-awareness remains (see Jackson and Scott 2010). In relation to heterosexuality, however, the picture changes, because children come to understand nonsexual aspects of heterosexuality—families, mothers and fathers, for example—before they gain access to specifically sexual scripts. Such knowledge is a resource available for reconceptualization as sexually significant once children become sexually self-aware.

This approach assumes variable outcomes in the process of self-formation; there is no single way of being heterosexual—or homosexual, lesbian, bisexual, or queer—although gender remains significant. While there are multiple ways of being male or female, for young heterosexuals becoming sexual is profoundly gendered and so are sexual relations in later life. Becoming lesbian or gay does not mean a loss of gender since same-sex sexuality, as much as heterosexuality, is defined by gender—but it does require negotiating different ways of investing gender with erotic significance and different forms of gendered self-understanding. How this occurs varies historically depending on the kinds of stories of becoming that are culturally available in any given time or place. It is significant, however, that lesbians and gay men are often called on to account for their sexuality, while heterosexuals generally are not, which is indicative of the consequences of heteronormative and gendered assumptions for the ways we understand ourselves and others.

Applying the Framework: Heterosexuality in Hong Kong and the United Kingdom

If, as I have argued, the institutionalization, practice, and meaning of heterosexuality are historically and culturally variable, then a comparative study of two differing locations should cast some light on this. In our research on women's experience of social change in Hong Kong and Britain, the ordering of heterosexual relations and the consequences of institutionalized heterosexuality have been key issues. We interviewed 14 university educated young women aged 20–26 and 12 of their mothers in Hong Kong and 13 similarly placed young women and 12 of their mothers in the UK and also conducted focus groups with young women. There were both similarities and differences between the Hong Kong and UK samples, as well as variations within them, but here I focus on some of the differences we found in "practices of intimacy" (Jamieson 2011), in particular mothers' attitudes to and regulation of their daughters' sexual lives (see Jackson and Ho 2014). The practices we identified were, of course, mediated through the accounts of our participants and therefore the way they reflexively make sense of them. Such qualitative data does not directly tell us about social structures, but in interpreting women's accounts it became clear that their lives were shaped by structural constraints as well as being imbued with meanings deriving from their specific cultural heritages and everyday interaction.

Although Hong Kong is now richer than the UK in terms of per capita GDP, an immense gulf between the rich and poor persists—one of the legacies of the colonial era in which the native population was largely left to fend for themselves, with very little welfare provision beyond (inadequate) public housing. The material consequences of this situation proved to be very important in understanding the lives of the women we interviewed. Partly as a result of this and partly as a legacy of different forms of family organization, the Hong Kong women relied far more on the wider family for economic and social support than the British women, and norms of filial obligation still affected how young Hong Kong women saw their responsibilities to their parents (see Jackson, Ho, and Na 2013). But how women practiced their intimate lives was not wholly determined by structural factors or cultural mores, nor were the meanings it had for them. It was clear that women were exercising considerable agency and reflexivity in negotiating their lives and relationships within given social structural and cultural contexts.

Generally, mothers exercised far stricter discipline over daughters in Hong Kong, in keeping with norms of filial piety but also because of the need to ensure their daughters' educational and future material success in the context of economic uncertainty, Hong Kong's fiercely competitive capitalist order, and their own likely dependence on their children in old age. This was reflected in their management of their daughters' sexuality, in that they had encouraged their daughters to concentrate on educational and career advancement rather than romantic attachments until they were deemed of marriageable age (in their late twenties). While British mothers were also concerned about the consequences of the economic climate for their daughters' futures, they were far more relaxed about their career aspirations, summed up by a frequently uttered phrase, "as long as she's happy." The British young women grew up with greater freedom and were also able to develop more independence from their parents on reaching adulthood. Most left home for good once they began higher education, though a few had become "boomerang" children, returning home because of lack of a job or relationship failure. All the Hong Kong young women, however, still lived with their parents, not only due to the cultural expectation that they would do so until they married but also because of the acute shortage of affordable housing (in the most expensive housing market in the world). This meant that their mothers continued exercising surveillance over daughters' conduct, including sexual conduct, into adulthood.

British women in both generations, with the exception of one deeply religious mother-daughter pair, seemed to accept teenage sexual experimentation as a "normal" aspect of growing up and took nonmarital sexuality for granted as part of life. The British mothers typically had allowed their daughters to sleep with their (predominantly male) sexual partners at home, to stay with them on weekends, or go on holiday with them—and this had often begun before daughters left home to attend universities. They were concerned about the risk of early pregnancy and most ensured their daughters had access to contraception, but otherwise did not interfere in their sexual lives, though permitting them to use the parental home for sexual encounters could be seen as a means of ensuring they were safe. As one mother noted, it also made it possible for a daughter to return to live in the parental home without it unduly constraining her social life. Nonetheless, heteronormativity was reinforced through the expectation that daughters would have boyfriends and would engage in (hetero)sexual activity. One young woman commented that her parents would be worried if she ended up as a "35-old virgin."

In Hong Kong virginity prior to marriage remains normative and part of the gendered meaning and practice of heterosexuality. Since all the young Hong Kong women lived with their parents, this severely limited their sexual opportunities—sleeping with partners in the parental home was out of the question. Many mothers assiduously policed their daughters' virginity; one told us that "virginity is a gift to your lifelong partner," while her daughter complained that her mother was constantly checking her virginity status. Young women gave many examples of how their mothers sought to discourage sexual activity, from dire warnings against losing their virginity to, in one case, telling a daughter's boyfriend not to have sex with her. Whether or not daughters complied with their mothers' wishes (they were not all avowed virgins), they revealed a high degree of reflexivity in discussing these issues with us, particularly in the focus group discussion, often distancing themselves from their mothers through the use of humor. Through this strategy they demonstrated relational selfhood—locating themselves in relation to their mothers and in relation to the other young women in the group, creating a shared sense of "what mothers were like" and how daughters could deal with this.

Hong Kong also remains far more heteronormative than Britain (see Kong 2011; Tang 2011). Its colonial laws against homosexuality survived until 1991, and there is no protection against discrimination for lesbians and gay men. Hong Kong mothers frequently saw lesbianism as "abnormal," though the daughters were more accepting of sexual diversity. There were two young lesbians in our Hong Kong sample: the mother of one of them said that it took her two years (and the fear of losing her daughter altogether) to accept it; the other does not acknowledge her daughter's sexuality. Both British generations expressed liberal attitudes to lesbianism; for example, one mother said "the gender of the person that loves your child is less important than the quality of the love." The British mothers also often referred directly to changing structural circumstances—that living as a lesbian today in Britain has become much easier than in their own youth as a result of increased sexual rights.

Some of the differences discussed here are products of meanings and practices derived from cultural heritage, such as the continued importance of filial piety in Chinese societies; others are adaptations to historical, socioeconomic, and political conditions. But these are always negotiated by women possessed of the ability to be reflexive about the constraints on their lives.

Conclusion

This brief discussion of differences between two territories is indicative of the range of aspects of the social that need to be taken into account in any analysis of heterosexuality. A full picture can only emerge through consideration of the structures, practices, and meanings of heterosexuality and gender and of subjective gendered and sexual selfhood in any given society. This is probably more than can be achieved within any single study, but it can serve to sensitize us to the limits of what can be discovered and how. It is also crucial to take account of gender hierarchy as well as heteronormativity and the complex interconnections between gender, sexuality, and heterosexuality within each dimension of the social.

This is why I claim that a focus on heteronormativity is not enough and why queer theory, while offering some useful insights, can never do as much as a more sociological analysis because of its limited appreciation of how heterosexuality works. Queer theorists are simply not interested in what goes on, for example, within "normal" heterosexual families (or, for that matter, in those founded on same-sex partnerships). The idea of discursively (and sometimes psychoanalytically) constituted subjectivity, deriving from poststructuralist theory, also leaves little room for agency or reflexivity. Finally, queer theory, because of the avoidance of totalizing claims about the social world, cannot deal with structural issues of power and domination and how gender hierarchy figures in the maintenance of institutionalized heterosexuality.

I am therefore arguing that we do still need social structural analysis: it is not outmoded and is, if anything, even more vital to understanding the many inequalities and oppressions that exist globally. A structural analysis alone, however, is not enough to explore all the complexities of human gendered and sexual social relations and therefore has to be open to supplementation by other forms of analysis. I have suggested that the linkages between gender and heterosexuality are structurally particularly strong, but specific structural linkages between gender and heterosexuality cannot be assumed to *determine* other points of connection within other dimensions of the social. We cannot deduce from structural arrangements how individuals practice heterosexuality or other sexualities, their meanings, or how they contribute to shaping the self even within one specific part of the world, let alone account for cross-national variations that might be affected by local cultures and practices as well as structural factors.

NOTE

1 The term "heteronormativity" refers to the taken for granted assumption that heterosexuality is the (only) natural form of sexuality and the (only) normal form of couple relationship and family formation. The term is generally extended to social institutions, practices, and laws or norms based on this assumption. Heteronormative ideas, practices, and institutions therefore serve to position anyone who is not 100 percent heterosexual as "other."

REFERENCES

Agustín, L. M. 2007. *Sex at the Margins: Migration, Labour Markets and the Rescue Industry*. London: Zed Books.

Aoyama, Kaoru. 2009. *Thai Migrant Sex Workers: From Modernisation to Globalisation*. Basingstoke: Palgrave Macmillan.

Beasley, C., H. Brook, and M. Holmes. 2011. *Heterosexuality in Theory and Practice*. New York: Routledge.

Butler, J. 1990. *Gender Trouble*. New York: Routledge.

———. 2004. *Undoing Gender*. New York: Routledge.

Chang Kyung-Sup. 2010. *South Korea under Compressed Modernity*. London: Routledge.

Chao, A. 2002. "'How Come I Can't Stand Guarantee for My Own Life?' Taiwan Citizenship and the Cultural Logic of Queer Identity." *Inter-Asia Cultural Studies* 3 (3): 369–381.

Connell, R. 1987. *Gender and Power*. Cambridge: Polity.

———. 2002. *Gender*. Cambridge: Polity.

Connell, R., and R. Pearce. 2015. *Gender in World Perspective*. 3rd ed. Cambridge: Polity.

Ding Yu and Ho Sik Ying. 2008. "Beyond Sex Work: An Analysis of *Xiaojies'* Understandings of Work in the Pearl River Delta Area, China." In *East Asian Sexualities*, edited by Stevi Jackson, Liu Jieyu, and Woo Juhyun. London: Zed Books.

Duncan, S., J. Carter, M. Phillips, S. Roseneil, and M. Stoilova. 2013. "Why Do People Live Apart Together?" *Families, Relationships and Societies* 2 (3): 323–338.

Evans, D. 1993. *Sexual Citizenship: The Material Construction of Sexualities*. London: Routledge.

Foucault, M. 1981. *The History of Sexuality Vol I*. Harmondsworth: Penguin.

Gagnon, J., and W. Simon. 1974. *Sexual Conduct*. London: Hutchinson.

———. 2004. *Sexual Conduct*. 2nd ed. New York: Aldine de Gruyter.

Gunkel, H. 2011. *The Cultural Politics of Female Sexuality in South Africa*. London: Routledge.

Hakim, C. 2011. *Honey Money: The Power of Erotic Capital*. London: Allen Lane.

Halperin, D. 1995. *Saint Foucault: Towards a Gay Hagiography*. Oxford: Oxford University Press.

Hennessy, R. 2000. *Profit and Pleasure*. New York: Routledge.

Hoang, K. K. 2015. *Dealing in Desire: Asian Ascendancy, Western Decline, and the Hidden Currencies of Sex Work*. Berkeley: University of California Press.

Holmes, M. 2004. "An Equal Distance? Individualisation, Gender and Intimacy in Distance Relationships." *Sociological Review* 52 (2): 180–200.

Ingraham, C. 1996. "The Heterosexual Imaginary." In *Queer Theory/Sociology*, edited by S. Seidman. Oxford: Blackwell.

Irwin, S. 2005. *Reshaping Social Life*. London: Routledge.

Itaborahy, P., and J. Zhu. 2015. "State Sponsored Homophobia: A World Survey of Laws: Criminalisation, Protection and Recognition of Same-Sex Love." Geneva: International Lesbian, Gay, Bisexual, Trans and Intersex Association. Accessed January 10, 2016. www.ilga.org.

Jackson, S. 1999. *Heterosexuality in Question*. London: Sage.

———. 2006. "Gender, Sexuality and Heterosexuality: The Complexity (and Limits) of Heteronormativity." *Feminist Theory* 7 (1): 105–121.

Jackson, S., and P. S. Y. Ho. 2014. "Mothers, Daughters and Sex: The Negotiation of Young Women's Sexuality in Hong Kong and Britain." *Families, Relationships, and Societies* 3 (3): 387–405.

Jackson, S., P. S. Y. Ho, and J. N. Na. 2013. "Reshaping Tradition? Women Negotiating the Boundaries of Tradition and Modernity in Hong Kong and British Families." *Sociological Review* 61 (4): 667–688.

Jackson, S., and S. Scott. 2010. *Theorizing Heterosexuality*. Maidenhead, UK: Open University Press.

Jamieson, Lynn. 2011. "Intimacy as a Concept: Explaining Social Change in the Context of Globalization or Another Form of Ethnocentrism?" *Sociological Research Online* 16 (4); www.socresonline.org.uk.

Johnson, C. 2006. "Analysing the Politics of Same-Sex Issues in a Comparative Perspective." *Intersections: Gender, History and Culture in the Asian Context* 14 (November). http://intersections.anu.edu.au.

Kempadoo, K., J. Sanghera, and B. Pattaniak, eds. 2012. *Trafficking and Prostitution Reconsidered: New Perspectives on Migration, Sex-Work and Human Rights*. Boulder, CO: Paradigm.

Kessler, S. J., and W. McKenna. 1978. *Gender: An Ethnomethodological Approach*. New York: Wiley.

Kong, T. S. K. 2011. *Chinese Male Homosexualities: Menba, Tongzhi and the Golden Boy*. London: Routledge.

Leeds Revolutionary Feminists. 1981. "Political Lesbianism: The Case against Heterosexuality." In *Love Your Enemy: The Debate between Heterosexual Feminism and Political Lesbianism*, edited by Onlywomen Press. London: Onlywomen Press.

McLaughlin, J. 2008. "The Return of the Material: Cycles of Theoretical Fashion in Lesbian, Gay and Queer Studies." In *Intersections between Feminism and Queer Theory*, edited by D. Richardson, J. McLaughlin, and M. Casey. Basingstoke: Palgrave Macmillan.

Mead, G. H. 1934. *Mind, Self, and Society*. Chicago: University of Chicago Press.

Mercer, C. H., C. Tanton, and P. Prah, et al. 2013. "Changes in Sexual Attitudes and Lifestyles in Britain through the Life Course and Over Time: Findings from the National Survey of Sexual Attitudes and Lifestyles (Natsal)." *Lancet* 382 (9907): 1781–1794.

Mkhize, N., J. Bennet, V. Reddy, and R. Moletsane. 2010. *The Country We Want to Live In: Hate Crimes and Homophobia in the Lives of Black Lesbian South Africans*. Cape Town: Human Sciences Research Council.

O'Connell Davidson, J. 2001. "The Sex Tourist, the Expatriate, His Ex-Wife and Her 'Other': The Politics of Loss, Difference and Desire." *Sexualities* 4 (5): 5–34.

Plummer, K. 1975. *Sexual Stigma*. London: RKP.

Rich, A. 1980. "Compulsory Heterosexuality and Lesbian Existence." *Signs* 5 (4): 631–660.

Richardson, D. 2005. "Desiring Sameness? The Rise of a Neoliberal Politics of Sameness." *Antipode* 37 (3): 515–535.

Sechiyama, K. 2013. *Patriarchy in East Asia: A Comparative Sociology of Gender*. Leiden: Brill.

Seidman, S. 2005. "From Polluted Homosexual to the Normal Gay: Changing Patterns of Sexual Regulation in America." In *Thinking Straight: New Work in Critical Heterosexuality Studies*, edited by Chrys Ingraham. New York: Routledge.

———. 2009. "Critique of Compulsory Heterosexuality." *Sexuality Research and Social Policy: Journal of NSRC* 6 (1): 18–28.

Simon, W., and J. Gagnon. 1969. "On Psychosexual Development." In *Handbook of Socialization Theory and Research*, edited by D. A. Goslin. Chicago: Rand McNally.

Stanley, L., and S. Wise. 1983. *Breaking Out*. London: Routledge and Kegan Paul.

Tang, D. T-S. 2011. *Conditional Spaces: Hong Kong Lesbian Desires and Everyday Life*. Hong Kong: University of Hong Kong Press.

Taylor, Y. 2004. "Negotiation and Navigation—an Exploration of the Spaces/Places of Working-Class Lesbians." *Sociological Research Online* (9) 1. www.socresonline.org.uk.

Warde, A. 2015. *The Practice of Eating*. Cambridge: Polity.

West, C., and D. Zimmerman. 1987. "Doing Gender." *Gender & Society* 1 (2): 125–151.

Whittier, D., and W. Simon. 2001. "The Fuzzy Matrix of 'My Type' in Intrapsychic Sexual Scripting." *Sexualities* 4 (2): 139–165.

Wittig, M. 1982. "The Category of Sex." *Feminist Issues* 2 (2): 63–68.

———. 1992. *The Straight Mind and Other Essays*. Hemel Hempstead, UK: Harvester Wheatsheaf.

8

Gender Inequality and Feminism in the New Economy

CHRISTINE L. WILLIAMS AND MEGAN TOBIAS NEELY

At the beginning of *Gender and Power*, Connell introduces the reader to 15-year-old Delia Prince to illustrate how the life of a "normal" teenager is a product of a gender regime. The case also demonstrates how much has changed in the last three decades. Delia lives with her family in a working class suburb in Australia. Her parents own their home and work in unionized jobs—her father as a tradesman and her mother as a part-time typist, having been dismissed from her previous job in a bank when she married. Delia's father is the family disciplinarian. In his leisure time, he coaches football and drinks beer at the pub. In addition to her paid work, Delia's mother performs the housework (she keeps the place "gleaming") and manages the accounts of the football team her husband coaches. For her part, Delia aspires to become a veterinarian, but she will settle for being a bank clerk if her grades are insufficient to get into the university. Delia has a boyfriend, and hopes to be married by age 20. Delia's parents are very protective and control who is in her peer group. Violent sexual assaults in their neighborhood mean that she is not allowed out at night.

Connell recounts these details of Delia's life to introduce her theory of gender. *Gender and Power* argues that gender inequality is reproduced by three "main structures": labor, power, and cathexis, or the expression of erotic desire. Labor practices contribute to male domination by excluding women from high-paying jobs and relegating them to housework and child care. These patterns are reflected in the different job opportunities, full-time versus part-time schedules, and the unequal division of housework and leisure time of Delia's parents, and in Delia's sense of her future career possibilities. The second structure upholding male domination is power, particularly men's monopoly on violence. Delia's father is the undisputed "head of the household" who sometimes uses physical violence to control his family, while her mother is "second-in-command" (5). Connell connects the violence in the Prince neighborhood to men's control of state power, noting that in Australia virtually no women serve in high political offices or military posts. Finally, Connell argues that cathexis promotes male domination, particularly through the heterosexual organization of emotional life. This is illustrated by the taken-for-granted heterosexuality of the Prince household, including the dream of an early marriage for Delia and the danger of sexual assault (including gay bashing) in the neighborhood. In Connell's view, these three structures of labor, power, and cathexis compose Delia's life and reproduce a gender regime that ensures men's domination of women in society.

Much has changed since Delia was a teenager. The institutions shaping Delia's life have been fundamentally reconfigured. Connell interviewed Delia's family during the apex of union density in Australia; since then, many working class jobs have been outsourced, eliminated, or transformed into part-time, temporary, or contract work. Families have become less stable, too. High rates of divorce and of births to single mothers mean that many children today grow up in a household without a father. Today's working class young adults suffer from job insecurity, housing insecurity (many live with a parent well into their 20s), and relationship insecurity (Waters, Carr, and Kefalas 2011). Instead of aspiring to early marriage, they seem to reject long-term relationships altogether (Silva 2013).

The intervening decades also witnessed significant progress for women. Barriers to women's employment have fallen (including in the military), the number of women political leaders has grown (Australia elected a woman prime minister in 2010), women now outnumber men in colleges and universities, and firms widely embrace "diversity" as an organizational goal. The U.S. and Australia have undergone remarkable changes in attitudes toward sexual minorities; the increasing recognition of lesbian and gay marriage rights is one example. Gender inequality has not been eliminated by any means, but the mechanisms driving women's oppression have changed since Delia's teenage years.

Although Connell could not have anticipated these changes, her theory does help to account for them. Connell argues that within the three main structures are "crisis tendencies" that constantly threaten to "de-compose" the system of male domination (117). Political struggles stemming from conflicts of interest can result in new institutional practices that challenge men's power and its legitimacy. Therein lies the hope of feminist movements: to exploit moments of crisis to envision and demand a more equal and just society. Unfortunately, according to Connell, the system of hegemonic masculinity (or the socially dominant discourses and practices that legitimize male domination) often diffuses and appropriates such challenges.

In this chapter, we examine the crisis tendencies emerging in one of the main structures—labor—with a focus on U.S. society.[1] In the first part, we explain how the pathways to economic security and leadership positions still favor men despite radical changes in the organization of work. In the second part, we discuss how increasing economic inequality in the U.S. constitutes a "crisis" fueling feminist demands for justice, but also exacerbates divisions among women. We argue that understanding and addressing conflicts of interest among women requires adopting an intersectional perspective, or understanding gender in the context of race, ethnicity, class, and other forms of inequality. To conclude, we return to Delia. Although the life of a typical teenager has changed, we argue that Connell's structural theory enhanced with an intersectional lens remains a valuable approach for understanding gender inequality today.

Gender Inequality in the New Economy

In work organizations of the postwar era, working class men like Delia's father anticipated a lifetime of loyal service to a single employer. Employers rewarded men for their loyalty with promotions, raises, benefits, and pensions. This standard employment contract was developed in the 1940s and '50s during the so-called golden age of capitalism (Reich 2007).

In the United States, this contract was available only to a select group, mostly white men employed by large oligopolistic firms. The "family wage" was a cornerstone of this contract. Acknowledging their dependence on women's domestic work, union members like Delia's father fought for and received an income deemed adequate to support a wife and children at home. Importantly, unions and employers initially excluded women and racialized minority men from receiving the family wage (Thistle 2006). During the "golden age," married white women were not supposed to work at all; those who did work typically did so in dead-end, temporary, or part-time positions to augment their husbands' earnings (Delia's mother is an example). Minority women were forced to work because their husbands were denied the family wage. In fact, it wasn't until the civil rights movement in the 1960s that significant numbers of black and Latino men gained access to well-paying unionized jobs.

Not surprisingly, as globalization, deregulation, and outsourcing whittled away the terms of the standard employment contract, working class men experienced the greatest declines. Black and Latino men who managed to make headway into unionized jobs were the first hit by these forces; they have since impacted white working class men as well. Over the past 30 years, men's jobs have become increasingly precarious—that is, more similar to women's jobs. In fact, some describe this as the "feminization of labor" (Standing 2011), claiming that all low-wage workers are becoming women workers, regardless of gender (McDowell 2014). This "feminization" does not imply that women encounter better working conditions, but that many of the advantages men—primarily white working class men—previously enjoyed are disappearing.

A number of statistical trends reflect these disappearing advantages. In the United States, significant gaps between men's and women's rates of labor force participation, job tenure, and perceived job insecurity are closing (Kalleberg 2011). The earnings gap for men and women has decreased, but for different reasons at the lower and upper strata of the workforce. The gender wage gap for workers at the middle and lower tiers of the labor force declined because men's wages dropped precipitously. For example, the median income of male high school graduates aged 25–34 fell 25 percent, from $41,000 in 1980 to $31,000 in 2010 (in constant dollars); women high school graduates in this age group experienced a decline from $26,500 to $24,000 over the same time period (Pedulla 2012, 29). Thus, the ratio of women's earnings to men's earnings for this group narrowed, from .65 to .77. Calling this an improvement in women's status would be a gross misrepresentation; rather, it indicates a decline in men's status due to the standard employment contract's demise.

In contrast, the incomes of the college educated have steadily increased over the past 30 years. Women have closed the gender education gap; they now outnumber men on American college campuses and receive the majority of degrees (England 2010). Kalleberg (2011, 106) shows that the incomes of men and women in the top 5 percent of earners have increased significantly, with men's wages growing from $39/hour in 1973 to $55/hour in 2009 (in constant dollars), and women's growing from $24 to $41 over the same time period (the corresponding ratios are .62 and .75). For elite workers, the declining gender wage gap reflects the steeper rise of women's incomes compared to men's.

Thus, the new economy has had uneven effects. For the majority of workers, job quality has deteriorated, a change felt most keenly by men without college degrees. Working class women also experienced losses, but their plight received less notice because they were already at the bottom of the labor market. For those at the top, the new economy has been a gold mine—although a significant gender wage gap persists. Who are these winners? What do we know about gender dynamics at the top of the labor market?

At the very top, the winners are virtually all white men. In 2014, women headed fewer than 5 percent of Fortune 500 companies; minority men also have dismal representation among CEOs. Executive compensation and corporate profits have soared in the new economy. And although executive turnover is high, job dislocation at the top is softened by generous separation packages, often called "golden parachutes."

Most high earners are not CEOs, but managers and professionals. The increase in women's incomes since 1980 is due almost entirely to women entering these male-dominated jobs (England 2010). While most women professionals do not work in these top careers, their numbers increased throughout the 1990s (although progress stalled in the 2000s). Most women professionals continue to work in nursing, teaching, and clerical positions—jobs that are practically as gender segregated today as they were in Delia's childhood (Williams 2013).

Women who enter male-dominated professions confront structural barriers to their achievement that result in gender inequality. Elite workers are typically required to work long hours (Correll et al. 2014), in stark contrast to low-wage workers who struggle to get enough hours (Lambert 2012). Salaried professionals may feel compelled to work long hours to prove their worth to their employers in an effort to avoid being laid off. This overwork is facilitated by new communications technology that makes workers available around the clock. Those with specialized skills may become consultants or start their own businesses, which can subject them to even greater precariousness and overwork.

The expectation for long hours has consequences for gender inequality because women still retain primary responsibility for child care and housework. Although elite workers can outsource these tasks (often to immigrant women in low-paid, precarious jobs), some women "opt out," or quit their jobs instead (Stone 2007). "Opting out" is thus a coping strategy for women facing insurmountable pressures to excel at home and at work, but it is only available to married women with high-earning husbands, a small and privileged group (Cha 2010). Furthermore, "opting out" may be a gendered cover story to hide job displacement. When women face the threat of layoffs, they may claim to leave work voluntarily to look after children to legitimize their absence to future employers.

Wage-earning women across the income spectrum experience conflicting demands of employment and of motherhood, but most women do not have the option to quit their jobs. Surviving employment insecurity for many families requires two incomes so that one spouse's earnings can act as a buffer if the other is laid off. Yet even dual-earner families cannot always meet the financial demands of raising a family in the new economy. Despite earning 75 percent more than the families of Delia's childhood, two-income families today have 25 percent less discretionary income (Warren and Tyagi 2004).

Of course, not all households contain two adults capable of earning wages. Marriage rates are falling in the U.S. for all groups except for the college educated. Rates of divorce and single motherhood are very high among the poor and less well educated (Thistle 2006). Mass incarceration of poor men in the U.S. further contributes to the increasing number of families composed of single mothers and their children. This disproportionately impacts black families. In major U.S. cities, roughly 80 percent of black men have criminal records and are 20 to 50 times more likely to go to prison for drug charges than white men (Alexander 2010). Structural racism in the labor market and the criminal justice system creates unique problems for black women, who increasingly bear the responsibility for raising children alone.

The economic situation of single mothers has always been fragile in the U.S., but diminishing welfare support worsened their plight.

To receive public assistance today, poor mothers must participate in paid work or job training. The jobs available pay very low wages; many "workfare" jobs are exempt from the federal minimum wage requirement. Moreover, as hourly workers, they are expected to be available at any time—to work late at short notice or to work nonstandard hours. Single mothers unable to cope with erratic schedules are forced to forfeit their meager welfare benefits (Collins and Mayer 2010).

The household division of labor thus remains a critical factor contributing to gender inequality today, just as it did when *Gender and Power* was written. Mothers' primary responsibility for child care in the U.S., as in many nations, perpetuates men's domination of women. However, in the past many mothers could rely on their husbands' income to support them and their children—an arrangement that buttressed a power structure in which men were "heads of household" and women were "second-in-command." Ironically, this arrangement is only available to the "winners" in the new economy. Unlike Delia, nearly a quarter of American children reside in father-less households, many depending solely on their mothers' meager incomes from precarious jobs (U.S. Census 2014; Thistle 2006).

Gender inequality stems not only from the gender division of household labor but also from the structure of jobs in the new economy. In particular, the institution of teamwork, career maps, and networking can disadvantage women's careers. These job features have become ubiquitous throughout the labor market, from manufacturing (e.g., Plankey-Videla 2012) and service sector jobs (e.g., Ollilainen and Calasanti 2007; Smith 1996), to high-level professional workplaces (Williams, Muller, and Kilanski 2012).

A recent study of scientists in the oil and gas industry illustrates how these new workplace practices can disadvantage women (Williams, Muller, and Kilanski 2012). In this industry, teamwork has been implemented in an effort to de-layer companies by transferring management to coworkers who monitor and evaluate one another. Gender inequality emerges when women fail to get recognition and credit for their contributions. Women who demand this attention may be stigmatized and marginalized further for violating "feminine" norms, especially if they work in male-dominated teams. Furthermore, career maps are replacing career ladders, which specify uniform requirements for advancement.

Because career maps are individually negotiated and because workers rarely know the details of the agreements negotiated by coworkers, supervisors' gender bias can flourish unchecked. Finally, networking has become the chief way that these workers gain exposure and locate job opportunities. In big firms, the networks of white men are both more powerful and extensive than those of other groups. Race and gender shape the experience of network ties: while weak network ties benefit white men in their careers, white women and people of color usually require powerful sponsors in top positions to promote them into higher-paying jobs and leadership roles (Ibarra, Carter, and Silva 2010).

Importantly, none of these workplace innovations *intentionally* promotes gender and racial inequality. Whereas traditional work organizations were designed to exclude white women and people of color, organizations in the new economy are resolutely "gender neutral" and "race blind," based on the principle of equal treatment. Virtually every major U.S. corporation proudly proclaims commitment to fostering a diverse workforce, even companies with few women and minority men in leadership positions (Collins 2011; Williams, Kilanski, and Muller 2014).

Companies demonstrate their commitment to diversity by featuring workers with a variety of demographic characteristics on their websites, advertisements, and recruitment literature, and by instituting programs to attract and retain workers from different backgrounds. These "diversity programs" include mentoring, affinity groups, and diversity training—none of which effectively promote women and minority men into leadership positions (Kalev, Dobbin, and Kelly 2006; Williams, Kilanski, and Muller 2014). Nevertheless, they remain extremely popular (Bielby, Krysan, and Herring 2013). Critics charge that these "feel good" programs mask persistent discrimination (Ahmed 2012; Bell and Hartmann 2007). Companies can "brand" themselves as inclusive (despite evidence to the contrary) to protect themselves from liability if they are ever charged with unlawful employment discrimination.

Thus, the new economy is "pro-diversity" but remains deeply structured by gender and other forms of inequality. The culture of insecurity, the expansion of precarious employment, the decline of welfare support, the changed structure of jobs, and the new discourse of diversity contribute to male domination and the economic oppression of women. None of these factors affected Delia when she was a teenager.

Feminism in the New Economy

When *Gender and Power* was first published, a key feminist demand was the abolition of the gender division of labor. Connell endorsed breaking down employment barriers to women and encouraged men to take on more domestic labor (280). In the United States, liberal feminists embraced these goals; socialist feminists and women of color feminists were more skeptical that increased labor force participation could liberate women (Davis 1983; Hartmann 1979; hooks 1981). Since then, the two sides have moved even further apart. In the current era of economic inequality, structural racism, and employment instability, the conflicts between elite women workers and other women appear irreconcilable.

At the top of the economic pyramid, we see the emergence of "neoliberal feminism" or "transnational business feminism" (Eisenstein 2009; Roberts 2014). Referring to a corporate-friendly approach to gender equality based on the business case for diversity, this paradigm equates women's empowerment with their right to participate in the market economy. This neoliberal approach trusts the market to absorb women on an equal footing with men because it will make companies more profitable; businesses that do not join the gender equality bandwagon will fail.

One key neoliberal feminist demand is to increase workplace flexibility through employer-sponsored policies that allow for part-time schedules, telecommuting arrangements, and temporary and extended periods of time off (Christensen and Schneider 2010). Implementing such options, it is argued, will promote gender equality by enabling workers to balance their work and family obligations. Like the business case for diversity, advocates believe these innovations will increase productivity and profits by improving employee retention and morale (Correll et al. 2014).

There are many reasons to doubt this approach to achieving gender equality in the workplace. First, research shows that those who use flexibility policies (mostly women, despite the gender neutral language) suffer economic penalties for doing so (Glass 2004; Noonan and Glass 2012). Second, "work-family balance" assumes the separation of spheres—a bounded work life that is separate from a bounded home life; that's an unrealistic idea for those laboring under the constant threat of downsizing whose employers expect round-the-clock availability (Adkins and Dever 2014). Finally, without government protections, expanding workplace flexibility will likely *increase* insecurity for many workers, especially in the low-wage labor market, where "flexibility" enables employers to manipulate employee schedules depending on workflow (Williams 2013). When neoliberal feminists advocate for flexibility, the interests of low-wage workers are not considered (Correll et al. 2014).

Neoliberal feminists believe that increasing the number of women in executive positions will address these concerns. Advocates believe that women are naturally more risk-averse, empathetic, and altruistic than men, so admitting more women into the C-suite of corporations' top executives would therefore result in policies that benefit workers, especially other women. This trickle-down approach to gender equality is believed to eliminate the need for governmental regulation of corporations, since women leaders will naturally implement socially responsible policies (Nelson 2013; Roberts 2014). Consequently—and paradoxically—neoliberal feminists exhort women to aggressively compete with men and to grasp every opportunity for advancement (e.g., to "lean in").

Some women who have gained entrance into the power elite have used their newfound wealth and status to invest in other women. Melissa Fisher (2012) finds a growing interest among women executives on Wall Street in economically empowering other women through microfinance, investment mandates, and corporate social responsibility programs. These efforts reflect broader initiatives to create "shared value," a dual emphasis on the bottom line and collective good driven by the belief that what's good for society is good for business (Pfitzer, Bockstette, and Stamp 2013). Women executives adapt these ideas with the goal of benefiting women's economic well-being (even though their fortunes have come from investment practices that produce the conditions they seek to ameliorate). The outcomes of shared value initiatives are difficult to measure (Beard and Hornik 2011). Like diversity programs, shared value and social responsibility campaigns may only further the interests of the corporations and investors sponsoring them, rather than address the underlying causes of gender inequality in the new economy.

For women struggling in low-wage precarious jobs, neoliberal feminist goals are at best irrelevant and at worst part of the problem. Encouraging women to work harder and promoting "flexible" working conditions only worsens the exploitation of those at the bottom end of the labor market. Furthermore, investment initiatives and corporate campaigns designed to empower women may reflect the concerns of the women driving them, but overlook their actual impact on low-wage women workers (Eisenstein 2009).

Instead of embracing neoliberal solutions to gender inequality, working class women have turned to labor organizing. Although not necessarily in the name of "feminism," unions have adopted women's demands for increased wages, equal opportunities, guaranteed hours and schedules, and the end to sexual harassment and assault in the workplace (Cobble 2007; Walby 2014). In the United States, this has been an uphill battle, as unions have fallen on especially hard times. Private sector employees have seen their unions decimated. In the public sector, unions are under attack by neoliberal politicians, especially the female-dominated teachers' and nurses' unions; the male-dominated police and firefighter unions have managed so far to retain their legitimacy (Farnham 2011; Greenhouse 2014b). Meanwhile, newly formed service unions in low-wage labor markets struggle against well-funded, organized, and unwavering corporate opposition; Walmart and Amazon, the largest private U.S. employers, are notorious examples (Kopytoff 2014; Lichtenstein 2009).

One bright spot for low-wage women workers in the U.S. is the recent success of voter initiatives to raise the minimum wage. With the support of nonunion worker advocacy groups, voters in 2014 approved increasing the minimum wage in a number of cities and states (Greenhouse 2014a). These victories represent an advance for gender equality because women are overrepresented among minimum-wage earners.

In the new economy, some feminists question whether activism should continue to focus on waged work (Adkins 2012; Weeks 2010). Instead of encouraging women to work harder, Nancy Fraser (2009) encourages women to demand limits to employers' control over their lives. She urges feminists to fight to valorize carework, including the unpaid domestic labor that women provide for their families. The goal is not to promote women's competitiveness in the workplace, but rather to shrink the power of employers over workers by opening up opportunities to pursue interests outside of work. Instead of focusing activism exclusively on access to jobs and improved working conditions, feminists should fight for sustainable hours at work—not too few or too many—and more control over their time.

An intersectional approach reveals what is at stake in recognizing the value of carework. As middle class women in the U.S. and elsewhere follow the neoliberal dream of emancipation through employment, their families outsource carework, often to women of color and women migrant laborers from the Global South (Glenn 1992; Hondagneu-Sotelo 2007). Evelyn Nakano Glenn (1992) argues that past feminist attempts to address the "universal needs of women" obscured differences and perpetuated abuses against poor women and women of color. Recognizing the value of carework would only begin to right this historical wrong.

At the minimum, valorizing carework would require paying domestic workers a living wage *and* providing them the time and space to care for their own families. If they too must outsource carework—a situation facing migrant domestic workers—then those workers must be guaranteed living wages and time to devote to their families as well. However, increasing the wages of domestic workers and providing them time for their own families would mean that middle class women likely could no longer afford their services. Thus, addressing the needs of women throughout the labor force will not only require a revaluation of carework but a redistribution of income so everyone has access to this vital resource. This model of "work-family balance" differs from the neoliberal version because it aims to provide all workers with ample time and money to care for themselves and others—a goal that requires mutual recognition across the divisions of class, race/ethnicity, and nationality.

The theory of intersectionality draws attention to how economic success for some women today is contingent on the hardship and exploitation of others. These conflicts of interest among women constitute what Connell calls "cracks" in the system of male domination. Because the organization of labor in the new economy does not provide adequate support for many women, a "main structure" of male domination is delegitimized and new demands for social justice can emerge. It is not surprising that feminist demands to restrict employer power are gaining traction at this historical moment.

Conclusion

In this chapter, we focused on labor, which is an important factor in reproducing gender inequality today. However, we have argued that changes in the new economy have altered the labor processes that promote men's advantages over women.

In the new economy, the life of a typical working class teenager in the U.S. differs from that of Delia Prince in significant ways. Today's teens are more likely to live with a single mother who supports the family on an insecure job with stagnant wages and unpredictable hours. Those lacking a college education face bleak employment prospects, while those who attend a university must incur debt to finance it themselves. Young women are encouraged to be economically self-sufficient and independent, yet they remain at a disadvantage in workplaces organized in ways that privilege men.

Gender inequality still structures the life of today's Delia Princes. But because the mechanisms of gender inequality have changed, feminism is also changing. Thirty years ago, feminists fought for women's access to paid work. Today, women are expected to have a job and to work all the time, while those without jobs are expected to undertake self-improvement projects to enhance their chances of employment. The only women exempt from these requirements are married to wealthy men.

Thirty years ago, feminists fought against the standard labor contract that explicitly endorsed male domination. Today, workers confront an employment culture that valorizes diversity and gender equality. While this is unquestionably a step forward for women, it does not solve the problem of male domination. The redesign of workplaces—in particular, the institution of teamwork, career maps, and networking—favors men and qualities associated with masculinity. Moreover, women's ongoing responsibility for domestic labor penalizes them in their paid jobs, virtually assuring the continuation of the gender wage gap.

These are the reasons why some feminists argue that paid work cannot liberate women. A job may be necessary for survival, but it does little to advance the cause of social justice for women. On the contrary, most women's jobs leave them exhausted and bereft. This is inevitable when employers have the upper hand, as in a neoliberal culture. Without unions or government regulations to restrain them, employers degrade working conditions, and, to paraphrase Marx, the more women work, the more impoverished they become.

Because the new economy breaks from the previous system of gender inequality, feminists have the opportunity to imagine alternatives. As Connell writes in *Gender and Power*, the historical condition of the gender order is "about change produced by human practice, about people being inside the process" (144). How are feminists using the current moment to forge alternatives to the prevailing gender order?

The intersectional turn in feminist theory is the key to this endeavor. In exposing how interests among women conflict, women of color feminists illuminate cracks in the gender system and envision viable alternatives. Instead of imploring women to work harder and "lean in," these feminists and their allies are demanding the reorganization of work, care, distribution, and recognition with the goal of inclusivity. Only by reducing income inequality, lessening employers' power, and alleviating the negative impacts of job insecurity will the dream of gender equality become reality.

NOTE

1 Parts of this chapter are derived from Christine L. Williams and Megan Tobias Neely, "Gender and Work: Precariousness and Inequality," in *Emerging Trends in the Social and Behavioral Sciences*, ed. Robert Scott and Stephen Kosslyn (New York: Sage, 2015).

REFERENCES

Adkins, Lisa. 2012. "Out of Work or Out of Time? Rethinking Labor after the Financial Crisis." *South Atlantic Quarterly* 111 (4): 621–41.

Adkins, Lisa, and Maryanne Dever. 2014. "Housework, Wages and Money." *Australian Feminist Studies* 29 (79): 50–66.

Ahmed, Sara. 2012. *On Being Included: Racism and Diversity in Institutional Life*. Durham, NC: Duke University Press.

Alexander, Michelle. 2010. *The New Jim Crow: Mass Incarceration in the Era of Colorblindness*. New York: New Press.

Beard, Alison, and Richard Hornik. 2011. "It's Hard to Be Good." *Harvard Business Review* (November): 88–96.

Bell, Joyce M., and Douglas Hartmann. 2007. "Diversity in Everyday Discourse: The Cultural Ambiguities and Consequences of 'Happy Talk.'" *American Sociological Review* 72 (6): 895–914.

Bielby, William T., Maria Krysan, and Cedric Herring. 2013. "How Americans View Workplace Antidiscrimination Interventions: Why We Need a New Conversation about Race, Gender, Who Wins, Who Loses, and What Works." Paper presented at Ford Foundation Research Workshop, New York.

Cha, Youngjoo. 2010. "Reinforcing Separate Spheres: The Effect of Spousal Overwork on Men's and Women's Employment in Dual-Earner Households." *American Sociological Review* 75 (2): 303–29.

Christensen, Kathleen, and Barbara Schneider. 2010. *Workplace Flexibility*. Ithaca: Cornell University Press.

Cobble, Dorothy Sue. 2007. *The Sex of Class: Women Transforming American Labor*. Ithaca: Cornell University Press.

Collins, Jane L., and Victoria Mayer. 2010. *Both Hands Tied: Welfare Reform and the Race to the Bottom in the Low-Wage Labor Market*. Chicago: University of Chicago Press.

Collins, Sharon M. 2011. "From Affirmative Action to Diversity: Erasing Inequality from Organizational Responsibility." *Critical Sociology* 37 (5): 517–20.

Connell, R. W. 1987. *Gender and Power: Society, the Person, and Sexual Politics*. Stanford: Stanford University Press.

Correll, Shelley, Erin Kelly, Lindsey Trimble O'Connor, and Joan Williams. 2014. "Redesigning, Redefining Work." *Work and Occupations* 41 (1): 3–17.

Davis, Angela Y. 1983. *Women, Race, and Class*. New York: Vintage.

Eisenstein, Hester. 2009. *Feminism Seduced: How Global Elites Use Women's Labor and Ideas to Exploit the World*. Boulder, CO: Paradigm Publishers.

England, Paula. 2010. "The Gender Revolution: Uneven and Stalled." *Gender & Society* 24 (2): 149–66.

Farnham, Alan. 2011. "Cops vs. Teachers: Who's Worth More in Tight Times?" *ABC-News*, February 28. Accessed December 1, 2014. www.abcnews.go.com.

Fisher, Melissa S. 2012. *Wall Street Women*. Durham, NC: Duke University Press.

Fraser, Nancy. 2009. "Feminism, Capitalism, and the Cunning of History." *New Left Review* 56:97–117.

Glass, Jennifer. 2004. "Blessing or Curse? Work-Family Policies and Mother's Wage Growth." *Work and Occupations* 31:367–94.

Glenn, Evelyn Nakano. 1992. "From Servitude to Service Work: Historical Continuities in the Racial Division of Paid Reproductive Labor." *Signs* 18 (1): 1–43.

Greenhouse, Steven. 2014a. "The Fight for $15.37 an Hour: How a Coalition Pushed for a Hotel Workers' Minimum Wage." *New York Times*, November 22. Accessed November 24, 2014. http://nyti.ms.

———. 2014b. "Wisconsin's Legacy for Unions." *New York Times*, February 23. Accessed December 1, 2014. http://nyti.ms.

Hartmann, Heidi. 1979. "The Unhappy Marriage of Marxism and Feminism: Towards a More Progressive Union." *Capital & Class* 3 (2): 1–33.

Hondagneu-Sotelo, Pierrette. 2007. *Domestica: Immigrant Workers Cleaning and Caring in the Shadows of Affluence*. Berkeley: University of California Press.

hooks, bell. 1981. *Ain't I a Woman: Black Women and Feminism*. New York: Routledge.

Ibarra, Herminia, Nancy M. Carter, and Christine Silva. 2010. "Why Men Still Get More Promotions Than Women." *Harvard Business Review* (September): 80–85.

Kalev, Alexandra, Frank Dobbin, and Erin Kelly. 2006. "Best Practices or Best Guesses? Assessing the Efficacy of Corporate Affirmative Action and Diversity Policies." *American Sociological Review* 71 (4): 589–617.

Kalleberg, Arne L. 2011. *Good Jobs, Bad Jobs: The Rise of Polarized and Precarious Employment Systems in the United States, 1970s–2000s*. New York: Russell Sage.

Kopytoff, Verne. 2014. "How Amazon Crushed the Union Movement." *Time Magazine*, January 16.

Lambert, Susan J. 2012. "Opting in to Full Labor Force Participation in Hourly Jobs." In *Women Who Opt Out: The Debate over Working Mothers and Work-Family Balance*, edited by B. D. Jones, 87–102. New York: New York University Press.

Lichtenstein, Nelson. 2009. *The Retail Revolution: How Walmart Created a Brave New World of Business*. New York: Metropolitan Books.

McDowell, Linda. 2014. "Gender, Work, Employment and Society: Feminist Reflections on Continuity and Change." *Work, Employment & Society* 28 (5): 825–37.

Nelson, Julie A. 2013. "'Would Women Leaders Have Prevented the Global Financial Crisis?' Teaching Critical Thinking by Questioning a Question." *International Journal of Pluralism and Economics Education* 4 (2): 192–209.

Noonan, Mary, and Jennifer Glass. 2012. "The Hard Truth about Telecommuting." *Monthly Labor Review* 135 (6): 38–45.

Ollilainen, Marjukka, and Toni Calasanti. 2007. "Metaphors at Work: Maintaining the Salience of Gender in Self-Managing Teams." *Gender & Society* 21 (1): 5–27.

Pedulla, David. 2012. "To Be Young and Unemployed." *New Labor Forum* 21 (3): 26–36.

Pfitzer, Marc, Valerie Bockstette, and Mike Stamp. 2013. "Innovating for Shared Value: Companies That Deliver Both Social Benefit and Business Value Rely on Five Mutually Reinforcing Elements." *Harvard Business Review* (September): 100–107.

Plankey-Videla, Nancy. 2012. *We Are in This Dance Together: Gender, Power, and Globalization at a Mexican Garment Firm*. New Brunswick, NJ: Rutgers University Press.

Reich, Robert. 2007. *Supercapitalism: The Transformation of Business, Democracy, and Everyday Life*. New York: Knopf.

Roberts, Adrienne. 2012. "Financing Social Reproduction: The Gendered Relations of Debt and Mortgage Finance in Twenty-First-Century America." *New Political Economy* 18 (1): 1–22.

———. 2014. "The Political Economy of Transnational Business Feminism: Problematizing the Corporate-Led Gender Equality Agenda." *International Feminist Journal of Politics* (online first) doi:10.1080/14616742.2013.849968.

Silva, Jennifer. 2013. *Coming Up Short: Working Class Adulthood in an Age of Uncertainty*. New York: Oxford University Press.

Smith, Vicki. 1996. "Employee Involvement, Involved Employees: Participative Work Arrangements in a White-Collar Service Occupation." *Social Problems* 43 (2): 166–79.

Standing, Guy. 2011. *The Precariat: The New Dangerous Class*. London: Bloomsbury Academic.

Stone, Pamela. 2007. *Opting Out? Why Women Really Quit Careers and Head Home.* Berkeley: University of California Press.

Thistle, Susan. 2006. *From Marriage to the Market: The Transformation of Women's Lives and Work.* Berkeley: University of California Press.

U.S. Census. 2014. "Current Population Survey, 2013. Annual Social and Economic Supplement." Accessed November 7, 2014.

Walby, Sylvia. 2014. "Regendering Unions: Changing Alliances and Agendas." Paper presented at the Annual Meeting of the American Sociological Association, San Francisco, August 16–19.

Warren, Elizabeth, and Amelia Warren Tyagi. 2004. *The Two-Income Trap: Why Middle-Class Parents Are Going Broke.* New York: Basic Books.

Waters, Mary, Patrick J. Carr, and Maria J. Kefalas. 2011. *Coming of Age in America: The Transition to Adulthood in the Twenty-First Century.* Berkeley: University of California Press.

Weeks, Kathi. 2010. *The Problem with Work.* Durham, NC: Duke University Press.

Williams, Christine L. 2013. "The Glass Escalator, Revisited: Gender Inequality in Neo-liberal Times." *Gender & Society* 27:609–29.

Williams, Christine L., Kristine Kilanski, and Chandra Muller. 2014. "Corporate Diversity and Gender Inequality in the Oil and Gas Industry." *Work and Occupations* 41:440–76.

Williams, Christine L., Chandra Muller, and Kristine Kilanski. 2012. "Gendered Organizations in the New Economy." *Gender & Society* 26:549–73.

9

Gender Politics in Academia in the Neoliberal Age

BARBARA POGGIO

Gender, Education, and Knowledge

One of Connell's key contributions to gender studies consists of her *in-depth* analysis of education, which she views as a primary arena for gender construction. Attention to how educational institutions contribute to the production and reproduction of gender asymmetries has been a constant of her studies and research since her earliest texts, such as *Making the Difference* (1982), to the more recent ones (Connell 1982, 2013). In these works gender and education are principally dealt with in relation to social justice issues. Education is viewed as a process that is able to produce capacities for practice and, as a result, to generate advantages and disadvantages for individuals and groups on the basis of specific differences such as gender, but also class and race.

To some extent, Connell's work on education represents an important basis for the development of her structural approach to gender analysis, where structure and practice concepts are closely interconnected. In this intertwining, situatedness and historical change are crucial dimensions. From the various studies and research carried out by Connell in educational contexts there emerges recurrent attention to how people's practices are constrained by educational structures, but at the same time to how they can change and shape those structures. A prime analytical construct with which to observe the configuration of gender relations in these contexts is the gender regime in educational institutions, which is based on four main components (Connell 1996): power relations, division of labor, patterns of emotions, and symbolization. One specific symbolic structure is represented by the gendering of knowledge through which certain characteristics and skills are constructed as male, and others as female. Connell refers on several occasions in her work to the intertwining of rationality and masculinity in Western thought and the patriarchal ideology. In Western philosophy, science and technology "are culturally defined as a masculine realm. Hegemonic masculinity established its hegemony partly by its claim to embody the power of reason. Masculine authority is connected with disembodied reason" (Connell 2005, 164). In advanced capitalism, men's domination of women is no longer legitimized by religion or physical force, but by the technical organization of production: efficiency of means prevails over the ultimate ends.

In recent work, Connell focuses on the subtle, and yet pervasive, dynamics that connote educational contexts in an era when the neoliberal agenda is becoming predominant. She seeks to show how the imbalances embedded in knowledge acquisition are exacerbated by the principles of neoliberalism, a paradigm for economic theory and policy-making and an agenda of social transformation driven by the ideas of individual entrepreneurial freedom and market deregulation. The results of neoliberal policies are, according to Connell, the commodification and privatization of public institutions and more and more spheres of social life, the accentuation of class exclusion, and the postfeminist ideology of gender neutrality. Her analyses consistently address the impact of the pervasive market logic on educational processes and practices, a scenario in which knowledge is increasingly rationalized and commodified. The new keywords have become privatization, competition, deregulation, quality assurance, performance management, and corporate branding, and the new totems are "league tables," indices, and the technologies of research and educational measurement.

Although market ideology presents itself as being gender-neutral, it is in fact fundamentally gendered. Connell (2013) illustrates the consequences of this above all in relation to first-level education, where the neoliberal program requires mothers who are pressured to support the participation of their children in a competitive education system. The gender implications of the affirmation of the neoliberal paradigm are, however, also present in the scientific and academic institutions on which the analysis developed in this chapter centers.

In what follows, I focus on the relationship between gender and science, and on gender construction processes within the domains of the formal production and legitimation of knowledge, namely universities.

I concentrate on the European context, with which I am most familiar because of my direct participation in projects supported by the European Commission and which involve diverse European universities and research centers.

The Persistence of Gender Asymmetries in Higher Education and Knowledge Production Contexts

There have been significant changes in participation by women and men in the various levels of education over the past thirty years. One phenomenon frequently noted today is the feminization of the student population, which also characterizes tertiary education. Yet statistical evidence continues to show the existence of gender disparities in participation in technical and scientific educational programs, as well as an imbalance in higher-status scientific careers.

The main reports on gender differences in science in Europe indicate that, despite some progress, gender inequalities in scientific contexts persist and have proved difficult to overcome. The so-called scissor trend still persists, and the tendency is for it to widen during the course of a person's working life. Even as female students and graduates outnumbered male students, and the gender gap among PhD students and graduates is now very small, women are still poorly represented in senior positions at scientific institutions and in the STEM fields (science, technology, engineering, and mathematics). Horizontal and vertical segregation reinforce each other, producing unequal job opportunities and careers for women compared with men. Data show relevant gender gaps even in salaries and in the allocation of research funding (European Commission 2009, 2016; European Research Council 2015).

Main Interpretive Lens for Gender Asymmetries in the Academy

There is a significant body of literature dealing with the topic of gender asymmetry in scientific contexts. The interpretations used to account for these asymmetries refer to a number of factors ranging from innate characteristics to the organizational practices of academic institutions.

The most traditional explanations of the gender gap in academia emphasize the role of inborn cognitive sex differences, which can be identified, for instance, in differing mathematical and spatial performances rather than verbal and written abilities, which are attributed to biological factors such as brain structure and function, or to hormonal composition or mental development (National Academies of Science 2007). Numerous studies have been conducted in this area to measure the differences in performance between girls and boys, and to explain differing educational choices on the basis of them. The most recent data, however, show a progressive decrease in this gap, which in some countries (such as Sweden, Norway, and Iceland) has disappeared (European Commission 2012). Moreover, it has been demonstrated that integrated educational systems and more equal societies correlate with smaller, or even nonexistent, gaps in scientific performance (Guiso et al. 2009).

A second theoretical approach, mainly based on cross-national studies and on the use of several kinds of indexes of gender equality, stresses the importance of macro-structural factors, such as the type of education system, the labor market, the care and welfare regimes, and the development of gender equality in countries. Even if gender asymmetries in scientific careers are common in various countries, women and men do not face the same structural and normative opportunities and constraints in every national context (Musselin 2005). The internal and external structure of the labor market, the position of the academic occupation in the socioeconomic hierarchy, and the support provided by the welfare system generate different experiences of academic work (Le Feuvre 2015).

A third body of research focuses on cultural determinants in socialization and gender identity construction processes. According to this perspective, a dichotomous, stereotypical view of gender differences underlies the divergence of career pathways, and it assigns different tasks and competences to women and men in society, associating women with reproduction and men with production, women with social skills and men with technical ones. Various socialization agents (such as the family, peers, teachers, and the mass media) cooperate in the construction of gender identity and influence the educational paths of girls and boys through stereotyped expectations, pressures on vocational choices, and different evaluation criteria that reinforce gender asymmetries (Cassell and Jenkins 2000; Xie and Shaumann 2003).

Moreover, many studies have shown that scientific careers reflect the traditional model of the male worker without domestic or familial obligations and totally committed to his work as the norm (Dean and Fleckenstein 2007). Attention to other spheres, such as the family, is seen as a limitation on total dedication to a scientific career. The prevalent career model in scientific contexts is based on the "long hours culture" (Currie, Harris, and Thiele 2000), constant availability (Ward 2000), and the linearity of the career pathway (National Academies of Science 2007). This therefore has negative implications for anyone—whether a woman or a man—who wants to combine professional and family commitments, but it penalizes females more severely because it is expected that women will give priority to caregiving. The difficulties associated with reconciling scientific work and caregiving duties are documented in a large body of literature, which has noted that often the dilemma is resolved by a woman's abandoning her career or temporarily suspending it. Some women (unlike men) decide not to have a family at all if they see doing so as incompatible with a having a career (Blackwell and Glover 2008).

Finally, a fourth strand of research includes studies focused on organizational practices, and therefore on how scientific and academic organizations behave, with specific regard to the gender and power dynamics. Studying academic institutions in this perspective means analyzing the norms that govern formal recruitment and promotion procedures, observing power relations and gatekeeping practices, and analyzing formal and informal networks (Bagilhole and Goode 2001; Benschop and Brouns 2003). Various studies have shed light on the presence of mechanisms deeply embedded in the cultures of scientific and academic organizations, mechanisms that are reproduced through homosocial practices, such as the informal male-dominated networks that perform a gatekeeping role by means of gendered mechanisms of inclusion and exclusion; biases in formal assessment procedures, such as peer review, recruitment, and evaluation, which give rise to unequal access to research funding or academic positions (European Commission 2012); asymmetries in the allocation of time to the different kinds of academic tasks performed by men and women (production/research tasks versus reproduction/teaching and administrative tasks), with differing consequences for career advancement; and isolation and discouragement, and even sexual harassment (De Welde and Stepnick 2014).

These various interpretations furnish a composite picture of the problem and highlight its multifaceted and multilayered nature. However, they should be considered in light of more general changes that characterize the world of science, producing new configurations affecting the various areas considered that, in general, have important implications for gender balance within scientific domains.

The Impact of the Neoliberal Model

The practices emerging in science production and the evaluation of scientific performances, as well as the new working arrangements in scientific organizations consequent on the growing hegemony of the neoliberal agenda, are not irrelevant from the point of view of gender asymmetries in academia.

The orientation of European education policies toward the neoliberal model was ratified in 1999 by the Bologna Declaration, which affirmed the need to rationalize and harmonize national university systems and to promote new procedures of accountability, quality assessment, funding, selection, and performance evaluation.

Neoliberal policies make research and scientific work increasingly rationalized and efficiency-driven in response to the urgent need to transfer new knowledge from academia to society, and to promote economic growth and competitiveness in global markets (Ylijoki and Ursin 2013). One important result of this change has been that universities are progressively changing "from institutions supporting and operating on social interests, public welfare and equality of opportunity to ones centred on the neoliberal values of individualism, competition, contractual relations and 'freedom of choice'" (Ward 2012). Academic organizations increasingly become "greedy institutions" with regard to the level of undivided loyalty, high work productivity, and emotional engagement that they expect of their members and the redefinition of the boundaries between personal and family life and work time (Currie, Harris, and Thiele 2000). On the one hand, universities require increasing workloads, greater flexibility and availability, and accelerated rhythms and time pressure, while on the other, instability is on the increase, salaries are falling, and career prospects and professional development are shrinking for the younger academic generations (Court and Kinman 2008).

The neoliberal turn has changed the model of university governance. It has led to the application of management methods similar to those used in private, for-profit companies, with a growing emphasis on managerialism and entrepreneurialism at the expense of the independence and collegiality of the teaching staff. Moreover, it has significantly affected the nature and content of academic work, in particular by severing the relationship between teaching and research (Barnett 2003).

These processes have remarkable gender implications. Some scholars have observed that the total commitment required in the neoliberal frame is closely associated with the male breadwinner model and the notion of heroic masculinity that excludes management of caregiving responsibilities (Bellavita 1991). The dominant model is no more that of science as an agora, where the social dimension of scholarship prevails, but an Olympian model, in which the dominant profile of a researcher is that of "a young man in solitude high on top of the Olympus, distanced from all everyday practices" (Benschop and Brouns 2003, 207). At the same time, the proliferation of seasonal, part-time, and contract employment seems more dramatically to affect women, who are more likely to be hired into such positions (Higher Education Statistics Agency 2014).

Managerialism is seen as imbued with masculine discourse and practices. As recognition and evaluation of merit gradually become more focused on productivity, performance, and entrepreneurship, other dimensions of academic work important in the past, such as teaching responsibilities, become more feminized, and progressively lose prestige (Thornton 2014). And the growing emphasis on STEM disciplines (science, technology, engineering, and mathematics), considered as engines of innovation and economic growth, has obvious consequences from a gender perspective because these disciplines are differently targeted.

If we consider in particular the neoliberal attitude to gender policies, on the one hand the increasing emphasis on performativity and cost cutting has reduced the attention to equity issues, which are seen as luxuries (Blackmore and Sachs 2003). On the other, greater benevolence is accorded to the gender mainstreaming strategy, as well as to approaches oriented to diversity management, where women are considered as potential resources that should be better exploited (Schunter-Kleemann and Plehwe 2006).

Policies to Combat Gender Asymmetries in Academia

Various policies intended to combat gender asymmetries in academic institutions have been formulated and implemented in many countries since the beginning of the new millennium. Initially, the actions and programs were mainly targeted at helping women to gain access to and pursue a scientific career, based on the assumption of their intrinsic weakness, through two different intervention methods. On the one hand, women's participation in tertiary scientific education is encouraged and promoted through actions to render the choice of scientific disciplines more appealing to women or to assist them in their academic pathways (for example, by implementing mentoring schemes), thereby combating the risk of dropping out. On the other hand, women's careers are supported by increasing their scientific productivity, promoting access to funding, incentivizing attention to gender equality in the preparation of projects, providing financial incentives to rebalance the gender presences in departments, introducing quota targets, enhancing female role models, facilitating networking among women, and providing support for maternity and maternal leave.

Over time, however, it was realized that these programs were not sufficient to close the gender gap in scientific careers, especially regarding women in positions of responsibility, and that the main focus should be not on women but on organizations. This realization led the European institutions to stress the need to make structural changes to educational institutions by employing a systemic and sustainable approach. In 2007, taking its lead from the U.S. National Science Foundation program that aims at Increasing the Participation and Advancement of Women in Academic Science and Engineering Careers (ADVANCE; begun in 2001) and has a strong emphasis on institutional transformation (Risman and Adkins 2014), the European Commission launched the Science in Society initiative, as a part of the broader 7th Framework Programme (FP7). Its aim was to foster greater gender equality in academic and scientific contexts through support for universities and research institutes that undertake to implement structural changes by the creation of consortia.

This program, which lasted until 2013, funded over twenty projects, many of which had the direct aim of promoting equal opportunities for men and women in scientific and research organizations, with a special emphasis on management changes (in the first phases) and structural transformations by the implementation of tailored gender equality plans (in the subsequent phases). Every project involved a partnership of different European universities and research organizations.

Because some of the projects have just concluded and others are still in progress, it is not possible to offer an overall evaluation of the program or its impact on European universities. However, by analyzing the documentation available on the respective websites and on the Community Research and Development Information Service (CORDIS) website,[1] we can consider their premises, objectives, and actions (as they are enunciated) and draw some preliminary conclusions.

The projects present a significant number of actions that fall within the two categories of intervention identified above: actions directed at women to increase their presence in scientific tracks, and actions to support women's careers in scientific institutions. However, as requested by the European Commission's calls, we can note an effort to formulate strategies and policies more directly tailored to the specific requirements and characteristics of the organizations concerned, starting from a situated analysis of the context, and also aimed at developing and implementing actions that focus on organizational structures and practices rather than on women. In almost all projects, there is an initial phase of quantitative survey data and sometimes a qualitative review of issues central to the objectives of the projects. The priority requirement of securing the support of decision makers and management for the objectives and planned actions is also often emphasized. The most frequently cited objectives are promotion of gender awareness at an individual and organizational level and changes in organizational settings.

Among the most significant and impactful actions mentioned are the integration of top-down and bottom-up approaches to create networks within universities in order to design and activate change in a gender-sensitive perspective (the STAGES[2] and TRIGGER[3] projects); the implementation of actions aimed at making decision making transparent, like gender budgeting[4] in the GENIS LAB[5] project, focused on the analysis and monitoring of how financial and time resources are distributed in the scientific organizations involved (assuming that allocations reflect power relationships); the integration of a gender perspective into research and curricula pursued by different projects; the analysis of resistance practices activated by organizations in relation to project initiatives aimed at introducing structural changes that might represent significant tools and processes for acquiring knowledge about and understanding of gender regimes and orders within the institutions involved (FESTA project[6]).

However, we can also identify issues that could limit the capacity of the organizations involved to produce profound, effective internal changes, in particular in light of the transformations that are now under way in scientific spheres as a result of the affirmation of a neoliberal agenda.

One of these can be identified in the same conditions under which the projects have been instituted and carried out. Strong pressures on universities to raise funds can represent a significant motive to participate in this kind of project, thus undermining the true willingness to produce structural changes and support policies and actions that are required for effectiveness and sustainability.

A second concern is the rationales sometimes used, both by the EU institutions and the funded projects, to argue for the need to rebalance the presence of women and men in scientific contexts, where a subtext emerges very similar to that used in the neoliberal debate: criteria such as competitiveness, success, and excellence are not necessarily critically described but they are identified as priorities, whereas equality is principally evaluated as a factor of productivity and efficacy rather than a right or a value as such (in the logic of the "business case"). In fact, in these discourses the principal framework of reference remains the one proposed by the neoliberal agenda, which is not disputed.

A third critical issue is the exclusive focus on STEM disciplines, which on one hand strengthens the perception of the centrality of these sectors within the current economic and research system, and on the other overshadows the overall impact of the ongoing changes also in more highly feminized sectors, like the social sciences and humanities (SSH), as well as the growing asymmetries between the two areas.

Moreover, a fourth critical issue is the scant attention paid to emerging work models in scientific organizations oriented to flexibility and fragmentation. Most of the projects concentrate on existing asymmetries in the scientific careers of women and men in permanent positions but tend to ignore the situations of the increasing numbers of individuals with temporary or precarious contracts—a phenomenon particularly important in the current scenario, all the more so from a gender perspective. One exception in this respect is the GARCIA[7] project focused on the early stages of academic and scientific careers and in particular on untenured researchers and their tenuous career prospects relating to differing gender regimes.

Research and change actions in the GARCIA project are undertaken at macro, meso, and micro levels in order to highlight the emergent criticalities that both STEM and SSH disciplines represent. The goals are to make the work of these researchers more visible within scientific organizations and counter the precariousness of their work and life experiences. The project pays particular attention to gender asymmetries and hopes to achieve concrete results including increased visibility for women researchers' work, management of the work-life balance, wider inclusion in welfare programs, and increased awareness and reflection about current evaluation/assessment processes.

Finally, it should be noted that in all such projects only cursory treatment is given to dimensions more closely associated with emotions and sexuality. For example, bullying and molestation remain common in academic institutions and indeed may be exacerbated by the vulnerabilities women have due to being in precarious positions. Furthermore, such issues are often made invisible by being treated as if they are individual, not organizational, in character. Questions connected with intersectionality, for example with regard to different race/ethnic, social class, age, and sexual orientation statuses, are also considered only cursorily if at all.

While the last group of projects of the 7th Framework program were still under way, 2014 saw the start of a new European program, Horizon 2020—Research and Innovation Framework Programme, which is in some respects significantly different from the previous ones. It is based in part on the results that have emerged from the projects already completed. It has among its declared objectives: (a) promoting equality in research groups; (b) promoting gender balance in decision making; and (c) integrating the gender dimension into research and innovations. The most important difference is that, in the new program, gender is treated as a cross-cutting issue from the mainstreaming perspective,[8] with the aim of integrating the gender dimension at each stage of the research cycle, in all activities where it may be relevant, from the research idea phase (generating gender-sensitive ideas and hypotheses), through the research proposal phase (formulating gender-sensitive research questions, selecting mixed teams of men and women, creating gender-equal working conditions), to the actual research phase (managing and monitoring gender equality, valuing women's and men's work equally), and to the dissemination phase (using gender impartial language and reporting data in gender-sensitive ways).

Applying Connell's Model to Academia

This chapter has considered the contribution of Connell's thought to gender studies with specific regard to education, in particular higher education and knowledge production contexts like universities. These institutions play a central role in Connell's research work and more generally in gender studies, because they are privileged contexts of gender production and reproduction (as well as possible deconstruction) of specific gender regimes that determine gender relationships both within organizations and in society at large.

Intervening in universities is particularly strategic for pursuit of a full institutional citizenship that "connects the project of inclusiveness to universities' core mission of advancing knowledge and preparing the future citizens and leaders of a different polity to address complex problems and entrenched injustices" (Sturm 2006, 250).

Over time, gender balances in educational institutions have changed as the number of women has increased significantly. Nevertheless, universities—and within them scientific faculties and departments—continue to be strongholds of men and masculinity/ies. Recent changes in the management models of educational institutions and the rise of neoliberal policies, with their emphasis on merit and the valorization of human capital, offer alternative scenarios than those of classical liberal discourse, based on women's exclusion and targeted on male networks and privileges. At the same time, they introduce values and practices that appear to lower the odds of gender equality improvements, such as the growing flexibilization and precarization of scientific careers, the affirmation of an individualistic and increasingly competitive model of scientific work, based on the idea of heroic masculinity and the request for a total and exclusive work commitment, without room for other aspects of social life.

In the foregoing pages, I focused on initiatives funded by the European Commission to tackle gender imbalances and support the presence of women in scientific research. In this section, I deepen this analysis in accord with Connell's "structural inventory" of the four main gender dimensions: power relations; production, consumption, and gendered accumulation; emotional relations; and symbolization. On a theoretical level, I try to systematize key issues emerging in the debate on the gender politics of higher education, and, on a political level, I propose a comprehensive rather than partial agenda for gender reform politics.

Power Relations

The rise of the neoliberal agenda in higher education has produced new power configurations. It has increased the power of central managers and academic administrators (rectors, deans, and heads of departments) and reduced that of teachers and students. It has generated an imbalance between the various curricula and disciplines (STEM vs. SSH) on the basis of their differing capacities to raise funds and generate profits. It has increased the amount of staff working on part-time and fixed-term contracts at or near the bottom of the organizations. The gender implications of these processes are manifest because women are largely underrepresented in dominant positions and in disciplines more tied to the market. Policies to counter the gender imbalance in higher education institutions should start from careful analysis of these processes and foresee rebalancing measures. Yet they should also support forms of collective decision making and the creation of new networks and communities. The experiences considered comprise analytical tools (such as gender budgeting) that move in this direction, although initiatives that effectively reallocate resources or foster participative management are still rare.

Production, Consumption, and Gendered Accumulation

The neoliberal production model has profound implications for the gender division of labor. It concerns not only the allocation of different roles and tasks within scientific organizations but also the structure of conditions that make scientific work possible. A growing emphasis on constant availability and total dedication to work involves an a priori division of labor, with one subject (usually the man) totally devoted to science and another (usually the woman) responsible for the domestic sphere. The division between production and reproduction is then metaphorically reiterated in how activities are allocated and valued within a scientific context. To counter structures of this type, it is necessary to conduct analyses of various asymmetries and their implications for development, valorization, and rebalancing measures. In the research projects to which I have referred, this was done through the analysis of data, processes, and policies. Yet this kind of work requires further effort, especially in light of various resistance measures. It is important to monitor how such projects are managed and whether project leaders are supported within an institution. Indeed, in a context of increasing cuts and financial difficulties, the risk to academic organizations of participating in these projects to raise funds, without a real commitment, is high. The risks could perhaps be reduced if the institutions were pressured by the funding entities to produce genuine change.

Emotional Relations

Emotions represent an area in need of action by projects designed to improve gender balance. Work intensification, the push for individualization, an intensely competitive climate, and an emphasis on evaluation typify scientific organizations within a neoliberal frame. These conditions are particularly problematic for academics and scientists in unstable jobs. Feelings of insecurity, precariousness, anxiety, and vulnerability characterize the experiences of many such people. Women are more subject to such pressures and risks for both structural and cultural reasons. Among the interventions that could be implemented to reduce these phenomena are activating spaces for scholarship, public dialogue, and discussion aimed at restoring relations of mutual cooperation and collegiality. Moreover, attention to bullying and sexual harassment is minimal to zero, despite concerns that these practices may be on the increase.

Symbolization

Gender symbolism is regularly used in academia to justify the different and dichotomous positions of men and women, for example, in distinctions between "hard" and "soft" data, mind and matter, reason and intuition, objectivity and subjectivity. A neoliberal paradigm introduces values and symbolic codes into scientific organizations that are laden with such gender implications. Representation of scientists as solitary heroes, associated with excellence, "performance," "ranking," "business," and "entrepreneurship," fosters a definition of scientific work as requiring men and masculinity/ies. In many projects reviewed here, little if any effort is made to deconstruct this kind of discourse. Indeed, in some cases neoliberal rhetoric of this sort is used to advocate for diversity in/ of management policies.

A case can be made that Connell's paradigm would be enriched by the construct of positioning or the discursive process whereby selves are located within cultural circulating discourses and narratives (Davies and Harré 1990). Considering the processes of subjectivation and positioning highlights the ways in which scientific organizations affect members' identities by encouraging a focus on performativity, competition, individualization and commodification. Focusing on these processes will allow us to observe the practices of adaptation or resistance implemented by individuals, men and women, toward the subject positions made available to them by the dominant discursive order.

Conclusion

Although it is impossible to provide a balance sheet for the effectiveness of gender equity projects funded in recent years by the EU Commission, I can highlight issues for readers to consider. Changing formal organizations and complex institutions such as the academy is difficult at best because it entails countering historical patterns and vested interests on the part of those in privileged positions who may passively resist or actively work against change. Universities are a relatively undisputed domain for men and hegemonic masculinity (see Messerschmidt and Messner, this volume). Thus, change toward greater gender equity is difficult in light of this gendered patterning and associated scientific practices. Neoliberalism also is difficult to counteract. The projects have paid the price of such difficulties and resistances, and their results may well fall short of their hoped for ends. Still, perhaps they will have raised awareness of gender issues and contribute to a climate that is more inclined to consider and implement change.

The choice by European institutions to move in the direction of *gender mainstreaming* entails both benefits and drawbacks.[9] On the one hand, this choice can be read as a response to the need to perform actions and interventions less directly focused on women yet that will take account of gender dynamics as they cross-cut the construction processes in science. Gender mainstreaming can be viewed as a strategy to remedy dissatisfaction and criticalities that have emerged from separate projects for women over the years and that will move even further in the direction of effective systemic and structural changes in scientific and academic institutions (Squires 2005). However, some critics of gender mainstreaming see it as a neoliberal reorganization strategy aimed at optimizing gender-specific human resources for the institution's welfare (including finances), thereby mooting its political potential (McRobbie 2009). According to these readings, gender mainstreaming risks becoming a technocratic exercise, implemented from the top down and realized through funded projects—reporting on actions and deliverables rather than producing sustainable changes in dominant gender regimes and orders. In this perspective, the strategy of gender mainstreaming blurs the issue of power in gender relations.

If gender mainstreaming and other gender equity approaches to academia are to avoid losing their transformative potential and become truly effective, constant attention must be paid to the processes and structures that regulate gender relations, as well as to changes generated by emerging structures whereby old inequalities are reinforced or new ones created relative to gender and other dimensions intertwined with it. Moreover, it will be necessary to maintain a balance between the different levels of intervention from the situated dimension of organizational micropractices to the system-wide implications of neoliberalism (Jeanes, Knights, and Martin 2011). Universities, Ferree and Zippel (2015, 562) claim, are "complex organizations for producing and reproducing knowledge as a form of power." They are arenas where different and often conflicting tensions coexist.

Connell's theory of gender provides a frame of reference that calls for a multidimensional reading of gender relations suited to understanding imbalances and dynamics in the academic world. It treats gender as a historically constituted relational structure that is in constant change, recognizes the probability of conflicts within each gender order and regime, and encourages attention to neoliberal as well as to other contextual influences on universities' practices and transformations. Interventions and actions aimed at fostering gender equality in higher education have necessarily to start from this awareness. They must avoid any shortcuts and temptations of celebration and demonization. Finally, they must acknowledge the existence of multiple narratives and discourses, each of which is rife with paradoxes and ambivalences and is situated within specific historical-political-cultural contexts. Without such awareness, the risk of meeting with failure and frustration seems assured.

NOTES

1 The website can be found at cordis.europa.eu.

2 STAGES—Structural Transformation to Achieve Gender Equality in Science—at www.stages.csmcd.ro.

3 TRIGGER—Transforming Institutions by Gendering Contents and Gaining Equality in Research—at www.fp7trigger.com.

4 Gender budgeting is an application of gender mainstreaming in the budgetary process. It means a gender-based assessment of budgets, incorporating a gender perspective at all levels of the budgetary process and restructuring revenues and expenditures in order to promote gender equality (Council of Europe 2010).

5 GENIS LAB—Gender in Science and Technology LAB—at www.genislab-fp7.eu.

6 FESTA—Female Empowerment in Science and Technology Academia—at www.festa-europa.eu.

7 GARCIA—Gendering the Academy and Research: Combating Career Instability and Asymmetry—at www.garciaproject.eu.

8 Gender mainstreaming is a strategy for promoting gender equality based on the integration of the gender perspective into every stage of policy processes.

9 Debates about the adoption by European institutions of this approach have focused on the conflicts between "gender equality" and "mainstreaming" and on the difference between transformation and integration. See Walby 2005; McGauran 2009.

REFERENCES

Bagilhole, B., and J. Goode. 2001. "The Contradiction of the Myth of Individual Merit and the Reality of a Patriarchal Support System in Academic Careers." *European Journal of Women's Studies* 8 (2): 161–180.

Barnett, R. 2003. *Beyond All Reason: Living with Ideology in the University*. Buckingham: Open University Press.

Bellavita, C. 1991. "The Public Administrator as Hero." *Administration & Society* 23 (2): 186–193.

Benschop, Y., and M. Brouns. 2003. "Crumbling Ivory Towers: Academic Organizing and Its Gender Effects." *Gender, Work and Organization* 10 (2): 194–212.

Blackmore, J., and J. Sachs. 2003. "Managing Equity in the Performative University." *Australian Feminist Studies* 18 (41): 141–162.

Blackwell, L., and J. Glover. 2008. "Women's Scientific Employment and Family Formation: A Longitudinal Perspective." *Gender, Work and Organization* 15 (6): 579–599.

Cassell, J., and H. Jenkins. 2000. *From Barbie to Mortal Combat: Gender and Computer Games*. Cambridge, MA: MIT Press.

Connell, R. 1982. *Making the Difference: School, Families and Social Division*. Sydney: Allen and Unwin.

———. 1987. *Gender and Power: Society, the Person and Sexual Politics*. Sydney: Allen and Unwin.

———. 1996. "Teaching the Boys: New Research on Masculinity, and Gender Strategies for Schools." *Teachers College Record* 98 (2): 206–235.

———. 2005. *Masculinities*. 2nd ed. Berkeley: University of California Press.

———. 2013. *Confronting Equality: Gender, Knowledge and Global Change*. Sydney: Allen and Unwin.

Connell, R. W., and R. Pearse. 2009. *Gender: In World Perspective*. Cambridge: Polity Press.

Council of Europe. 2010. "Parliamentary Assembly: Recommendation 1921 (2010)." Strasbourg.

Court, S., and G. Kinman. 2008. *Tackling Stress in Higher Education*. London: University and College Union.

Currie, J., P. Harris, and B. Thiele. 2000. "Sacrifices in Greedy Universities: Are They Gendered?" *Gender and Education* 12 (3): 269–291.

Davies, B., and R. Harré. 1990. "Positioning: The Discursive Production of Selves." *Journal for the Theory of Social Behavior* 20 (1): 43–63.

Dean, D. J., and A. Fleckenstein. 2007. "Keys to Success for Women in Science." In *Women and Minorities in Science, Technology, Engineering and Mathematics*, edited by R. J. Burke and M. C. Mattis, 28–46. Cheltenham: Edward Elgar.

De Welde, K., and A. Stepnick. 2014. *Disrupting the Culture of Silence: Confronting Gender Inequality and Making Change in Higher Education*. Sterling, VA: Stylus.

European Commission. 2009. *She Figures 2009: Statistics and Indicators on Gender Equality in Science*. Luxembourg: Publications Office of the European Union.

———. 2012. *Meta-analysis of Gender and Science Research*. Luxembourg: Publications Office of the European Union.

———. 2016. *She Figures 2015*. Brussels: Directorate General for Research and Innovation.

European Research Council. 2015. *Annual Report on the ERC Activities and Achievements in 2014.* Luxembourg: Publications Office of the European Union.

Ferree, M. M., and K. Zippel. 2015. "Gender Equality in the Age of Academic Capitalism: Cassandra and Pollyanna Interpret University Restructuring." *Social Politics* 22 (4): 561–584.

Gherardi, S. 2010. "Ways of Knowing: Gender as a Politics of Knowledge." In *Handbook of Gender, Work and Organization*, edited by E. Jeanes, D. Knights, and P. Y. Martin, 37–50. Chichester: Wiley and Sons.

Guiso, L., F. Monte, P. Sapienza, and L. Zingales. 2009. "Culture, Gender and Math." *Science* 320 (5880): 1164–1165.

Higher Education Statistics Agency. 2014. *Staff in Higher Education Institutions 2012/13.* Cheltenham: HESA.

Jeanes, E. L., D. Knights, and P. Y. Martin. 2011. "Editorial Introduction." *Handbook of Gender, Work and Organization.* Chichester: John Wiley and Sons.

Le Feuvre, N., ed. 2015. *Contextualizing Women's Academic Careers: Comparative Perspectives on Gender, Care and Employment Regimes in Seven European Countries.* Garcia Working Papers no. 1. Trento: University of Trento.

McGauran, A. M. 2009. "Gender Mainstreaming and the Public Policy Implementation Process: Round Pegs in Square Holes?" *Policy & Politics* 37 (2): 215–233.

McRobbie, A. 2009. *The Aftermath of Feminism: Gender, Culture and Social Change.* London: Sage.

Musselin, C. 2005. "European Academic Labour Markets in Transition." *Higher Education* 49: 135–154.

National Academies of Science, Committee on Science, Engineering, and Public Policy. 2007. *Beyond Bias and Barriers: Fulfilling the Potential of Women in Academic Science and Engineering.* Washington, DC: National Academies Press.

Risman, B. J., and T. Adkins. 2014. "The Goal of Gender Transformation in American Universities: Toward Social Justice for Women in the Academy." In *Social Justice and the University: Globalization, Human Rights and the Future of Democracy*, edited by J. Shefner, H. Dahms, R. E. Jones, and A. Jalata, 99–113. New York: Palgrave Macmillan.

Schunter-Kleemann, S., and D. Plehwe. 2006. "Gender Mainstreaming: Integrating Women into a Neoliberal Europe?" In *Neoliberal Hegemony: A Global Critique*, edited by D. Plehwe, B. Walpen, and G. Neunhöffer, 188–203. London: Routledge.

Squires, J. 2005. "Is Mainstreaming Transformative? Theorizing Mainstreaming in the Context of Diversity and Deliberation." *Social Politics* 12 (3): 366–388.

Sturm, S. 2006. "The Architecture of Inclusion: Advancing Workplace Equity in Higher Education." *Harvard Journal of Law and Gender* 29: 248–334.

Thornton, M. 2014. "The Changing Gender Regime in the Neoliberal Legal Academy." *Zeischrift für Rechtssoziologie* 33: 235–251.

Walby, S. 2005. "Gender Mainstreaming: Productive Tension in Theory and Practice." *Social Politics* 12 (3): 321–343.

Ward, M. 2000. "Gender and Promotion in the Academic Profession." *Scottish Journal of Political Economy* 48 (3): 283–302.

Ward, S. C. 2012. *Neoliberalism and the Global Restructuring of Knowledge and Education*. New York: Routledge.

Xie, Y., and K. A. Shaumann. 2003. *Women in Science: Career Processes and Outcomes*. Cambridge: Harvard University Press.

Ylijoki, O-H., and J. Ursin. 2013. "The Construction of Academic Identity in the Changes of Finnish Higher Education." *Studies in Higher Education* 38 (8): 1135–1149.

10

The Holy Grail of Organizational Change

Toward Gender Equality at Work

YVONNE BENSCHOP AND MARIEKE VAN DEN BRINK

After 30 years of feminist research and actions, we still have not reached the Holy Grail of gender equality at work. In this chapter, we theorize one of the major problems today: the slow progress toward gender equality in contemporary work organizations. Such a theory contributes to the general interdisciplinary field of gender studies, fitting in particular into the subfield of "gendered organizations," which is at the crossroads of (critical) management and organization studies and gender studies. Concepts such as gender regimes or inequality regimes have been helpful to understanding the systematic, overall pattern of interlocked practices and processes of gender, class, and race relations in organizations continuously producing inequalities (Acker 2006; Connell 2006). Yet the academic knowledge on how to make changes toward gender equality[1] in organizations has lagged seriously behind. This chapter sets out to contribute to the development of a feminist theory of change toward gender equality in organizations.[2]

We start by identifying the different actors involved in organizational change toward gender equality and their take on the subject. Several authors have hinted that the academic–practitioner divide hinders fruitful knowledge exchange and collaboration (Benschop and Verloo 2011; De Vries 2015; Kulik 2014). This divide between feminist research and activism is apparent in other fields such as violence against women and education. Yet in the context of organizations it seems that a rather strict division of labor occurred between the academy and practice, with practitioners in the mud of organizational change, academics in the ivory tower of analysis, and consultants running up and down the stairs to connect the two. These major players all seem to have their own perspectives on organizational change toward gender equality. As Connell (2006, 837) notes, "The way we think about gender is a key to the way we act on gender reform." We examine the local gender knowledge (Cavaghan 2012) of these different actors.

We argue that there is a politics to this local gender knowledge, in the sense that some bits of knowledge are seen as more legitimate and visible and carry more weight with decision makers on organizational change. This affects the progress of change and should be taken into account in any theory of change. These are the two core questions of our chapter: How do different key actors envision organizational change toward gender equality? How do their perspectives facilitate or hinder change toward gender equality in organizations? The answers to those questions relate to the politics of knowledge and contribute to a theory of change toward gender equality generally.

We distinguish between two groups of actors involved in creating knowledge for theory and the practice of change processes toward gender equality in organizations: academics theorizing organizational change and consultants researching and advising organizations to change. We note that of course the boundaries between these two perspectives are blurred and that there are academics who engage in consultancy and consultants who cross over to academia. In order to capture the local gender knowledge available, we analyze academic writings and consultancy reports on organizational change toward gender equality. We access the practitioner perspective in this chapter through the academic and consultancy publications about practices of change and the role of organizational change agents, such as diversity professionals, managers, ambassadors, or champions (Kirton, Greene, and Dean 2007). It is clearly beyond the scope of a single chapter to discuss all the local gender knowledge available. Therefore, we focus on three core issues that feature most prominently in current writings about organizational change toward gender equality and are presented as the crucial elements of any attempt to change. The first issue concerns the change of organizational cultures and structures. When thinking about changing gendered cultures and structures, specific issues arise around the commitment of top management (second issue) and the engagement of men in change efforts (third issue).

Short Note on Methodology

To provide a comprehensive and critical review of the literature on gender/diversity and organizational change, we conducted a series of searches using the Institute for Scientific Information's Web of Knowledge database. We used the following keywords in different combinations: organizational change, gender equality, diversity, inclusion, commitment, top management, leadership, champions, engaging men, men in gender equality, organizational culture change, structural change organizations. To cover books and book chapters as well, we additionally searched on Google Scholar with similar keywords. We refined our search to select material published in the period 1995–2015 because (a) an analysis of the first selection of publications showed a growing academic interest in changing organizations from 1995 onwards, and (b) similarly the data show that the year also corresponds to the time when diversity research started to proliferate in management studies (Özbilgin et al. 2011). The vast majority of the articles and book chapters we found documented and analyzed gender *inequalities* in various sectors of the labor market, from sports to the financial sector, and from health care to development. In contrast, we were looking for academic work that specifically and explicitly centered on instruments for or accounts of organizational *change* programs or projects on gender inequalities. We therefore only included academic publications that concern actual organizational change efforts toward gender equality, diversity, and inclusion. By going through these publications and their reference lists, we added publications that were considered relevant but that had not showed up in our initial search. The result is a vast array of publications on gender and change in organizations from different disciplines and perspectives.

For consultancy publications, we identified global consultancy firms that publish research and advice about gender equality change projects. Two such companies regularly report on gender equality: Catalyst and McKinsey, both originally from the United States but also active across the Western world. We searched their websites and publications to identify reports on strategies for creating inclusive cultures or workplaces, or both, including changing organizational cultures and ways to engage men in gender equality work. Our analysis begins with a review of the competing perspectives of academia and consultants regarding organizational change toward gender equality.

Changing Organizational Processes

The first key issue we discuss concerns the different perspectives of academics and consultants on changing organizational processes. For academics, the focus on organizational processes was a new alternative strategy for creating gender equality in organizations, differing from earlier approaches such as "fixing the women" and "valuing differences" (for an overview of approaches, see Ely and Meyerson 2000). Both are strategies focused on the individual that forget to target the organizational cultures and structures that reproduce the hierarchical valuing of gender difference in organizations (Meyerson and Kolb 2000; Zanoni et al. 2010). Acker (2006) was one of the pioneers arguing that organizations systematically produce inequality because organizational structures and cultures are not gender neutral. Ely and Meyerson (2000) argued that making the workplace more inclusive entails a postequity approach that changes core organizational processes, beliefs, cultures, routines, and structures. Changing these taken-for-granted organizational routines and practices attempts to undermine the roots of inequality by fundamentally altering the way work is defined, executed, and evaluated (Ely and Meyerson 2000). This approach advocated action research and close collaboration with organizational "change agents" to change gendered structures and cultures as the most effective way to enhance gender equality (Liff and Cameron 1997; Nentwich 2006). Little empirical work has been published on how exactly these organizational processes can be changed (Benschop et al. 2012; De Vries 2010), and which initiatives and practices have proven the most effective in different settings (Kalev, Dobbin, and Kelly 2006). The research that does exist mainly highlights the reasons for the limited success of change initiatives (Eriksson-Zetterquist and Styhre 2008; Liff and Cameron 1997).

Another strand of literature that focuses on changing organization processes stems from (critical) diversity studies and uses the concept of inclusion (Holvino, Ferdman, and Merrill-Sands 2004; Mor-Barak and Cherin 1998; Roberson 2006). Inclusion shifts attention to creating an organizational context in which everybody feels like an insider and "encompasses involvement, engagement, and the integration of diversity into organizational processes" (Roberson 2006, 228). These changes in organizational processes must lead to an inclusive culture in which employees must be able to both bring their "uniqueness" to work and have a feeling of belonging (Shore et al. 2011). Organizations that are inclusive involve employees in critical organizational processes such as decision making (Mor-Barak and Cherin 1998), encourage equal treatment of all employees, and simultaneously recognize and acknowledge individual differences (Zanoni and Janssens 2007). In line with the literature on organizational processes described above, work on inclusiveness has not yet yielded comprehensive knowledge about how to create such an inclusive culture. An exception is inductive identification of the organizational practices that foster the valuing of multiple competencies (uniqueness) and the ability to express multiple identities (belongingness), two key markers of inclusiveness (Janssens and Zanoni 2014).

All in all, the academic perspective on organizational change toward gender equality advocates transformational change of organizational structures and cultures. The core idea is that persistent inequalities and their underlying power processes can be changed only if organizational processes are transformed, because the interventions geared at changing individual employees or managers will leave the gendered system intact.

The emphasis on organizational processes, culture, and inclusiveness is also reflected in consultancy reports. Catalyst published a series of reports on inclusive workplaces and cultures (Catalyst 2015), introducing change models that are applied to member organizations. These models are based on literature on organizational change, but they hardly engage research from academic gender and diversity studies. As a consequence, these reports use the concept of inclusiveness and inclusion as key but fail to clarify what an inclusive culture entails. For instance, one report introduces a model for creating inclusive workplaces that includes leadership, change commitment, and developing a business case. This report builds on field-based insights about the effective management of change initiatives. However, no specific attention is paid to what inclusiveness entails.

McKinsey's *Women Matter* report (McKinsey 2015) focuses on gender equality at the top of corporations. A study of 1,400 managers from a wide range of companies worldwide points toward the need to create an "ecosystem" of measures including strong chief executive officer/top management commitment, human resource policies, development programs, and performance indicators on diversity. In addition, the report suggests that gaps in the corporate culture and mind-sets can be addressed by "inclusive programs" that can build awareness among men about the greater difficulties women face in reaching the top. These inclusiveness programs thus seem to be focused on bias training for men.

Summarizing, we observe that the perspective of consultants presents inclusive cultures in a positive light, primarily as good for business, and remains largely silent about gender inequalities and underlying power processes. Inclusiveness equates to women's participation at the decision-making table, a participation in business as usual without changing the gender order.

Creating inclusive workplaces and changing core organizational processes have been a dominant topic in both academic and consultancy literature. Both stress the need to change organizational practices and beliefs, such as leadership and cultural notions about the quality of employees. In the academic literature changes in practices and beliefs are needed to counter power inequalities; in consultancy publications, changes are geared to the realization of members' full human potential, ultimately providing competitive advantage to the employer. Neither academic nor consultancy publications have answers for how to accomplish these difficult change efforts, but consultancy reports have a more positive and instrumental tone of voice, and they propose models and stories to show that change is possible. This pattern may be related to the fact that consultancies' core business is selling advice to corporations. The need to sell advice limits the opportunities for profound critique or acknowledgment that change is difficult and multifaceted. Consultants may play down critique because it is risky to bite the hand that feeds. Also, an inclusive workplace, in the consultants' view, is a workplace with women participating in top management. Inclusion is thus restricted to giving women a boost up the ladder, leaving intact the ladder that hindered them in the first place (Cockburn 1989). Contradictorily, the academic literature targets that ladder, emphasizing the difficulties that arise when changing organizational processes, structures, and cultures. These studies have been critiqued for not being practically oriented and lacking guidelines on how to make organizations more gender equal (Benschop et al. 2012). Another striking difference is that consultants talk about the fashionable topic of inclusiveness but do not explicate what it is beyond mere participation. They hardly address "belonging" and "uniqueness," both of which are central to the academic notion of inclusion among diversity scholars.

Commitment from the Top

The second core issue is the commitment of top management. Turning to academic literature about organizational change generally and gender equality more specifically, the premise of the commitment of top management stands out. This commitment is seen as important not only because of symbolic effects but also because it increases the odds that equality actions are taken. The importance of top management support for diversity is highlighted in the diversity literature (DiTomaso and Hooijberg 1996, 169), but what this support entails is not elaborated.

The commitment of top management to gender equality, diversity, and inclusion is expected to lead to diversity practices and outcomes (Dansky et al. 2003; Leo and Barton 2006). Studies on the leadership of organizational change efforts point to leaders' responsibilities as shapers and framers of organizations and to their role as champions for equality and diversity in their organizations (Ng 2008). Van den Brink (2015) argues that, for successful gender interventions, leaders must prioritize gender equality, create a sense of urgency, provide financial and personnel resources, and display gender-aware leadership. Scholars also point to tensions between commitment and action. Some studies show that leaders may express positive attitudes toward gender equality as a principle but resist when it comes to concrete actions (Wahl and Holgersson 2003). This suggests that the commitment of top management to gender equality is not self-evident. Commitment may be only of a rhetorical nature, as it seems to be a challenge to engage leaders into action that goes beyond sloganism (Cox and Blake 1991), verbal and symbolic support (Holvino, Ferdman, and Merrill-Sands 2004), or lip service (Benschop 2000).

All in all, academic literature generally underlines the importance of commitment by top management for gender equality change. Yet, in most studies, leadership commitment is problematized, and no studies confirm that leadership is a success factor for change. This means that we need to develop more knowledge about how and when leadership makes a difference in gender equality change.

The claim that leadership is crucial can also be found in any consultancy report on gender equality. Both Catalyst and McKinsey frame the commitment of top management as a sine qua non condition for change to happen. The chief executive officer (CEO) is seen as the primary role model who must be involved for the rest of the organization to follow his/her example. Catalyst emphasizes a transformational leadership style in which leaders communicate about the vision, establish coalitions, empower the change agents, and negotiate conflicts. McKinsey stresses that senior executives need to tell stories, preferably personal and emotional ones, about their engagement, experiences, and beliefs about gender diversity to strengthen the case for diversity and to prompt more people commit to it. Interestingly, consultancy reports typically lack information about the concrete actions that top managers must take in order to act upon this commitment. They are vague about actions needed from leadership to advance gender equality. After all, any change project benefits from a transformational, visionary leader who sets a strategy, tells stories, and empowers the change agents. Two core issues are silenced in this nostalgic call for a strong leader. One is that men who care enough about gender equality to act upon it are as scarce as the men and masculinities literature on organizations illustrates (Collinson and Hearn 1994; Connell 1987; Martin 2001). The second is the naïveté of relying on a strong leader and a top-down approach to organizational change. The latter overestimates the relative power of a leader in multifaceted and complex organizational change processes.

Commitment from the top for organizational change toward gender equality is, in our view, an underresearched premise. Specification as to what this commitment of top management to gender and diversity change initiatives actually entails is lacking in both academia and consultancy. Furthermore, it is striking that the importance of commitment at the top is so readily and widely accepted when change projects are often initiated elsewhere. Unions, for instance, play a role in advancing gender equality in organizations through collective bargaining (Kirton and Healy 2013). Diversity networks and employee affinity groups in organizations are drivers for change (Dennissen, Benschop, and Van den Brink 2014). And, finally, some governments, notably Norway, en-force quota laws to increase the number of women in top management positions.

Engaging Men

The third issue in changing organizations is the engagement of men in gender equality initiatives. This relates to the issue of commitment at the top, as top managers tend to be men, but it goes beyond the top lay-ers of management to the involvement of all men. This issue has gained momentum in academic work, particularly in more recent years. Con-nell (2005, 1801) notes how gender equality was placed on the agenda of society, politics, and management by women, but stresses that men are necessarily involved in gender equality reform because widespread support from both women and men is required. Furthermore, current power relations have men in the control seat. As such, men act as gate-keepers for gender equality (Connell 2005, 1802) and as the purported drivers and champions of gender change (De Vries 2015). However, Wahl (2014) notes that male managers with basic levels of gender awareness do not necessarily "have the required competence, or will, actually to become change-agents and initiate organizational change" (143). Another rationale for engaging men reflects the belief that women who push for gender equality are biased and primarily self-interested, whereas men can do so from an impartial standpoint with only the best interest of the organization in mind (Van den Brink 2015). Ironically, this casts men as the more legitimate champions of gender equality and adds another layer to the marginalization of women. De Vries (2015) offers a more nuanced account, seeing two sides to this claim. On the one hand, the call for engaging men can be framed as a way to make gender change an organizational problem instead of a woman's problem, stressing the organization's responsibility and accountability for gen-der change in organizations. On the other hand, De Vries stresses that engaging men cannot be set apart from gendered notions of leadership that privilege men, notions that strengthen rather than undermine the gendered status quo. Her study of Australian executives championing a gender change process shows the complexities of gendered leadership of change in organizations.

The classic feminist adage that the master's tools will never dismantle the master's house (Lorde 2003) still features in the background of discussions of engaging men in gender equality changes. Yet reducing men to protectors of male privilege is a simplified representation of men's role in organizational change. It fails to do justice to their importance in successful change and the genuine engagement of some men in gender equality efforts (see, for instance, McKearney 2014), to the disadvantages men face in the gendered division of labor (Connell 2005), or to the perils of masculine stereotypes for men who do dangerous work when guided by macho masculinity norms (Ely and Meyerson 2010). Indeed, such categorical thinking obscures the profound differences between men and the multiplicity of masculinities (Collinson and Hearn 1994; Martin 2001), with some benefitting from the privileges and others bearing the costs of gender inequality and with some actively advocating and others actively resisting gender change. Several studies recognize and encourage strategic alliances between women and men as the way forward for gender change in their organizations (Benschop and Verloo 2006; Van den Brink and Benschop 2012).

Summarizing, the academic literature acknowledges the need to engage men in gender equality change. Academic visions differentiate between men and masculinities, differentiating between men who benefit and those who experience the disadvantages of gender inequality. It is the latter group that is expected to contribute to changing organizations.

Turning to the consultancy publications, we find similar arguments for engaging men, such as the mutual responsibility of women and men for gender equality change, and the leadership positions of men. McKinsey (2015) reports on how the low level of engagement of men, men's less favorable perceptions of women's leadership abilities, and men's skepticism about the value of diversity initiatives are important barriers to cultural change toward gender equality. They emphasize the necessity to move mind-sets, stating that "ultimately, what is good for women will also be good for men—and for corporations" (7), but without further substantiation. Catalyst has made the engagement of men a cornerstone of their activities, publishing multiple reports and tools on the subject of engaging men (Catalyst 2015). Their key arguments are that men are a largely untapped resource, and that male champions can be role models who influence other men who are not convinced of equality. The reports result from a hybrid collaboration between Catalyst researchers and gender studies academics, pairing scholarly research to consultancy advice. The research exposes restrictive masculine norms that affect men in organizations, identifies barriers (apathy, fear, ignorance) that prevent men from taking action, and offers ideas on how to raise men's awareness of gender inequality by defying some masculine norms, encouraging men to mentor women, and promoting a strong sense of fair play. Catalyst presents concrete actions men can take to create an inclusive workplace, and has developed a Diversity and Inclusion training program to increase men's gender awareness, examining what drives men's interest in training and the perceived effects of a specific training program on the attitudes and behavior of white men toward inclusion.

Summarizing, the consultants stress that men have to and can be engaged in gender equality work when they are made aware of the benefits that gender equality has for them. While some publications analyze masculine norms and inequalities, they remain largely silent about the loss of privilege that comes with the change.

Engaging men in gender equality change is thus a topic of debate in both the consultancy and scholarly literatures. Academics tend to acknowledge the legacies of feminism, the women's movement, and feminist scholarship that complicate men's involvement in gender equality change projects (Hearn 2014). In the consultancy publications we observe a preferred presentation of gender equality as a win-win project benefitting men as well as women and not as a zero-sum game that only women benefit from and men stand to lose. Further theorizing is necessary to substantiate these benefits for men, as changing inequalities inevitably calls for a redivision of power along gender lines, and thus some men will have to give up privileges. Simultaneously, the lack of progress on gender equality at work gives rise to the development of strategies to include men in gender change projects. Especially alluring is involving men in leadership positions to advance gender equality and move the project forward energetically. Of course new complexities and dilemmas develop around what De Vries (2015) calls the gendered nature of executive leadership for gender change and, more practically, around the gender awareness or lack thereof of the men who lead.

Facilitating or Hindering Change?

Now that we have analyzed the perspectives of the key actors on three core issues, we come to the second research question: How do the different perspectives facilitate or hinder change toward gender equality in organizations? Academics tend to focus on the persistent and systematic nature of gender inequality, and have little to say on how to change inequalities. As for the consultants' perspective, they have a lot to say about changing organizations, providing tools to change organizations to a certain extent, but without addressing the issues of power and inequality.

Our position is that organizational change toward gender equality is hindered by the politics of knowledge inherent in both perspectives. Politics drive academics to problematize organizational processes to build theoretical contributions. Theory gets them published in international A+ journals, often leading to inaccessible jargon that escapes practical significance (Sinclair 2004). Even with open access publishing on the rise, the focus on theoretical contributions is hindering dissemination among a wider nonacademic public. An incentive to bridge the gap to practice is lacking when academic survival depends on international top publications as an end in itself, and not as a means to create knowledge that can be used by change agents in organizations to make a difference. Kulik (2014) argues that academics fail to deliver on the knowledge needs of practitioners.

Consultants are also tied to their politics of knowledge, regulated by the neoliberal commercialism of the business market. They seek to be hired by the powers that be, and thus are immediately implicated in the management of the organizations they work for, even if they are presented as the outside innovators of business (Sturdy et al. 2009). Consultants refrain from drastic critique or measures. They need to keep their clients happy either as a matter of self-policing to secure the business relation, as a response to clients' refusal of all too critical measures, or as a form of impression management promoting their capability to make organizations change. Whereas scholars can boast academic independence, consultants need to produce palatable results, preferably in the form of practical toolkits, checklists, and in-step recipes.

We thus note that the knowledge in both perspectives is limited. The different goals of academia and consultancy hinder interchange and crossover between academic and consultancy knowledge. So, we are left with the question of whether a feminist theory of organizational change for gender equality calls for a critical dialogue between academics and consultants.

Conclusion

The goal of this chapter is to contribute to the development of a feminist theory of change toward gender equality in organizations. We have shown that current theories about changing organizations toward gender equality are hindered by the politics of knowledge among both academics and consultants. Academic research lacks tangible starting points to bring about change. Consultants sell positive stories about the possibilities for organizational change by providing clear-cut models and recipes. Yet their understanding of cultural change valorizes change accelerators and key milestones, but fails to specify what constitutes these accelerators and milestones for gender change. Since there is no one-size-fits-all change recipe for all organizations, theoretical work should be informed by situated knowledge from the inside of organizations. We thus argue that the knowledge from both groups of actors is necessary to develop a feminist theory that can actually be useful for changing gender regimes in organizations.

In order to ensure the mutual learning and collaboration of the different actors, we need to work with the politics of knowledge. Multiple perspectives are needed to grasp the complexity of change both theoretically and practically. For feminist academics, this means a more pronounced engagement with practical change agendas as well as with theoretical contributions. The work of feminist consultants would benefit from a more realistic perspective on nonlinear, messy, and complex change processes. Commitment to feminist principles may help to bridge the two perspectives, since they share the quest for the Holy Grail of gender equality. Because of these shared goals, we are optimistic about the opportunities for collaboration between feminist academics and feminist consultants. Action research projects provide a learning environment in which collaboration can thrive when both parties are willing to transcend their own perspectives, to be open to not-knowing, and to explore new roads to organizational change.

We conclude that a feminist theory of change needs to target organizational processes that reproduce gender inequalities, needs the commitment of top management, and the active engagement of both women and men. In Connell's terms, this means a change in the gender division of labor, in gender relations of power, and in gender culture and symbolism (Connell 2002). We concur with Connell (2005, 1819) who emphasizes the need for widespread social support for gender equality and wants to treat men systematically as agents in gender equality processes in organizations. After all, both women and men stand to gain from changing gender relations in hegemonic masculine cultures that can be dysfunctional and dangerous (Ely and Meyerson 2010). We have demonstrated that we currently are missing in-depth knowledge on the form of leadership required to realize this kind of gender change. The issue is preeminently an area for dialogue and collaboration between academics and consultants who are driven by a feminist agenda. They can collectively provide insights into the specificity of gender change processes in comparison to other change agendas. This will help us understand which strategies, interventions, and actions of leaders are needed and what dilemmas they encounter. We realize that overcoming the politics of knowledge is no easy endeavor, but one that just may set us on the right path to the Holy Grail.

NOTES

1 We define gender equality in organizations as the equal access of participants to power and control over goals, resources, outcomes, influence on decisions, opportunities, security and benefits, and pleasures (cf. Acker 2006).

2 We would like to thank the editors and especially Pat Martin for her thoughtful comments and suggestions to improve this chapter.

REFERENCES

Acker, J. 2006. Inequality regimes: Gender, class, and race in organizations. *Gender & Society* 20 (4): 441–464.

Benschop, Y. 2000. *Van lippendienst tot tegengas: Een kritische benadering van gender in organisatieverandering.* Nijmegen: Radboud Universiteit Nijmegen.

Benschop, Y., J. Mills, A. J. Mills, and J. Tienari. 2012. Editorial: Gendering change: The next step. *Gender, Work and Organization* 19 (1): 1–9.

Benschop, Y., and M. Verloo. 2006. Sisyphus' sisters: Can gender mainstreaming escape the genderedness of organizations? *Journal of Gender Studies* 15 (1): 19–33. doi:10.1080/09589230500486884.

———. 2011. Gender change, organizational change, and gender equality strategies. In *Handbook of gender, work and organization*, edited by E. Jeanes, D. Knights, and P. Y. Martin. London: Wiley-Blackwell.

Catalyst. 2015. Engaging men in gender initiatives. Accessed 15 November 2015. www.catalyst.org.

Cavaghan, R. 2012. Gender mainstreaming as a knowledge process: Towards an understanding of perpetuation and change in gender blindness and gender bias. PhD diss., University of Edinburgh, Edinburgh.

Cockburn, C. 1989. Equality: The long and short agenda. *Industrial Relations Journal* (Autumn): 213–225.

Collinson, D., and J. Hearn. 1994. Naming men as men: Implications for work, organization and management. *Gender, Work and Organization* 1 (1): 2–22.

Connell, R. W. 1987. *Gender and power: Society, the person and sexual politics*. Redwood City, CA: Stanford University Press.

———. 2002. *Gender*. Cambridge: Polity Press.

———. 2005. Change among the gatekeepers: Men, masculinities, and gender equality in the global arena. *Signs* 40 (1): 1801–1825.

———. 2006. The experience of gender change in public sector organizations. *Gender, Work and Organization* 13 (5): 435–452.

Cox, T. H., and S. Blake. 1991. Managing cultural diversity: Implications for organizational competitiveness. *Academy of Management Executive* 5 (3): 45–56.

Dansky, K. H., R. Weech-Maldonado, G. De Souza, and J. L. Dreachslin. 2003. Organizational strategy and diversity management: Diversity-sensitive orientation as a moderating influence. *Health Care Management Review* 28 (3): 243–253.

De Vries, J. 2010. *A realistic agenda? Women only programs as strategic interventions for building gender equitable workplaces*. Perth: University of Western Australia.

———. 2015. Champions of gender equality: Female and male executives as leaders of gender change. *Equality, Diversity and Inclusion: An International Journal* 34 (1): 21–36.

Dennissen, M., Y. Benschop, and M. Van den Brink. 2014. *Diversity networks: Networking for equality?* Paper presented at the European Group for Organizational Studies, Rotterdam, July 3–5.

DiTomaso, N., and R. Hooijberg. 1996. Diversity and the demands of leadership. *Leadership Quarterly* 7 (2): 163–187.

Ely, R. J., and D. E. Meyerson. 2000. Advancing gender equity in organizations: The challenge and importance of maintaining a gender narrative. *Organization* 7 (4): 589–608.

———. 2010. An organizational approach to undoing gender: The unlikely case of offshore oil platforms. *Research in Organizational Behavior* 30: 3–34.

Eriksson-Zetterquist, U., and A. Styhre. 2008. Overcoming the glass barriers: Reflection and action in the "Women to the Top" programme. *Gender, Work and Organization* 15 (2): 133–160.

Hearn, J. 2014. Introduction: International studies on men, masculinities, and gender equality. *Men and Masculinities* 17 (5): 455–466.

Holvino, E., B. Ferdman, and D. Merrill-Sands. 2004. Creating and sustaining diversity and inclusion in organizations: Strategies and approaches. In *The psychology and management of workplace diversity*, edited by M. S. Stockdale and F. J. Crosby, 245–276. Malden, MA: Blackwell.

Janssens, M., and P. Zanoni. 2014. Alternative diversity management: Organizational practices fostering ethnic equality at work. *Scandinavian Journal of Management* 30 (3): 317–331.

Kalev, A., F. Dobbin, and E. Kelly. 2006. Best practices or best guesses? Assessing the efficacy of corporate affirmative action and diversity policies. *American Sociological Review* 71 (4): 589–617.

Kirton, G., A. M. Greene, and D. Dean. 2007. British diversity professionals as change agents—radicals, tempered radicals or liberal reformers? *International Journal of Human Resource Management* 18 (11): 1979–1994. doi:10.1080/09585190701638226.

Kirton, G., and G. Healy. 2013. Commitment and collective identity of long-term union participation: The case of women union leaders in the UK and USA. *Work, Employment & Society* 27 (2): 195–212.

Kulik, C. T. 2014. Working below and above the line: The research–practice gap in diversity management. *Human Resource Management Journal* 24 (2): 129–144.

Leo, E., and L. Barton. 2006. Inclusion, diversity and leadership perspectives, possibilities and contradictions. *Educational Management Administration & Leadership* 34 (2): 167–180.

Liff, S., and I. Cameron. 1997. Changing equality cultures to move beyond "women's problems." *Gender, Work and Organization* 4 (1): 35–46.

Lorde, A. 2003. The master's tools will never dismantle the master's house. In *Feminist postcolonial theory: A reader*, edited by Reina Lewis and Sara Mills, 25–29. London: Routledge.

Martin, P. Y. 2001. "Mobilizing masculinities": Women's experiences of men at work. *Organization* 8 (4): 587–618.

McKearney, A. 2014. Critical reflections from men in the field. *Equality, Diversity and Inclusion: An International Journal* 33 (5): 406–413.

McKinsey. 2015. *Women matter*. Accessed 15 November 2015. www.mckinsey.com.

Meyerson, D. E., and D. M. Kolb. 2000. Moving out of the "armchair": Developing a framework to bridge the gap between feminist theory and practice. *Organization* 7 (4): 553–571.

Mor-Barak, M., and D. A. Cherin. 1998. A tool to expand organizational understanding of workforce diversity: Exploring a measure of inclusion-exclusion. *Administration in Social Work* 22 (1): 47–64.

Nentwich, J. C. 2006. Changing gender: The discursive construction of equal opportunities. *Gender, Work and Organization* 13 (6): 499–521.

Ng, E. 2008. Why organizations choose to manage diversity? Toward a leadership-based theoretical framework. *Human Resource Development Review* 7 (1): 58–78.

Özbilgin, M., T. Beauregard, A. Tatli, and M. Bell. 2011. Work-life, diversity and inter-sectionality: A critical review and research agenda. *International Journal of Management Reviews* 13 (2): 177–198.

Roberson, Q. M. 2006. Disentangling the meanings of diversity and inclusion in organizations. *Group & Organization Management* 31 (2): 212.

Shore, L. M., A. E. Randel, B. G. Chung, M. A. Dean, K. H. Ehrhart, and G. Singh. 2011. Inclusion and diversity in work groups: A review and model for future research. *Journal of Management* 37 (4): 1262–1289. doi:10.1177/0149206310385943.

Sinclair, A. 2004. Journey around leadership. *Discourse: Studies in the Cultural Politics of Education* 25 (1): 7–19.

Sturdy, A., T. Clark, R. Fincham, and K. Handley. 2009. Between innovation and legitimation—boundaries and knowledge flow in management consultancy. *Organization* 16 (5): 627–653.

Van den Brink, M. 2015. The politics of knowledge: The responses to feminist research from academic leaders. *Equality, Diversity and Inclusion: An International Journal* 34 (6): 483–495.

Van den Brink, M., and Y. Benschop. 2012. Gender practices in the construction of academic excellence: Sheep with five legs. *Organization* 19 (4): 507–524.

Wahl, A. 2014. Male managers challenging and reinforcing the male norm in management. *NORA–Nordic Journal of Feminist and Gender Research* 22 (2): 131–146.

Wahl, A., and C. Holgersson. 2003. Male managers' reactions to gender diversity activities in organizations. In *Individual diversity and psychology in organizations*, edited by M. Davidson and S. Fielden, 313–330. Chichester: Wiley.

Zanoni, P., and M. Janssens. 2007. Minority employees engaging with (diversity) management: An analysis of control, agency, and micro-emancipation. *Journal of Management Studies* 44 (8): 1371–1397.

Zanoni, P., M. Janssens, Y. Benschop, and S. Nkomo. 2010. Unpacking diversity, grasping inequality: Rethinking difference through critical perspectives. *Organization* 17 (1): 9–29. doi:10.1177/1350508409350344.

PART IV

Dynamics of Masculinities

The chapters in this section concentrate on masculinities—and demonstrate how far research on this topic has traveled in the past thirty years. In the first chapter, Kopano Ratele argues that since all practices are embedded with past traditions and all traditions are gendered, masculinities scholars should not, as they often do, equate "traditional masculinity" with patriarchy and domination. Specifically, Ratele critically assesses the notion of tradition for men in societies that were formerly colonized and now are subject to globalization forces that are "modernizing" masculinity conceptions. Colonization and globalization have placed African men under multiple pressures that affect their relationship to community culture and practices. The issue is dramatized by the life and death of Nelson Mandela, who valued deep ties to his community of origin but faced very different demands in the world of national and international politics. Ratele advises viewing tradition as an open question, not as a given, and concludes that traditions in masculinity are multiple, uncertain, and contestable.

The second chapter, by Gul Ozyegin, reassesses the place of *patriarchy* in gender theory. Ozyegin investigates this through new and emerging masculine practices, focusing on the "unpatriarchal desires" of young adult Turkish men who publicly disavow patriarchy while in practice constructing unequal gender relations—reproducing a masculine-patriarchy nexus in new ways. Ozyegin reports a case study of a young couple—Oktay is the man, Sezen the woman—to explore how patriarchal values associated with "protecting" a woman operate in a new context. Oktay wants a "modern" young woman but he also wants Sezen to subordinate her interests (and time) to his. The existence of patriarchy in a society where legally women and men have equal legal rights causes dilemmas for young men like Oktay. Ozyegin's conclusion is that Sezen has undergone liberation in her life options while Oktay has garnered conflict and confusion in his.

A third chapter by Tristan Bridges and C. J. Pascoe takes the idea of newly emerging masculinities a step further (this time in the global North) by examining the meanings of contemporary transformations of masculinity. Bridges and Pascoe explore how distinct *hybrid masculinities* both accomplish and obscure gender inequality and how they can be understood through Connell's notion of "symbolic relations." They ask if nonhegemonic masculinities are truly on the increase, thus creating a chink in men's privileges relative to women's. The answer is no: the emergence of hybrid masculinities is not a sign of improving gender equality. The apparent loosening of masculinity norms, rules, and policing that hybrid masculinities are said to offer is primarily an increase in flexibility for privileged white men (and boys). They add options for how these men can act and show that they are "being men." They do not challenge hegemonic masculinity as we know it nor the gender system that exploits and subordinates women as well as gay and racial minority men. Bridges and Pascoe call into question any assertions that hegemonic masculinity is on the decline.

11

Concerning Tradition in Studies on Men and Masculinities in Ex-Colonies

KOPANO RATELE

Following his death on December 2013, the first president of postapartheid South Africa was laid to rest in Qunu, the Eastern Cape Province, where he had spent part of his boyhood. Nelson Rolihlahla Mandela's passing generated massive international coverage. Messages of condolence and support for his family, his comrades in the African National Congress (ANC), and the country over which he governed came from all over the world. Many of the world's premiers came to honor him for his statesmanship. International and local celebrities paid homage to his acts as a man who forgave his white oppressors. His personal development and political leadership in moving blacks and whites toward reconciliation were liberally praised in global and local media.

The numerous well-deserved tributes notwithstanding, some observers reminded us of the many turns, contradictions, and dilemmas that characterized the man's life. Among these was that Mandela was born of the royal house of abaThembu people in rural Eastern Cape where he herded cattle as a boy, grew up into a radical African nationalist who at one stage took up armed struggle, served a very long prison term for his political beliefs, and became a globally recognized icon of peace and forgiveness. Given where he came from, a turn that Mandela had to negotiate relatively early in his life was that he could have become a chief among the abaThembu but was pulled toward the pursuit of national liberation. Another noteworthy contradiction was the apparent tug between self and group in Mandela's life, between being a charismatic personality and a dedicated member of the groups to which he belonged (e.g., the ANC and abaThembu).

While these slices of Mandela's life reference aspects of tradition, the dilemmas of interest in this chapter are those that signal moments where *cultural* traditions knock against other social forces and institutions.[1] An example is when the command of a king bumps up against the laws of the state, or when a practice seen as part of tradition (such as the practice of *ukuthwala*, meaning heterosexual marriage via abduction among some Nguni communities) runs afoul of the law of a country. When Mandela died, then, a question that had to be answered was how he would be buried: according to the customs of the abaThembu royal house, or would he be given a state funeral (Ndeze 2013)? The key dilemma analyzed in this chapter is how to understand tradition and men's genders in ways that are not alienating to one's tradition or to one's commitment to the ideals of men's equality with women.

The notion of tradition attaches itself to various phenomena, including family, politics, gender, and theory. All traditions are, however, ultimately about something handed down from previous generations (e.g., parents, teachers, theories), a sense of belonging (to a place or group), a shared continuity of experience (what does it mean to be a man or woman among abaThembu?). Defined as a historical discursive and material resource, tradition is key (like nationality, race, or religion, for example) to a sense of belonging and experience from which members of a group draw to apprehend the present, past, and future. Crisply captured in the Sesotho language, *setso* (meaning where things or people come from), tradition is indicative of not only extraindividual experience as a symbolic resource but of temporality too (Glassie 1995). Speaking of Sesotho, language is, to be sure, a vital part of tradition, and therefore vital in fully understanding traditions. The focus here is on *cultural* sorts of traditions, how they are considered in theories, research, and activism around men and masculinities. By masculinities, following Connell and Messerschmidt (2005, 836), is meant "configurations of practice that are accomplished in social action and, therefore, can differ according to the gender relations in a particular social setting."

The fascinating thing about using Mandela as an example of the conceptual question at the center of the chapter is precisely that, in contradistinction with a figure such as Jacob Gedleyihlekisa Zuma, the fourth president of democratic South Africa, the former seemed to have found answers to the apparent tensions raised by his pride in his traditional Thembu customs and his role as a president of a multiracial/cultural country that constitutionally upholds equal rights on the basis of, among others, race, belief, gender, and sexuality (Ratele 2013). Working through such dilemmas might be productive in efforts toward a situated *and* dynamic appreciation of traditions in studies on men and masculinities— not as more primary than race, class, religion, sexuality, or age, but as one other vital social force that is co-constitutive with gender. Mandela's apparent reconciliation of the predicaments between "the traditional" and modern constitutionalism notwithstanding, the chapter proposes that such tradition-inscribed dilemmas were never fully worked out in his life and thus returned to haunt the man at the end. More abstractly, it is contended that such predicaments are not restricted to men and women who are born outside major cities of the world—the cities usually (self-)identified as modern or postmodern—even though they may be magnified in the lives of subjects who have experienced colonial disruptions of the continuity of their "traditional" social structures, relations, desires, and identities. "Colonial disruptions" signal colonization and coloniality. A product of the conquest of the native by the colonizer, colonialism refers to a situation whereby one national or subnational group is economically, politically, and culturally dominated and exploited by another (Bulhan 2015; Ndlovu-Gatsheni 2007). As relations that emerge from a specific period in history yet outlast it, coloniality "refers to long-standing patterns of power that emerged as a result of colonialism, but that define culture, labour, intersubjective relations, and knowledge production well beyond the strict limits of colonial administrations" (Maldonado-Torres 2007, 243; see also Quijano 2000).

Although he is not a gender scholar, Paulin Hountondji's work (1983, 2000) has been useful for situating an engagement with tradition as part of a larger critique of the global neoliberal structures of knowledge-making, including the international division of intellectual labor whereby the global South produces raw data and the global North produces concepts (see Connell 2014b). Regarding *cultural* tradition per se, Hountondji's intervention is useful in challenging dominant thought and prevalent studies on tradition. He has suggested that when we take on the task of analyzing the meanings of tradition in play, we must always begin by resisting the temptation of instinctive justification but also that of irrational contempt. The latter temptation he refers to as cultural imperialism based on first-order ethnocentrism, most visible in a sense of superiority in Western traditions cultivated by scholars, writers, artists, journalists, and ideologists, evident in Euro/American-centrism. The former temptation he calls cultural nationalism, an unreflective re-action to the historical inferiorization and persistent marginalization of cultures by Euro/American powers and Western hegemonies. This temptation takes the form of excessive identification with one's own cul-ture. Hountondji (2000, 6) advises ridding ourselves of "the obsession of the Other and develop again a free and critical relationship to our own cultures."

Another theorist useful in approaching tradition is Sabelo Ndlovu-Gatsheni (2013), whose work draws on the critical coloniality "school." He illuminates how coloniality has been constitutive of what he calls "post-colonial neocolonised" African cultural and gender relations and thought. Anibal Quijano (2007), who is central to this school, has pos-ited that while European cultural colonization was not as destructive in Africa as it was in Latin America, it was intensive, delegitimating, and oppressive over African cultures and modes of knowing and producing knowledge.

Part of the answer to neo/postcolonial African cultural and gen-der relations is to develop dynamically situated anti/post/decolonial theories of culture and gender. By this is meant theories and tools to analyze gender that take full recognition of the colonial disruption and the persistence of the ongoing coloniality of cultural and subjective realities; theories and tools that begin from the concession of the inter-ruption of the continuity of some men's and women's lived experiences and sense of belonging by colonial invasion as well as the durability of that interruption (see also Césaire 1972; Fanon 1965). Tools and theo-ries like these, focused on African realities, are not abundant. How-ever, there are useful existing elements. I think, for example, that a theory that offers a grip on the interweaving of personal life and social structure, such as that of Connell (1987)—in particular the notions of gender as a social practice and hegemonic masculinity—is very help-ful. For gender thought centered on neo/postcolonial African social realities, however, we need other elements—for example, gender-critical work on African masculinities (e.g., Morrell 1998), and work on women that contests Western feminist thought (e.g., Amadiume 1987; Oyěwùmí 1997).

This chapter does not attempt to analyze the relationship of tradition to masculinity in Mandela's own life. Neither does it dwell on the subject of gender within the traditions of abaThembu. Instead, the chapter engages in further reflections (see Everitt-Penhale and Ratele 2015; Ratele 2013) on the entanglement of masculinity and tradition as signaled in discourses such as those by Mbanjwa, Ngcukana, and Ndlangisa (2013). The seeming shifts and paradoxes that featured in Mandela's life, and his relationships as an individual with his *political* vis-à-vis his cultural traditions, are of interest because they appear to confirm the finding that lived experiences of masculinities are characterized by multiplicity and change, but also because they suggest that the relationship of individual men to traditions can be dynamic and complex. On this basis, a number of proposals are made in this chapter. A reconsideration of the notion that there is a special category of men and masculinity (and women and femininity) to be referred to as traditional men or traditional masculinity (traditional women or femininity) is warranted. A need exists to consider the significance of tradition in the constitution of masculinities, but chiefly of men's and women's practices in former colonies and neocolonies. We have to admit that all gender practices have traditions, and all traditions embed implicit or explicit gender theories. And all concepts used to understand men and women and their relations emerge out of particular cultures. Therefore, there is enormous need to undertake theoretical and empirical work to undo the misrecognition of the traditional evident in a broad swath of scholarship on men (cf., e.g., Levant et al. 1992; Mahalik et al. 2003), particularly subjects from the former European colonies where tradition can be one of the bulwarks against contemporary Western Euro-American economic and cultural colonization (see Quijano 2007).

This chapter seeks to carve out a clearer position for tradition within the field of men. The first section stays with one of Mandela's apparent dilemmas. Next I point out a need to cultivate space for the concept of tradition within critical studies on men. I then suggest that tradition is a body of beliefs with associated acts that have to be thought of as a resource. In that section I consider how, instead of misreading "the traditional" (as in the concept of "traditional men"), what's missing is thinking on time—how time, generation, or history, are imperative in considering tradition in studies of men in neo/postcolonial societies.

Mandela's Dilemma

A starting point into the key dilemma at the center of the chapter and apparently inscribed into Mandela's struggles is something noted by Mbanjwa, Ngcukana, and Ndlangisa (2013). These journalists were reporting on events surrounding the journey of Mandela's body toward its final resting place in Qunu. The newspaper article itself is a study of the multiple ties, identities, roles, and affiliations that defined Mandela. From a critical masculinities perspective one sentence was striking in conveying the dilemma at issue: "As only male relatives can accompany the plane according to abaThembu tradition, his grandsons[2] Mandla, Ndaba and Zondwa Mandela travelled with the body" (n.p.). Immediately, a gender-critical question about tradition pressed itself upon us: Why can't females accompany the body of the deceased?

Others followed. Why do abaThembu send members of their group who die elsewhere back "home"? Given the colonial and apartheid damage of African families and communities in South Africa and the scattering of people around the world, where is home and who decides? Does the custom apply to all the abaThembu or only to men born into royalty?

Intentional or not, the effect of that sentence was not only to provoke questions on gender and tradition. It also suggested that the customary practice of male relatives being able to accompany bodies of deceased was unchanged, absolute.

In the case of Zuma, he, the presidency, or the ruling party has had to recant, explain, or apologize for his views on women and gays that undermine the Constitution and specific laws on equality and nondiscrimination.[3] In contrast to Zuma, Mandela appeared to have worked out the apparent dilemma that emerges when one takes pride in cultural traditions but also leads a modern multicultural polity that guarantees gender and sexual rights (Republic of South Africa 1996). Yet Mandela had not fully resolved the dilemma between his devotion to political liberation, in particular the liberation of women, and his obvious fondness toward his boyhood traditional customs, as is apparent in his acclaimed autobiography, *Long Walk to Freedom*. In the early part of the book Mandela reflects on his childhood growing up among the Xhosas:

> My life, and that of most Xhosas at the time, was shaped by custom, ritual and taboo. This was the alpha and omega of our existence and went unquestioned. Men followed the path laid out for them by their fathers; women led the same lives as their mothers before them. Without being told, I soon assimilated the elaborate rules that governed the relations between men and women. (Mandela 1994, 13)

The insinuation in this extract is that the singular path followed by most Xhosa men or women was fixed, that the rules that govern gender relations were unquestioned. In Xhosa tradition, men follow(ed) the path of the fathers and women that of their mothers. Mandela assimilated the rules of how to be a Xhosa man. Yet the point of this narrative is that Mandela would question. He became something other than what custom intended. He was a different man—although it can be argued that it was because he left the village for the city, even if he remained Xhosa.

Mandela misconstrued tradition, understanding it in too deterministic a way. Some boys do/did not follow their fathers, and some girls do/did not lead the same lives as their mothers. Even in villages where life is slow to change, there is always a questioning both of custom and the gender order (Connell 1987). While he nursed a fondness for his childhood, Mandela sets up custom, ritual, taboo, and rules to make up a straw man against somewhere else where subjects question and change is commonplace. More crucially, Mandela misreads how gender arises from a given cultural tradition and in turn shapes tradition. To change cultural tradition requires a study of how men and women are defined and relate to each other within that tradition. To achieve fundamental change in gender relations demands an inquiry into traditions.

Other moments that indicate that Mandela misread tradition appear throughout the book and his documented life. Zolani Ngwane (2014) has remarked that the contestation of Mandela's divorce from Winnie Madikizela-Mandela, his second wife, was on the grounds that the husband had neglected abaThembu custom whereby tribal elders should have been asked to mediate the dispute between wife and husband. In his response during the trial, Mandela said: "I respect custom, but I am not a tribalist. I fought as an African nationalist and I have no commitment to the custom of any particular tribe" (Ngwane 2014, 115). Ngwane sees Mandela's words as indicative of his ambivalent attitude toward tradition. Certainly, but it is tradition in relation to something else: African nationalism, global politics, relations between women and men. For instance, Mandela's ambivalence crops up from not having fully worked out the relation between one's (anti)"tribalist"[4] sentiments and pronationalist commitments. In other cases the contradiction might emerge from not having worked out the relationship between "traditionalist" family relations and egalitarian masculinities.

It would be inaccurate to consider these instances from Mandela's life as expressive of a prototypical member of abaThembu, even though he would have been a chief had his father not been deposed by the colonial administration, or as an expression of hegemonic masculinity among abaThembu men, postcolonial African political leaders, or black men. The dilemma reveals the difficulty of fully grasping constructions of masculinity outside of traditions.

Awareness about the place of cultural processes also clarifies how Mandela, or some African political leaders, could be powerful without embodying hegemonic masculinity in their nation. "Constructed in relation to women and to subordinated masculinities," hegemonic masculinity refers here to "the cultural ideal (or ideals) of masculinity," as Connell (1987, 186 and 184) observed. She also stated that although hegemony does not preclude force, a masculinity achieves a hegemonic social position that reaches "into the organization of private life and cultural processes" (Connell 1987, 184). The choice of *culture* by Connell seems significant. At various places in *Gender and Power* there is awareness of the cultural locatedness and limits of Western gender theory. For instance, Connell contends:

Social scientific theories of gender are a Western invention, as far as I know, and definitely a modern one. Other civilisations have had their own ways of dealing with human sexuality and the relations between the sexes. As Indian eroticism and Chinese family codes illustrate, these can be as sophisticated and elaborate as anything the West has created. But they are different kinds of cultural formation. (1987, 24)

And she adds: "When relations between cultural elements change, new conditions for practice are created and new patterns of practice become possible" (ibid., 289).

An analysis of Mandela's gender ideas and cultural politics would certainly be interesting as he offers—in a context of cultural change—a potentially different model of manhood and cultural subjectivity, particularly as he was a politically powerful man. There are also several moments in his (auto)biography that illustrate this constant movement in and out of psycho-discursive practices of "traditional," "modern," powerful, and marginal masculinity (Wetherell 2008; Wetherell and Edley 1999). What I wish to stress is that Mandela was mistaken in his notion about the indisputability of custom, ritual, and taboo, and his incorrect analysis of the relation between tradition and gender was based on his ambivalent refusal to engage tradition. As Ngwane (2014) contended, "Like most intellectuals, Mandela believed he could patronise or pay tribute to tradition (by engaging an *imbongi*, paying *lobola* or hosting a ritual slaughtering) while retaining his independence from its precepts." In short, the notion that the traditional is never questioned misrecognizes the social, political, and ideological character of tradition.

The dilemma of abaThembu custom pitted against nationalism may be particular to Mandela; however, the general outline of the predicament, where local beliefs, ideas, or practices come up against globally powerful ones, is widely observable. The challenge is to think of tradition in the light of gender theory and gender as a constitutive element of culture.

Clearing a Space for the Concept of Tradition in Critical Studies on Men

Debates on the concept of tradition in discipines such as anthropology, folklore studies, and cognate disciplines have been extensive, and it would be difficult to present a comprehensive review of the literature (e.g., Ben-Amos 1984; Handler and Linnekin 1984; Gusfield 1967; Soares 1997). In research on masculinities, tradition usually turns up as a term to distinguish some men/women and masculinities/femininities from "others"—in terms such as "traditional men/women" and "traditional masculinity/femininity" (see Carrigan, Connell, and Lee 1985). Pierrette

Hondagneu-Sotelo and Michael Messner (1994, 200) noted that in the context of the university classes they teach in the United States, classes populated mainly by white and upper-middle-class students, traditional men would be "black men, Latino men, immigrant men, and working-class men." In a global context, the "others" include men in the global South, homeless men, and rural men. It is crucial to also note that the figure of the "traditional man" is not just used by students and nonresearchers but is also common among masculinity researchers (Everitt-Penhale and Ratele 2015). Whether in everyday conversation or academic spaces, the injudicious use of concepts like traditional men, and opposing it to modern or new men, tends to misrepresent gender realities and ignore men's structural positions (Hondagneu-Sotelo and Messner 1994). Clearly, there is a need to clear space for and bring new insights about tradition onto the field of men, so that we may ask questions such as can "traditional men" mobilize against gender-based violence, and, vice versa, can egalitarian men like tradition?

Tradition is fascinating precisely because within the body of work on men, even though commonly alluded to, it is less common to find work that theorizes the concept (Santaularia 2010). Several reasons may underpin the lack of engagment with the concept of tradition in studies of men (Everitt-Penhale and Ratele 2015). Among these is a tendency to interpret the concept to refer to mere factitiousness or convention. Too often, to cherish tradition is conflated with a lack of critical thought. Often identifying with tradition is confounded with authoritarianism and conservatism. Although conservatism and authoritarianism can be a feature of traditionalism, they do not exhaust tradition.

With regard to gender theory on men in former colonial contexts, because conservative patriarchal traditions of the colonized had been appropriated by the colonizers as a key apparatus "to rationalise domination by a minority over the rest of the population and thereby to justify social control through a variety of political and directly coercive institutions" (Spiegel 1989, 49), scholarship on men's gender practices has largely disregarded contestations within traditions (but see Walker 1994, 2013).

Where people identify themselves with the dominant form of globalized Western modernity, traditions tend to be treated as what "others" have. Conversely, in some parts of the world where there is a strong identification with tradition as a bulwark, tradition as what "we" have. Yet all men and women have a past, as Edward Shils (1971) said about all things. And, even while he cast it aside, Foucault (2002, 23) observed that "tradition enables us to locate the new against a background of permanence." To recognize when and in what ways men change we need theories, research, and politics that recognize that all men and masculinities, women and femininities—"new," queer, and "traditional," or African, American, or "modern"—are embedded in traditions. Just as masculinities positioned as "modern" have been readily seen as constructed, masculinity characterized as "traditional" cannot be conceived as the only ones with a tradition; there are in fact plural "traditional" masculinities. The common deployment of "traditional masculinity" is often inconsistent with some of the basic conceptualizations of masculinities studies. Instead of taking tradition as ancient views from the past restricted to some men and women, masculinities and femininities said to be traditional ought to be seen as socially constructed in the present, as historically contingent, and as being impossible if not characterized by mutability.

The prevalent view of tradition in masculinity studies is of something fixed, a trait that only some men have. Whereas masculinity is commonly accepted to be a cultural fact arising from gender relations, masculinity defined as "traditional" tends to be something almost outside of time. Those who use the concept of the "traditional" in this manner unconsciously, or consciously, sneak in classist, racist, or ethnocentric prejudices about "othered" men and cultures (Hondagneu-Sotelo and Messner 1994). A space to study "traditional" masculinity/ies as something more than merely "invented" (Hobsbawm and Ranger 1983) but constantly shifting, heterogeneous, and as emergent from contemporary cultural relations of gender is therefore desirable.

While the reification of tradition in relation to gender is evident in several disciplines, "traditional masculinity" seen as a form of masculinity characterized by archaic attitudes and conduct is evident within psychological studies of men, emanating largely from the United States (e.g., Burn and Ward 2005). There is a US/Western European and usually urban, often white, and mainly middle class-centred view regarding the concept of "the traditional" with respect to masculinities. However, psychological studies of men too tend to individualize and pathologize traditional masculinity. Masculinity in general, and traditional masculinity specifically, is seen as a personality trait, or an attitude, or something in the mind of "backward" individuals (Mahalik et al. 2003; Thompson and Pleck 1995). For example, traditional masculinity ideology has been associated with "restricted emotionality," "self-reliance through mechanical skills," "negativity toward sexual minorities," "avoidance of femininity," "importance of sex," "toughness," and "dominance" (Levant et al. 2010, 33). In this measure, traditional masculinity ideology is turned into a property of individuals instead of ideas about tradition and gender. This strand of work on tradition does not merely fail to recognize the intense debates on tradition in fields such as anthropology, ethnology, and folklore, but also that what is called "traditional masculinity" is profoundly misleading. *Authoritarian* masculinity is a better term.

Tradition emerges as a social problem precisely at the moment of change—whether in the nation, in subnational groups, or among women or queers. It surfaces with queer struggles, with women's liberation, with the birth of the postcolonial nation—that is, at decisive ruptures in internal struggles around recognition of a people, ethnicity, and language, women's rights, and nonheteronormative sexualities.

Tradition as Particular Kinds of Beliefs

Tradition is a highly elusive and contentious concept. There are, however, several commonly accepted meanings from which we can found a beachhead toward a more useful working concept. Tradition is usually associated with words such as custom, lore, ritual, heritage, habit, taboo, common law, rules, "tribal" identification, and belief. This is how Mandela seemed to understand tradition. However, all of these are loose and unsatisfactory equivalents. Not all rules or habits are part of tradition. If tradition is the same thing as, for instance, belief, then what kind of belief is tradition?

Tradition may be considered to be a set of shared beliefs, and accompanying acts, that the actors who identify with the tradition take to be a resource in making sense of, and acting in, the present—a resource that has social, political, symbolic, or ideological functions (cf., e.g., Hobsbawm and Ranger 1983; Glassie 1995; Shils 1971). A distinctive characteristic of these beliefs is that they are inherited. They are usually tacit, but not always so. These beliefs make up one of the major social forces that operate in a given place.

Similar to religion, class, race, or gender, tradition can be deployed to segregate between in-group and out-group members. It can be used to bring people together. It can be called forth when people need others to help mark death, marriage, birth, or graduation into manhood (as done among amaXhosa when males are sent for *ulwaluko* at a certain point of their lives; see Mandela 1994). It can be used to maintain hierarchies within the group. It can be used to enhance personal standing in society.

Accounts of tradition have therefore to be understood as indicative of how the practices and experiences of individuals, in the context of life with or against others and a collective past, are authorized, contested, transmitted, inherited, interpreted, and reinvented. Beliefs taken to be part of a tradition are therefore always a social enterprise. They are not psychological creations. Their principal value is that they are a socio-symbolic resource for "believers."

Tradition is also distinguishable from other kinds of habits in that it tends to more readily elicit a sense of "us" or "them." In this way it can be as powerful as, for instance, sexuality, socioeconomic status, religion, or race. Tradition is raised when people wish to self-consciously locate themselves or others in relation to the past, concerning how the present came about.

As earlier noted, the meaning of the term for "tradition" in Sesotho, a South African indigenous language, refers to where a group of people or their ways of life, beliefs, customs, rituals, practices, and so forth *come from*. This term signals how Basotho (speakers of the language Sesotho) comprehend tradition as implicating generational movement. It points to history and the temporality that defines beliefs that make up tradition. This insight makes history or social time an indispensable perspective in studying masculinities and femininities in relation to tradition. Time is one of the two intertwined elements that I would like to underscore. To speak of the "traditional," I contend, without acccounting for social temporality and history is absurd.

The second element requiring emphasis is the act of passing something down between generations. Tradition is always intergenerational. How, though, are we to understand tradition in those cases where intergenerational ties have been discontinuous? Such a question arises in the context where societies have been disturbed by major social upheaval. But it also crops up where the transmission of tradition between parents and children is rendered more complex because parents have died or left home. South Africa is a dense example of such societies. Not only is it a former colony, currently approximately a million children in the country are growing up in child-headed households (Hall, Meintjes, and Sambu 2014). I would like to turn in the last part of this section and consider how these elements are crucial in thinking about tradition, in studies of men, in neo/postcolonial societies.

An examination of where people come from and the inherited "things" that make up tradition becomes at once imperative and demanding, because of intergenerational discontinuities and impaired bonds between parents and children, and a widely shared sense of void where something ought to be (the absence of a significant proportion of fathers, for example). While South African research on fatherhood has problematized the discourse of absent fathers (e.g., Clowes, Ratele, and Shefer 2013; Langa 2014; Richter and Morrell 2006), it has not thoroughly placed "fatherlessness" within the context of the impairment of "traditional" cultural bonds, and of the colonial and apartheid evisceration of tradition as a shared social and psychological resource. In trying to apprehend topics like fatherhood in neo/postcolonial contexts, with tradition in sight, it seems necessary therefore to give serious consideration to interrupted historical time, discontinuous intergenerational memory, and cultural disruption.

Among the effects of colonialism and apartheid was the degradation of the traditions of the colonized and blacks. Colonialism and apartheid were purposefully geared toward the deformation of the cultural worlds of the indigenous people, besides land robbery and labor exploitation. More precisely, the distortion of tradition was the result of at least three interrelated processes.

First, aspects of tradition were pressed into the service of white capital accumulation. Able-bodied men were forced or induced (usually under threat, but sometimes with the collusion of headmen) to leave their families for superexploitative work in the growing mining industry. Migrancy in turn had myriad unfavorable relationship-related consequences—besides interrupting intergenerational ties.

Second, tradition was vulgarized in order to serve the racial subordination of blacks to whites. White men literally installed themselves as chiefs over black cultural affairs. Mandela (1994) remarks on this in his autobiography in regard to the authority of white civil servants over tribal affairs, including the powers allocated to them by law to depose and appoint chiefs.

Third, patterns of authority within black families were unhinged. White men, it could be said, in view of patriarchal relations in white and black families, arrogated the roles of the father over black fathers and by implication over all black subjects. Mohamed and Ratele (2012) have suggested that the history and experience of becoming men and women under colonialism or apartheid pose a problem for black subjects as they cannot return to the past without complication.

The interruption of cutural time by colonial conquest and apartheid policies—that is, the disruption of socialized temporality as an element of tradition—implies that the inheritors of tradition may be uncertain about their past even while they want to claim it. It means that contestations around tradition are more complex and potentially unresolvable, but troubling for understanding gender relations on such a terrain, because the disruption of tradition was a disruption of what it is to be a man and woman. Under colonial and apartheid rule some men were refused the status of adult manhood. For men subjugated by colonialism and apartheid, claims about a culturally valued masculinity were mixed with feelings of historical humiliation and a desire to remember tradition.

It seems that without a historical perspective on tradition, analyses of masculinities in former colonies remain very partial. A number of scholars who can be brought under the broad rubric of anti/post/de-colonial theory may be of help in theorizing and researching masculinities in neo/postcolonies as they have as one of their aims the examination of the historical and contemporary economic, political, cultural, and social relations as constituted by imperialism, colonialism, and apartheid (cf., e.g., de Sousa Santos 2010; Go 2013; Ndlovu-Gatsheni 2013). Some postcolonial theorists, such as Achille Mbembe (2001), have called for investigations of how the former subjects of colonialism exist in and negotiate different temporalities. Mbembe (2001, 8) has observed how "social theory has failed to account for time as lived in its multiplicity and simultaneities, its presences and absences." Viewed as chacterized by the question of temporality, traditions in neo/postcolonial societies are enfolded in "an entanglement of presents, past, and futures that retain their depths of other presents, pasts and future" (Mbembe 2001, 16).

A key concern in analyses of masculinities in neo/postcolonial cultures thus ought to be men's and women's struggles precisely *about* and *with* tradition as a resource in the face of the power of globalized Western European and American cultural hegemony. The questioning of the significance of tradition happens even while they hold to some bits of their inherited beliefs (such as holding on to the value of *lebollo*—a Sesotho term meaning the ritual initiation of boys into manhood). Men's and women's struggles around tradition are attempts to recover lost time and restitch the continuity between generations. These struggles may be examined as to how they speak to the intimate association of historical time, of the disruption of the continuity between a generation of fathers and children. The invocation of tradition needs to be analyzed for how it works to suture a ruptured sense of time in the life of indiviuals, groups, and society. Individuals and groups are of course continually trying to reposition themselves in the flow of disrupted time/temporalities. Thus, to speak of traditions may be one attempt to revive a sense of collective and subjective time, to reclaim the continuity of experience between generations, between parents and children, while also recovering memories and remaking a sense of commonality.

When Mandela said "men followed the path laid out for them by their fathers; women led the same lives as their mothers before them," he was betraying how the development of masculinities and femininities is indispensable to tradition-making, and simultaneously how tradition is entwined with gender-making. Gender relations do not sit outside of tradition, and instead are constitutive of that which is seen as traditional. Tradition in turn authorizes proper and improper gender relations, constitutive of masculinities and femininities. Gender relations, as Connell (1987) observed, are present throughout all of cultural life. Therefore, conscious of some men's and women's deployment of the language of tradition to assert and maintain gender patterns and ideologies, it is clear that in order for studies of gender in the global South to realize their transformative potential it is necessary to consider discourses on traditions, to analyze ideas of tradition in masculinity politics, theories, and research. Working on changing regimes of gender and sexualities seems to imply usually indirect involvement with tradition. However, it seems preferable to get more directly involved with tradition—that is, for critical masculinity scholars to deliberately aim to transform the space of (gendered) tradition itself. It is vital to engage tradition because, while true for many countries around the world, it is particularly in the global economic peripheries where tradition gets more of a salient role as a resource to contest subjective and structural power, construct an original, meaningful identity, consciously produce a life with others, and sustain a sense of continuity between present, past, and future.

NOTES

1 Grateful acknowledgement is due to Raewyn Connell, Michael Messner, James Messerschmidt, and Patricia Martin for the kind invitation, gentle questioning, and editorial input that helped me in shaping this chapter.

2 Mandela had six children: two girls (one deceased) and two boys (both deceased) with his first wife, Evelyn Mase; and two girls with his second wife, Winnie Madikizela Mandela. It was because the sons were deceased that the grandsons took the place of their fathers.

3 For example, Zuma was challenged by gender activists on his comments that it is "not right" for women to be single, childless, and that having children is extra training for a woman (Pillay 2012).

4 The "tribe" (and associated words like tribalist) is ill-advised. As Archie Mafeje observed, "In many instances the colonial authorities helped to create the things called 'tribes,' in the sense of political communities; this process coincided with and was helped along by the anthropologists' preoccupation with 'tribes'" (Mafeje 1971, 254).

REFERENCES

Amadiume, Ifi. 1987. *Male Daughters, Female Husbands: Gender and Sex in an African Society*. London: Zed Books.

Ben-Amos, D. 1984. The Seven Strands of Tradition: Varieties in Its Meaning in American Folklore Studies. *Folklore Research* 21: 97–131.

Bulhan, Hussein A. 2015. Stages of Colonialism in Africa: From Occupation of Land to Occupation of Being. *Journal of Social and Political Psychology* 3 (1): 239–256. doi:10.5964/jspp.v3i1.143.

Burn, S. M., and A. Z. Ward. 2005. Men's Conformity to Traditional Masculinity and Relationship Satisfaction. *Psychology of Men & Masculinity* 6 (4): 254–263.

Carrigan, Tim, Raewyn Connell, and John Lee. 1985. Toward a New Sociology of Masculinity. *Theory and Society* 14 (5): 551–604.

Césaire, Aimé. (1955) 1972. *Discourse on Colonialism*. New York: Monthly Review Press.

Clowes, Lindsay, Kopano Ratele, and Tammy Shefer. 2013. Who Needs a Father? South African Men Reflect on Being Fathered. *Journal of Gender Studies* 22 (3): 255–267.

Connell, R. W. 1987. *Gender and Power: Society, the Person, and Sexual Politics*. Sydney: Polity Press.

Connell, Raewyn. 2007. *Southern Theory: The Global Dynamics of Knowledge in Social Science*. Sydney: Allen and Unwin.

———. 2014a. The Study of Masculinities. *Qualitative Research Journal* 14 (1): 5–15.

———. 2014b. Using Southern Theory: Decolonizing Social Thought in Theory, Research and Application. *Planning Theory* 13 (2): 210–223.

Connell, Raewyn, and James W. Messerschmidt. 2005. Hegemonic Masculinity: Rethinking the Concept. *Gender & Society* 19 (6): 829–859.

de Sousa Santos, Boaventura. 2010. From the Postmodern to the Post-colonial—and beyond Both. In *Decolonizing European Sociology: Transdisciplinary Approaches*, edited by Encarnación Gutiérrez Rodriquez, Manuela Boatcǎ, and Sérgio Costa. Surrey: Ashgate.

Everitt-Penhale, Brittany, and Kopano Ratele. 2015. Rethinking "Traditional Masculinity" as Constructed, Multiple, and Hegemonic Masculinity. *South African Review of Sociology* 46 (2): 4–22.

Fanon, Frantz. (1959) 1965. *A Dying Colonialism*. New York: Grove Press.

Foucault, Michel. (1969) 2002. *The Archaeology of Knowledge*. Translated by A. M. Sheridan Smith. London: Routledge.

Glassie, H. 1995. Tradition. *Journal of American Folklore* 108 (430): 395–412.

Go, Julian. 2013. For a Post-colonial Sociology. *Theory and Society* 42 (1): 235–255.

Gusfield, J. R. 1967. Tradition and Modernity: Misplaced Polarities in the Study of Social Change. *American Journal of Sociology* 72 (4): 351–362.

Hall, Katharine, Helen Meintjes, and Winnie Sambu. 2014. Demography of South Africa's Children. *South African Child Gauge 2014*: 90–93.

Handler, R., and J. Linnekin. 1984. Tradition, Genuine or Spurious. *Journal of American Folklore* 97: 273–290.

Hobsbawm, Eric. 1983. Introduction: Inventing Tradition. In *The Invention of Tradition*, edited by Eric Hobsbawm and Terence Ranger. Cambridge: Cambridge University Press.

Hobsbawm, Eric, and Terence Ranger, eds. 1983. *The Invention of Tradition*. Cambridge: Cambridge University Press.

Hondagneu-Sotelo, Pierrette, and Michael A. Messner. 1994. Gender Displays and Men's Power: The "New Man" and the Mexican Immigrant Man. In *Theorizing Masculinities*, edited by Harry Brod and Michael Kaufman. London: Sage Publications.

Hountondji, Paulin J. 1983. *African Philosophy: Myth and Reality*. London: Hutchinson University Library for Africa.

———. 2000. Tradition: Hindrance or Inspiration? *Quest* 14 (1–2): 5–11.

Langa, Malose. 2014. Meaning Making in Growing Up without a Father: Narratives of Young Adolescent Boys. *Open Family Studies Journal* 6 (Suppl 1: M7): 56–61.

Levant, Roland F., L. S. Hirsch, E. Celentano, and T. M. Cozza. 1992. The Male Role: An Investigation of Contemporary Norms. *Journal of Mental Health Counseling* 14: 325–337.

Levant, Ronald F., Thomas J. Rankin, Christine M. Williams, Nadia T. Hasan, and K. Bryant Smalley. 2010. Evaluation of the Factor Structure and Construct Validity of Scores on the Male Role Norms Inventory—Revised (MRNI-R). *Psychology of Men and Masculinity* 11: 25–37.

Linnekin, J. S. 1983. Defining Tradition: Variations on the Hawaiian Identity. *American Ethnologist* 10: 241–252.

Mafeje, Archie. 1971. The Ideology of "Tribalism." *Journal of Modern African Studies* 9 (2): 253–261.

Mahalik, J., B. Locke, L. Ludlow, M. Diemer, and R. Scott, et al. 2003. Development of the Conformity to Masculine Norms Inventory. *Psychology of Men and Masculinity* 4 (1): 3–25.

Maldonado-Torres, Nelson. 2007. On the Coloniality of Being: Contributions to the Development of a Concept. *Cultural Studies* 21 (2–3): 240–270.

Mandela, Nelson. 1994. *Long Walk to Freedom: The Autobiography of Nelson Mandela.* London: Little, Brown and Company.

Mbanjwa, Xolani, Lubabalo Ngcukana, and Sabelo Ndlangisa. 2013. Ah! Dalibhunga It's Time to Rest. *City Press*, December 15. www.citypress.co.za.

Mbembe, Achille. 2001. *On the Postcolony.* Berkeley: University of California Press.

Mohamed, Kharnita, and Kopano Ratele. 2012. Where My Dad Was From He Was Quite a Respected Man. *Peace and Conflict: Journal of Peace Psychology* 18 (3): 282–293.

Morrell, Robert. 1998. Of Boys and Men: Masculinity and Gender in Southern African Studies. *Journal of Southern African Studies* 24 (4): 605–630.

Ndenze, Babalo. 2013. Tata's Burial Ritual Explained. December 13. Accessed May 19, 2016. www.iol.co.za.

Ndlovu-Gatsheni, Sabelo J. 2007. Re-Thinking the Colonial Encounter in Zimbabwe in the Early Twentieth Century. *Journal of Southern African Studies* 33 (1): 173–191.

———. 2013. *Coloniality of Power in Post-colonial Africa: Myths of Decolonization.* Dakar: Codesria.

Ngwane, Zolani. 2014. Mandela and Tradition. In *The Cambridge Companion to Nelson Mandela*, edited by Rita Barnard. Cambridge: Cambridge University Press

Oyěwùmí, Oyèrónkẹ. 1997. *The Invention of Women: Making an African Sense of Western Gender Discourses.* Minneapolis: University of Minnesota Press.

Pillay, Verashni. 2012. Zuma: Women Must Have Children. *Mail and Guardian*, August 22. mg.co.za.

Quijano, Anibal. 2000. Coloniality of power, Eurocentrism and Latin America. *Nepantla: Views from South* 1 (3): 533–580.

———. 2007. Coloniality and Modernity/Rationality. *Cultural Studies* 21 (2–3): 168–178.

Ratele, Kopano. 2013. Masculinity without Tradition. *Politikon: South African Journal of Political Studies* 40 (1): 133–156.

Republic of South Africa. 1996. *Constitution of the Republic of South Africa Act, No. 108 of 1996*. Cape Town: Republic of South Africa.

Richter, Linda, and Robert Morrell, eds. 2006. *Baba: Men and Fatherhood in South Africa*. Human Sciences Research Council. Cape Town: HSRC Press.

Santaularia, I. 2010. Dexter: Villain, Hero or Simply a Man? The Perpetuation of Traditional Masculinity in Dexter. *Atlantis: Journal of the Spanish Association of Anglo-American Studies* 32: 57–71.

Shils, Edward. 1971. *Tradition*. Chicago: University of Chicago Press.

Shotter, Jonathan, and Margaret Wetherell. 1987. *Discourse and Social Psychology: Beyond Attitudes and Behaviour*. London: Sage.

Soares, J. A. 1997. A Reformulation of the Concept of Tradition. *International Journal of Sociology and Social Policy* 17: 6–21.

Spiegel, Andrew. 1989. Towards an Understanding of Tradition: Use of Tradition(al) in Apartheid South Africa. *Critique of Anthropology* 9: 49–74.

Thompson, Edward H., and Joseph Pleck. 1995. Masculinity Ideologies: A Review of Research Instrumentation on Men and Masculinities. In *A New Psychology of Men*, edited by Ronald F. Levant and William S. Pollack. New York: Basic Books.

Walker, Cherryl. 1994. Women, "Tradition" and Reconstruction. *Review of African Political Economy* 21 (61): 347–358.

———. 2013. Uneasy Relations: Women, Gender Equality and Tradition. *Thesis Eleven* 115 (1): 77–94.

Wetherell, Margaret. 2008. Subjectivity or Psychodiscursive Practices? Investigating Complex Intersectional Identities. *Subjectivity* 22: 73–81.

Wetherell, Margaret, and Nigel Edley. 1999. Negotiating Hegemonic Masculinity: Imaginary Positions and Psycho-discursive Practices. *Feminism & Psychology* 9 (3): 335–356.

12

Rethinking Patriarchy through Unpatriarchal Male Desires

GUL OZYEGIN

Is patriarchy a useful concept for analysis of gender? How should we understand its relation to gender theory? How does the concept of patriarchy as a system of male domination, neither uniform nor static, figure into various domains of gender and gender vocabularies?

I employ the term "rethinking patriarchy" in my title to orient the reader to the particularities of the Turkish case, but more importantly my usage is intended to recall a notable absence in gender theory. I advocate a conceptual framework that can address a missing domain in gender theory: gender domination. When patriarchy was expelled from Northern gender theory as too abstract, too broad, and ahistorical, it seems we also vacated the domain of gender domination altogether from our theorical vocabularly and dropped it from our conceptual toolkit. With the rise of the intersectionality paradigm,[1] the anaytical power of investigating how gender domination comes to be constituted, maintained, and transformed in particular ways was diminished.

An important category of analysis, patriarchy is notably absent from the burgeoning literature on gender in the West. The hegemonic intellectual categories of gender in contemporary feminist scholarship take us away from explorations of the nature and dynamics of patriarchy. Now the paradigm of intersectionality provides the dominant concepts of gender with a seemingly infinite and flexible capacity to animate research and theory. Postcolonial feminist scholars have pointed out the growing strategic use and transnational circulation of critiques of patriarchy as a strong marker of the boundaries between the global North and South (the absence of patriarchy in the West but the existence of "patriarchy elsewhere") in the service of various economic and political global neoliberalization projects. Indeed, Inderpal Grewal (2013) argues that "patriarchy" has been outsourced to the global South.

I propose that it would constitute a vital omission to our building of gender theory and politics to leave out of our research and theory the experiences of those individuals who intrinsically link domains of gender to patriarchy and who see themselves, their gender arrangements, and their struggles through a prism of patriarchy.

Like Raewyn Connell, I see a major task in taking account of the theoretical concepts and methods produced in the global South in the elaboration of gender as an analytic paradigm. Connell sees rendering visible theories and concepts produced in the global South and bringing them into the center as the most difficult contemporary challenge to the social sciences in which practices of Eurocentric knowledge production rule. As she puts it cogently, feminist literature "works on the tacit assumption that the global South produces data and politics, but doesn't produce theory" (2014, 520). Actively privileging plurality and the permeability of different theoretical voices to allow for the cultivation of a mode of knowledge production, what Connell calls "cross-fertilization," is a formidable task for it hinges on so many radical institutional and political transformations. Cross-fertilization requires forging links that allow understanding connected and mutually constitutive processes and, more importantly, as Connell underlines, recognizing theory and concepts produced in the global South. Seeing, naming, and theorizing the connections, I want to suggest, is also fundamentally dependent on theory embedded in substantive empirical interrogation that captures experience in actually lived terms.

My goal in this chapter is to participate in the effort to build cross-fertilization and to deepen the challenges of this concern with an illustration from my research. The task of this chapter is to reevaluate the place of patriarchy in gender theory from the perspective of heterosexual young men in Turkey who are the subjects of, and mediums for, (re)producing patriarchy but who have unpatriarchal desires and struggle to enact unpatriarchal identities and gender practices. It is toward this end that I approach the narratives of love, sex, and self-making the young men shared with me.[2] These men's narratives provide a useful point of entry for understanding historically and culturally specific configurations of masculinity and patriarchy. Their narrated experiences of sex, love, and romance are telling, constituting a rich site for furthering the theorization of the masculinity-patriarchy nexus, how they come together, and how they are uncoupled or recoupled in speech, action, and intimate relations.

Patriarchy as "Elsewhere": The Expulsion of Patriarchy from Northern Theory

Feminist scholars have used the concept of patriarchy as a foundational concept to describe and analyze what they see as simultaneously an ideology, structure, and organizing force in social institutions and practices for women's gender-based subordination and oppression. While the patriarchy paradigm framed many studies in the formative years of feminist scholarship, increasing debates among feminists about how to define the category of "woman" formed a significant impetus for disowning interest in the concept of patriarchy during the last decades of the twentieth century. Black and Third World feminists' challenges to the Euro-American second-wave feminist movement—its construction of white middle class heterosexual women as the "unmarked" subject and object of feminist analysis—generated efforts to theorize differences of race/ethnicity between women and to examine how these differences modify our conceptions of subordination based on gender (Crenshaw 1989; Mohanty 1988; Spelman 1988). The concept of patriarchy has come to be regarded as ahistorical, apolitical, homogenizing, lacking cultural specificity, too abstract, and too broad—an imprecise category not useful in understanding the gender order. It served to underlie white women's oppression to the exclusion of other oppressions, obscuring the complexities of class and racial oppression and Western colonialism.

Out of these concerns, a new paradigm—intersectionality—gained currency, seeming more commensurate with the emergent queer movements, masculinity studies, the global women's movement, and postcolonial feminism. Feminist scholarship has placed the concept of intersectionality at the core of feminist theory and politics, and intersectionality has excited feminist inquiry in many disciplines. Now considered the basic building block of feminist theory, the intersectionality paradigm has, not surprisingly, generated a great deal of discussion regarding how it should be precisely defined and where and how it should be studied (McCall 2005; Davis 2008). The question emerges whether, by using intersectionality as a theoretical tool, we are eliminating the analytical power of investigating how each category of difference or inequality comes to be constituted and historically transformed in particular ways.

Two recent articles by postcolonial feminist scholars Inderpal Grewal (2013) and Vrushali Patil (2013) reflect new and productive destabilizations of core assumptions about the decline of patriarchy in feminist scholarship. Grewal notes that while we see an acknowledged abandonment of the concept of patriarchy by theorists in the West, the relevance of patriarchy to describe "others" outside the American-European contexts has been on the rise: "an essentialist notion of the term 'patriarchy' has become naturalized in relation to the 'Global South'"(7), serving to buttress and legitimate all kinds of projects for fiscal gain (including wars waged to save women, as a contemporary version of the saving "brown women from brown men"). Patil (2013) argues that in spite of the well-established critiques of the concept of patriarchy, there is an unfinished agenda because much Western feminist writing has evaded the intellectual and political challenges of investigating patriarchies working relationally on a transnational scale and scope. She asks theorists to expand feminist inquiries beyond particular national settings, taking up questions about how patriarchies were and are located in transnational contexts.

The Turkish Case

Turkey offers a transformative setting for reconsidering patriarchy in gender theory. Historically in Turkey patriarchy and paternalism have been intertwined and the definition of masculinity has been imbued with dominance and a strong emphasis on men's roles as protectors. As such, this specific constellation of patriarchy and paternalism implicates traditional masculinity, like femininity, as "selfless"—a linkage that, as we will see, forms a strong impetus for young men to actively disinherit traditional masculinity and pursue self-consciously unpatriarchal selves. The Turkish case also helps unpack the ways young men come to be invested in romance, over sex, as sources of recognition, challenging our understanding of patriarchal desires and highlighting the importance of incorporating notions of patriarchy in gender theory.

At the present historical moment, we see the coproduction of global neoliberalism and local "neoconservative familialism" (Korkman 2015), which together have led to the emergence of a new mode of patriarchy (Coşar and Yeğenoğlu 2011; Kandiyoti 2011; Acar and Altunok 2012) in Turkey.[3] The Islamist government of the Justice and Development Party (AKP), which has been in power for the last 13 years, promotes a new Turkey that fosters piety based on Sunni Islam by the top-down imposition of Islamic morality. The government advances a pronatalist agenda and policies, prioritizing procreation in heterosexual marriage, actively encouraging early marriage and at least three children, restricting abortion rights, and challenging working mothers to part-time employment and work in the informal economy. In short, the suturing of global neoliberalization with Islamization is a project linked to the fortification of patriarchal familialism. At the same time the strong dissension and resistance to this fortification animates and shapes feminist and LGBTQ movements.

While melding neoliberalism with neoconservatism is remaking patriarchy, during the last two decades the patriarchal underpinnings of law have been marginalized or eliminated. During the early 2000s, a strong feminist campaign within the context of the EU accession process resulted in gender-egalitarian legal and policy reforms that have granted women equal citizenship rights. The new civil code of 2001 equalized the status of husband and wife in the conjugal union by abolishing the concept of the head of family, establishing full equality with respect to rights over the family abode, marital property, divorce, child custody, and rights to work and travel. The new penal code of 2005 reclassifies sexual crimes like rape as crimes against the individual rather than as crimes against "public morality" or "community order."

During this time state paternalism has also undergone a process of dismantling. Historically, the Turkish welfare system has been structured around a patriarchal male-breadwinner family norm in which women's dependence on male protection formed a vital source of security (social security, health insurance, and the pension system). The AKP's reform of the welfare system was instigated by gender-neutral neoliberal policies, with an emphasis on the privatization of the benefits systems. The reforms eliminated women's privileged access to social transfers. However, this dismantling of the paternalistic welfare state is increasing women's vulnerability to economic and social risks precisely because with new economic policies women are being pushed to part-time employment in the formal sector and work in the informal sector that more than ever is reinforcing patriarchal gender identities and roles, particularly the valorization of motherhood and caregiving as women's central roles and identities in Turkey, while (re)constructing men as protectors of women (Dayıoğlu and Başlevent 2012; Toksöz 2012).

The most recent perspectives on men and masculinities in Turkey bring our attention to a crisis of hegemonic masculinity. They highlight the ever-increasing global centrality of neoliberal economic transformations, the newly enacted conservative national policies, the altered forms of the gendered division of labor, fatherhood, and militarism and warfare, and how these processes destabilize the reproduction of hegemonic masculinity. Importantly, these perspectives aim precisely to grasp the native self-understanding and practical realizations of this crisis as they are worked out on the ground. This approach involves an emphasis on subjectivity and attention to the interconnections between the global and local, the role of the state, and how these factors come together to shape the types and forms of (re)negotiations and enactments of masculine identities (Açıksöz 2015; Beşpınar 2015; Özbay 2015).

Imported Vernaculars

Turkey also provides an important context for discussing the ways experience is retained and theorized in actual analysis. There is considerable distance between theorizations of gender in the North and importation of its terms from English and the vernacular feelings their adaptations create. "Gender" is a relatively recent coinage in Turkey, translated from English. Gender as translated in Turkish is *toplumsal cinsiyet*, literally meaning "societal sex." Transforming a genderless meaning of sex into gendered *toplumsal cinsiyet* constructs categories that allow us to speak about socially constructed experiences and identities. However, the specific vernacular feelings *toplumsal cinsiyet* create are awkward and do not lend themselves to easy mobilization in creating discursivity for social movements. For instance, instead of gender-based inequalities (*toplumsal–cinsiyete dayalı eşitsizlik*), the feminist movement uses the expression *kadın erkek eşitsizliği* (inequality between men and women) or *erkek devlet* (male State). The common vernacular words *patriarki* or *erkek iktidarı* (male power or *ataerkil*, paternal power), on the other hand, allow us to speak about lived experiences. They are versatile in referencing perceptions and symbolic inferences, forming a core imaginary and providing the images, norms, and ideals for people's self-understanding of their struggles. In short, not gender but notions of patriarchy and practices of patriarchy in creating gender-based system of domination provide a language and symbolism with which to imagine and represent experiences. Thus, the concept/critique of patriarchy is an anchor of local feminist movements and theory. I propose that we should not underestimate the importance of political attachment to patriarchy as a struggle term deployed within feminist/women's movements. It would constitute a vital omission to our building of gender theory and politics to leave out the experiences of those individuals who intrinsically link domains of gender to patriarchy and who see themselves, their gender arrangements, and their struggles through a prism of patriarchy. We should not also underestimate the effective significance of the vocabulary of patriarchy on the ground in contexts in which feminism and its movements have been posed explicitly against patriarchy.

My perspective on theory construction is that theory is produced within a dialogical realm, a form of interpretive and imaginative exchange between the analytical tools we employ and the experiences of the subjects of our studies as narrated to us or observed by us. In order to be locally and politically relevant, feminist theory must both sustain and critique the terms of reference of our ethnographic subjects and their experiences while "also lead[ing] fruitfully beyond it" (Connell 2014, 539). Otherwise, in reference to this discussion here, women and men who believe that their relations are defined by patriarchy find themselves unrepresented, and indeed unpresentable, within a theoretical language devoid of the key terms of patriarchy.

Unpatriarchal Male Desires

The young men I interviewed came of age amid Turkish society's pivot away from state-based paternalism and have been intensely subjected to the ethos of neoliberalism. Accordingly, they see themselves as embarking on projects of "entrepreneurship of the self" where old ideals of paternal selflessness are replaced by new ideals of masculine individualism, ambition, and pleasure seeking. The young men I spoke with believe that their fathers' lives followed a predetermined teleological course imbricated in patriarchal history. Their lives were marked by the conformity of protective paternalism and structured by a patriarchal order that devalued male passion, emotionality, creativity, and authenticity. Although the impact of fathers is complex and dynamic, what remains consistent across the young men's narratives is the sense that adhering to the patriarchal association between masculinity and protection provided their fathers with narrow ranges of identity. By contrast, these young men's identity-making hinges on self-expansion through the invention of new forms of subjectivities, pleasures, and relationships.

As these men reject the patriarchal modes of masculinity modeled by their fathers, they explicitly seek new types of affective relationships with "selfish" women who break with the traditional models of female selflessness embodied by their mothers by privileging their own desires and ambitions. Especially for those upwardly mobile men from traditional family backgrounds who lack suitable others to confer recognition on their new masculine selves, relationships with such women become important sites upon which they confirm the success of their self-making. Yet, as we will see, even as these men seek recognition and support for their own self-making from women who are equally driven and independent, they cannot completely repudiate the maternal model, longing at the same time for "positive" "selfless" girls who subordinate their desires to the needs of the relationship. The tension of this paradox is felt most acutely by men from conservative and rural family backgrounds whose desire to be recognized as desirable and important in intimate relationships with young women who have their own desires for recognition can lead to male domination, jeopardizing these men's projects of creating unpatriarchal male identities.

Precisely because these men are authoring new types of masculine selves, dependent on recognition from suitable others, the desire for intimacy and recognition emerges as more important than the desire for sex in their narratives. The desire for recognition is a powerful formative force in structuring masculinities in a cultural context that steeps desire in a patriarchal tradition, a tradition of motherly devotion and of the privileging and adulation of sons' desires and needs. I examine the terrain of these anxious boundaries and how they are experienced from the point of view of one 23-year-old man: Oktay.[4] The stories and themes I draw upon from my research in this section bring Oktay into the foreground in ways that help make concrete theoretical points about what interrupts or changes the patriarchal construction of masculinity as dominant and protective in Turkish society.

(Re)Making Male Dominance: Oktay's Story

In our interview, Oktay declared that "the woman I will marry [will] have a different life than my mother's," signaling his self-conscious and active rejection of paternal masculinity. An ambitious, high-achieving 23 year old, Oktay was raised in a traditional home structured by patriarchal gender and sexual values. According to Oktay, dominating intimate female others is central to his father's identity. Oktay described his mother, a homemaker with limited formal education, as a typical selfless mother. In our interview, Oktay revealed that he does not feel he really knows his mother, a fact he attributed to her total selflessness: "Because, I think, it is not permitted to know her; she makes herself obliterate, puts her desires in the background, because she is someone who sacrifices herself for her children and her husband." Although Oktay blamed larger cultural patterns of male domination and the all-consuming role of motherhood for women's selflessness, he had nevertheless lost personal respect for his mother. As he put it, "I cannot receive [or gain] anything from my mother anymore."

In rejecting his mother's selflessness, Oktay simultaneously rejected the mode of masculinity upheld by his father. His efforts to reflexively constitute an alternative masculinity are thus steeped in a rejection of the mutually reinforcing traditions of selfless femininity and patriarchal masculinity. While away at college he forged a deep desire "not to become like [his] father." One telling motivation in Oktay's self-reimaging was the revelation that his sister did not love his father, something that provoked a fear in Oktay that a future daughter might not love him. Imagining himself as not being loved and admired remained Oktay's emotional point of reference for his romantic aspirations, development, and identity.

Oktay met his girlfriend, Sezen, during their freshman year at Bogazici. According to Oktay, they love each other deeply, and Oktay values her in large part because he can be totally himself around her: "Anything I can experience and feel I can tell her without becoming uncomfortable because I think she understands me. That is, I can let myself go." Oktay and Sezen have been together for three years and explore embodied sexuality but haven't experienced sexual coitus. A key episode of their relationship was an eight-month separation, linked, as Oktay put it, to his "curtailment" of Sezen's freedoms. Despite his resistance to inheriting his father's oppressive masculinity, Oktay consistently sought dominance in his relationship with Sezen, disapproving, for instance, of Sezen visiting male friends at their houses to play cards or staying out later than she promised.

Despite his professed rejection of the masculine practices of domination, Oktay's motivation to control Sezen's mobility and relationships arose out of a discourse of masculine protection (the critical but unnamed term in his narrative, I observed). In Oktay's view, Sezen's unsuspecting and warm personality and her inclination to become close with people easily (the exact qualities that made Oktay fall in love with her) rendered her vulnerable and in need of his protection and control. He said that he had no objection to Sezen's socializing and staying out late with friends in their own circle: "She can do anything with friends I know." He saw the issue as Sezen's innocence in dealing with outsiders and her tendency to approach people with open arms without recognizing that men might have ulterior motives.

Oktay also developed an intense preoccupation with what he saw as Sezen's selfishness, which, over time, fostered feelings of insignificance in him. As he put it, "I desire to feel important. . . . I desire for her to respect my values. Maybe even I want her to live by my values." A variety of situations connected with this desire "to feel important" surfaced in Oktay's narrative, indicating that Sezen's "selfishness" was, in Oktay's estimation, a function of her prioritizing her own desires. For example,

> even cooking together can be a problem. For instance, she likes spinach and I don't like it. . . . I love pasta. She was taking care of the spinach dish when I asked her to watch the pasta, but she didn't hear me because she likes spinach. I coded this as evidence that she doesn't value my desires; she values her own desires.

Oktay's need for Sezen to reassure him that she desired him even extended to the academic environment they share—Oktay reports feeling jealous when Sezen pays too much attention in lecture, ignoring him: "We are taking the same classes; she is listening to the lectures, and taking notes. She is disinterested in me during classes." Oktay feels entitled to constant, public assurances that he is at the center of Sezen's attention: "For instance, let's say five of us are studying together and trying to understand something at the same moment. If she understands first, I want her to explain it to me first. That is, I want to know that I am the top priority among other people in her life." Importantly, Oktay values Sezen's attention precisely because she is a modern, unsubordinated woman. She can provide the recognition men like him need to support their new selves—the love, desire, and understanding of a high-achieving, independent woman. Yet, paradoxically, these same qualities meant that Sezen prioritized her desires over his, making him feel unimportant, unloved, and, unrecognized.

As dominance is conveyed and practiced within relationships, it can be contested, accepted, challenged, or assimilated with complete acquiescence or all-around conflict. Oktay and Sezen's experience was all-around conflict. Oktay's desire to restrict Sezen's freedom upset her, but, according to Oktay, "She wasn't telling me because she feared that I'd be angry. And because we love each other, we avoid fights." Instead, she apologized for her "transgressions" so as not to upset him. In time, however, "She realized that her freedoms were curtailed and she found herself apologizing to me too much because of my reactions." According to Oktay, she eventually couldn't stand to remain quiescent while her freedoms were subjugated, and she left him.

Oktay's eight-month separation from Sezen helped him gain a critical distance on his relationship. Despite having a brief affair with another young woman during this separation, Oktay was reminded of the exclusiveness of his devotion to Sezen. The separation led him to reassess how he should deal with his intense desire to control her. Knowing he would need to change his behavior in order to rekindle and preserve their romance, he committed to quashing these controlling impulses. Now back together with Sezen, however, he sees himself as keeping his "desires captive in the background." While backgrounding his desires offers Oktay a solution to sustain his relationship, he claimed that he could not help but continue to think about Sezen's selfishness, and this trait haunts him when he envisions his future with her, believing that "in a marital relationship, selfishness would bring harm to the relationship."

Oktay comes across as brutish and narcissistic, consumed by his desire to be recognized as special and driven by open displays of superiority—when I asked him if Sezen also engaged in another relationship when they were apart, he said that she hadn't but that he wished that she had "for the sake of her understanding of my specialness." This stance can be understood as a specific expression of the more general phenomenon of the desire for recognition: it is symptomatic of an uncertainty of rank and porous dividing lines between different types of masculinities. Oktay lacks familial others with "suitable selves" to confer recognition for the man he wants to become. All he wants to be is a man who is loved and admired by women for his nonoppressive behavior, but this dimension of ideal masculinity is one that neither his oppressive father nor his selfless mother is equipped to affirm. The intimate, gendered other thus becomes crucial to the development of the self—with paradoxical effect.

Oktay's story challenges assumptions we make when we constrain our analysis to the gendered dichotomies of yearning for love and sex that prevail in the literature. Longings for love and sex are not independent from but are in fact complicated by other significant longings—like the longing for recognition. However, as we have seen in Oktay's account, this longing for recognition can lead to masculine domination, when, as Benjamin (1988) suggests, young men wish to be recognized as subjects without returning that recognition. Oktay's story not only highlights practices of domination but may also helps nuance the dialectics of male ambivalence when girls claim selfishness in relationships and refuse to make "meaningful the feelings, actions, and intentions" (Benjamin 1988, 21) of the masculine self.

The path young men, like Oktay, desire to traverse in placing themselves out of patriarchy highlights the potential for the analytic refinement of patriarchy in gender theory.

A Dialogical Approach to Gender

Connell's theorization of hegemonic masculinity addresses a foundational question in gender theory: What are the relationships between forms of male dominance and gender relations? Her formulation of the concept of hegemonic masculinity is dependent upon and reflects the centrality of patriarchy itself. She defines hegemonic masculinity "as the configuration of gender practice which embodies the currently accepted answer to the problem of the legitimacy of patriarchy" (2005, 77). Her definition of hegemony in terms of the successful correspondence of "cultural ideal" and collective "institutional power" recognized the significance of the institutional materialization of patriarchy. Furthermore, her stress on "correspondence" gives historicity and specificity to patriarchy, which is determined through specific institutional and organizational forms and underwrites the hegemony of certain groups of men. Her theory also emphasizes how the patriarchal dividend— "the advantage men in general gain from the overall subordination of women" (79)—provides the matrix within which hegemony, the distinctive form of domination in the gender order, occurs. In particular, the hegemonic capacities of the dominant form depend on its contribution to men's gender cohesion—that is, the complicity of other, subordinated masculinities (despite their deep contradictions), who benefit from the patriarchal dividend. In other words, patriarchy guarantees (at least in an abstract manner) the universal general interest, advantage, and privilege of all men.

However, Connell's conceptualization of the relationship between hegemony, domination, and femininity remains underdeveloped (a fact she herself acknowledges in a footnote). In her theory, femininity is always organized as an adaptation to men's power (1987, 188). She defines "emphasized femininity" as "compliance with subordination" and argues that it "is oriented to accommodating the interests and desires of men" (1987, 183). Connell ignored the problem of how different femininities are articulated or dislocated in specific conjunctures across different fields of domination and hegemony. Femininity is thus treated as a residual category and conceptualized with no sustained attention to different forms of patriarchy and women's varied responses to them. Despite the fact that in Connell's theory hegemony, subordination, and complicity as relations are fundamentally rooted and always present in the gender order, an account of how femininity's relationality to masculinity enters into the complex links among hegemony, subordination, and complicity remains unexplored. This lack of attention to femininity results, in Connell's work, in the conflation of hegemony and domination and, perhaps more importantly, undermines a theorization of gender relationally.

Indeed, it is exactly for this reason that gender scholars who approach their research in various geographies with theoretical tools borrowed from Connell study masculinity and femininity as typologies: hegemonic, complicit, emphasized, exaggerated, marginalized, and subordinated. Furthermore, as Michael Moller (2007) argues, "the conceptual mobility" of these typologies "may also conceal important aspects of the knowledge thus produced; namely the exclusion of those practices, statements and feelings which do not fit this typology of masculine objects" (268). Such practices would include the strong desires of some young men, like Oktay, *not* to be dominant, controlling, and protective when young men attempt to escape from hegemonic masculinity because it is, like femininity, aligned with selflessness due to the interlinkage of paternalism and patriarchy. As such, this specific constellation of patriarchy and paternalism implicates traditional masculinity, like femininity, as "selfless"—a linkage that, as we will see, forms a strong impetus for young men to actively disinherit traditional masculinity and pursue self-consciously unpatriarchal selves. In addition to encouraging a limited disciplinary field of vision that overdetermines male identity, changes in the construction of masculinity are often articulated as changes in the relation between masculinities (Collinson and Hearn 1994).

Indeed, explicitly stated in Connell's later work (Connell and Messerschmidt 2005, 848) is the realization that femininity must be examined not only from the viewpoint of compliance with patriarchy but also from that of the new identities and practices of young women.

I propose a dialogical approach to gender in which gender is theorized relationally. I emphasize the importance of pursuing gender relationally because attention to how practices of domination and subordination are constructed and experienced is important to transforming the relations of domination, and to capturing to the ways women and men contest the boundaries of their transformative capacities both in relation to each other and in relation to the structural and institutional materiality of patriarchy. This is particularly crucial in a societal context like Turkey in which the gender order is destabilized and the stability of hegemonic masculinity is being contested and strongly critiqued in both local practices and discourses like those explored here by young men who question the paternalistic construction of masculinity.

I apply such a dialogical approach to gender and conceptualize men and women as coproducers of masculine and feminine ideals. I also conceptualize intimate romantic and sexual relationships as sites both for the reproduction of patriarchy and for challenges to it. Romance and sex as an intersubjective terrain shapes young people's perceptions of who they are and generates experiences that reinforce or contradict the enactments of patriarchal gender identities and sexual selves (Ozyegin 2015).

One of the most striking features of the gender transformation across all classes in my larger research is the merging of young men's and women's desires for expanded selfhoods beyond the selflessness implied in both the protective masculine and the maternal feminine models. Men in Turkey are deemed appropriately masculine when they are protective and carry the power to define the boundaries of action and conduct of the girls and women under their protection. The renunciation of this model by young men is propelled by Turkey's neoliberal turn within the context of globalization and the changing structures of career trajectories propelled by massive privatization. However, the building of male self-expansion is organically linked to and dependent on a vision of the feminine other who provokes and nurtures these male desires for layered selves. The male narratives described a vision of desired femininity that was marked by opposing dualities of, on the one hand, ambitious, charismatic, sexually desiring, and self-possessed women and, on the other hand, positive, alturistic, "energy-giving" women.

The emergence of the new definition of masculinity has occurred simultaneously with the appearance of a new construction of femininity among young women. This new femininity constitutes its identity not through maternal roles but through a shared desire for individualized selves defined against other-directedness, self-sacrifice, and female subservience to the desires of others. The desire for self-governance and the rejection of male intrusion on female sovereignty in the name of protection mark the most important constitutive dimensions of the new femininity. Like its male counterpart, this new femininty also has its cocreators. The desired man in the female narratives is constructed dualistically as someone who seeks power and creativity for self-expansion and who has strong ambitions to become a dominant actor in society, while simultaneously disavowing gender-based traditional privileges to control and dominate women.

I conclude that these nonpatriarchal gender projects should not be read necessarily as a promise of democratic gender relations. The very notions of desirable femininity, the dialectic between charismatic and engery-giving women in male narratives that would help make expanded male selves possible, might ultimately undermine young women's claims to a new femininity untied to maternal selflessness and female altruism. In the same fashion, the female constructions of ideal masculinity, the dialectic between power in the public sphere and escaping power and domination in intimate relations and the private sphere, might actually serve to undermine female desire for noncontrolling men.

I consider bringing the rich dimensions of "undoing" patriarchy to gender theory as a distinct analytical pathway. This pathway also addresses the methodological question of how we might continue to investigate the link between gender and patriarchy.

Conclusion: From Gender Domination to Rethinking Patriarchy

Focusing on the identification of selfhood with unpatriarchal values among men raises particular questions and new analytical openings for a feminist theory of gender, lending a valuable paradigm that can reveal the relevance, complexities, and contradictions of the concept of "patriarchy" in gender theory. I have proposed an integration of the language of patriarchy via the example of young men in Turkey who self-consciously disavow patriarchy and paternalism while simultaneously giving it new forms and subtle expressions. I suggest that their stories cannot be told at all without representing the subjects' explicit engagement with patriarchal ideals and the cognitive and emotional narrative sources that guide their vocabularies. This is not just a challenge for a simple recognition of experience in theory or a claim that experience itself is either a superior or entirely sufficient form for theoretical representation or, as Connell says, "theory is the moment in a larger social process of knowledge formation that transforms data or experience, always in some way moving beyond the given" (Connell 2014, 521).

Focusing on a nation such as Turkey highlights the complex and multifaceted domain of patriarchy and provides strong justification for approaches that challenge nation-based boundaries and stress interrelationships rather than ahistorical and preconstituted categories of patriarchy. In particular, it offers an important vantage point from which to view the historical specificities and transformations of Turkish conceptions of patriarchy and state paternalism in relation to global neoliberalism, a complex alignment in the making that is both destroying and remaking the patriarchy-paternalism couple simultaneously in different realms. The ongoing presence of building hegemony to create a new Turkey, the strong resistance to neoconservative patriarchal familialism from feminist and LGBTQ movements, and unpatriarchal desires among young adults offer a transformative setting for a reconsideration of patriarchy in gender theory.

If the aim of gender theory is to generate explanations and imaginaries of change that are indeed politically meaningful and transformative, the basis for achieving that end will depend on its epistemological principles and categories being informed across time, global locations, and cultural particularities. Patriarchy is now conceived as a dangerous traditional form of gender- and aged-based domination that has been supposedly eradicated in the global North, while, as Gwepal illustrates in the quotation with which I begin this chapter, "an essentialist notion of the term 'patriarchy' has become naturalized in relation to the 'Global South.'" We must reject the false certainties and the temptation to construct an "epistemological other" in the service of collective projects of domination by the global North. In the same vein, how we deploy conceptions of the "transnational" in relation to patriarchy is important. Limiting the Southern voice to a critique and an exposé (of how contemporary transnational connections operate as neocolonial projects) without tracing in practical terms the real and varying relationships in local patriarchies, which have such a formative place in constructing gender, risks becoming reductive, and actually has the potential to disempower and short-circuit the integration of theories produced by the global South.

In urging a focus on rethinking patriarchy, I am not suggesting that there is an effective universal, singular form of patriarchy that encompasses all gender relations and constructs male power and privilege the same way, and shapes how gender is defined, constituted, identified with, and reproduced. Patriarchy is a particular system of gender domination, neither uniform nor static. However, without refining and studying the term "patriarchy," we run the risk of reifying, dehistoricizing, and valorizing patriarchy in the global South and discounting patriarchy in the global North. Critically extending and developing the concept of patriarchy in gender theory makes one more attentive to the project of creating new integrative paths (cross-fertilization, in Connell's terms), by which Southern theory can be incorporated into Northern theory. The Turkish case illuminates the ways in which the concept of patriarchy can help address the incompleteness of gender theory, which currently leaves vast numbers of social actors and political practices thoroughly unaccounted for and constructs a false universalism. It also builds upon the strength of gender theory developed by Connell by providing avenues to address and elaborate the relationality of gender in a more systematic way.

We should devise a theory of gender domination to describe and theorize sites of domination-subordination, practices intimately associated in the creation of gender relations based on domination, finding new ways both to map variations among the domination of men and the subordination of women and to incorporate a focus on interaction/intersection with other systems of domination. Whatever the approach, we must open a thread via gender domination that can provide the anaytical template to link theories produced in different locations that contextualize and particularize gender domination spatially and epistemologically. Gender relations as relations of domination enter into and help to constitute other collective relations and institutional arrangements. *Gender domination* in gender theory thus provides a larger conceptual canvas and inclusive epistemological and political agenda. The richness that can be garnered from such a theoretical incorporation helps us articulate transformative projects at the systemic macro-structural or institutional level and at the micro-interpersonal or individual level, locally, globally, and transnationally.

NOTES

1 Originally proposed by black feminists, as way to interpret the effects of race, gender, and class, the intersection theory suggests that instead of looking at race, gender, and class as separate entities, they need to be looked at as interactive, multiplicative, and mutually amplifying experiences and processes that create unique locations of subordination and domination, privilege and disadvantage. Kathy

Davis (2008) brilliantly argues that it is the very ambiguity and epistemological vacuity and methodological rootlessness of the concept of intersectionality that in fact defines its success. She argues that the concept's undefined parameters powerfully invite inclusion of different epistemological traditions and methodological strategies.

2 In this chapter, I focus on one such narrative. My larger research includes 87 upwardly mobile young adults interviewed between 2002 and 2006 in Istanbul, of which 22 were heterosexually identified men.

3 Neoliberalism is considered as a major governing force in the world today, but the concept lacks a precise definition applicable to every case. My usage of this concept is derived from David Harvey who stresses that neoliberalism is better understood as "a theory of political economic practices" that emphasizes that "human well-being can best be advanced by liberating individual entrepreneurial freedoms and skills within an institutional framework characterized by strong private property rights, free markets and free trade" (2005, 2). While this definition is illuminating, it needs further explication as the practical implementation of neoliberal policies and practices depends on cultural and historical particularities. For example, in the Turkish version we see a lack of correspondence between neoliberal economic practices and a weakening of the role of the state, in contradiction with one of core neoliberal tenets. During the early 1980s neoliberalism gained prevalence in Turkey where a privatized and liberalized market economy replaced state-controlled capitalism. Neoliberal transformations are marked by a new economic and cultural configuration and legal changes, broadly characterized by the global opening of markets, a radical process of privatization (selling state-owned enterprises, goods, and services to private companies), and establishing and preserving foreign capital investments. The concept of neoliberalism also includes a perspective on changing notions of selfhood, the production of the presupposed neoliberal subject centered on the ideals of entrepreneurial freedom, self-invention, flexibility, autonomy, and self-realization. Exploration of the complex social, psychological, and material processes that collectively foster the formation of the neoliberal subject now occupies the research agendas of a growing number of scholars across a number of social science disciplines. This chapter situates itself in the framework of this contemporary concern and offers the voices of educationally advantaged young men in Turkey. These men are not only intensely subjected to neoliberal images, ideologies, and institutions but also have the ability to appropriate, reject, or reshape the ethos of neoliberalism in a plurality of contexts.

I use the expression "local neoconservatism" to highlight the wide application of neoliberal policies and the Islamist project of reconstructing patriarchy to control and regulate women's sexuality, labor, and feminine bodily modalities within the context of globalization. It is "neoconservative" because the Islamist government vigorously advocates quite extensive top-down policies to cultivate Islamic piety by focusing on gender relations and sexuality. These new state policies are designed to facilitate a pronationalist agenda of sexual reproduction, promotion of (heterosexual) early marriage, gender segregation in the public sphere, and the control and regulation of public life—particularly the elimination of sexually animated environments. Also, the very existence of new gender conservatism in Turkey is a testament to the advances made by the feminists and how they articulated a powerful critique of patriarchal institutions, ideology, and practices.

4 Fictitious name.

REFERENCES

Acar, Feride, and Gülbanu Altunok. 2012. "The 'Politics of Intimate' at the Intersection of Neo-liberalism and Neo-conservatism in Contemporary Turkey." *Women's Studies International Forum* 41 (1): 14–23.

Açıksöz, Salih Can. 2015. "In Vitro Nationalism: Masculinity, Disability, and Assisted Reproduction in War-Torn Turkey." In *Gender and Sexuality in Muslim Cultures*, edited by Gul Ozyegin, 19–37. Burlington, VT: Ashgate.

Benjamin, Jessica. 1988. *The Bonds of Love: Psychoanalysis, Feminism, and the Problem of Domination.* New York: Pantheon.

Beşpınar, Fatma Umut. 2015. "Between Ideals and Enactments: The Experience of 'New Fatherhood' among Middle-Class Men in Turkey." In *Gender and Sexuality in Muslim Cultures*, edited by Gul Ozyegin, 95–115. Burlington, VT: Ashgate.

Collinson, D. L., and J. Hearn. 1994. "Naming Men as Men: Implications for Work, Organization and Management." *Gender, Work and Organization* 1 (1): 2–22.

Connell, R. W. 1987. *Gender and Power.* Stanford, CA: Stanford University Press.

———. 2005. *Masculinities.* 2nd ed. Berkeley: University of California Press.

Connell, Raewyn. 2007. *Southern Theory.* Cambridge: Polity.

———.2014. "Rethinking Gender from the South." *Feminist Studies* 40 (3): 518–539.

Connell, Raewyn, and J. W. Messerschmidt. 2005. "Hegemonic Masculinity: Rethinking the Concept. " *Gender & Society* 19: 829–859.

Coşar, Simten, and Metin Yeğenoğlu. 2011. "New Grounds for Patriarchy in Turkey? Gender Policy in the Age of AKP." *South European Society and Politics* 16 (4): 555–573.

Crenshaw, Kimberlé. 1989. "Demarginalizing the Intersection of Race and Sex: A Black Feminist Critique of Antidiscrimination Doctrine, Feminist Theory, and Antracist Politics." In *Feminist Legal Theory: Foundations*, edited by D. Kelley Weisberg. Philadelphia: Temple University Press.

Davis, Kathy. 2008. "Intersectionality as Buzzword: A Sociology of Science Perspective on What Makes a Feminist Theory Successful." *Feminist Theory* 9: 67–85.

Dayıoğlu, Meltem, and Cem Başlevent. 2012. "Gender Aspects of Income Distribution and Poverty in Turkey." In *Gender and Society in Turkey: The Impact of Neoliberal Policies, Political Islam, and EU Accession*, edited by Saniye Dedeoglu and Adem Elveren, 65–86. London: I. B. Tauris.

Dedeoglu, Saniye, and Adem Elveren, eds. 2012. *Gender and Society in Turkey.* London: I. B. Tauris.

Grewal, Inderpal. 2013. "Outsourcing Patriarchy." *International Feminist Journal of Politics* 15 (1): 1–19.

Hartmann, Heidi. 1981. "The Unhappy Marriage of Marxism and Feminism: Towards a More Progressive Union." In *Women and Revolution*, edited by Lydia Sargent. Boston: South End Press.

Harvey, David. 2005. *A Brief History of Neoliberalism*. Oxford: Oxford University Press.

Kandiyoti, Deniz. 2011. "A Tangled Web: The Politics of Gender in Turkey." *OpenDemocracy*, January 5. Accessed October 12, 2014. www.opendemocracy.net.

Korkman, Zeynep. 2015 "Blessing Neoliberalism: Economy, Family, and the Occult in Millennial Turkey." *Journal of the Ottoman and Turkish Studies Association* 3 (1).

McCall, Leslie. 2005. "The Complexity of Intersectionality." *Signs: Journal of Women in Culture and Society* 30: 1771–1800.

Mohanty, Chandra Talpade. 1988. "Under Western Eyes: Feminist Scholarship and Colonial Discourse." *Feminist Review* 30 (Autumn): 61–88.

Moller, Michael. 2007. "Exploiting Patterns: A Critique of Hegemonic Masculinity." *Journal of Gender Studies* 16 (3): 263–276.

Özbay, Cenk. 2015. "'Men Are Less Manly, Women Are More Feminine': The Shopping Mall as a Site for Gender Crisis in Istanbul." In *Gender and Sexuality in Muslim Cultures*, edited by Gul Ozyegin, 73–95. Burlington, VT: Ashgate.

Ozyegin, Gul. 2015. *New Desires, New Selves: Sex, Love, and Piety among Turkish Youth*. New York: New York University Press.

Patil, Vrushali. 2013. "From Patriarchy to Intersectionality: A Transnational Feminist Assessment of How Far We've Really Come." *Signs: Journal of Women in Culture and Society* 38 (4): 847–867.

Spelman, Elizabeth V. 1988. *Inessential Woman: Problems of Exclusion in Feminist Thought*. Boston: Beacon Press.

Toksöz, Gulay. 2012. "The State of Female Labour in the Impasse of the Neoliberal Market and the Patriarchal Family." In *Gender and Society in Turkey: The Impact of Neoliberal Policies, Political Islam, and EU Accession*, edited by Saniye Dedeoglu and Adem Y. Elveren, 47–64. London: I. B. Tauris.

Women for Women's Human Rights. 2002. *The New Legal Status of Women in Turkey*. Istanbul: WWHER–New Ways.

———. 2006. *Turkish Civil and Penal Code Reforms from a Gender Perspective: The Success of Two Nationwide Campaigns*. Istanbul: WWHER–New Ways.

13

On the Elasticity of Gender Hegemony

Why Hybrid Masculinities Fail to Undermine Gender and Sexual Inequality

TRISTAN BRIDGES AND C. J. PASCOE

Gender is susceptible to extraordinary change; gender inequality is, by comparison, much more durable. Indeed, shifting gendered styles have been at the center of discussion among masculinities scholars and contemporary social commentators, many claiming that the days of emotional repression, homophobia, and sexism are nearing their end. Consider, for example, some recent trends in masculine expression: the "metrosexual," the "hipster," and the "bro."

The earliest of these, the *metrosexual*, emerged in 1994 (Simpson 1999 [1994]; Barber 2016). This well-coiffed twenty- or thirtysomething, white, educated, professional man likely lived in a city and stylistically laid claim to symbolic territory typically associated with women and gay men (de Casanova, Wetzel, and Speice 2016). This "new heterosexual masculinity, one rooted in consumption and vanity" (Barber 2016) purchased grooming products, wore designer clothing, and spent a great deal of time and money on hygiene and appearance (e.g., Whitehead 2007; Coad 2008; Shugart 2008).

Appearing on the heels of the metrosexual (though echoing earlier gendered expressions [Mailer 1957]), the *hipster* is a white, usually college educated, 20–30-year-old, city-dwelling man, distinguished by tastes such as musical interests, hairstyles, grooming habits, clothing, literary and artistic curiosities, as well as culinary and libation preferences. More countercultural, androgynous, intellectual, creative, and independent than the metrosexual, the hipster draws on a gendered form of nostalgia for masculinities of old—embracing styles of facial hair, dress, or particular cultural artifacts from specific historical periods (at least as those periods are collectively imagined). The rise of the artisanal hipster aesthetic is part of a more general elevation of all manner of "geek masculinities" to new heights of gendered status (Bell 2013).

Other recent expressions of masculinity, such as the *bro*, seem to be less indicative of change. "Bro" is most often used to describe young, white men, connoting a playful, immature, hypermasculine, frat boy, party culture (e.g., Ward 2008, 2015). As a prefix or suffix, "bro" masculinizes all sorts of identities, objects, relationships, and behaviors: "laxbros" (lacrosse players), "brogrammers" (computer programmers), "dudebros" (generic, hypermasculine twentysomethings), "brogurt" (yogurt for men), "brotein" (protein as a dietary supplement), "broga" (yoga for men), and, perhaps most conspicuously, the "bromance." From movies (*I Love You, Man*, 2009) to social media hashtags (#mancrushmonday), "bromance" describes intense emotional bonds and perhaps even intimate touch between young, straight-identified men (e.g., DeAngelis 2014), forms of homosociality that seem to share little in common with similar relations in relatively recent history (e.g., Bird 1996; Grazian 2007).[1]

While by no means an exhaustive list, taken together we suggest that these three emergent configurations of gender illustrate that masculinity is changing. What does it mean for heterosexual men to care deeply about their appearance in ways that are typically associated with women or gay men? What does it mean when men proudly announce intimate relationships with other straight men? Do they herald larger changes in the structure and organization of gender relations and inequality? Can they be seen as evidence of a general demise of homophobia or sexism? The answer to all of these questions is both "Yes" and "No." Indeed, the larger question—and one that is more challenging to answer—is what do contemporary transformations in masculinity among historically privileged groups of men *mean*?

The sense that masculinity is changing is nothing new (e.g., Rotundo 1993; Segal 1990; Kimmel 2012). Over a half century ago, Helen Hacker (1957) asked why and how masculinity was transforming, what kinds of new dilemmas and burdens awaited men navigating emerging gendered expectations, and whether changes in masculinity might foreshadow transformations in inequality. Historical evidence suggests that gendered anxieties and discourses that follow shifts in gender relations are recycled. Indeed, while the examples of the metrosexual, the hipster, and the bro are contemporary ones, they indicate that gender is a historical *process*, and that some configurations of practice are more likely during some historical periods than others as patterned responses to transformations in gender relations.

As with previous historical periods during which masculinities were being redefined, the extent of contemporary transformations and their impact and meaning is the source of a great deal of theory, research, and debate (e.g., Connell 1985, 1987, 1995, 2002; Messner 1993; Anderson 2009; Bridges and Pascoe 2014). What we are interested in here is not the fact that change is happening, but how to interpret the *meanings* of these changes. It is tempting to read the metrosexual, the hipster, and the bro as part of a narrative of extraordinary and progressive change—men seem less inhibited by strict expectations of manliness. Indeed, some scholars suggest that the transformations associated with young, white, educated, and class-privileged men are signs of "the declining significance of homophobia" (McCormack 2012). Others argue that contemporary masculinities are no longer organized hierarchically; rather, they are "inclusive" (Anderson 2009) and represent a fundamental challenge to systems of power and inequality. We suggest that symbolic changes in the gender order need to be understood in terms of what they accomplish, but also what they obscure.

To understand these emerging identities as both accomplishing and obscuring gender inequality, we bring Raewyn Connell's theorization of "symbolic relations" into dialogue with our conceptualization of "hybrid masculinities"--the selective incorporation of identity elements typically associated with various marginalized and subordinated masculinities or femininities into privileged men's gendered performances and identities (e.g., Demetriou 2001; Messner 2007; Messerschmidt 2010; Arxer 2011; Bridges 2014; Bridges and Pascoe 2014, 2015). By drawing on the substructures of Connell's theory of gender relations, we articulate how flexibility in some substructures can work in ways that conceal the resilience of others.

Gender Relations

Drawing on Juliet Mitchells's (1966) insight that gender inequality was established by a complex yet "specific structure" made up of distinct components, Connell makes sense of gender relations as composed of four constituent parts: power relations, production relations, emotional relations, and symbolic relations (Connell 1987, 2002). These four dimensions of gender relations are interconnected and mutually constitutive. As with other understandings of gender as a social structure (e.g., Lorber 1993; Risman 2004), the identification of these four substructures emerged out of previous feminist theorizing.

As "substructures" (Connell 2004), Connell understood these dimensions of gender relations as working together, though not always to the same ends or with the same means. As such Connell's theory makes possible an understanding of gender inequality as capable of being challenged and reproduced simultaneously. As Connell notes, however:

> The argument does not assume that they are the only discoverable structures, that they exhaust the field. Nor does it claim that they are necessary structures. . . . The argument rests on a gentler, more pragmatic but perhaps more demonstrable claim that with a framework like this we can come to a serviceable understanding of current history. (1987, 97)

Intentionally leaving a theory open like this speaks to this framework's ability to adapt to new contexts and contingencies. Connell's theory of gender relations does more than simply account for change; it actively anticipates change.

Not only do gender relations change, but these changes actually *constitute* gender relations. Gender relations are historically unstable and prone toward crisis, something Connell calls "crisis tendencies." Crisis tendencies are uneven, often affecting gender relations incompletely. While the gender order continually tends toward crisis, Connell suggests that this propensity may have intensified in recent history, producing "a major loss of legitimacy for patriarchy," such that "different groups of men are now negotiating this loss in very different ways" (1995, 202).

Conceptualizing crisis tendencies as an integral feature of gender relations allows us to make sense of historical change by considering the diverse potential embedded within any historical transformation in gender relations. Crisis tendencies speak to the flexibility of systems of power and inequality. Though the history of gender inequality is sometimes presented as a slow but steady march toward equality, Connell's theory makes possible an understanding of progress while contextualizing this potential with a conceptualization of inequality as flexible and adaptive.

Hybrid Masculinities

As relations of power, production, emotions, and symbols change, these changes reverberate throughout the gender order. Building on the dimension of symbolic relations in particular, the concept of hybrid masculinities attests to the flexibility of gender inequality. Hybrid masculinities illustrate a great deal of change among symbolic and emotional relations—transformations that obscure the fact that power relations have been less challenged than it initially seems.

Hybrid masculinities refer to the selective incorporation of elements of identity typically associated with various marginalized and subordinated masculinities and—at times—femininities into privileged men's gender performances and identities (e.g., Demetriou 2001; Messner 2007; Messerschmidt 2010; Arxer 2011; Bridges 2014; Bridges and Pascoe 2014).[2] These transformations include men's assimilation, among others, of "bits and pieces" (Demetriou 2001, 350) of identity projects coded as "gay" (e.g., Hennessy 1995; Demetriou 2001; Heasley 2005; Bridges 2014; Bridges and Pascoe 2015), "Black" (e.g., Ward 2008; Hughey 2012), or "feminine" (e.g., Arxer 2011; Wilkins 2009; Schippers 2000; Messerschmidt 2010).

Research on hybrid masculinities points to a patterned set of consequences associated with the processes of incorporating elements of the identities of various Others. Hybrid masculinities work in ways that reproduce contemporary systems of gender, race, class, and sexual inequality, but, importantly, obscure this process as it is happening. The emergence of hybrid masculinities indicates that normative constraints associated with masculinity are shifting, and shows that these shifts have largely taken place in ways that have sustained existing ideologies and systems of power and inequality (e.g., Messner 1993, 2007; Demetriou 2001; Messerschmidt 2010; Bridges 2014; Bridges and Pascoe 2014, 2015).

The interpretation of changes in gender relations provided by our conceptualization of "hybrid masculinity" directly critiques a growing body of literature that suggests that new configurations of identity and practice are best understood as *resistance* to gender and sexual inequality. This "inclusivity" framework (Anderson 2009; McCormack 2012) suggests that these changes in gender relations represent important, lasting, and serious changes in various dimensions of gender inequality. Yet historical work on masculinity documents that it is a category of identity characterized by internal and dialectical contradictions (e.g., Kimmel 2012; Aboim 2010) and that hegemonic configurations have demonstrated extraordinary elastic properties over time, incorporating new modes of behavior and practice in periods of crisis (e.g., Messner 1993, 2007; Connell 1995; Demetriou 2001; Bridges 2014; Bridges and Pascoe 2014, 2015; de Boise 2015), and taking on unique forms in different regions and local contexts (Connell and Messerschmidt 2005). This chapter provides an alternate analysis of contemporary shifts in masculinities not as uniform challenges to gender and sexual inequality, but as complicated processes that have the collective effect of obscuring inequality.

The concept of hybrid masculinities grew out of analytic limitations associated with Connell's theorization of hegemonic masculinity (Demetriou 2001). In analyzing straight-identified men's assimilation of elements of "gay male culture," Demetriou suggested that the concept of hegemonic masculinity, which had at its core a symbolic distance from "subordinated masculinity" (a configuration Connell [1987, 1992, 1995] argued was best represented by gay men), could not account for why straight men might adopt the styles of subordinated men. This is, for Demetriou, inconsistent with a Gramscian conceptualization of "hegemony":

> Whereas for Gramsci the process is essentially a dialectical one that involves reciprocity and mutual interaction between the class that is leading and the groups that are led, Connell understands the process in a more elitist way where subordinate and marginalized masculinities have no effect on the construction of the hegemonic model. (Demetriou 2001, 345)

As such, Demetriou suggests that hegemonic masculinity is better understood as a "hegemonic masculine bloc" capable of appropriating "what appears pragmatically useful and constructive for the project of domination at a particular historical moment" (2001, 345). While it may seem that the adoption of elements associated with gay men by straight men is a significant movement away from hierarchical gendered relations, Demetriou suggests something much more dynamic—that the incorporation of "bits and pieces [of gay male culture] . . . [produce] new, hybrid configurations of gender practice that enable them to reproduce their dominance over women [and other men] in historically novel ways" (2001, 350–51). The appropriation of elements of subordinated and marginalized "Others" into configurations of hegemonic masculinities works to recuperate existing systems of power and inequality.

Demetriou's understanding, however, presupposes concrete social groups in definite relations of alliance and subordination. Our identity-based approach situates these practices as much more fluid and dynamic. As such, our theorizing of hybrid masculinities builds on— rather than opposes—Connell's framework. It is not the case, for instance, that young, straight, white men are the only ones "playing" with masculinity. Nor is it necessarily true that young men are *intentionally* playing with masculinity in ways that either maintain or conceal gender inequality. Our conceptualization of "hybrid masculinities" captures the dynamic processes through which some groups receive a qualitatively different set of patterned consequences for their participation and have a qualitatively different set of considerations at stake in participating in the first place.

Our theorization of "hybrid masculinity" connects a consistent finding across a collection of research that has shown that hybrid masculinities are broadly associated with at least three distinct consequences that exacerbate, reflect, and conceal existing inequalities in patterned ways (e.g., Bridges and Pascoe 2014). First, hybrid masculine practices often work in ways that create discursive space between privileged groups of men and hegemonic masculinity, enabling some to frame themselves as outside of existing systems of privilege and inequality—something we label *discursive distancing*. Second, contemporary hybrid masculinities are often premised on the notion that the masculinities available to young, white, straight men are less meaningful than the identities of various Others, whose identities were at least partially produced by collective struggles for rights and recognition. We call this process *strategic borrowing*. Third, hybrid masculinities work to fortify symbolic and social boundaries between (racial, gender, sexual, class-based) groups—

further entrenching, and often concealing, inequality in historically novel ways. We refer to this consequence as *fortifying boundaries*.

Collectively, these patterned consequences exemplify the processes by which meanings and practices of hegemonic masculinity change over time in ways that have sustained the structure of institutionalized gender regimes to advantage men collectively over women and some men over others (Connell and Messerschmidt 2005). Similar to Connell's (1987, 1995) conceptualization of the four substructures of gender relations as interrelated and overlapping, we see each of the consequences we identify here as heuristic devices that enable us to examine the meanings of contemporary shifts in gender identities, relations, and inequality. Below, we provide more detail from research that highlights the three processes as interrelated, yet distinct.

Discursive Distancing

Research on men's profeminist, political, and grooming activities illustrates how hybrid masculinities can work in ways that discursively distance men from hegemonic masculinity as they also (often more subtly) align themselves with it. "Bromances," for instance, are instructive—they are, on the surface, a relationship that would seem to reduce the distance between hegemonic masculinity and intimacy between men in a way that questions the centrality of homophobia to contemporary masculinities. Yet the very language to describe these relationships—"bro"—works to symbolically enshrine heterosexuality by establishing distance from same-sex eroticism even while seemingly engaging in same-sex intimacy. In this way, "bro" works as a both a symbol and discourse associated with a dominant configuration of white, heterosexual masculinity (Ward 2015). An analysis of men's antisexist work and beauty practices documents a similar process of change in symbolic relations that does little to disrupt the systems of power that structure gender and sexual relations more broadly.

Men's participation in antiviolence movements such as Walk a Mile in Her Shoes marches (Bridges 2010) or My Strength Is Not for Hurting campaigns (Masters 2010) illustrates discursive distancing. Walk a Mile marches require that men wear high-heeled shoes and walk one mile protesting violence against women and pledging support to end it. These men are standing in solidarity with women, actively opposing men's violence, and wearing women's clothing—all practices that seem to distance them from hegemonic masculinity. As Bridges (2010) observed, however, march participants can reproduce gender and sexual inequality even as they actively resist it. Participants regularly joked about wearing women's clothing, their (in)ability to walk in heels, and same-sex sexual desire—all of which worked to align them with hegemonic masculinity even as their participation in antiviolence activism distances them from it.

The My Strength Is Not for Hurting campaign—one of few antirape campaigns explicitly directed at men—also works to distance men from hegemonic masculinity through framing rapists as pathological men while depicting the nonrapist as hegemonically masculine. The nonrapist is a "real," "strong" man who is fundamentally different from (the presumably weak and unmanly) rapist. The campaign draws on ideologies about men's inherent "strength" and protectionism (". . . is not for hurting") in a way that symbolically reinscribes unequal gender relations. Campaigns like this separate "good" from "bad" men and fail to account for the ways that presenting strength and power as natural resources for men perpetuates gender and sexual inequality even as they are called into question (Murphy 2009; Pascoe and Hollander 2016). Both Walk a Mile marches and the My Strength Is Not for Hurting campaign create some distance between these (good) men who oppose gendered violence and (bad) hegemonically masculine men who presumably support it. Yet, in challenging men's violence against women, both campaigns simultaneously reaffirm hegemonic masculine forms.

Other boundary blurring projects accomplish similar ends. Kristen Barber's (2008, 2016) study of white, middle-class, heterosexual men's interactions with workers in professional men's hair salons illustrates a related dynamic in which some men engage in beauty work formerly coded "feminine." Barber shows how men rely on a rhetoric of expectations associated with professional-class masculinities to justify their participation in the beauty industry while simultaneously naturalizing distinctions between themselves and working-class men, framing the latter as misogynistic and responsible for reproducing gender inequality. Barber highlights the ways these men avoid feminization while simultaneously strengthening their status as class-privileged men. The cost of the salon services excludes working-class men; but more than this, the salons' clients position themselves as more gender and sexually progressive than the nonwhite and working-class men not represented in these places. Thus, the straight, white, educated, and elite men in Barber's study frame costly salon haircuts as a sign of progressive masculinity—a potent symbol they frame as illustrating their status as "new" men (see Messner and Messerschmidt's chapter in this volume).

While bromances, men's prowomen activism, and beauty work may appear to be new, the process of *discursive distancing* is not. As Pierette Hondagneu-Sotelo and Mike Messner argued:

> Too often critical discussions of masculinity tend to project atavistic hypermasculine, aggressive, misogynistic masculinity onto relatively powerless men. By comparison, the masculine gender displays of educated, privileged New Men are too often uncritically applauded, rather than skeptically and critically examined. (1994, 215)

Ignoring the intersectional dynamics that inequitably distribute access to specific hybrid masculine forms risks presenting contemporary changes as indicative of transformations in systems of inequality that still exist—albeit in new forms. As Hondagneu-Sotelo and Messner (1994) suggest, men of color, working-class men, and immigrant men, among others, are often implicitly cast as the possessors of regressive masculinities. In fact, when groups of marginalized and subordinated Others craft hybrid gender identities, they often do so with very different consequences and concerns than those of white, middle-class, young, urban men. *Discursive distancing* provides a sensitizing concept to analyze these intersections in finer detail. Part of analyzing transformations in symbolic gender relations must involve a critical assessment of the work accomplished for the groups who get labeled as transformed.

Strategic Borrowing

Configurations of hybrid masculinity associated with privileged groups of men are often premised on the notion that the masculinities they perceive as available to them are meaningless when compared with various "Others." Indeed, cultural appropriation is a defining characteristic of processes of hybridization—domination through "negotiation" rather than "negation" (e.g., Sinfield 1996; Burke 2009). Research on hybrid masculinities has shown that men who occupy privileged social categories "strategically borrow" symbols associated with various Others in ways that work to reframe themselves as symbolically part of socially subordinated groups.

While challenging inequality may be part of the motivation driving hybrid masculine configurations, research suggests that these practices may also have to do with exploring pleasures that powerful men have been denied by gendered expectations. Relatively privileged men who mobilize hybrid configurations of masculinity gain access to some of the symbolic and emotional pleasures associated with transgression. In this way, hybrid masculinities can also be seen as a form of symbolic tourism—enjoying the pleasures associated with transgressing normative gender and sexual boundaries, but avoiding much of the injustice and pain.

Once made visible by feminist challenge and critique, privileged configurations of masculinity are capable of dramatically reworking the meaning associated with that visibility to recuperate privilege in new ways. Through this process, white men are presented as victims (Messner 1993) and inequality becomes less easily identified. Like Mary Waters's (1990) research documenting white people's relative ignorance of the ethnic flexibility they are afforded, the hybrid identities available to young, straight, white men may be very different from those available to marginalized and subordinated groups. As Patricia Hill Collins writes, "Authentic Black people must be contained—their authentic culture can enter white controlled spaces, but they cannot" (Collins 2004, 177). The strategic borrowing of symbols and styles associated with various marginalized and subordinated "Others" has a patterned set of consequences, research documents. One manifestation of this are hipster masculinities, which borrow bits and pieces from working-class, white masculinity as a way of symbolically laying claim to masculine authenticity.

Strategic borrowing is also at work in the incorporation of gay culture by straight-identified men. The emergence of the identity of the metrosexual seems perhaps the best example of this. Indeed, de Casanova, Wetzel, and Speice's (2015) interviews with metrosexual-identified men indicate that white-collar men embraced this configuration of gender strategically (for career advancement) "rather than [out of] a collective rethinking of masculine norms or a challenge to hegemonic masculinity" (2015, 78). As culturally dominant models of masculinity assimilate symbols associated with subordinated "Others" and alter the look and feel of contemporary performances of gender, however, these practices do little to challenge men's structural position of power and authority (Demetriou 2001). Rather, as Demetriou writes,

[w]e are used to seeing masculine power as a closed, coherent, and unified totality that embraces no otherness, no contradiction. This is an illusion that must be done away with because it is precisely through its hybrid and apparently contradictory content that hegemonic masculinity reproduces itself. (2001, 355)

Similarly, by theorizing the symbolic elements of sexuality, Bridges (2014) analyzes the causes and consequences of heterosexual men subjectively identifying aspects of themselves as "gay" in ways that preserve their heterosexuality and simultaneously reinforce existing boundaries between gay and straight individuals and cultures.

Steven Arxer's (2011) study of interactions between heterosexual men at a college bar documents an analogous practice. The behavior of the men in Arxer's study is surprisingly different from the competitive, emotionally detached, sexually objectifying practices that characterize straight men's interactions in Bird's (1996) or Grazian's (2007) research. Instead, these men draw on the emotionality presumably displayed by gay men (illustrating flexibility within Connell's "emotional relations") to increase their chances of sexually "scoring" with women (providing no real challenge to "power relations"). Thus, while a different collective performance of masculinity than the "the girl hunt" that Grazian (2007) examined or Bird's (1996) analysis of the "men's club," the consequences of performing emotional sensitivity are strikingly similar in terms of sustaining existing systems of power and inequality. Similar consequences occur with racial strategic borrowing among white men (e.g., Hughey 2012; Bridges and Pascoe 2014).

When we frame young, straight, class-privileged, educated, white men's "new" performances of masculinity solely as indicators of a decline in gender and sexual inequality (e.g., Anderson 2009; McCormack 2012), already marginalized groups of men often end up situated as playing a greater role in perpetuating inequality (Messner 1993; Hondagneu-Sotelo and Messner 1994; Bridges and Pascoe 2014). By framing an extraordinarily privileged group of men as both the embodiment and harbinger of feminist change, social scientists participate in further marginalizing poor men, working-class men, religious men, undereducated men, rural men, and men of color (among others). Even as young, straight, white men borrow from young, gay, black, working-class, rural, or urban men to symbolically boost their masculine capital, research shows that these practices often work to reaffirm these subordinate and marginalized groups as deviant, shoring up existing relations of power and dominance.

Fortifying Boundaries

By co-opting elements of style and performance from less powerful masculinities, young, straight, white men's hybridizations often obscure the symbolic and social boundaries between groups upon which such practices rely. Through a process we call *fortifying boundaries*, hybrid masculinities further entrench and conceal systems of inequality in historically new ways, often along lines of race, gender, sexuality, and class.

For instance, when men engage in sexual practices that challenge the relationship between normative masculinity and homophobia, they may reify inequality. Jane Ward's (2008, 2015) research on white straight-identifying men who have sex with other straight-identifying men illustrates this process. Ward documents the ways that, in their search for sexual partners, these men objectify women, reject effeminacy among men, and hypereroticize men of color. They talk about hooking up with other men while watching "pussy porn," say they do not want to have sex with men who are feminine "sissy la las," and use stigmatizing language to describe their ideal men-of-color sex partners. Ward calls this particular configuration of practices "dude sex," implicitly suggesting that sex between men *might* challenge contemporary gender relations, but sex between "dudes" does not. Similar to the "bromance," "dude sex" relies on symbolic relations to simultaneously challenge and reinforce systems of power and inequality. Though violating the "one-act rule"

(Schilt and Westbrook 2009) of men's homosexuality by participating in same-sex sex, these men simultaneously reinforce gendered and raced inequality. In fact, according to Ward's research, engaging in same-sex sex is *proof* of their masculinity precisely because of their race and class position—a process Ward (2015) calls "hetero-exceptionalism." Their identity projects are situated as having a better political and cultural "fit" with heterosexuality, relying on symbols and stereotypes of gendered and racialized performances of masculinity to authenticate their *hetero-sexual* masculine identities.

Some of men's practices that initially appear to be feminist also perpetuate gender inequality even as they obscure it. Recent changes in the ideologies and practices of fathering may seem progressive—such as increasing levels of emotionality and time spent with children. But, upon closer investigation, they also often entrench gender inequality. The new fathering movement of the twentieth century, for instance, was not necessarily about challenging gender inequality in families, but about a particular *style* of men's parenting (Messner 1993), that, as Stein (2005) argues, redraws boundaries around men's heterosexuality and masculine authority. In her study of the Promise Keepers movement, Heath (2003) examines the ways that men embody "new fathering" by playing larger roles in their children's lives and increasing their emotional availability while also enforcing gender inequality by espousing a "biblical" notion of "the family" in which women submit to their husbands (see also Donovan 1998).

Groups of evangelical Christian men exemplify the processes by which hybrid masculinities can be understood to fortify boundaries between groups even as they appear to challenge those boundaries (e.g., Diefendorf 2015; Wilkins 2009; Gerber 2015). For instance, Diefendorf's (2015) analysis of young evangelical Christian men's claims to sexual abstinence before marriage appear to be a fundamental departure from hegemonic configurations of masculinity, which emphasize sexual experience. She shows, however, that such claims are better understood as enabling these men to continue to collect on forms of gendered entitlement that have arguably been more successfully challenged outside of these groups. Thus, Diefendorf shows that rather than resisting hegemonic masculinity, this strategy is a hybrid configuration of masculinity that fortifies boundaries and systems of inequality between these men and "Other" men and between men and women in ways that work to these men's collective (and continued) advantage.

While diverse boundary-blurring work is accomplished in many contemporary configurations of masculinity, much of this blurring is best understood as superficial. Within Connell's framework, research on hybrid masculinities illustrates an extraordinary flexibility in symbolic and emotional relations. But this flexibility often works in ways that conceal the continued resilience of power relations. This makes the gender order appear to have transformed a great deal, when less has actually changed than these practices appear (and are sometimes used as evidence) to demonstrate.

Conclusion

Connell (1995) theorized something she calls "gender vertigo" as accompanying periods of change—the sense of unease as gendered personality structures and relations transform.[3] It is associated with public challenges to cultural conceptualizations of masculinity and femininity and the experiences associated with charting new gender projects under shifting systems of opportunity and constraint—liberating for some, disorienting for others, and potentially infuriating for those who refuse to acknowledge change. As Connell writes,

> The pattern of difference/dominance is so deeply embedded in culture, institutions and body-reflexive practices that it functions as a limit to the rights-based politics of reform. Beyond a certain point, the critique of dominance is rejected as an attack on difference—a project that risks gender vertigo and violence. (Connell 1995, 232)

Because crisis tendencies are a fundamental feature of the structure of gender relations, gender vertigo is a historically recycled set of anxieties that accompany transformation. Hybrid masculinities are gender projects that offer *some* men new tools to navigate the gender vertigo accompanying periods of crisis in gender relations. The hipster, the metrosexual, and the bromance, as well as other gendered configurations in this chapter, are gender strategies that accompany transformations. Our theorization of hybrid masculinities, however, situates them as more than this as well: hybrid masculinities are strategies with patterned consequences for groups of men who hold concentrated constellations of power and authority.

Recent changes—produced both by structural change and feminist critique and reform—have shed light on masculinity and gender privilege in historically unprecedented ways. Privilege works best when it is invisible, when it goes unrecognized by those who benefit the most. When the experiences of privilege are fundamentally altered, so too are the "legitimating stories" that justify systems of gendered power and inequality. The concept of hybrid masculinities offers a framework within which we can better assess how privilege adapts to structural and sociopolitical change by highlighting these emergent strategies of action and legitimating stories and strategies.

Research on hybrid masculinity suggests that we should be careful when assessing whether these transformations are best understood as challenges to systems of power and inequality or simply shifts in the ways those systems are perpetuated (e.g., Bridges 2014; Bridges and Pascoe 2014; Budgeon 2014). Legal scholar Reva Siegel (1996) refers to processes of social reproduction involving the appearance of social transformation that share some of the patterns we have identified here as "preservation-through-transformation." Similarly, we suggest that it is critically important to separate an analysis of the motivations and the consequences of hybrid masculinities—recognizing patterned consequences even when individuals may be unaware of their participation or even their interests in reproducing existing structures of power and inequality.[4] While the motivations behind hybrid configurations of masculinity may be to challenge inequality or explore pleasures men have been denied by stoic configurations of masculinity, research suggests three separate dimensions of hybrid masculinities that have the collective consequence of obscuring power and inequality. Indeed, rather than challenging inequality, they are better understood as what Kandiyoti (1988) referred to as "patriarchal bargains."

Hybrid masculinity helps us recognize that meaningful changes in or successful challenges to systems of gendered power and inequality are more complex than they may at first appear. Considerations of what real (not simply stylistic) change will look like is an open question and must be answered with a framework capable of making sense of the elasticity of gender and sexual inequality.

GLOSSARY OF KEY TERMS

Discursive distancing—hybrid masculine practices that create symbolic space between privileged groups of men and hegemonic masculinity, enabling some men to frame themselves as outside of existing systems of privilege and inequality.

Fortifying boundaries—hybrid masculine practices that entrench and conceal systems of inequality in historically new ways, often along lines of race, gender, sexuality, and class.

Gender and sexual inequality—the organization of social relations through which heteronormative and patriarchal ideals become part of the structure of society, embedded in social institutions, interactions, identities, and culture.

Gender hegemony—the process by which gender inequality is justified through social structures, interactions, and institutions—a process that is continually transforming as it adapts to new historical circumstances, challenges, and social contexts.

Hegemonic masculinities—configurations of masculinity that symbolically organize inequalities among men and legitimate inequality between men and women.

Hybrid masculinity—the selective incorporation of identity elements typically associated with various marginalized and subordinated masculinities or femininities into privileged men's gendered enactments and identities.

Strategic borrowing—hybrid masculine practices of cultural appropriation by which privileged groups claim ownership of cultural symbols associated with subordinated and marginalized social groups.

NOTES

1 This type of intimacy—both emotional and physical—is not historically unique. A great deal of scholarship documents intimate relationships between men throughout U.S. history. See, for instance, E. Anthony Rotundo's (1993) and John Ibson's (2002) work on emotional and physical intimacy between men in the 19th and early 20th centuries as well as Jane Ward's (2015) work, which documents same-sex intimacy as consistently part of heterosexual masculinity. What we are seeing today are contemporary expressions of a long-standing pattern of relationships among men rather than something historically unprecedented.

2 Subordinated and marginalized groups also incorporate elements associated with dominant groups as well. Consider Messerschmidt's (1997) analysis of Malcolm X and his participation in a form of zoot-suit "hipster" masculinity among African American men in the 1930s and '40s in the United States as well as Nandy's (1983) analysis of British colonialism in India. While they illustrate a process of hybridization of masculinity as well, African Americans and Indians are here motivated by very different concerns and operating under dramatically different constraints than the hybrid masculinities we analyze in this chapter. We are suggesting that this form of hybridization (involving dominant groups appropriating cultural elements of various Others) often works in ways that do not resist systems of inequality.

3 While "gender vertigo" is now primarily associated with Barbara Risman's (2004) work on challenges to gender relations within the family, she borrows the concept from Connell's theory.

4 Discussions of "men's interests" are necessarily complex (e.g., Messner 2004). Connell discusses men's "interests" in ways that do not necessarily demand conscious reflection or malicious intentions. As she writes, "Interests are formed in any structure of inequality, which necessarily defines groups that will gain and lose differently by sustaining or by changing the structure" (1995, 82). Our examination of hybrid masculinities considers them as working "in men's interest" in a similar manner.

REFERENCES

Aboim, Sofia. 2010. *Plural Masculinities*. Burlington, VT: Ashgate.

Anderson, Eric. 2009. *Inclusive Masculinity*. New York: Routledge.

Arxer, Steven. 2011. "Hybrid Masculine Power: Reconceptualizing the Relationship between Homosociality and Hegemonic Masculinity." *Humanity & Society* 35: 390–422.

Barber, Kristen. 2008. "The Well-Coiffed Man: Class, Race, and Heterosexual Masculinity in the Hair Salon." *Gender & Society* 22: 455–76.

———. 2016. *Styling Masculinity*. New Brunswick, NJ: Rutgers University Press.

Bell, David. 2013. "Geek Myths." In *Rethinking Transnational Men*, edited by Jeff Hearn, Marina Blagojević, and Katherine Harrison, 76–90. London: Routledge.

Bird, Sharon. 1996. "Welcome to the Men's Club: Homosociality and the Maintenance of Hegemonic Masculinity." *Gender & Society* 10: 120–32.

Bridges, Tristan. 2010. "Men Just Weren't Made to Do This: Performances of Drag at 'Walk a Mile in Her Shoes' Marches." *Gender & Society* 24: 5–30.

———. 2014. "A Very 'Gay' Straight? Hybrid Masculinities, Sexual Aesthetics, and the Changing Relationship between Masculinity and Homophobia." *Gender & Society* 28: 58–82.

Bridges, Tristan, and C. J. Pascoe. 2014. "Hybrid Masculinities: New Directions in the Sociology of Men and Masculinities." *Sociology Compass* 8: 246–58.

————. 2015. "Masculinities and Post-Homophobias?" In *Exploring Masculinities*, edited by C. J. Pascoe and Tristan Bridges, 412–23. New York: Oxford University Press.

Budgeon, Shelley. 2014. "The Dynamics of Gender Hegemony." *Sociology* 48: 317–34.

Burke, Peter. 2009. *Cultural Hybridity*. New York: Polity.

Coad, David. 2008. *The Metrosexual*. New York: SUNY Press.

Collins, Patricia Hill. 2004. *Black Sexual Politics*. New York: Routledge.

Connell, Raewyn. 1985. "Theorising Gender." *Sociology* 19: 260–72.

————. 1987. *Gender and Power*. Stanford: Stanford University Press.

————. 1992. "A Very Straight Gay." *American Sociological Review* 57: 735–51.

————. 1995. *Masculinities*. Berkeley: University of California Press.

————. 2002. *Gender*. London: Polity Press.

————. 2004. "Encounters with Structure." *International Journal of Qualitative Studies in Education* 17: 10–27.

Connell, Raewyn, and James Messerschmidt. 2005. "Hegemonic Masculinity: Rethinking the Concept." *Gender & Society* 19: 829–59.

DeAngelis, Michael. 2014. *Reading the Bromance*. Detroit: Wayne State University Press.

de Boise, Sam. 2015. "I'm Not Homophobic, 'I've Got Gay Friends': Evaluating the Validity of Inclusive Masculinity." *Men and Masculinities* 18: 318–39.

de Casanova, Erynn Masi, Emily Wetzel, and Travis Speice. 2016. "Looking at the Label: White-Collar Men and the Meanings of 'Metrosexual.'" *Sexualities* 19: 64–82.

Demetriou, Demetrakis. 2001. "Connell's Concept of Hegemonic Masculinity: A Critique." *Theory and Society* 30: 337–61.

Diefendorf, Sarah. 2015. "After the Wedding Night: Sexual Abstinence and Masculinities over the Life Course." *Gender & Society* 29: 647–69.

Donovan, Brian. 1998. "Political Consequences of Private Authority." *Theory and Society* 27: 817–43.

Gerber, Lynne. 2015. "Grit, Guts, and Vanilla Beans: Godly Masculinity in the Ex-Gay Movement." *Gender & Society* 29: 26–50.

Grazian, David. 2007. "The Girl Hunt." *Symbolic Interaction* 30: 221–43.

Hacker, Helen. 1957. "The New Burdens of Masculinity." *Marriage and Family Living* 19: 227–33.

Heasley, Robert. 2005. "Crossing the Borders of Gendered Sexuality." In *Thinking Straight*, edited by Chrys Ingraham, 109–30. New York: Routledge.

Heath, Melanie. 2003. "Soft-Boiled Masculinity: Renegotiating Gender and Racial Ideologies in the Promise Keepers Movement." *Gender & Society* 17: 423–44.

Hennessy, Rosemary. 1995. "Queer Visibility in Commodity Culture." In *Social Postmodernism*, edited by Linda Nicholson and Steven Seidman, 142–83. New York: Cambridge University Press.

Hondagneu-Sotello, Pierrette, and Michael Messner. 1994. "Gender Displays and Men's Power: The 'New Man' and the Mexican Immigrant Man." In *Theorizing Masculinities*, edited by Harry Brod and Michael Kaufman, 200–218. Thousand Oaks, CA: Sage.

Hughey, Matthew. 2012. *White Bound*. Stanford: Stanford University Press.

Ibson, John. 2002. *Picturing Men*. Washington, DC: Smithsonian Institution Press.

Kandiyoti, Deniz. 1988. "Bargaining with Patriarchy." *Gender & Society* 2: 274–90.

Kimmel, Michael. 2012. *Manhood in America*. 3rd ed. New York: Oxford University Press.

Lorber, Judith. 1993. *Paradoxes of Gender*. New Haven: Yale University Press.

Mailer, Norman. 1957. "The White Negro: Superficial Reflection on the Hipster." In *Advertisements for Myself*, 337–58. New York: G. P. Putnam's Sons.

Masters, N. Tatiana. 2010. "'My Strength Is Not for Hurting': Men's Anti-Rape Websites and Their Construction of Masculinity and Male Sexuality." *Sexualities* 13 (1): 33–46.

McCormack, Mark. 2012. *The Declining Significance of Homophobia*. New York: Oxford University Press.

Messerschmidt, James. 1997. *Crime as Structured Action*. London: Sage.

———. 2010. *Hegemonic Masculinities and Camouflaged Politics*. Boulder, CO: Paradigm.

Messner, Michael. 1993. "'Changing Men' and Feminist Politics in the United States." *Theory and Society* 22: 723–37.

———. 2004. "On Patriarchs and Losers." *Berkeley Journal of Sociology* 48: 74–88.

———. 2007. "The Masculinity of the Governator: Muscle and Compassion in American Politics." *Gender & Society* 21: 461–80.

Mitchell, Juliet. 1966. "Women: The Longest Revolution." *New Left Review* 40: 11–37.

Murphy, Michael. 2009. "Can 'Men' Stop Rape?" *Men and Masculinities* 12: 113–30.

Nandy, Ashis. 1983. *The Intimate Enemy*. Ann Arbor: University of Michigan Press.

Pascoe, C. J. 2007. *Dude, You're a Fag: Masculinity and Sexuality in High School*. Berkeley: University of California Press.

Pascoe, C. J., and Jocelyn A. Hollander. 2016. "Good Guys Don't Rape: Gender, Domination and Mobilizing Rape." *Gender & Society* 30: 67–79.

Risman, Barbara. 2004. "Gender as a Social Structure." *Gender & Society* 18: 429–50.

Rotundo, E. Anthony. 1993. *American Manhood*. New York: Basic Books.

Schilt, Kristen, and Laurel Westbrook. 2009. "Doing Gender, Doing Heteronormativity: 'Gender Normals,' Transgender People, and the Social Maintenance of Heterosexuality." *Gender & Society* 23: 440–64.

Schippers, Mimi. 2000. "The Social Organization of Sexuality and Gender in Alternative Hard Rock." *Gender & Society* 14: 747–64.

Segal, Lynne. 1990. *Slow Motion*. New Brunswick, NJ: Rutgers University Press.

Shugart, Helene. 2008. "Managing Masculinities: The Metrosexual Moment." *Communication and Critical/Cultural Studies* 5: 280–300.

Siegel, Reva. 1996. "'The Rule of Love': Wife Beating as Prerogative and Privacy." *Yale Law Journal* 105: 2117–207.

Simpson, Mark. (1994) 1999. "Metrosexuals: Male Vanity Steps out of the Closet." In *It's a Queer World: Deviant Adventures in Pop Culture*, 207–10. New York: Harrington Park Press.

Sinfield, Alan. 1996. "Diaspora and Hybridity." *Textual Practice* 10: 271–93.

Stein, Arlene. 2005. "Make Room for Daddy." *Gender & Society* 19: 601–20.

Ward, Jane. 2008. "Dude-Sex." *Sexualities* 11: 414–34.

———. 2015. *Not Gay: Sex between Straight White Men.* New York: New York University Press.

Waters, Mary. 1990. *Ethnic Options.* Berkeley: University of California Press.

Whitehead, Stephen. 2007. "Metrosexuality! Cameron, Brown and the Politics of 'New Masculinity.'" *Public Policy Research* 14: 234–39.

Wilkins, Amy. 2009. "Masculinity Dilemmas." *Signs* 34: 343–68.

PART V

Agendas for Theory

In this final section of the book, the chapters propose ideas for how gender theory should develop in the future. The first chapter, by Barbara J. Risman, Kristen Myers, and Ray Sin, argues for a theoretical "(re) turn" to gender as a social structure. Risman, Myers, and Sin examine the current neoliberal context that emphasizes how *individual choice* creates the danger of promoting *nonreflexive celebrations of diversity* while ignoring ongoing structural inequalities. Risman, Myers, and Sin call for viewing gender as a system of stratification while simultaneously resisting essentialist ideas—including the concept of *cisgender*—that create oversimplified umbrella categories. They urge prioritizing the deconstruction of gender structure as a precursor to creating a world characterized by greater equality in relation to gender and other categorical distinctions.

In the next chapter, Judith Lorber, in a return to her previous work on gender paradoxes, ponders the question of how—under what structural conditions—the emergence of multiple genders, and chosen gender displays, challenges structured social inequalities in workplaces, families, or other social institutions. Similar to what Bridges and Pascoe (in this volume) say about hybrid masculinities, *multiple genders*, Lorber warns, are not in and of themselves revolutionary. Lorber argues that the recent spate of multiple genders being hailed by some as a sign of degendering—a development that could undermine the current binary gender order—is in fact no such thing. Multiple genders not only fail to free people from gendered distinctions and norms, they help shore them up. Lorber favors the option of degendering the many realms of social life where we now place great emphasis on gender divisions.

Finally, the chapter by Mimi Schippers examines sexuality by arguing that the monogamous couple is a discursively constructed ideal and compulsory structure for sexual and emotional intimacy that simultaneously legitimates gender hegemony. Schippers examines polyamory, which refers to an intimate relationship—physical or emotional, or both—with more than one person at a time and to which all involved actively consent. She suggests that consensual nonmonogamies, such as polyamory, can develop new forms of intimate and sexual relationships by stressing gender egalitarianism, thereby becoming a fruitful area of empirical research and gender theory development. Schippers concludes that monogamy fosters unequal gender relations whereas polyamory has the potential to subvert inequality and promote egalitarian relations between women and men.

14

Limitations of the Neoliberal Turn in Gender Theory

(Re)Turning to Gender as a Social Structure

BARBARA J. RISMAN, KRISTEN MYERS, AND RAY SIN

Choice feminism has co-opted feminist language in a way
that takes the political out of the personal.
—Meghan Murphy, "Choice Feminism"

In 1987, Raewyn Connell published *Gender and Power,* introducing a
new approach to understanding gender as *inequality.* She insisted on
the importance of everyday practices and structural constraints, push-
ing us beyond individualistic approaches to gender. In this chapter we
argue that advances first pioneered by Connell, the integration of structure and practice, highlighting the co-construction of individuals and
society, are in danger of being reversed by a neoliberal[1] turn in gender
theory.[2] To make this argument, we provide a brief history of gender
scholarship. We then show how gender scholarship has recently veered
away from concerns about sexism and inequality to focus on questions
of identity and agentic gender performance as part of narrowing concerns to the individual, a shift at least compatible with a neoliberal turn.

We provide three different kinds of evidence for our concern: (1)
recent research published in feminist journals that situates gender as
individual identity or strategy with little attention to gender inequality (Bantjes and Nieuwoudt 2014; Mora 2012; Balogun 2012; Kim and
Pike 2015; Gimlin 2013); (2) a recent focus on individual rights to choose
pronouns and the identification of a new identity binary based on individual identity ("cis" as the opposite of trans) (Schilt and Westbrook
2009); and (3) the popularization of "born that way" rhetoric for gender, borrowed from the gay rights movement (Khan 2015). Using data
from a collaborative research project studying Millennials,[3] we show one

limitation of the neoliberal turn toward identity in feminist writing: it cannot do justice to the complexity of young adult lives. We show that relying upon neoliberal concepts at the individual level of analysis hampers our understanding of the persistence of gender inequality even in the face of an increasing spectrum of gender performances. Finally, we conclude by suggesting a return to feminist scholarship that continues to celebrate diversity at the individual level while refocusing attention on feminist attempts to dismantle gender as a structure itself.

From Sex Roles to Stratification: A Brief History of Gender

During the heyday of functionalist sociology, only those writing about the family (e.g., Parsons and Bales 1955; Zelditch 1955) were interested in sex and gender. They theorized that sex roles should socialize girls for domesticity and boys for labor force participation and patriarchal fatherhood. Once the second wave of feminism crashed the gates of social science, women pointed out that gender is not about roles but primarily about inequality (England et al. 2007; Lorber 1994). Psychologists (e.g., Bem 1974, 1981; Spence, Helmreich, and Holahan 1975; Spence, Helmreich, and Stapp 1975) began to measure sex role attitudes using scales derived from old personality and employment tests (Terman and Miles 1936). Within a few years, however, it became clear that femininity and masculinity were not actually opposites (Locksley and Colten 1979; Pedhazur and Tetenbaum 1979; Edwards and Ashworth 1977), and Bem (1981, 1993) reconceptualized gender in what was then a novel way: she posited that masculinity and femininity were two different personality dimensions distinct from bodies. This became the accepted understanding used by psychologists and sociologists alike.

Early feminist sociologists used sex role theory to show how gender socialization disadvantaged girls (Lever 1974; Stockard and Johnson 1980; Weitzman 1979) by socializing them into femininity as a personality trait, presuming gender training embedded societal norms deep inside of us. Psychologists and sociologists alike implied that the key to eradicating gender inequality was to raise a new generation without gender limits and to resocialize adults. Soon, however, feminist sociologists began to critique this approach that reduced gender to personality. Lopata and Thorne (1978) published a now classic article showing the functionalist presumptions underlying "sex role" explanations for differences between women and men: the very rhetorical use of the language of "role" requires conceptualizing a complementarity devoid of questions of power and privilege. Social scientists would never use the language of "race roles" to explain the differential opportunities and constraints of majority and minority members of a Western society. The language of "sex role" presumed a stability of behavior across the life cycle and gender patterns that are similar across class, sexuality, and race and ethnic groups. It became clear that gender was not only about socialized personalities and identities but that a more deeply sociological analysis was needed.

Two distinct sociological theoretical alternatives developed: an interactionist framework, "doing gender," and a focus on how organizational structure shapes people, the new "structuralists." The interactionist "doing gender" framework introduced by West and Zimmerman (1987) argued that gender is something we are held morally accountable to *perform*, something we do, not something we are. At the same time, a structural focus on workplace organizations was introduced by Kanter (1977) to explain inequality between women and men with organizational characteristics such as differential opportunity and tokenism. Apparent sex differences in leadership style represented women's disadvantaged organizational placement, not their gendered personalities. Epstein (1988) supported this argument, suggesting that most of the differences between men and women were deceptive distinctions: if men and women were given the same opportunities and constraints, the differences between them would vanish. Much research ensued suggesting that male advantage remains even when men and women fill identical structural roles (Williams 1992). Purely social-structural variables cannot explain the power of gender.

Emerging during this period, Connell's *Gender and Power* represented a shift in the paradigm of gender scholarship. Connell drew on historical cross-cultural research to argue that it was with the urban revolution and the development of bureaucratized state capitalism in Western Europe that gender inequality was institutionalized into the particular sexual division of labor we now recognize. The proliferation of trade and colonialism led to a global diffusion of colonial versions of gender, although always in conversation with local cultures. Connell concluded that gender is socially constructed, historically contingent, culturally specific, and about power. Connell offered a complex view of gender that included individual psychology, social structure, and the relationship between them. Connell's work complicated feminist theorizing about gender, incorporating recursive models of structure and practice. Soon thereafter, Lorber (1994) suggested that gender difference itself was socially constructed, specifically as a legitimation for inequality. Similarly, Messerschmidt's (1997, 2016) structured action theory also pushed the integrative envelope. He emphasized the "construction of sex, gender, and sexuality as situated social, interactional and embodied accomplishments" (2016, 37). Together these works shifted the ground: gender could no longer be understood entirely as psychology, nor entirely as structure (see Risman and Davis 2013 for a more detailed intellectual history of gender scholarship).

From the end of the 20th century onwards, the conceptualization of gender as a stratification system that exists outside of individual characteristics and varies along other axes of inequality became the new consensus (Lorber 1994; Martin 2004; Risman 1998, 2004; Collins 1990; Crenshaw 1989; Harris 1990; Ingraham 1994; Mohanty 2003; Nakano Glenn 1999). Theorists turned their attention to gender as an institutional structure of inequality across different levels of analysis (Lorber 1994; Martin 2003, 2004, 2006; Risman 1998, 2004; Acker 1990, 1992). Gender can be conceptualized as a social structure, integrating social processes that occur at the individual, interactional, and macro levels of analysis without claiming a priori any more significant explanatory power (Risman 1998, 2004). The gender structure is dynamic and change in any aspect will reverberate throughout. Moreover, Connell's recognition of the global nature of the gender order has inspired scholars from different countries to understand how local gender structures interact with the gender orders from other countries, which, in turn, constitute a global gender regime (O'Connor, Orloff, and Shaver 1999; Walby 2004).

The Neoliberal Turn in Gender Scholarship: From Multilevel Stratification Systems to Choice Feminism's Essentialist Authentic Self

In the 21st century, there has been renewed attention to the individual level of analysis, to a concern with identities and the authenticity of gendered selves. While such issues are critically important, the increasing focus on diversity of gender identities and performances without linking them back to the social structure may have the unintended consequence of essentializing femininity and masculinity within the body. This returns us to a view of gender that is primarily about individuals, personalities, and selves and not a concern with societal stratification. The short history above provides evidence that this is not the first time that social science has struggled with gender essentialism. But this recent iteration seems to be distinct, spawned by the current influence of neoliberalism. Within a neoliberalist framework, attention is shifted to the "choice" and responsibility of individuals, with less attention to the governmental and other social-structural explanations for social life. While few feminist sociologists identify themselves as neoliberals, it seems as if there has been an unreflexive importation of neoliberal thought into the study of gender that is problematic both as an analytic strategy and as an effective collective feminist project to eradicate gender inequalities.

We provide three different kinds of evidence for our concern: (1) recent research published in feminist journals that highlight gender as individual identity or strategy with little attention to inequality; (2) the social construction of a new gender binary with the linguistic adoption of the term "cisgender" as an opposite of transgender and an array of new identity pronouns; and (3) a reliance upon "born that way" rhetoric, which requires essentialist presumptions.

Femininities and Masculinities

Much recent research focuses on the varieties of femininities and masculinities constructed by those in marginalized social groups, often providing thick description of masculinities and femininities of all varieties, with perfunctory concern for gender inequality or the processes of the social construction of gender itself (Bantjes and Nieuwoudt 2014; Mora 2012; Balogun 2012; Williams 2002; Gimlin 2013; Paechter 2007). For example, Kim and Pike (2015) critique the Father School movement in Korea for stigmatizing how Korean men "do gender" and for promoting Western hegemonic masculinity. But they do not much wrestle with how enactment of alternative masculinities might increase or decrease women's power in Korean families, the sexism women face in Korean society, or the homophobia faced by gender nonconforming men. Similarly, Gimlin (2013) examines narratives of women undergoing breast augmentation as aesthetic surgery and reports that the cultural narrative of desired femininity has shifted from authenticity to intervention and improvement. She suggests that the desire to improve oneself may signify empowerment and agency. What goes underexamined is that breast augmentation is another manifestation of the imposition of almost impossible standards of beauty upon women, standards that cannot be achieved without the burden of medical risks and exorbitant cost. Such burdens of beauty are primarily the work of women (and not men), and even among women such work further stratifies femininity by social class.

While description of the varieties of masculinities and femininities does help decenter the white middle class from the study of gender, what remains underanalyzed is how these varieties of "doing gender" connect to inequality between the sexes, or even between the varieties of gender. Research on gender that focuses on cultural variations of femininities and masculinities, devoid of concern for the structure of inequality, is one kind of evidence of a global neoliberal worldview colonizing the study of gender.

Freedom from Old Binaries: Choosing New Pronouns and Identities and New Binaries

A second kind of evidence of an encroaching neoliberal focus on the individual is an increasing tendency to study the choices of individuals, while allowing social-structural analysis to recede into the murky background. Although sociologists have critiqued choice models for decades, there has been an increasing emphasis on choice in recent scholarship and activism (see Budgeon 2003; Baumgardner and Richards 2000). While choice may seem liberating and socially progressive, we agree with critics who have argued that it is a mistake to lose the forest while we study the trees (see Groenveld 2009; Murphy 2012; Zimmerman, McDermott, and Gould 2009). For example, the freedom for those who reject the binary of male/female (or men/women) to use new pronouns (e.g., *ze* and *hir*) may shake up the binary logic that presumes gender can only be about men and women. And yet the new ability to choose gender pronouns that evade the binary may ironically preserve the larger system of meaningful gender categories. When people resist gender categories because they are too limiting, pressure builds to shatter the stereotypes that bind. But if those most miserable within the categories as they now exist can opt out, then the pressure needed for stereotypes to lose power is lessened, leaving them intact. For those most oppressed, opting out eases the pain, which is important. Opting out itself can be revolutionary. If *everyone* were to opt out of gendered pronouns, the gender structure itself might crack down to its foundation. But does the recent proliferation of categories portend such an imminent collapse? We think not. Most people unreflexively inhabit the gendered binary, and those who opt out of male or female opt into a rebel category. Despite expanded choices for the few, the categories of women and men have remained intact, and stereotypes attached to gender continue to constrain the majority who remain identified as male or female. Rather than exploding gender categories altogether, choice allows liberty for some without attacking stereotypes or constraints for most others. Further, the rhetoric of cisgender makes intersex people invisible. There isn't an agreed-upon "sex category" to which intersex people "should" have been labeled at birth, as they are quite literally between the binary of sex categories (see Viloria 2014).[4] In fact, intersex scholars and activists point out that the sex categories themselves are social constructions used to oppress people who don't fit (Davis 2015; Fausto-Sterling 2012).

Neoliberal "choice" ideology has also trickled into feminist research on gender identities. One example of the individualist turn by gender scholars is the construction of the new category "cisgender," a term that refers to anyone who identifies with the gender that aligns with the sex they were assigned at birth (Schilt and Westbrook 2009). The term has recently come into popular use as more attention is given to people who transition from the sex assigned at birth to another sex (transgender), as well as those who reject the binary entirely (using identities such as genderqueer and agender). Indeed, the term has recently been added to the Oxford English Dictionary. Despite its popularity—or perhaps because if it—the rhetorical language of cisgender needs some deconstruction.

The earliest written record of using "cis" as a prefix related to gender can be traced to a German physician, Ernst Burchard, in a sexology textbook in 1914 (Williams 2013). Burchard used "cisvestitismus" to refer to human beings who dress in gender-normative clothing. But "cis" did not become popular for 80 years, until biologist Dana Leland Defosse used the term "cisgender" as a linguistic term within molecular biology. He used "cis" as a prefix to describe action from the same molecule, while "trans" refers to action from a different molecule. Organic chemistry uses the terms similarly (within and across). Cisgender as a term was only recently adopted by activists in the transgender rights movement to differentiate themselves from the majority (Enke 2012). In 2009, Schilt and Westbrook introduced cisgender to the sociological community as "individuals who have a match between the gender they were assigned at birth, their bodies, and their personal identity" (461).

This new terminology is useful in conversations about trans issues as it disrupts assumptions of gender normality. It acknowledges that trans people face especially pernicious, dehumanizing gender policing (see Schilt and Westbrook 2009; Westbrook and Schilt 2013; Schilt 2011). Yet the term cisgender also creates a new binary, dividing those who are cisgender from those who are not. What it does not do is help us understand the increasing fluidity of bodies, identities, and performances in contemporary society. For example, children who identify as transgender may remain so identified for life, while others may not (Drescher and Pula 2014; Wallien and Cohen-Kettenis 2008). Some experience gender dysphoria only later in life. In Messerschmidt's 2016 book, *Masculinities in the Making*, some respondents are very clear that they have held a variety of identities and are open to the possibility of other identities in the future. How does a trans/cis divide help us or them chart new insights into gender fluidity, or ambiguity? What if the new binary itself simply adds another set of expectations on today's youth, instructing them to figure out who they "really" are and stay there?

The current concept of cisgender is limited in three major ways. First, the cis-trans language introduces yet another binary, oversimplifying gender complexity for all people, including ignoring those actually born intersex. Second, the concept presumes a certain gender essentialism, at least for those who are not trans. Third, and perhaps most problematic, is that this new language leaves the other gender inequality unmarked: between men and women (whether they are those assigned the category at birth or not), and between those who conform to gender stereotypes and those who do not. While the point of this new binary is to underscore that cisgender people are privileged, and transgender people are not, the articulation of that privilege with male privilege and gender conformity is often left unexplored (for an exception, see Schilt 2011).

It is very clear that the language of cisgender and the new gender binary is useful for transgender activism. The very existence of a rhetoric for "marking" what Schilt and Westbrook (2009) refer to as "gender normals" highlights the argument that neither group is more normal than the other. Both cis and trans people need to be identified by an identity label for trans activism. What is less clear is whether such a new binary is useful for social science.

"Born That Way" Rhetoric: From Sexual to Gender Identities

In a neoliberal framework, where individual choice and freedom are at the center of attention, conflicts among social scientists can indeed erupt. We see this happening in research on sexual orientation and political activism. Khan (2015) argues that while the "born this way" explanation for lesbian and gay identities has been effective in the marriage equality movement, it obfuscates the strong social science that has shown that sexuality is culturally variable and that homosexuality as an identity is a modern invention. Extending this same logic to gender, Khan contrasts basic sociological evidence about gender as socially constructed with the strongly held opinions of those who believe that masculinity or femininity is their only biologically "authentic" self. That belief can be as strongly held by those assigned male at birth and by transmen, or by those assigned female at birth and by transwomen And, yet, much research in social science shows that biological determinants explain a small variance of gendered responses and identities (Cohen-Bendahan, van de Beek, and Berenbaum, 2005; Davis and Risman 2014; Jordan-Young 2010). The meanings attached to gender and the ways gender is manifested are culturally shaped, historically contingent, and variable. Still, gender (like sexuality) is often experienced as a deeply essential authentic core self. To the extent that we uncritically accept the essential need to be masculine or feminine as biologically "authentic," we support individuals' right to self-determination. But to do so as social scientists requires us to ignore what is at the moment the state of the art social scientific evidence. We agree with Khan (and also see D'Emilio 2002) that most social scientists remained silent regarding their knowledge about sexual plasticity because of the political efficacy in doing so. To remain silent in a political movement may be efficacious, but social scientists have not remained silent about the social construction of sexual identities within the social scientific community. We fear the silencing of social science in the face of the rhetoric of a new essentialist gender binary (cis/trans). Surely there are better ways to affirm and support the rights of transgender and genderqueer people without creating a binary that ignores the variation in gendered selves among the many who are not transgender and challenges the theoretical power of the social construction of gender. To concretely illustrate the problem of narrowing attention to gender identity once again, we turn to an overview of a study we have conducted of U.S. Millennial youth.

Millennials and the Gender Structure: The Limitations of Neoliberal Conceptualizations of Gender

In order to explain the empirical limitations of neoliberal frameworks on our understanding of gender complexity, we use data from a research project on which we collaborated. In this project, we collected 116 interviews with mostly working class minority Chicagoland Millennials. The sample was also gender diverse, with over 15 percent respondents who were genderqueer or trans. Their stories illustrate how focusing on individual identity, choice, and the rhetoric of cisgender would create far more confusion than clarification.

In analyzing our data, if we were to apply the cis/trans binary to our sample, we would be unable to understand the experiences of all of our subjects. Cis people are not at all a homogenous, monolithic group. They do not share some attribute that provides them a common privilege. Too broad an array of people are currently defined as cis: effeminate men, butch women, tough guys, and feminine ladies. Men and women who do not conform to gender stereotypes may challenge the gender structure even as they claim a gender category that aligns with their assigned sex. For example, we talked to a self-identified butch lesbian woman who had always felt constrained by gender norms and oppressed by her body. Once she had her breasts removed, she was at peace with being female and was distressed when panhandlers addressed her as "sir." Why is it helpful to label this woman as cisgender? Her struggles are ignored if we lump her into this amorphous category.

Similarly, the cis/trans dichotomy also has the unintended consequence of essentializing the trans community as undifferentiated. Some trans people seek to pass, while others want to disrupt gender categories altogether. We found the stories told by transgender respondents who were in transition and wanted very much to pass as "the opposite sex" were very different from the transgender respondents who were rebels against the gender structure and were comfortable being publicly and openly identified as transwomen or transmen. Both were quite distinct from those who held a genderqueer identity, or were neither male nor female identified. The Millennials who opted for a genderqueer identity and who wanted to smash the binary are also sometimes categorized within the broad "trans" label in that they rejected the sex category assigned at birth. Our genderqueer respondents were quite different from the transgender ones, however, as they reported far less childhood trauma and were far more political in their conceptualization of gender politics.

In order to apply the cis/trans lens to our sample, we would be forced to categorize our subjects as either cis or trans. How do we determine this? Categorizing people into the cis/trans dichotomy involves exploring how they align their "true selves" with their gender performances. Assuming that people have an essential gendered nature flies in the face of theoretical insights of the past four decades, and it collapses the complexity that Connell herself helped us to understand. A focus on people's true selves pushes us backward toward a biological essentialism that research does not support. For example, gender nonconforming respondents talked very openly about having held a variety of gender identities. A self-identified genderqueer female had previously identified as a butch lesbian, and then as a transboy. She wanted us to know that her gender was a journey, and she did not know where it might lead. But she was very open to yet another identity still in the future. The creation of a category of "cis" versus "trans" presumes a stability that simply does not exist, at least not for all of our respondents. And how can it be applied to the intersex? Are intersex people who align their gender identity with the sex category that was imposed by their medical doctors during infancy cisgender (see Costello 2015)?[5]

And finally, were we to rely on a neoliberal analytical framework, we would fail to examine the structural consequences of gender. The gender structure bifurcates and stratifies people as women and men regardless of whether or not they self-identify as such. For example, Pfeffer (2014) writes about how misrecognition of transmen and their partners as normatively heterosexual renders their queer identities invisible. Schilt (2011) shows that male privilege is accorded to transmen who pass as men but not to those who do not. Perhaps transmen men have more in common—in the workplace—with hegemonic men who do gender in a socially valuable way than with others who display gender nonconformity, even if their gender performance doesn't match their sex assigned at birth. In our research, the young men who broke gender norms told gut-wrenching stories about being bullied by other boys, and about being sometimes stigmatized by their own families. Transgender Millennials told such stories but so did boys, gay and straight, who didn't "man up," who rejected team sports for fashion interests, or wanted the freedom to wear bright colors and makeup. Stigma is experienced by those who reject gender-normative lives, whether they are transgender, genderqueer, effeminate men, butch women, or anyone else. Patriarchal dividends are awarded to those who subscribe to gender-normative behavior. We must use theoretical lenses that enable us to critique the gender structure. Despite the promise of personal freedom, the ability to choose your gender, from an increasing array of possibilities, as your authentic gender does not free one from gender inequality.

Ongoing and Future Debates: Where Should We Go from Here?

The landscape of gender identities is growing ever more complicated. Some people enjoy "doing gender," especially the aspects that are not inherently stratification markers, such as makeup, pumping iron, and fashion. Others strongly identify with gender categories distinct from sex assignment at birth, and, for them, gender is a source of liberation from imprisonment in bodies that do not match their identities. In our technologically sophisticated society, bodies seem more malleable than selves. There are also now genderqueer or agender identity people who deny the binary of male/female and occupy the space between the categories. We have no longitudinal data to know if previous generations had equal numbers of gender nonconformists hidden in closets or whether this era allows more exploration of all facets of the self. But we can hypothesize that the cracks in our gender structure (language first offered by Connell and now a part of our shared theoretical language) have allowed feminist and queer theories to develop, and with those theories the very possibility of imagining new ways to live across and between the binary has emerged.

Research is needed to even hazard a guess whether the defiance of assigned gender categories, identities, and statuses reflects dissatisfaction with the gender structure as we know it or simply dissatisfaction with one's own gendered expectations. We see far more divorce in modern societies than in more traditional ones, but that does not mean that a divorcing spouse rejects marriage as an institution, only that they don't like the particular person to whom they are married at the moment. Perhaps for some trans people, gender is entirely a personal issue, and the gender structure ceases to feel oppressive once they change categories. In our study of Millennials, however, some transgender and genderqueer youth reject the notion that there should be gender categories and see their choices in opposition to a binary gender structure. Perhaps the category of transgender is insufficient for transgender men and women and genderqueer people to coexist within it. Identity categories are always socially constructed, contested, and historically contingent, and our research simply illustrates that this is also true for our current crop of gender identities.

In this chapter, we have argued that there has been a neoliberal turn in gender scholarship. This neoliberal turn is evidenced by all the scholarly attention to individual identities without clear analysis of the relationship between individuals and the social structure, and the relationship between them. Attention must still be paid to gender inequality across sex categories and to inequality between gender identities. It is important to link a focus on the diversity of gender identities and performances back to the gender structure. If we focus only on identities and individuals' right to name their own gender, we risk the unintended consequence of essentializing femininity and masculinity within the body. This returns us to a view of gender that is primarily about individuals and not about stratification. Within a neoliberal framework, attention is narrowed to the "choice" of individuals with less attention to the governmental and other social-structural explanations for social life. Neoliberalism is in the intellectual air we breathe in the 21st century. In a world with increasingly fewer unions or pensions or stable employment contracts, the individual managing his or her own trajectory has become routine. Individuals are responsible for choosing everything from religious denominations to health care plans to identities. We suggest this individualist focus has been imported into the study of gender. This is problematic both as an analytic strategy and for a collective feminist project to eradicate gender inequalities.

We can envision two possible future scenarios as a result of more gender categories. First, we foresee that those who now "choose" to use male- or female-identified pronouns that align with the sex ascribed to them at birth will be under more pressure to behave in stereotypically masculine or feminine ways. If male, to be tough and sturdy, agentic, and emotionally repressed, and, if female, to be empathetic, nurturing, and avoid being "bossy." Those who "choose" new gender-neutral pronouns are freed to be who they want to be. In such a scenario, choosing gender-alternative pronouns creates comfort and a sense of belonging for those who do so. That is useful, but it is far less radical a solution to gender inequality than a challenge to the very gender expectations attached to categories themselves. The need to focus on structural inequality and the social construction of gendered categories may recede if those most oppressed by them have a personal choice to opt out. A second possible scenario, and our advice to activists, is to use the proliferation of gender identities to critique the need for categories themselves. Bem (1995) once suggested that the explosion of sexual identities would eventually lead us to realize that sexuality needn't be organized by types of people at all, but by relationships between them. So, too, an explosion of gender identities should lead to questioning whether we need gender categories and their attendant stereotypes at all.

What will the future bring? Nothing is inevitable because, as Connell notes, the present moment "is not a culmination but a point of choice" (279). We worry that interactional expectations, cultural ideology, and institutional constraints may become nearly invisible in a neoliberal framework that orients us entirely to the politics of individual choice. If gender is reduced to a quest for authentic identity among individuals, we have reverted to an essentialist belief about "real" gender essence, even if we expand the conversation to include people whose "real" gender does not match their assigned sex.

The need for feminist social action is as necessary as ever. Gender inequality between women and men, and within gender categories, is still rampant. We believe the most radical way forward is to destabilize the gender structure: to dismantle the binary categories upon which the gender structure is based. Gender transgressions of all sorts can push toward this goal: genderqueer youth destabilize taken-for-granted presumptions when they demand gender-neutral pronouns. Transgender community members demanding equality under the law and in civil society destabilize the presumption that gender must conform to biological bodies. Male caretakers and female leaders smash stereotypes as well. While expanding the list of categories that we use to denote gender *may* help to disrupt the gender structure, it cannot do so if those categories simply defuse tension for the most oppressed, leaving the categories themselves unchallenged. We cannot achieve a feminist utopia without more critical research on sexism and gender as a social structure. We have hardly moved beyond the paradox of gender (Lorber 1994). We must continue to make gender inequality visible before we can dismantle it. While we support each individual's right to live with an authentic identity, we suggest that no one is truly free to do so as long as gender as a social structure persists.

It is imperative that gender scholars continue to study, and support, those who reject gender norms, who change their sex category, and genderqueers who reject binary categories entirely. But we cannot do so with a focus only on individual-level identity politics. As feminist analysts, we must understand gender rebellion as a response to a repressive gender structure, not merely a desire to live authentically according to an essential presocial self. We hope this is a transitional moment in history, where new categories help explode the expectations attached to sex categories, so that masculinity and femininity have little social meaning, and are not attached to male or female bodies, or to the categories of man and woman. As such, we can create a bridge to a future with a less oppressive gender structure.

With this chapter, we have attempted to foster a respectful dialogue among gender scholars with different perspectives but who share the feminist goal that everyone should have freedom to live authentic lives within, beyond, or between gender categories. We are committed to a feminist vision of a society with gender equality. As long as people assigned as female at birth face differential expectations compared to those labeled male at birth, our society will remain gender stratified with inequality embodied at the individual level, policed at the interactional level, and accepted as cultural logic and official policy at the macro level. Only when the sex category assigned at birth has no more power than the color of one's eyes (Okin 1989) will we have gender equality. Perhaps when that time comes, gender can be reconstituted without inequality. But why would anyone then want to do so?

NOTES

1 There is no one definition of neoliberalism. On a broad conceptual level, neoliberal ideology is the injection of market principles into all aspects of society and its attendant implications for geopolitics across nations, local domestic politics, and the individual. In this chapter, we focus on the implications of neoliberalism on the individual when it comes to gender. As Peters (2001) argues, neoliberalism on the individual level represents a shift toward individualizing social problems as personal responsibilities and choices. Hence solutions to social problems such as gender inequality are now placed on self-help, self-empowerment, and self-reliance.

2 Barbara J. Risman thanks both the University of Illinois at Chicago and the Center for Advanced Study in the Behavioral Sciences at Stanford for support during a sabbatical year in 2015–16 during which this article was written.

3 Millennials are a demographic cohort. While there are no precise agreed-upon dates, they range from those born in the early 1980s until the end of the 20th century. The label implies that they came of age in this new millennium.

4 See www.hidaviloria.com.

5 See trans-fusion.blogspot.com.

REFERENCES

Acker, J. 1990. "Hierarchies, jobs, bodies: A theory of gendered organizations." *Gender & Society* 4: 139–158.

———. 1992. "From sex roles to gendered institutions." *Contemporary Sociology* 21 (5): 565–569.

Balogun, O. M. 2012. "Idealized femininity and embodied nationalism in Nigerian beauty pageants." *Gender & Society* 26: 357–381.

Bantjes, J., and J. Nieuwoudt. 2014. "Masculinity and mayhem: The performance of gender in a South African boys' school." *Men and Masculinities* 17: 376–395.

Baumgardner, J., and A. Richards. 2000. *Manifesta: Young women, feminism, and the future.* New York: Farrar, Straus and Giroux.

Bem, S. 1974. "The measurement of psychological androgyny." *Journal of Consulting and Clinical Psychology* 42: 65–82.

———. 1981. "Gender schema theory: A cognitive account of sex typing." *Psychological Review* 88: 354–364.

———. 1993. *The lenses of gender: Transforming the debate on sexual inequality.* New Haven: Yale University Press.

———. 1995. "Dismantling gender polzarization and compulsory heterosexuality: Should we turn the volume down or up?" *Journal of Sex Research* 32 (4): 329–334.

Budgeon, S. 2003. *Choosing a self: Young women and the individualization of identity.* Westport, CT: Praeger.

Chen, A. 1999. "Lives at the center of the periphery: Chinese American masculinities and bargaining with hegemony." *Gender & Society* 13: 584–607.

Cohen-Bendahan, C. C. C., C. van de Beek, and S. A. Berenbaum. 2005. "Prenatal sex hormone effects on child and adult sex-typed behavior: Methods and findings." *Neuroscience and Biobehavioral Reviews* 29: 353–384.

Collins, P. H. 1990. *Black feminist thought.* New York: Routledge.

Connell, R.W. 1987. *Gender and power: Society, the person, and sexual politics.* Palo Alto, CA: Stanford University Press.

Costello, C. G. 2015. "Cis gender, ipso gender." June. http://trans-fusion.blogspot.com.

Crenshaw, K. 1989. "Demarginalizing the intersection of race and sex: A black feminist critique of antidiscrimination doctrine, feminist theory, and antiracist politics." *University of Chicago Legal Forum*: 1 (8): 139–167.

Davis, G. 2015. *Contesting intersex: The dubious diagnosis.* New York: New York University Press.

Davis, S., and B. J. Risman. 2014. "Feminists wrestle with testosterone: Hormones, socialization and cultural interactions as predictors of women's gendered selves." *Social Science Research* 49: 110–125.

D'Emilio, J. 2002. "Born gay?" In *The world turned: Essays on gay history, politics, and culture*, 154–164. Durham: Duke University Press.

Drescher, J., and J. Pula. 2014. "Ethical issues raised by the treatment of gender-variant prepubescent children." *Hastings Center Report* 44: S17-S22.

Edwards, A., and C. Ashworth. 1977. "A replication study of item selection for the Bem sex role inventory." *Applied Psychological Measurement* 1 (4): 501–507.

England, P., P. Allison, S. Li, N. Mark, J. Thompson, M. J. Budig, and H. Sun. 2007. "Why are some academic fields tipping toward female? The sex composition of U.S. fields of doctoral degree receipt, 1971–2002." *Sociology of Education* 80: 23–42.

Enke, A. F. 2012. "The education of little cis: Cisgender and the discipline of opposing bodies." In *Transfeminist perspectives in and beyond transgender and gender studies*, edited by A. F. Enke, 59–80. Philadelphia: Temple University Press.

Epstein, C. F. 1988. *Deceptive distinctions: Sex, gender, and the social order.* New Haven: Yale University Press.

Fausto-Sterling, A. 2012. *Sex/gender: Biology in a social world.* New York: Routledge.

Gimlin, D. L. 2013. "'Too good to be real': The obviously augmented breast in women's narratives of cosmetic surgery." *Gender & Society* 27: 913–934.

Groenveld, E. 2009. "'Be a feminist or just dress like one': BUST, fashion and feminism as lifestyle." *Journal of Gender Studies* 18: 179–190.

Harris, A. 1990. "Race and essentialism in feminist legal theory." *Stanford Law Review* 42: 581–616.

Ingraham, C. 1994. "The heterosexual imaginary: Feminist sociology and theories of gender." *Sociological Theory* 12 (2): 203–219.

Jordan-Young, R. M. 2010. *Brain storm: The flaws in the science of sex differences.* Cambridge: Harvard University Press.

Kanter, R. M. 1977. *Men and women of the corporation.* New York: Basic Books.

Khan, S. 2015. "Not born this way." *Aeon*, July 23. www.aeon.co.

Kim, A., and B. Pike. 2015. "Hegemonic American masculinity and South Korea's father school." *Gender & Society* 29 (4): 509–533.

Lever, J. 1974. *Games children play: Sex differences and the development of role skills.* New Haven: Yale University Press.

Locksley, A., and M. E. Colten. 1979. "Psychological androgyny: A case of mistaken identity?" 37 (6): 1017–1031.

Lopata, H. Z., and B. Thorne. 1978. "On the term 'sex roles.'" *Signs* 3: 718–721.

Lorber, J. 1994. *Paradoxes of gender.* New Haven: Yale University Press.

Martin, P. Y. 2003. "Said and done vs. saying and doing: Gender practices/practicing gender and work." *Gender & Society* 17 (3): 342–366.

———. 2004. "Gender as social institution." *Social Forces* 82 (4): 1249–1273.

———. 2006. "Practicing gender at work: Further thoughts on reflexivity." *Gender, Work and Organization* 13: 254–275.

Messerschmidt, J. W. 1997. *Crime as structured action: Gender, race, class, and crime in the making.* Thousand Oaks, CA: Sage.

———. 2016. *Masculinities in the making: From the local to the global.* Lanham, MD: Rowman and Littlefield.

Mohanty, C. 2003. *Feminism without borders: Decolonizing theory, practicing solidarity.* Durham: Duke University Press.

Mora, R. 2012. "'Do it all for your pubic hairs!' Latino boys, masculinity, and puberty." *Gender & Society* 26 (6): 433–460.

Murphy, M. 2012. "Choice feminism: How our rallying cry got co-opted and why we need to take it back." *Herizons* 26: 20–23.

Nakano Glenn, E. 1999. "The social construction and institutionalization of gender and race: An integrative framework." In *The gender lens: Revisioning gender,* edited by M. M. Ferree, J. Lorber, and B. Hess. Lanham, MD: Rowman and Littlefield.

O'Connor, Julia S., Ann Shola Orloff, and Sheila Shaver. 1999. *States, markets, families: Gender, liberalism and social policy in Australia, Canada, Great Britain and the United States.* Cambridge: Cambridge University Press.

Okin, S. 1989. *Justice, gender, and the family.* New York: Basic Books.

Paechter, C. 2007. *Being boys, being girls: Learning masculinities and femininities.* New York: Open University Press.

Parsons, T., and R. Bales. 1955. *Family, socialization, and interaction process*. New York: Free Press.

Pedhazur, E. J., and T. J. Tetenbaum. 1979. "Bem sex role inventory: A theoretical and methodological critique." *Journal of Personality and Social Psychology* 37 (6): 996–1016.

Peters, M. A. 2001. *Poststructuralism, Marxism and neoliberalism: Between theory and politics*. New York: Rowman and Littlefield.

Pfeffer, C. 2014. "I don't like passing as a straight women: Queer negotiations of identity and social group membership." *American Journal of Sociology* 120 (1): 1–44.

Risman, B. J. 1998. *Gender vertigo: American families in transition*. New Haven: Yale University Press.

———. 2004. "Gender as a social structure: Theory wrestling with activism." *Gender & Society* 18 (4): 429–451.

Risman, B. J., and G. Davis. 2013. "From sex roles to gender structure." *Current Sociology* 61: 733–755.

Schilt, K. 2011. *Just one of the guys? Transgender men and the persistence of gender inequality*. Chicago: University of Chicago Press.

Schilt, K., and L. Westbrook. 2009. "Doing gender, doing heteronormativity: 'Gender normals,' transgender people, and the social maintenance of heterosexuality." *Gender & Society* 23: 440–464.

Spence, J. T., R. Helmreich, and C. K. Holahan. 1975. "Negative and positive components of psychological masculinity and femininity and their relationships to self-reports of neurotic and acting out behaviors." *Journal of Personality and Social Psychology* 37 (10): 1673–1682.

Spence, J. T., R. Helmreich, and J. Stapp. 1975. "Ratings of self and peers on sex role attributes and their relation to self-esteem and conceptions of masculinity and femininity." *Journal of Personality and Social Psychology* 32 (1): 29–39.

Stockard, J., and M. M. Johnson. 1980. *Sex roles: Sex inequality and sex role development*. New York: Prentice Hall.

Terman, L., and C. Miles. 1936. *Sex and personality: Studies in masculinity and femininity*. New York: McGraw Hill.

Viloria, H. 2014. "Caught in the gender binary blind spot: Intersex erasure in cisgender rhetoric." http://hidaviloria.com.

Walby, Sylvia. 2004. "The European Union and gender equality: Emergent varieties of gender regime." *Social Politics* 11 (1): 4–29.

Wallien, M. S. C., and P. T. Cohen-Kettenis. 2008. "Psychosexual outcome of gender-dysphoric children." *Journal of the American Academy of Child and Adolescent Psychiatry* 47 (12): 1413–1423.

Weitzman, L. J. 1979. *Sex role socialization: A focus on women*. Palo Alto, CA: Mayfield.

West, C., and D. H. Zimmerman. 1987. "Doing gender." *Gender & Society* 1: 125–151.

Westbrook, L., and K. Schilt. 2014. "Doing gender, determining gender: Transgender people, gender panics, and the maintenance of the sex/gender/sexuality system." *Gender & Society* 28: 32–57.

Williams, C. 1992. "The glass escalator: Hidden advantages for men in the 'female' professions." *Social Problems* 39: 253–267.

———. 2013. "So, I hear trans people recently invented this whole cis/trans thing . . ." *Transadvocate*, August 12. www.transadvocate.com.

Williams, L. S. 2002. "Trying on gender, gender regimes and the process of becoming a woman." *Gender & Society* 16: 29–52.

Zelditch, M. 1955. "Role differentiation in the nuclear family: A comparative study." In *Family, Socialization, and Interaction Process*, edited by T. Parsons and R. Bales, 307–352. New York: Free Press.

Zimmerman, A. L., J. McDermott, and C. Gould. 2009. "The local is global: Third wave feminism, peace, and social justice." *Contemporary Justice Review* 12: 77–90.

15

Paradoxes of Gender Redux

Multiple Genders and the Persistence of the Binary

JUDITH LORBER

I have been out as an agender, or genderless, person for about a year now. To me, this simply means having the freedom to exist as a person without being confined by the limits of the western gender binary. . . . People don't know what to make of me when they see me, because they feel my features contradict one another. They see no room for the curve of my hips to coexist with my facial hair; they desperately want me to be someone they can easily categorise. My existence causes people to question everything they have been taught about gender, which in turn inspires them to question what they know about themselves, and that scares them. Strangers are often desperate to figure out what genitalia I have.
—Tyler Ford, "My Life without Gender"

Within the space of two weeks in 2014, the *New York Times* published several pieces on multiple genders. One was on the fiftysome choices of gender identity for Facebook users (Ball 2014; Herbenick and Baldwin 2014). These could be bigender, agender, gender fluid, variant, questioning, queer, transman, transwoman, intersex, neutrois, two-spirit, and variations of each. Another article reported that Australia's High Court has allowed someone to register their gender officially as "nonspecific" (Baird 2014) and another that India's Supreme Court had recognized transgender as a third gender (Varma and Najar 2014). In 2013, Germany allowed parents of intersexed babies to register them as "indeterminate" (Nandi 2013). "Queer," once a radical identity, has almost become the new normal (Wortham 2016). These are twenty-first-century iterations of going beyond the binary, the strict division of people into two and only two sexes or genders, a subject I've been exploring for twenty years (Lorber 1996, 2001). They are indicators of multiple personal genders and much more limited official third genders.

Despite the blurring of boundaries in chosen gender identities, there does not seem to be very much actual, lived erasure of gender displays. At an art exhibit in New York City not long ago, I was struck by the way the gender of the members of the avant-garde crowd was clearly identifiable as "man" or "woman." There were no "nonspecifics," let alone fifty varieties of gender.

Theoretically, the erosion of gender boundaries should undercut gendered power inequalities and sustain the thrust toward a gender-equal social order. In the social construction conceptualization of gender, processes and practices ("doing gender") that are repeated and ritualized congeal into a structure that encourages further repetition of gendered practices (Butler 2004; Lorber 2008; West and Zimmerman 1987). These practices create the differences between women and men that justify the inequities of power and privilege embedded in gender regimes. Personally chosen genders should affect the interactive processes that sustain social action and that ultimately influence practices in workplaces, families, and other social institutions. But the multiplicity of genders that supposedly has undermined the gender binary in Western cultures does not seem to have a positive interactive or structural effect. Rather, gender-variant appearances incur more opprobrium and violence than those experienced by transgendered people (Harrison, Grant, and Herman 2011–12; Vaid-Menon 2015). The most benign result seems to be the increasingly common designation of single-use bathrooms as M/F (Smith 2015) but not the spread of gender-neutral multiple-use facilities (Molotch and Norén 2010).

The gender paradox I explored over twenty years ago focused on the rhetoric of gender equality made meaningless by a total system that rendered women unequal and exploited (Lorber 1994). Today's gender paradox is a rhetoric of gender multiplicity made meaningless by a continuing system of bigendered social structures that support continued gender inequality. Underneath the seeming erasure of a rigid gender binary and its discriminatory norms and expectations lurks the persistence of men's power and privilege (Connell and Messerschmidt 2005; Kent 2015).

The revolutionary acceptance of homosexual and transgender women and men has ended there—with acceptance but without structural change (Walters 2014). Gays, lesbians, and transgendered people fit right into the gender binary. Homosexuality does not seem to diminish masculinity anymore (Browne 2014). Lesbians are women first and foremost; indeed, lesbianism has been defined as a continuum of women's emotional gamut (Rich 1980). Transgender men are coached in masculinity (Schilt 2011) and transgender women in femininity (Rogers 1992); both seek to legitimize bureaucratically and legally their chosen gender as man or woman (Currah, Juang, and Minter 2006). In short, what seems to be revolutionary—valorization of coming out as homosexual, same-sex marriage, and open transgender identity—has not changed the structure of binary gender regimes. Insidiously, these gender regimes, even those that are seemingly the most gender-equal in resource distribution, political power, and social privileges, such as those of Scandinavia, often still favor men (Borchorst 2009; Borchorst and Siim 2008).

The problem is that the popular concept of gender currently is what you believe you are and how you present yourself. It's not relational, social, structural, or institutional, but purely personal. Throwing gender back into personal identity ignores what feminists have learned about state gender regimes and the bureaucratic and legal imposition of binary categories. It also ignores the interactional and behavioral norms and expectations that validate personal gender identities. Another throwback is the resurgence of supposedly scientific support for male-female hardwiring of the brain and the subsequent behavior of immutably patterned children and adults that is often invoked to justify the choice of gender identity and sexuality (Jordan-Young 2011).

Where is the gender revolution feminists sought? Where is the thrust for a weakening of gender's pervasiveness? Interpersonally, "woman" and "man" are still enacted and maintained, and gender inequality persists.

How Could Multiple Gendering Have a Structural Effect?

At the end of *Gender and Power*, Raewyn Connell proposes two scenarios for change: abolition of gender and playing with gender (1987, 286–293). Abolition of gender could be accomplished by relegating sex differences to physical procreation, so that they are not "a cosmic division or a social fate" (287). Sexual and emotional binaries would be irrelevant, and masculinity and femininity would be meaningless. Instead, we would have "open-ended variety." That sounds like multiple gendering. Connell says that, without gender, it would be a "seriously impoverished" world (288). A more palatable alternative would be playing with gender and sexuality, or, as we would put it today, queering them: "Elements of sexual character, gender practice or sexual ideology are often disconnected and recombined for enjoyment, erotic tension, subversion or convenience" (289). That also sounds like multiple gendering.

Let's consider multiple gendering as an opening wedge of gender change, a precursor to abolishing gender as a binary social institution. Consistent presentation of self as not specifically a man or a woman would affect interaction, which should then in turn affect gender as a building block of social structure. There have been many real-life instances of parents raising a Baby X (Green and Friedman 2013) and many accounts of the liminal phases of gender transitioning, when the person is not easily identifiable as a man or a woman (Ames 2005). Despite the current climate of transgender acceptance, blurred gender identities seem to generate hostility and discomfort, especially in body-germane settings, such as bathrooms (Cavanagh 2010).

I am going to infer some possible effects of nonbinary gendering from research on sexual borderlands (Callis 2014), Patricia Hill Collins's analysis of how Black women could become empowered (2000, 275–290), Cecilia Ridgeway's discussion of a possible end to the pervasive gender frame (2011, 190–200), and consequences of nongendered bathrooms (Cavanagh 2010; Molotch and Norén 2010).

Borderlands

Those who are not conventionally gendered live in a borderland between men and women. Drawing on the borderlands theory of Gloria Anzuldúa (1987) and the work of Pablo Vila (2000), April Scarlette Callis (2014) explored how people sexually identifying as bisexual, pansexual, queer, and other nonbinaries inhabit the borderland between heterosexuality and homosexuality. Callis notes that, theoretically, "borderlands simultaneously develop their own cultures while challenging hegemonic ideology" (68). By this analogy, those who inhabit sexual borderlands should be creating new forms of being sexual and eventually open a space for an institutionalized "third sexuality." What she found was the other way around: the sexual borderland was created by the structures of heterosexuality and homosexuality. The thirty-seven people with non-binary sexualities she interviewed "used 21 different terms or phrases in multiple combinations to label their sexual identities. Despite the wide array of labels used, all of these identities were formed as a reaction to the binary of heterosexual/homosexual, and each moved within and beyond this binary" (78).

Multiple genders, I would argue, exist in a borderland similarly constrained by a powerful binary frame. Like those with nonbinary sexualities, those who invoke nonstandard gender identities have not developed a shared identity or culture. They include transpeople who alter their bodies in order to transition and live as women or men, those with intersexed bodies who want a third gender or X identity, and those with the bodies they were born with who have adopted alternative gender identities. They are too heterogenous and too fragmented to challenge the binary hegemony. Transpeople may support the gender binary, but do people who don't want to be tied down to hegemonic labels of "man," "woman," "male," "female" want to destroy it? It is oppressive and it does deprive those who live outside the heteronormative sexual and gender binary of rights, resources, and social power. Transgendered and intersexual people have generated substantial activism for rights specific to their physical and social situations, but the advocates of multiple gendering have not produced a unified standpoint or a revolutionary politics that might more generally undermine binary gendering.

The Politics of Empowerment

Hill Collins (2000, 274) asks, "But how does one develop a politics of empowerment without understanding how power is organized and operates?" Those invoking multiple genders may see themselves as rebels, but are they drawing on knowledge of the politics of empowerment to make real change? According to Hill Collins,

Whether viewed through the lens of a single system of power or through that of intersecting oppressions, any particular matrix of domination is organized via four interrelated domains of power, namely, the structural, disciplinary, hegemonic, and interpersonal domains. . . . The structural domain organizes oppression, whereas the disciplinary domain manages it. The hegemonic domain justifies oppression, and the interpersonal domain influences everyday lived experience and the individual consciousness that ensues. (2000, 276)

Let's take each domain in turn to see how multiple gendering could be empowered to change it.

Multiple gendering could affect the structure of the gender binary if there were a concerted effort to either abolish bureaucratic gender identities or to legally and medically recognize the range of sexed bodies. Despite the biological challenges of intersexed anatomies and anomalous hormonal and chromosomal development, each body is forced into a procrustean legal gender identity. Ambiguous infantile genitalia are surgically altered to look "normal" soon after birth (Dreger 1998; Kessler 1998). Anomalies continuously plague gender categorization in sports, with forced body changes rather than challenges to the intensely gendered structure of this powerful and pervasive institution (Dreger 2009; Karkazis and Jordan-Young 2014).

Hill Collins (2000) notes the conflicts of "outsiders within," those who have been able to move into positions of power in dominant institutions, but who are in danger of co-optation to maintain their positions and who therefore do not use their different perspectives to alter policies and practices. Transgendered people and homosexuals have made their identities visible and have promulgated nondiscriminatory laws, legal identity change, and marriage equality, but just adopting a variant gender identity does not seem consequential or revolutionary. It seems to be a matter of individual consciousness—not the end point of a process of change, but the beginning. However, after consciousness of the strictures of the two-gender social structure and the adoption of a gender-variant personal identity, there does not seem to be a path of rebellion. The two areas that should get shaken up by the open invocation and adoption of nonbinary gender identities are interpersonal interaction and hegemonic thinking about gender. Are they?

The Gender Frame

Ridgeway (2011, 190–192) argues that to make gender less powerful as a frame for most interaction, people would have to stop automatically categorizing everyone as a man or a woman. She feels this is highly unlikely since it creates too much social confusion and even anxiety in others because it "challenges the stability and validity of their own identity as a man or woman" (191). Of course, if others' gender identity was irrelevant to the interaction, then no one's gender would be of consequence. For that to happen, gender status beliefs and relevance would have to alter substantially (193).

If men did more of women's work and women more of men's work both in the workforce and at home, Ridgeway argues, conventional gender beliefs would be challenged and gradually made less relevant. In actuality, what has happened is that when men do what has been conventionally seen as "women's work," such as nursing or child care, it is reframed in gendered ways: men in nursing do more physical work or get rapidly promoted to administrative positions, and they do child care in masculine ways—roughhousing, sports, physical play. Women doing men's work, such as military combat, going into space, and ruling countries, are seen as remarkable innovators, but not the norm. Women now dominate in previously masculine professions, such as Western medicine, and have changed curricula and ways of practice, turning it into women's work, but men still predominate in the more lucrative specialties—surgery, neurology, and sports medicine. Thus, gendered cultural overlays persist, even as practices have shifted.

Bathrooms: Confronting the Material Binary

One of the arenas where gender-variant people have interacted with the conventionally gendered is multiuse bathrooms. The confrontations do not augur well for cultural change.

The demand for gender-neutral single-use bathrooms and then multiple-use bathrooms used to come from feminist women tired of waiting in long lines while men's rooms were empty. It was an integral part of the fight for gender equality (Edwards and McKie 1996; Molotch

1988). The current demand is coming from people who are gender-variant as well as from women (Brown 2005; Weiner 2015). In the United States, the demands for gender-neutral bathrooms are still seen as so radical as to continue to warrant public comment (Chemaly 2015; Smith 2015) and legal battles (Liptak 2016; Suk Gersen 2016).

Gender-variant users of multiple-use bathrooms visibly confront the binary gender social order. They violate what is to many people the psychological and biological immutability of their own sex and gender identity. In *Queering Bathrooms*, Sheila L. Cavanagh (2010) explored the shocked responses to the use of conventional bathrooms by people whose gender appearance is problematic or ambiguous. She suggests that being in a bathroom with someone of a seemingly different gender disrupts the psyche's carefully developed gender identity, achieved in great part through toilet training. The confrontation challenges the expectation that everyone is the same gender since they were born and have bodies congruent with gender appearance. Cavanagh interviewed 100 mostly white, able-bodied, middle-to-upper-class graduate students and others aged 18–59 who identified as transsexual or transgender, as gender queer, and as gay, lesbian, and bisexual. Three self-identified as intersex. Their experiences were with multiuse Western bathrooms. Many were activists, so they were able to analyze the reaction to their bathroom use. They reported double takes, verbal challenges, the calling of security guards, and even arrests.

Thus, conventional users of gendered bathrooms uphold the binary and the clear segregation of women and men in certain public spaces. Safety is invoked, although women would be safer in bathrooms where there are several of each gender. The comfort of being with "one's own" in a private space is also an issue. There is no official mandate for non-gendered, multiuse bathrooms, the way legal racial desegregation and laws governing access for the disabled altered bathroom use. In "On Not Making History," Harvey Molotch (2010) described a unisex bathroom that never got built at New York University's new facilities for a Department of Social and Cultural Analysis. He says, "It was a lost opportunity to inscribe social change into architectural form and to use form to facilitate intellectual growth" (264). But it didn't have enough supporters who were willing to fight for it.

The Paradox of Multiple Genders

The idea of multiple sexualities and multiple genders is not a twenty-first century invention. Early in the last century, Magnus Hirschfeld argued for sexual diversity. According to Alex Ross (2015), reviewing Robert Beachy's *Gay Berlin: Birthplace of a Modern Identity* (2014) in the *New Yorker*:

> The good doctor . . . preached the gorgeousness of difference, of deviations from the norm. From the beginning, he insisted on the idiosyncrasy of sexual identity, resisting any attempt to press men and women into fixed categories. To Hirschfeld, gender was an unstable, fluctuating entity; the male and the female were "abstractions, invented extremes." He once calculated that there were 43,046,721 possible combinations of sexual characteristics, then indicated that the number was probably too small. (77)

But the gay rights movement, then and now, had to present a unified face to fight for an end to stigmatization and discrimination.

The politics of identity demand that you know who is "us" and who is "them." As William Connelly says in *Identity/Difference*, "Identity requires difference in order to be, and it conveys difference into otherness in order to secure its own self-certainty" (1991, 94). Joan Wallach Scott calls it an inevitable feminist paradox that to fight to erase the effects of sex differences, you have to invoke them:

> To the extent that it acted for "women," feminism produced the "sexual difference" it sought to eliminate. This paradox—the need both to accept *and* to refuse "sexual difference"—was the constitutive condition of feminism as a political movement throughout its history. (Scott 1996, 3–4)

Sometimes differences need to be created to make a place for women. Radical feminists in particular valorized women's ways—caring, emotionality—as equal to if not superior to men's focus on rationality, objectivity, and physical violence. Maya Maor (2015) found an example of such a practice in martial arts, where women teachers create their own more relational, emotional, and less brutal style of karate and tae kwon do to make themselves visible.

Another paradox in the politics of identity is that acceptance and integration often produce what Urvashi Vaid (1995) calls virtual equality, the erasure of differences without changes in the social structure that make it possible to live differently. For the group, however, the marks of differentness may help their members identify one another as sources of help. As Suzanna Danuta Walters says of the gay and lesbian community in the United States, "One of the positive 'fallouts' of discrimination is the forging of community and the development of a concern for others, activism, a culture of responsibility. The response to AIDS is only one example" (2001, 19). However, Jane Ward's research (2004) on an AIDS service organization found that Latina lesbian women felt their health-care needs were neglected because most of the money went to gay Latino men. Obviously, differences must be bracketed off for some political actions and invoked when it is politically necessary to counter invisibility.

The question is, can "multiple gender" be a unified identity around which to rally to make structural change? What do those espousing multiple gender identities want? Just the right to call themselves a nonbinary name? To act it out? To legalize it? The first is a matter of personal identity; the second would challenge conventional face-to-face interaction; the third would disrupt the structure of the gender binary. The first and second goals don't need political unification; the third does. It would, ironically, establish a new boundary—between those who categorize by gender and those who do not (once a joke of bathroom identification with a long history).

Those who queer the gender and sexuality binaries rebel against the strictures of two and only two oppositional and fixed categories (Beemyn and Eliason 1996; Castro-Varela, Dhawan, and Engel 2011; Elliot 2010). They construct ambiguities and blur borders, but they haven't undermined the structural or interactional foundations of gender as a binary institution. Queer theory has argued that change will come when there are so many sexualities and genders that one cannot be played against the other as normal and deviant, valued and stigmatized.

The problem is that multiple gender identities exist within the gender binary and are informed by it. Multiple genders have not been frequently used in face-to-face interaction, although they may be invoked on the Internet and in bathroom use. To make structural change, people with various nonbinary gender identifications would have to perform their genders of choice openly, confront conventional others in interaction, coalesce into a unified force, bring new knowledge to bear on gender issues, and insist on bureaucratic and legal recognition.

The paradox of multiple gendering is that a politics of identity demands clear boundaries of "us" and "them." There may be coalitions and eventual erasure of the boundaries, but, for the purposes of resistance and rebellion, those insisting on multiple genders would be in the paradoxical position of establishing a new gender category.

Multiple Genders and Gender Equality

A further question is whether the current blurring of gender identities has the potential of enhancing gender equality. If we argue that gender as an institution is built on the construction of a gender binary, and that evident differences between the genders allow for the subsequent hegemony of men and masculinity and the exploitation of women's paid work and unpaid domestic labor and sexuality, then the blurring of the binary should lead to greater equality. If we can't tell or don't remark on gender in face-to-face interaction, women and men should be social equals. I have argued that with that goal in mind, everyone should practice degendering—consciously act and talk and behave as if everyone had no gender (Lorber 2000, 2005). It should be everyone's revolution, not just those who deliberately queer gender. But it needs legal and bureaucratic degendering as well, as in the gender-equal countries, where men and women are comparably educated, work in comparable occupations and professions for equal pay, have comparable political power, and share responsibility for the care of children. In short, if gender is irrelevant, not just multiple, then gender equality should follow.

This argument is testable. My hypothesis is that the more gender boundaries are blurred in attitudes, interaction, and identity, the greater the actual gender equality. The World Economic Forum's Global Gender Gap Index measures gender equality in the relative gaps between women and men in health, education, economy, and politics. According to the 2015 Global Gender Gap report, educational attainment and health and survival are close to parity globally—women and men share equally in whatever resources are available in a country. The economic participation and opportunity gender gap closed by 59 percent in the last decade but the political empowerment gap closed by only 23 percent (World Economic Forum 2015). Ranked on a combined index where gender-equal parity is 1, the highest scoring countries in 2015 were Iceland (0.881), Norway and Finland (0.850), Sweden (0.823), and Ireland (0.807). The United States is 28th with an index of 0.740; it scores well in all respects except political empowerment, where its score is a dismal 0.162.

How do gender egalitarian values compare with these measures of gender equality? My argument is that you can predict the extent of structural gender equality from the extent of how egalitarian gender attitudes are. A recent global survey asked women and men in twenty-four countries to answer ten questions about gender norms and expectations for men and women; the countries were ranked on the level of progressive gender attitudes. Matching the index of gender equality, the Nordic countries had the highest level of progressive gender attitudes (YouGov 2015). In Sweden, there was very little difference between women's and men's attitudes. The United States ranked ninth.

Other correlations of gender equality and progressive gender attitudes could be devised. In the United States, for instance, corporations could be ranked on the extent of their paid parental leave and the percentage of women executives. I would expect slippage in the correlations, which could then be explored in greater depth.

Avoiding Gender Binaries in Research and Practice

Queer studies has been a concerted effort to interrogate sexuality and gender and to deconstruct their normative assumptions of heterosexuality and binary gender but there has been a concomitant critique that "desire for gender" reinstates heterosexuality and its normativeness (Jeffreys 1996; Wiegman 2006).

Sociological research has expanded binary genders through intersectionality, where gender is sliced up by categories of race, ethnicity, social class, place of residence, and so on (McCall 2001). Gender begins as a binary variable, but it is broken up by the other variables so that the end result is multiple statuses in a stratified social structure, the equivalent of multiple genders that are not just individual identities. That is, the comparisons are not global categories of men versus women but categories such as White working class single mother and Black married woman executive. These are individual and group identities with behavioral sequelae and material effects. However, initial categorizations of gender in major survey research instruments are conceptually flawed in that they often do not clearly distinguish sex and gender or recognize gender variations, nor do they allow for changes in gender over time (Westbrook and Saperstein 2015).

It is possible to do research that does not start with binary gender categories but predicts behavior from processes and social locations, examining what people do to and with whom and how these processes construct institutional rules and social structures (Lorber 1996). Gender and other status variables can be correlated to emergent patterns later in the analysis, rather than beginning with the assumption that these variables are the starting point for behavior. Among useful methodologies are analysis of positions in a social network (Knoke and Yang 2008) and grounded theory (Charmaz 2014).

On the level of interactional practices that could undercut the gendering that supports gender-unequal policies I have proposed degendering focused on sorting people and allocating tasks in work organizations, schools, small groups, families, and other familiar social groupings (Lorber 2005). Degendered practices would encourage a gender-neutral division of labor in the home and gender-neutral jobs in workplaces, not grouping children by gender in schools, confronting gender expectations in face-to-face interaction, underplaying gender categories in language, and using gender-neutral kinship and relational designations.

Theoretically, degendered practices should feed into degendered official policies and ultimately into legal and bureaucratic statuses, but without a concerted movement for change, I do not think there will ever be a gradual progression into a social structure without gender.

Conclusion

Multiple genders may seem revolutionary, but they are not. First, they are personal identities, not legal or bureaucratic statuses. As such, they are not getting built into the structure of gender, which remains binary. Second, their individualistic rebelliousness does not encourage coalescence into a gender-resistant movement.

Queer studies, intersectionality, and nongendered research methods provide a basis for a transformation of sociological research and theorizing on gender. They could give us the data for policies that advance gender equality by challenging the legal rigidity of gender statuses, their constant use in the allocation of family work and paid jobs, and the consequent imbalance of economic resources and political power. At the same time, everyone, not just those who adopt nonbinary gender identities, could challenge the gender binary by not doing gender. Paradoxically, it's possible to be gendered and to try as much as possible to make one's gender irrelevant.

REFERENCES

Ames, Jonathan, ed. 2005. *Sexual Metamorphosis: An Anthology of Transsexual Memoirs.* New York: Vintage.

Anzaldúa, Gloria. 1987. *Borderlands/La Frontera.* San Francisco: Aunt Lute Books.

Baird, Julia. 2014. "Neither Female nor Male." *New York Times,* 7 April, A23.

Ball, Aimee Lee. 2014. "Who Are You on Facebook Now? Facebook Customizes Gender with 50 Different Choices." *New York Times,* 6 April, ST16.

Beachy, Robert. 2014. *Gay Berlin: Birthplace of a Modern Identity.* New York: Alfred A. Knopf.

Beasley, Chris. 2013. "Mind the Gap? Masculinity Studies and Contemporary Gender/Sexuality Thinking." *Australian Feminist Studies* 28 (75): 108–124.

Beemyn, Brett, and Mickey Eliason, eds. 1996. *Queer Studies: A Lesbian, Gay, Bisexual, and Transgender Anthology.* New York: New York University Press.

Borchorst, Anette. 2009. "Scandinavian Gender Equality: Competing Discourses and Paradoxes." Aalborg: Institut for Historie, Internationale Studier og Samfundsforhold, Aalborg Universitet.

Borchorst, Anette, and Birte Siim. 2008. "Woman-Friendly Policies and State Feminism: Theorizing Scandinavian Gender Equality." *Feminist Theory* 9: 207–224.

Brown, Patricia Leigh. 2005. "A Quest for a Restroom That's Neither Men's Room nor Women's Room." *New York Times,* 4 March. www.nytimes.com.

Browne, John. 2014. *The Glass Closet: Why Coming Out Is Good Business.* New York: HarperCollins.

Butler, Judith. 2004. *Undoing Gender.* New York: Routledge.

Callis, April Scarlette. 2014. "Bisexual, Pansexual, Queer: Non-binary Identities and the Sexual Borderlands." *Sexualities* 17: 63–80.

Castro Varela, María do Mar, Nikita Dhawan, and Antke Engel, eds. 2011. *Hegemony and Heteronormativity: Revisiting "The Political" in Queer Politics.* Burlington, VT: Ashgate.

Cavanagh, Sheila L. 2010. *Queering Bathrooms: Gender, Sexuality, and the Hygenic Imagination.* Toronto: University of Toronto Press.

Charmaz, Kathy. 2014. *Constructing Grounded Theory*. 2nd ed. Thousand Oaks, CA: Sage.

Chemaly, Soraya. 2015. "The Everyday Sexism of Women Waiting in Public Toilet Lines." *Time Magazine*, 5 January. www.time.com.

Connell, Raewyn. 1987. *Gender and Power: Society, the Person, and Sexual Politics*. Stanford, CA: Stanford University Press.

Connell, Raewyn, and James Messerschmidt. 2005. "Hegemonic Masculinity: Rethinking the Concept." *Gender & Society* 19: 829–859.

Connelly, William. 1991. *Identity/Difference: Democratic Negotiations of Political Paradox*. New York: Cornell University Press.

Currah, Paisley, Richard M. Juang, and Shannon Price Minter, eds. 2006. *Transgender Rights*. Minneapolis: University of Minnesota Press.

Dreger, Alice Domurat. 1998. *Hermaphrodites and the Medical Invention of Sex*. Cambridge: Harvard University Press.

———. 2009. "Seeking Simple Rules in Complex Gender Realities." *New York Times*, 25 October, 8.

Edwards, Julie, and Linda McKie. 1996. "Women's Public Toilets: A Serious Issue for the Body Politic." *European Journal of Women's Studies* 3 (3): 215–230.

Elliot, Patricia. 2010. *Debates in Transgender, Queer, and Feminist Theory: Contested Sites*. Burlington, VT: Ashgate.

Ford, Tyler. 2015. "My Life without Gender: 'Strangers Are Desperate to Know What Genitalia I Have.'" *Guardian*, 7 August. www.theguardian.com.

Green, Fiona J., and May Friedman, eds. 2013. *Chasing Rainbows: Exploring Gender Fluid Parenting Practices*. Bradford, ON: Demeter Press.

Harrison, Jack, Jaime Grant, and Jody L. Herman. 2011–12. "A Gender Not Listed Here: Genderqueers, Gender Rebels, and OtherWise in the National Transgender Discrimination Survey." *LBGTQ Policy Journal at the Harvard Kennedy School* 2: 13–24.

Herbenick, Debby, and Aleta Baldwin. 2014. "It's Complicated: What Each of Facebook's 51 New Gender Options Means." *Daily Beast*, 15 February. www.thedailybeast.com.

Hill Collins, Patricia. 2000. *Black Feminist Thought: Knowledge, Consciousness, and the Politics of Empowerment*. Rev. 10th anniversary 2nd ed. New York: Routledge.

Jeffreys, Sheila. 1996. "Heterosexuality and the Desire for Gender." In *Theorizing Heterosexuality: Telling It Straight*, edited by Diane Richardson. Buckingham, UK: Open University Press.

Jordan-Young, Rebecca M. 2011. *Brain Storm: The Flaws in the Science of Sex Differences*. Cambridge: Harvard University Press.

Karkazis, Katrina, and Rebecca Jordan-Young. 2014. "The Trouble with Too Much T." *New York Times*, 12 April, A21.

Kent, Lauren. 2015. "Number of Women Leaders around the World Has Grown, but They're Still a Small Group." Pew Research Fact Tank, 30 July. www.pewresearch.org.

Kessler, Suzanne J. 1998. *Lessons from the Intersexed*. New Brunswick, NJ: Rutgers University Press.

Knoke, David, and Song Yang. 2008. *Social Network Analysis*. 2nd ed. Thousand Oaks, CA: Sage.

Liptak, Adam. 2016. "Supreme Court Blocks Order Allowing Transgender Student Restroom Choice." *New York Times*, 3 August. www.nytimes.com.

Lorber, Judith. 1994. *Paradoxes of Gender*. New Haven: Yale University Press.

———. 1996. "Beyond the Binaries: Depolarizing the Categories of Sex, Sexuality, and Gender." *Sociological Inquiry* 66: 143–159.

———. 2000. "Using Gender to Undo Gender: A Feminist Degendering Movement." *Feminist Theory* 1: 101–118.

———. 2001. "It's the 21st Century—Do You Know What Gender You Are?" In *An International Feminist Challenge to Theory*, edited by Marcia Texler Segal and Vasilikie Demos. Advances in Gender Research, vol. 5. Greenwich, CT: JAI Press.

———. 2005. *Breaking the Bowls: Degendering and Feminist Change*. New York: W. W. Norton.

———. 2008. "Constructing Gender: The Dancer and the Dance." In *Handbook of Constructionist Research*, edited by James A. Holstein and Jaber F. Gubrium. New York: Guilford Publications.

Maor, Maya. 2015. "How Does Practicing Martial Arts Change Women? And How Do Women Change the Practice of Martial Arts?" Presented at the Center for the Study of Women and Society, City University of New York Graduate Center, 19 October.

McCall, Leslie. 2001. *Complex Inequality: Gender, Class, and Race in the New Economy*. New York: Routledge.

Molotch, Harvey. 1988. "The Restroom and Equal Opportunity." *Sociological Forum* 3: 128–132.

———. 2010. "On Not Making History." In *Toilet: Public Restrooms and the Politics of Sharing*, edited by Harvey Molotch and Laura Norén. New York: New York University Press.

Molotch, Harvey, and Laura Norén, eds. 2010. *Toilet: Public Restrooms and the Politics of Sharing*. New York: New York University Press.

Nandi, Jacinta. 2013. "Germany Got It Right by Offering a Third Gender Option on Birth Certificate." *Guardian*, 10 November. www.theguardian.com.

Preves, Sharon E. 2003. *Intersex and Identity: The Contested Self*. New Brunswick, NJ: Rutgers University Press.

Quote Investigator. 2014. "There Are Two Classes of People in the World; Those Who Divide People into Two Classes and Those Who Do Not." 7 February. www.quoteinvestigator.com.

Rich, Adrienne. 1980. "Compulsory Heterosexuality and Lesbian Existence." *Signs: Journal of Women in Culture and Society* 5: 631–660.

Ridgeway, Cecilia L. 2011. *Framed by Gender: How Gender Inequality Persists in the Modern World*. New York: Oxford University Press.

Rogers, Mary F. 1992. "They Were All Passing: Agnes, Garfinkel, and Company." *Gender & Society* 6: 169–191.

Ross, Alex. 2015. "Berlin Story." *New Yorker*, 26 January, 73–77.

Schilt, Kristen. 2011. *Just One of the Guys? Transgender Men and the Persistence of Gender Inequality*. Chicago: University of Chicago Press.

Scott, Joan Wallach. 1996. *Only Paradoxes to Offer: French Feminists and the Rights of Man*. Cambridge: Harvard University Press.

Smith, Noah. 2015. "Restroom Ordinance Is Just the Latest Sign of a City's Acceptance." *New York Times*, 18 January, A19.

Suk Gersen, Jeannie. 2016. "The Transgender Bathroom Debate and the Looming Title IX Crisis." *New Yorker*, 24 May. www.newyorker.com.

YouGov. 2015. "Global Report: Attitudes to Gender." September–October. yougov.co.uk.

Vaid, Urvashi. 1995. *Virtual Equality: The Mainstreaming of Gay and Lesbian Liberation*. New York: Doubleday Anchor.

Vaid-Menon, Alok. 2015. "Greater Transgender Visibility Hasn't Helped Nonbinary People—Like Me." *Guardian*, 13 October. www.theguardian.com.

Varma, Vishnu, and Nida Najar. 2014. "India's Supreme Court Recognizes 3rd Gender." *New York Times*, 15 April. india.blogs.nytimes.com.

Vila, Pablo. 2000. *Crossing Borders, Reinforcing Borders: Social Categories, Metaphors, and Narrative Identities on the US–Mexico Frontier*. Austin: University of Texas Press.

Walters, Suzanna Danuta. 2001. *All the Rage: The Story of Gay Visibility in America*. Chicago: University of Chicago Press.

———. 2014. *The Tolerance Trap: How God, Genes, and Good Intentions Are Sabotaging Gay Equality*. New York: New York University Press.

Ward, Jane. 2004. "'Not All Differences Are Created Equal': Multiple Jeopardy in a Gendered Organization." *Gender & Society* 18: 82–102.

Weiner, Jennifer. 2015. "The Year of the Toilet." *New York Times*, 22 December. www.nytimes.com.

West, Candace, and Don Zimmerman. 1987. "Doing Gender." *Gender & Society* 1: 125–151.

Westbrook, Laurel, and Aliya Saperstein. 2015. "New Categories Are Not Enough: Rethinking the Measurement of Sex and Gender in Social Surveys." *Gender & Society* 29: 534–560.

Wiegman, Robyn. 2006. "Heteronormativity and the Desire for Gender." *Feminist Theory* 7: 89–103.

World Economic Forum. 2015. "Global Gender Gap Report." www3.weforum.org.

Wortham, Jenna. 2016. "When Everyone Can Be 'Queer,' Is Anyone?" *New York Times*, 12 July. www.nytimes.com.

16

The Monogamous Couple, Gender Hegemony, and Polyamory

MIMI SCHIPPERS

In *Gender and Power,* Raewyn Connell (1987) introduces a theory of masculinity and femininity as central to and constitutive of hegemonic gender relations. Connell focuses on how gender hegemony—the relationship between a superior and dominant masculinity and a subordinate and complacent femininity—structures three[1] specific areas of social life: the division of labor, power relations, and what Connell calls "cathexis," or "relationships organized around one person's emotional attachment to another" (112). The relationship between masculinity and femininity structures desire in that "[o]bjects of desire are generally defined by the dichotomy and opposition of feminine and masculine; and sexual practice is mainly organized in couple relationships" (112). Connell goes on to write, "Though coupling is often seen as the basic structure of attachment, the gender dichotomy of desire seems to have some priority. When couples break up and their members form new attachments, it is almost universal practice for the new companion to be of the same sex as the old one, whichever that was" (113).

In this chapter, I want to pick up "coupling" and its relationship to the gender dichotomy and gender hegemony. While Connell suggests that the gender dichotomy is more central to the structure of cathexis than is the couple, I wish to make the argument that the couple matters. The *monogamous couple* is a discursively constructed ideal and an institutionalized and compulsory structure for sexual and emotional intimacy, and, as such, is a fruitful but oft neglected area for gender theorizing.

I refract gender hegemony through the prism of the *monogamous couple* for several reasons. First, feminist critique and theory have, since the first wave of the women's movement, placed critical focus on monogamy and its role in male dominance and patriarchy (e.g., De Beauvoir 1949; Firestone 1970; Kandiyoti 1988; Rich 1983 Robinson 1997). They have done so, however, episodically and, as Jackson and Scott (2004) lament, not with collective focus since the 1980s. Second, and as I will suggest below, the *monogamous couple* as an idealized structure for intimacy is implicated not only in gender inequality within monogamous relationships, as identified by feminist theorists, but also in broader relations of domination.[2] That is, the *monogamous couple* has been and continues to be discursively deployed to legitimate hegemonic constructions of gender difference and hierarchies as well as broader relations of domination along the lines of global imperialism and white supremacy. Third, consensually nonmonogamous (CNM) relationships in which partners agree that having sexual relations with people outside the relationship is acceptable have emerged as not only a viable relationship strategy but also as emergent subcultures (Coontz 2005; Sheff 2014; Ritchie and Barker 2006). For example, one of these emergent CNM relationship forms is polyamory, a relationship structure that includes committed or romantic partnerships, or both, with more than one person and in which all who are involved are aware of and consent to the arrangement. As I will show below, polyamory is nondyadic, has developed new languages for intimate and sexual relationships, and stresses gender egalitarianism, yet there is relatively little empirical research (Barker and Langdridge 2010a is an exception) on these kinds of relationships, including how they are shaped by and influence gender relations and structures.

Finally, the establishment of collective norms, relationship ethics, and shared meanings attached to polyamory is dominated by white, middle class, largely heterosexual populations in the U.S., Canada, Australia, and Western Europe (Sheff 2013) and focus largely on individual autonomy and choice rather than the social dynamics and political implications of polyamorous relationships (Rambukkana 2015; Wilkinson 2010). For these reasons, I believe there is far too little, yet much to be done, in terms of researching and theorizing the relationships among and between gender, other systems of domination and inequality, mononormativity, and polyamory.

To begin, my focus is on gender, race, and sexual politics in a global context and how the discursive construction of the *monogamous couple* supports, legitimizes, and naturalizes white, middle class, and

Western constructions of gender and intimacy as superior to those of non-Western, nonwhite populations. I will then turn my attention to polyamory as an emergent subculture to identify a few ways in which subcultural norms for gender, relationships, and intimacy offer a discursive intervention in the hegemonic relationship between masculinity and femininity.[3] Finally, I suggest that new lines of theory and research on the structural features of polyamory are necessary for not only understanding but also for shaping polyamory and its potential effects on broader relations of inequality.

Compulsory Monogamy, Mononormativity, and the Monogamous Couple

Within a growing scholarly and popular literature on consensual nonmonogamies, researchers and activists build on the concept of compulsory heterosexuality (Rich 1983) to identify *compulsory monogamy* as the institutionalized arrangements that encourage or force people into monogamous, dyadic relationships (see Mint 2004). Building on queer theory's critique of sexual normalcy and heteronormativity, a small but burgeoning academic literature focuses on *mononormativity* (see Barker and Langdridge 2010b). Mononormativity refers to institutionalized arrangements and cultural narratives that situate the monogamous dyad as the only legitimate, natural, or desirable structure for mature, emotionally fulfilling, intimate relationships (Pieper and Bauer 2005). Like other groups marginalized by their sexual practices or intimate relationships, those in consensually nonmonogamous and polyamorous relationships are an invisible sexual minority (Kleinplatz and Diamond 2014). For instance, because there are no laws outlawing discrimination on the basis of relationship status, polyamorists are usually not "out" about being poly (a shorthand adjective for "polyamorous" used by polyamorists, as in "I am poly" or "I am currently in a poly relationship") because there are real risks for employment and housing discrimination or losing custody of children. Because of stereotypes about and prejudice toward people practicing CNM (Conley et al. 2013), managing stigma or experiencing negative or discriminatory treatment, or both, are common experiences for polyamorists (Pallotta-Chiarolli 2010; Sheff and Hammers 2011; Sheff 2013).

In Pieper and Bauer's and others' discussions of mononormativity, the emphasis is not on sexual identities or practices, but instead on *relationship form* as variable and central to the operations of social privilege and disadvantage. Though mononormativity intersects with hetero-normativity, institutionalized dyadic monogamy confers privileges and advantages to people in or perceived to be in long-term, monogamous couple relationships regardless of the race, gender, or sexual identities of partners. If the gender binary is the basic structure of cathexis, as Connell suggests, then mononormativity and compulsory monogamy provide the organizing logic for ensuring dyadic intimacy and prohibiting plurality.

Deconstructing the Monogamous Couple as Gender Hegemony

What significance do mononormativity and the prohibition on plurality have for gender theory? Mononormativity is gendered in that the *monogamous couple*, as a discursively constructed ideal, reflects and maintains a complementary and hierarchical relationship between masculinity and femininity. As an organizing rationale for social life, the hegemonic relationship between the masculine and feminine manifests in culturally specific collective beliefs about erotic and emotional interactions and attachment to define what is a "good" relationship, who "belongs" together, and what are the behavioral and emotional expectations for individuals in a "good" relationship. While Connell identifies the gender dichotomy as the basic structure for cathexis, my focus here is on the gender structure of *monogamy* specifically to suggest that *mononormativity* (as opposed to the practice of monogamy) is constitutive of and reflects hegemonic gender relations.

First, the *monogamous couple*, as an imagined, glorified, and compulsory relationship form, mirrors and supports the discursively constructed relationship between hetero-masculinity and hetero-femininity. For instance, to the extent that it sutures one man and one woman together as "the one-and-only" true love, mononormativity supports the collective assumption that the *monogamous couple* is the only "good" relationship, while also naturalizing and providing cultural legitimacy to the construction of gender difference as consisting of *two and only two*, complementary and hierarchical opposites that belong together. In other words, *monogamy* as a hegemonic feature of sexual intimacy and relationships closes off the dyad as a unified and singular unit that both reflects and sustains the idea that the *gender binary* is natural and desirable. As I will discuss below, opening up relationships to include more than two people breaks open the dyad in ways that require new ways of thinking and talking about the relationship between hegemonic masculinities and femininities, gender and sexual identities, and the structures of intimacy.

In addition to closing off the dyad as a singular unit, monogamy is laced with gender meaning, and, as such, mirrors culturally specific constructions of hegemonic masculinity and hegemonic femininity. For example, the paradigmatic theoretical framework for family and kinship structure in evolutionary anthropology is that humans have evolved to form monogamous, heterosexual pair bonds (Ryan and Jetha 2010; Starkweather and Hames 2012). The theoretical narrative for how humans evolved to be monogamous relies upon and rearticulates widespread and culturally specific notions of gender difference as hierarchical and complementary. Specifically, evolutionary anthropologists argue that monogamous marriage is an evolved adaptation to men's natural propensity for sexual promiscuity and women's evolved desire for long-term protection and provision (see Symons 1979). The theory goes something like this: because male reproductive fitness lies in copulating with as many females as possible, men have evolved to be predisposed for nonmonogamy. In contrast, because the survival of a female's offspring depends on the father providing resources and protection, women evolved to seek and prefer long-term monogamy. Because men do not want to invest time, energy, and resources in the survival of another man's offspring—no payoff for a big investment—they are sexually jealous and protective of the women with whom they mate. In exchange for their investment of resources and protection, men demand monogamy from women and place tight controls on women's sexual behavior. From this evolutionary perspective, monogamous marriage is an evolved compromise to compel men to provide for and protect their mates and offspring and for women to be monogamous. This is the reason, evolutionary anthropologists hypothesize, that in contemporary society, men crave sexual novelty and are prone to infidelity while, at the same time, they demand and enforce monogamy from women, and why women desire emotional connection within the context of dyadic relationships and acquiesce to men's control.[4]

As a dominant discourse about *monogamy*, evolutionary theory establishes a set of complementary, hierarchical, and relational constructions of masculinity and femininity as also natural and beneficial: men have evolved to be sexual, possessive, jealous, and controlling. Women have evolved to be relationship oriented and compliant to men's control. These expectations for men and women are "coupled" together as complementary opposites and legitimate men's dominance through control and women's subordination through compliance. In this example, *monogamy* is the constitutive feature that binds the masculine and feminine together in a hierarchical and complementary relationship— the definition of hegemonic gender relations. The gender structure of the theory relies as much on mononormativity as it does on heteronormativity. While this example deconstructs evolutionary anthropological discourse in particular, it is the role of gender theorists to unpack how other scientific, literary, economic, historical, or legal theories and paradigms rely upon mononormative assumptions to mask or legitimate hegemonic notions of gender difference and inequalities.

Deconstructing the Monogamous Couple as Intersectional Gender Hegemony

To the extent that the *monogamous couple* is held up as the ideal and only viable relationship structure for emotionally and sexually intimate relationships, those who violate the norm of monogamy are often constructed as immoral or inferior, or both, because of the violation of natural or normal gender relations. That is, nonmonogamy in the form of polygamy or infidelity is sometimes constructed as a *gender failure* in order to secure race, ethnic, or national superiority and to legitimate imperialist and racist policy.

If we look closely at Western or white supremacist discursive constructions of the *ethno-sexual abject other*, they often rely upon the *monogamous couple* as normal, moral, and natural in order to cast imagined or real sexual practices or kinship structures of nonwhite or non-Western populations as deviant or immoral. For instance, while much has been written about controlling images of African American women as the "jezebel" or "mammy" and African American men as sexual predators (Hill Collins 2005), elsewhere I emphasized the pathologization of African American families and kinship structures as incapable of long-term, marital monogamy (Schippers 2016). During Jim Crow, for instance, images of hypersexualized African American masculinities and femininities included representations of "the acquiescence of the black husband to his wife's infidelity" (Higginbotham 1993, 190). Not only did this stereotype cast African American women as promiscuous and unfaithful to their husbands, it also emasculated African American husbands in their "acquiescence" to being cuckolded. By attaching "acquiescence to infidelity" to African American masculinities and promiscuity to African American femininities, the *monogamous couple* was established as superior and equated with whiteness and deployed to render African Americans as immoral or inferior.

The *monogamous couple* has also served colonial and imperialist Western constructions of polygamous societies as backwards, primitive, and immoral. James Messerschmidt's (2010, 2015) concept of "toxic masculinities" captures this discursive maneuver in the contemporary U.S. context. According to Messerschmidt, U.S. imperialist militarism depends on constructions of the "enemy" as sexist men who are brutal to "their" women. For instance, in the U.S., Muslim men are held up as dangerous, backwards, brutal, and violent toward women for practicing and enforcing polygamy, while American men are constructed as more enlightened, "civilized," and just because they embrace dyadic, monogamous, and supposedly egalitarian relationships with women[5] (Puar 2007). In other words, mononormativity intersects with gender hegemony to play at least some part in the narrative rationale for war and U.S. global imperialism, but it is not explicitly acknowledged as such. In what other ways and in what contexts is the *monogamous couple* as a gender ideal deployed to legitimate racial-ethnic, imperialistic, or other forms of domination? This is a question best answered by deconstructing the operations of mononormativity in gendered discourses about racial, ethnic, and national differences and hierarchies in order to develop and build intersectional theories of domination.

In addition to deconstructing mononormativity as central to gender, racial, and imperial hegemony, sociologists might turn an empirical lens on polyamory in order to better understand or develop new conceptual frameworks, or both, for the relationships among and between gender subjectivity, the gender structure of interpersonal relationships, and intimacy. I turn now to polyamory as a specific structure for intimate relationships to show how this can be done.

Polyamory and Gender Discourse

The word "polyamory" means multiple loves and refers to emotionally and sometimes sexually intimate relationships with more than one person. Though we don't have numbers on the extent of polyamory,[6] it is estimated that people in consensually nonmonogamous relationships number in the millions (Sheff 2013), and in one online survey, 3 percent of respondents said they were currently in consensually nonmonogamous or open relationships and an additional 10 percent said that they had been at one time (Moore 2015).

Elisabeth Sheff (2014a) suggests that there have been three waves of countercultural subcultures that emphasize and advocate consensual nonmonogamy. Contemporary polyamory follows and builds upon the ideals and political philosophies of nineteenth-century transcendentalist communes such as the Oneidas, and on twentieth-century countercultures associated with the sexual revolution, including the sexual liberation movement among gay men and lesbians, swinging subcultures, communes, and "free love."

Though polyamorists borrow from and build upon these previous subcultures, the social context in which polyamory has emerged is quite different in three ways. First, polyamory emerges in the wake of second and third wave feminist critiques of the nuclear family and politicization of women's sexual subjectivity. Second, high rates of divorce and infidelity, serial monogamy, and blended families have complicated notions of family and lifelong monogamy with one person (Stacey 2011). Third, unlike previous nonmonogamous subcultures, polyamory has emerged in the digital era. Not only does this make the subcultural norms, ethics, and practices readily available to anyone who has access to a computer,[7] it also allows for the development and cultivation of a consensus about those norms and ethics that stretch across time and space (Sheff 2013).

The confluence of feminism, changes in family structures, and the Internet not only distinguishes contemporary poly subcultures from previous nonmonogamous communities and subcultures; feminism, changing family forms including gay and lesbian households, and the Internet also shape the collective meanings and relationship ethics developed by polyamorists (e.g., Anapol 2010; Easton and Hardy 2009; Taormino 2008; Veaux and Rickert 2014).

Because mainstream and dominant relationship norms are mononormative, polyamorists have used online blogs, podcasts, forums, and how-to books to develop their own language and set of shared meanings and norms for how to do intimate relationships (Ritchie and Barker 2006). As a relationship structure that requires a new language and a new set of expectations, collective meanings, and practices, polyamory offers interesting opportunities to resist, challenge, and reconfigure the hegemonic relationship between masculinity and femininity as they structure and take shape in intimate relationships.

For instance, rejecting mononormativity while embracing gender egalitarianism requires alternative discourses and understandings of sexual jealousy. "Compersion" in the American and "frubbly" in the British contexts are words used by polyamorists to refer to feeling pleasure (rather than fear or anger) when one's partner experiences sexual pleasure or emotional intimacy with another person. Because poly subcultural norms insist upon gender egalitarianism, everyone, regardless of gender, is encouraged to cultivate compersion rather than jealousy and feel frubbly rather than frightened or angry when a partner is involved with another person. This subcultural understanding of jealousy offers a counternarrative to the evolutionary anthropological assumptions that sexual jealousy is "natural" or inevitable in men, that men need to control women's sexual behavior, and that women should acquiesce to men's control.

Although there is very little empirical research on the effects of these norms and expectations on how possessiveness manifests within the everyday, interpersonal lives of polyamorists, one study suggests that new meanings for and normative expectations about sexual jealousy were experienced by men as a catalyst for changes in their sense of masculinity. Because they no longer felt entitled to jealous feelings or a need to maintain control of their partners' social or sexual lives, these men no longer defined masculinity in terms of possessive control as constitutive of manliness (Sheff 2006). In the same study, polyamorous women experienced a shift in their sense of feminine subjectivity. Being relatively freed from men's jealousy and control, they reported feeling a sense of agency, autonomy, and entitlement to sexual pleasure (Sheff 2005). In other words, this research suggests that rejecting the mononormative assumptions that sexual jealousy is natural, inevitable, and structured by gender challenges and facilitates a rejection of the hegemonic construction of masculinity as possessive, competitive, and dominant over the possessed, complaisant feminine object.

Polyamorists also have developed a new language for recognizing and cultivating relationships with one's partners' partners. For example, two people who are in an intimate and committed relationship with the same person would be considered "metamours." The label situates a partner's partner in a recognizable and legitimate social location in intimate relationships and establishes specific role expectations and responsibilities. While there is variability in the extent of involvement between metamours (anywhere from being acquaintances to integrated family members), these role expectations include open lines of communication and some measure of interpersonal responsibility and accountability between metamours (see Veaux and Rickert 2014). Again, within the context of subcultural norms for gender egalitarianism, there are strong expectations that metamours develop lines of communication, if not emotional ties, across and within gender difference. How might cultivating metamour relationships change men's relationships with each other? How do metamour relationships change women's relationships to each other as competitors for the attention of men? These are just two among many questions in need of theory and research.

Polyamory and Gender Structure

The commitment to gender equality described above, however, is an ideological ideal, not a structural reality. There is no guarantee that the lived experience of metamour relationships or feeling less entitled to jealousy and possessiveness translates into ungendered or egalitarian interpersonal interactions and household practices. If Risman's (1999) research on feminist families is any indication, a commitment to gender equality can only go so far when dealing with the everyday constraints, pressures, and institutional structures of doing intimate relationships and households.

Elisabeth Sheff's (2013) extensive research on poly families suggests that poly family structure does have a transforming effect on some, but not all, aspects of gender in her sample of mostly white, middle class families. For instance, women and men in her sample report feeling a sense of relief from family responsibilities when there are multiple adults in the household, and children benefit from having several caretakers.[8] At the same time, Sheff finds that a gendered division of labor persists in poly households despite ideologies of gender equality. For instance, although there might be multiple adults living in a household, certain tasks like emotional labor and planning often fall on the shoulders of women. Some dynamics, however, seem to play out differently in poly households compared to two-adult households. For example, while multiple women in a household might reduce an individual woman's labor, men in poly families are relieved from the burdens of household labor even more so than men in monogamous, heterosexual households. This suggests that opening dyadic relationships to more than two adults might foster different interpersonal dynamics and challenges when confronting or resisting constraints, pressures, and structures. Gender theory and research are needed to better understand not just the dynamics and structures of poly households and practices but also what poly households might teach us about gender more generally.

Conclusion: Polynormativity and Gender Theory

In this chapter, I presented the *monogamous couple* as an important but neglected subject of gender theory. I also introduced the polyamory subculture as one example of how opening up relationships to include more than two might disrupt the hegemonic relationship between masculinities and femininities and offer opportunities to reconfigure gendered subjectivity and the gender structure of intimate relationships.

While there is some research on the effects of multiadult household structure on the division of labor, most notably the work of Sheff (2013) and Pallotta-Chiarolli (2010), polyamory is relatively absent from sociological gender theory and research. We know that polyamory as a subculture emphasizes equality and open communication, but we know little about how gender structures poly relationships in practice. Moreover, we know too little about how poly intimacies affect the structure of gendered subjectivities, interpersonal relationships, and household structures. Polyamory and poly relationships offer an opportunity to learn about and build new theories of how gender organizes intimate relationships, the relationship between feminist ideology and gender practice, and how we might do things differently—all of which are of central concern in gender theory and research.

Finally, I believe polyamory is relevant to gender theory because, unless they are academics or activists, many polyamorists (like most citizens in a late capitalist, neoliberal, global world) lack both a sociological self-reflexivity about their own relationships and a social justice understanding or narrative for polyamory in the broader context of gender, race, class, and national inequalities. In the how-to poly literature and in mainstream treatments of polyamory, for instance, there is a neoliberal emphasis on polyamory as an individual choice and a matter of taste or relationship orientation rather than on the potentially radicalizing way poly intimacies can transform gender, race, and class relations (see Schippers 2016) or about how it might lead to rethinking intimacy more generally (see Rambukkana 2015; Wilkinson 2010).

Moreover, public discourse about and community building around poly living are overwhelmingly dominated by white, middle class, and Western European, Canadian, Australian, and American polyamorists (Sheff 2013, Sheff and Hammers 2011), and all too frequently these conversations do not consider or confront racism, classism, global imperialism, or other systems of inequality (Rambukkana 2015). In the mainstream poly literature, for instance, there is little discussion of how race, class, and gender structure poly relationships and subcultures or how polyamory as a relationship form and subcultural practice might be forged in ways that do not reproduce but instead undermine or challenge structural inequalities.

Feminist theorists and sociologists, including Raewyn Connell (1987), fought for and succeeded in placing the gender structure of sex and intimate relationships squarely inside and relevant to the sociological study of not just family, kinships, and interpersonal sexual relations but also to broader relations of inequality and domination at all levels of social organization. Likewise, queer theorists and sexuality researchers have successfully argued and demonstrated how the study of heteronormativity, heterosexism, and the lived experiences of LGBTQ individuals, groups, and subcultures enhances not just our understanding of heterosexist prejudice and discrimination but also how the operations and institution-alization of heteronormativity have broader implications for relations of domination at all levels of social organization. Similarly, I believe that the study of *mononormativity* as an organizing feature of not just intimate re-lationships, but also social relations of domination more broadly, can lead to new gender theory. I also strongly believe that research on *polyamory* as a nondyadic and emergent structure for sex and intimate relationships practiced by a silent sexual minority is relevant to gender theory.

Finally, queer theorists point to and warn against "homonormativity" or efforts to normalize Western, monogamous, middle class, white gay and lesbian families. Likewise, I hope to convince my readers that study-ing the dynamics of *polynormativity*, which refers to the normalization of a particular kind of polyamory—one that reinforces rather than chal-lenges hegemonic gender relations, racism, class inequality, heterosex-ism, and Western imperialism—can open up new understanding and theorizing of gender as it intersects with other systems of inequality and at multiple levels of social organization. Without a sociological lens and without queer, critical race, and feminist theory we may miss the oppor-tunity to not only document but also to shape this poly moment in ways that subvert or disrupt social inequalities and transform the meaning and structure of intimate relationships.

NOTES

1 In later work, Connell and Messerschmidt (2005) add a fourth dimension of gender hegemony, specifically cultural representation.

2 There is some disagreement among feminist theorists and researchers about whether or not monogamy is harmful or beneficial to women. Just as Adrienne Rich focused on compulsory heterosexuality as an organizing feature of social structure and not a sexual practice, my focus in this chapter is less on the practice of monogamy, and more on mononormativity and compulsory monogamy as a broader structure for intimacy. For a conceptual framework for monogamy as a "patriarchal bargain," see Kandiyoti 1988.

3 For a definition of gender hegemony that focuses on *relationality* between the masculine and feminine, see Schippers 2007.

4 For an alternative interpretation of the anthropological data, see Ryan and Jetha 2010 and Starkweather and Hames 2012. For a more in-depth discussion of the mononormativity of this paradigm, see Schippers 2016.

5 Certainly male dominance correlates with polygyny and reflects and maintains men's dominance over women in many cultures (Zeitzen 2008). However, the

conflation of monogamy with egalitarianism and plural marriage with male dominance ignores the ways in which monogamy serves masculine interests, as has been identified by feminists. The mononormative assumption that plural marriage is, by definition, worse than monogamy for women constructs and oversimplifies the false binary between Western, feminist monogamy as qualitatively different from and superior to non-Western, patriarchal polygamy. This reproduces imperialist, colonizing feminist discourses that situate the "Western Woman" as more advanced or politically savvy compared to the "Third World Woman" (see Mohanty 1984, and, more recently, Pedwell 2008) and ignores the feminist critique of heterosexual monogamy and polygamy by women in non-Western contexts as well as the existence of nonmonogamous relationship forms in Western contexts. It also renders invisible the ways in which some plural relationship structures like polyandry (Starkweather and Hames 2012) and polyamory (Sheff 2005, 2006, 2011; Schippers 2016) correlate with more egalitarian gender relations.

6 There is no national level demographic information on the extent or characteristics of people in polyamorous relationships. Most research relies upon online or snowball sampling recruitment and cannot be generalized to larger populations. At the time of writing this chapter, there are no national random surveys that include questions with which we can make estimates of the numbers of polyamorists.

7 Because polyamory subcultures are largely online phenomena, access to a computer would be another stratifying feature of polyamory and mediated by geography, class, and nation.

8 Although beyond the scope of this chapter, research suggests that there are no significant adverse outcomes for children in poly households (Pallotta-Chiarolli 2010; Sheff 2013).

REFERENCES

Anapol, Deborah. 2010. *Polyamory in the 21st Century: Love and Intimacy with Multiple Partners*. New York: Rowman and Littlefield.

Barker, Meg, and Darren Langdridge. 2010a. "Whatever Happened to Non-Monogamies? Critical Reflections on Recent Research and Theory." *Sexualities* 13 (6): 748–772.

———, eds. 2010b. *Understanding Non-Monogamies*. New York: Routledge.

Conley, Terri D., Ali Ziegler, Amy C. Moors, Jes L. Matsick, and Brandon Valentine. 2013. "A Critical Examination of Popular Assumptions about the Benefits and Outcomes of Monogamous Relationships." *Personality and Social Psychology Review* 17 (2): 124–141.

Connell, R. W. 1987. *Gender and Power: Society, the Person, and Sexual Politics*. Cambridge: Polity.

Connell, R. W., and James Messerschmidt. 2005. "Hegemonic Masculinity: Rethinking the Concept." *Gender & Society* 19 (6): 829–859.

Coontz, Stephanie. 2005. *Marriage, a History: How Love Conquered Marriage*. New York: Penguin Books.

De Beauvoir, Simone. 1949. *The Second Sex*. New York: Vintage.

Easton, Dossie, and Janet W. Hardy. 2009. *The Ethical Slut: A Practical Guide to Polyamory, Open Relationships, and Other Adventures*. 2nd ed. Berkeley, CA: Celestial Arts.

Firestone, Shulamith. 1970. *The Dialectic of Sex: The Case for Feminist Revolution*. New York: Bantam.

Higginbotham, Evelyn Brooks. 1993. *Righteous Discontent: The Women's Movement in the Black Baptist Church, 1880–1920*. Cambridge: Harvard University Press.

Hill Collins, Patricia. 2005. *Black Sexual Politics: African Americans, Gender, and the New Racism*. New York: Routledge.

Jackson, Stevi, and Sue Scott. 2004. "The Personal Is Still Political: Heterosexuality, Feminism and Monogamy." *Feminism & Psychology* 14 (1): 151–157.

Kandiyoti, Deniz. 1988. "Bargaining with Patriarchy." *Gender & Society* 2 (3): 274–290.

Kleinplatz, Peggy J., and Lisa M. Diamond. 2014. "Sexual Diversity." In *APA Handbook of Sexuality and Psychology: Vol. 1*, edited by Debra L. Tolman and Lisa M. Diamond. Washington DC: American Psychological Association: 245–267.

McBride, Dwight. 2005. *Why I Hate Abercrombie and Fitch: Essays on Race and Sexuality*. New York: New York University Press.

Messerschmidt, James. 2010. *Hegemonic Masculinities and Camouflaged Politics: Unmasking the Bush Dynasty and Its War against Iraq*. Boulder, CO: Paradigm Publishers.

———. 2015. *Masculinities in the Making: From the Local to the Global*. Lanham, MD: Rowman and Littlefield.

Mint, Pepper. 2004. "The Power Dynamics of Cheating." *Journal of Bisexuality* 4 (3–4): 55–76.

Mohanty, Chandra Talpade. 1984. "Under Western Eyes: Feminist Scholarship and Colonial Discourses." *Boundary* 2 (12:3–13:1): 333–358.

Moore, Peter. 2015. "Poll Results: Open Relationships." *Huffington Post*, March 20. www.today.yougov.com.

Moynahan, Patrick. 1965. "The Negro Family: The Case for National Action." Washington, DC: Office of Policy Planning and Research, United States Department of Labor.

Pallotta-Chiarolli, Maria. 2010. *Border Sexualities, Border Families in Schools*. NewYork: Rowman and Littlefield.

Pedwell, Carolyn. 2008. "Weaving Relational Webs: Theorizing Cultural Difference and Embodied Practice." *Feminist Theory* 9 (1): 87–107.

Pieper, Marianne, and Robin Bauer. 2005. "Call for Papers: International Conference on Polyamory and Mono-normativity." Research Centre for Feminist, Gender & Queer Studies, University of Hamburg, November 5–6.

Puar, Jaspir. 2007. *Terrorist Assemblages: Homonationalism in Queer Times*. Durham: Duke University Press.

Rambukkana, Nathan. 2015. *Fraught Intimacies: Non/Monogamy in the Public Sphere*. Vancouver: UBC Press.

Rich, Adrienne. 1983. "Compulsory Heterosexuality and Lesbian Existence." In *Powers of Desire: The Politics of Sexuality*, edited by Ann Snitow, Christine Stansell, and Sharon Thompson. New York: Monthly Review Press.

Risman, Barbara. 1999. *Gender Vertigo: American Families in Transition*. New Haven: Yale University Press.

Ritchie, Ani, and Meg Barker. 2006. "'There Aren't Words for What We Do or How We Feel So We Have to Make Them Up': Constructing Polyamorous Languages in a Culture of Compulsory Monogamy." *Sexualities* 9 (5): 584–601.

Robinson, Victoria. 1997. "My Baby Just Cares for Me: Feminism, Heterosexuality, and Non-Monogamy." *Journal of Gender Studies* 6 (2): 143–158.

Ryan, Christopher, and Casilda Jetha. 2010. *Sex at Dawn: The Prehistoric Origins of Modern Sexuality*. New York: Harper.

Schippers, Mimi. 2007. "Recovering the Feminine Other: Femininity, Masculinity, and Gender Hegemony." *Theory and Society* 36 (1): 85–102.

———. 2016. *Beyond Monogamy: Polyamory and the Future of Polyqueer Sexualities*. New York: New York University Press.

Sheff, Elisabeth. 2005. "Polyamorous Women, Sexual Subjectivity and Power." *Journal of Contemporary Ethnography* 34 (3): 251–283.

———. 2006. "Poly-Hegemonic Masculinities." *Sexualities* 9 (5): 621–642.

———. 2011. "Polyamorous Families, Same-Sex Marriage, and the Slippery Slope." *Journal of Contemporary Ethnography* 40 (5): 487–520.

———. 2013. *The Polyamorist Next Door: Inside Multiple-Partner Relationships and Families*. New York: Rowman and Littlefield.

———. 2014. "How Many Polyamorists Are There in the U.S.?" *Psychology Today*, May 9. www.psychologytoday.com.

Sheff, Elisabeth, and Corrie Hammers. 2011. "The Privilege of Perversities: Race, Class and Education among Polyamorists and Kinksters." *Psychology & Sexuality* 2 (3): 198–223.

Stacy, Judith. 2011. *Unhitched: Love, Marriage, and Family Values from West Hollywood to Western China*. New York: New York University Press.

Starkweather, Katherine E., and Raymond Hames. 2012. "A Survey of Non-Classical Polyandry." *Human Nature* 23 (1): 49–172.

Symons, Donald. 1979. *The Evolution of Human Sexuality*. New York: Oxford University Press.

Taormino, Tristan. 2008. *Opening Up: A Guide to Creating and Sustaining Open Relationships*. San Francisco: Cleis Press.

Veaux, Franklin, and Eve Rickert. 2014. *More Than Two: A Practical Guide to Ethical Polyamory*. Portland: Thorntree Press.

Wilkinson, Eleanor. 2010. "What's Queer About Non-Monogamy Now?" In *Understanding Non-Monagamies*, edited by Meg Barker and Darren Langdridge. New York: Routledge: 243–254.

Zeitzen, Miriam. 2008. *Polygamy: A Cross-Cultural Analysis*. London: Bloomsbury.

Conclusion: Reckoning with Gender

RAEWYN CONNELL

At the time this book was being written, the Syrian civil war was deepening and the refugee stream to Lebanon, Turkey, and Europe was widening. A violent stalemate had arisen between Bashar al-Assad's regime, its Shiite backers, its Sunni rebels, and the Islamic State movement. A growing number of the world's nuclear powers leaned in: Barack Obama's United States, Nicolas Sarkozy's and François Hollande's France, Vladimir Putin's Russia, and Xi Jinping's China.

In the flood of commentary about this terrifying situation, one striking fact went almost unmentioned. All of the contending parties were headed by groups of men, and almost all the military forces involved were men. The rhetoric of power, confrontation, combat, victory, dominance, and defeat is coded masculine. But this is so familiar, so *ordinary*, that even in this extraordinary situation the fact hardly registered—except with a few feminist agitators for peace.

Why the outside involvement in a small country's conflicts? There are religious connections, certainly. There are some devious geopolitical maneuvers going on. But the main reason is that Syria is next door to the world's largest oil province, major new pipelines are planned to go through it, and the transnational corporate economy utterly depends on oil.

Who holds power in this transnational corporate economy? We have statistics on a key group, the CEOs of the world's 500 biggest corporations; and it turns out that 96 percent of them are men. Indeed, wherever we look among global elites—the transnational managers, the super-rich oligarchs, the dictators, the neoliberal state elites—there is a similar picture: a predominance of men, and heavily masculinized organizational cultures.

There is a claim, often made in journalism and politics and even in academia, that "gender doesn't matter now." On this view gender binaries, legal discrimination, and the oppression of women may have existed in the past, but are fading away. Modern women have equal rights, gender identities have become fluid, homophobia is fading, and men now change diapers. On this basis there is no more need for feminism, affirmative action, or gender studies programs.

It's perfectly true that laws, economies, and cultures have changed. Angela Merkel has Otto von Bismarck's job and has been doing it rather well; Hillary Clinton nearly got Teddy Roosevelt's. Over the past two generations, enormous investment in schools and adult education in developing countries has brought literacy to most of the world's women—perhaps the biggest change in gender patterns in our lifetime. Globally, women's participation in the paid labor force has been rising as men's has been falling.

But evidence of *change* in gender patterns is a far cry from the *disappearance* of gender. Change may mean that gender hierarchy is more emphatically present. The rise of fundamentalist movements in Christendom and Islam has dramatized gender; indeed the desire to recuperate troubled masculinities is one of the reasons for current religious and nationalist revivals. A display of exaggerated masculinity is a feature of new authoritarian politics, from Putin in Russia to Rodrigo Duterte in the Philippines to Donald Trump in the United States. Even technological advances may have regressive gender effects. The growth of the Internet immediately produced a vast surge of sexist pornography—now a main source of sex education for a whole generation of youth.

If we look into the boring details of economic life, we certainly do not see a genderless world. The usual assumption of a small and declining "gender gap" is quite wrong. The aggregate income of women as a group, so far as one can tell from erratic official statistics, is around 60 percent of the aggregate income globally of men as a group. The neoliberal corporate economy rests on stark gender divisions of labor and gendered hierarchies of power, from the clothing factories of Bangladesh and south China to the oil industries of the Gulf and the Caribbean. Gender division in the economy is by no means confined to old industries or poor countries. It runs high in Silicon Valley and on Wall Street.

The gender structuring of human life remains an important determinant of people's experiences and—to use old-fashioned language—their fates. Situation in the gender order affects people's access to income; their likelihood of owning land; their education; their nutrition, health, and illness; their exposure to violence; the way they are treated by police and by employers. It's not surprising that gender is so important in their personal identities, and persistently affirmed, or troubled, by the way they act in everyday life.

The gender structuring of social life matters not only because of gender differences but also because gender patterns affect our common fate. Those bombs falling in Aleppo are launched by men following a masculinized logic of conflict. But once dropped, the bombs don't discriminate. Media releases complain of attacks on "women and children," a clichéd way of saying that civilians were killed. But men are civilians too. Whole communities are blown away by modern warfare. And whole societies are at risk from the generals' nuclear missiles, from the corporate managers' relentless assault on the environment, and from the political elite's ruthless pursuit of power. Gender matters for the survival of human society. The stakes are as high as that.

Social Science and Gender

That is the reason we have written this book. Social science is an essential tool for understanding gender questions, but a tool not easy to use. Fifty years ago it did seem easy, when the theory of "sex roles" was popular. Gender was defined by social norms, children were socialized into those norms, grown men and women performed the male role or the female role accordingly, and they transmitted the norms to the next generation. For many scholars and activists this model provided a satisfying alternative to biological determinism. Gender was socially constructed, and gender inequality could be ended by changing the role norms.

Sex-role theory has not died. Perhaps it still has a role to play, since the ideology it contested, the belief in fixed natural sex differences in mentality and behavior, remains alive and well. But role theory never provided an adequate account of social life. It ignored the contradictions uncovered by psychoanalysis, it gave no account of the power structures familiar in sociology, and it dealt with the body by the drastic device of walling it off from the social. Not surprisingly, feminists concerned with emotion, power, or body politics turned to other resources.

In Anglophone social science, the 1980s were a time of consolidating and rethinking the experience of the Women's Liberation movement. Out of this a number of sociological perspectives on gender emerged. They included Dorothy Smith's subtle critique of gendered forms of knowledge; Sylvia Walby's structural approach to power; and the collective project of *Gender & Society*, the journal that took a central place in the field, not least because it promptly published Candace West and Don Zimmerman's previously unpublishable paper "Doing Gender."

Gender and Power was written in 1984 and published in 1987. The first three chapters of *Gender Reckonings* (part I above) discuss its theorizing and context. Myra Marx Ferree traces the combination of historical and structural ideas that went into *Gender and Power*. She shows, very perceptively I think, how these reflected the experience of Anglophone feminism up to that time; and then how changed political circumstances, new intellectual tools, and more global perspectives were reflected in my second attempt at a general theory. James Messerschmidt and Michael Messner look closely at the most influential passage in *Gender and Power*, the sketch of multiple masculinities and femininities, and trace the strange career of the concept of hegemonic masculinity. They rightly emphasize the structural basis of that concept, and the need to distinguish between crude domination in gender relations and the idea of hegemony, which is a much more complex and dynamic concept. They show particularly how to understand the appearance of new patterns of masculinity.

Kristen Schilt's contribution to part I surprised and delighted me. She has done a Sherlockian job of decoding the subtext in *Gender and Power* that gives an account of transsexuality. There were some quietly anguished sentences about personal experience in the preface to *Gender and Power*, too well coded to make much sense at the time. I don't think being a transsexual woman committed me to any specific view of gender, but it doubtless made me more aware of the tension and complexity in real-life gender patterns—which have never been binary. I am grateful to Kristen for showing how the broader approach of *Gender and Power* helps a sociological understanding of gender transition.

We can tell the story of gender theory as if the whole thing happened inside a library. In fact all the attempts at gender theory in the 1980s grew out of the political struggle, and represented attempts to construct knowledge for social change. Along with academics and students, their audiences included movement activists, public officials, teachers, counselors, and health workers. Feminist social science in the 1980s was close to feminist policy work, trying to shape policy and practice in schools and universities, health services, employment, and legal systems. This work has continued since, though the political scene has become grimmer. The trajectory of gender theory includes engaged texts such as the splendid 2003 UNESCO report *Gender and Education for All.*

The social science of gender is also affected by changes in knowledge-making institutions, notably universities and the state. The last generation has witnessed the dismantling of welfare states in the global North and autonomous development projects in the global South. Both have been replaced by a neoliberal world order based on immense unrestricted flows of capital and goods—and more restricted flows of labor. Universities are increasingly defined as firms competing in a market, subject to managerial control, and desperate to improve their ranking in competitive league tables. States themselves are increasingly managed as rival corporations, shedding unprofitable activities like caring for the poor, and outsourcing to other corporations functions like managing their prisons and their data.

There was a moment when sociology might have allied itself conceptually with the neoliberal order, borrowing the market-based model of the person. But rational-choice theory, which did this, now looks like a blind alley. What managers in the new order want is not ideology but data, lots of it, and the result is a surge of neopositivism in the social sciences. The excited talk about the wonders of "big data" is one sign of this, quantitative modeling in climate-change impact research is another, the focus on competitive test outcomes in educational research is yet another. Sixty years after C. Wright Mills's famous denunciation of abstracted empiricism, the *American Sociological Review* remains No. 1 in the sociological league tables.

This matters for gender analysis, because abstracted empiricism does have a view of gender. I discussed it in *Gender and Power* under the name of "categoricalism." Gender is simply a variable, one among many ways of categorizing people as data points in a population. Usually it's a variable with two possible states: male, coded 1, and female, coded 0—easy to feed into a multivariate analysis. The amount of variance attributable to being 1 or 0 is calculated; age, race, SES, and religion are partialled out; and presto! we have a social science of gender. This may sound like a parody. But in truth whole books, and an impressive number of journal articles and policy documents, have been written using this logic. If little green women from Mars arrived tomorrow to investigate Planet Earth's understanding of gender, this is the main model they would find.

To criticize such impoverished thinking is by no means to reject quantitative methods. Counting carefully provides crucial evidence about gender inequalities and changes over time, and sometimes starkly challenges mainstream ideology. The huge psychological literature of "sex difference" research, more aptly called "sex similarity" research, is a striking example. Surveys and censuses do matter for gender analysis. But they take their place among other powerful research methods, including historical documentation, organizational ethnography, textual studies, life-history work, and analysis of discourse—a number of which are illustrated in this book. Social science works most productively through combined methods.

The Changing Substance of Gender Analysis

The dynamism of social science is well shown by changes in the sociology of gender over the last three decades. Perhaps the most important change is simply the deepening of knowledge across many subfields. To blow a little fanfare for the March of Science, the collective labor of thousands of researchers has constructed knowledge about gender relations and processes on a scale, and with a sophistication, never seen before. This is well shown by the four chapters in part III of this book.

Sexuality was a concern in the Women's Liberation movement, which opposed abortion laws and celebrated women's right to sexual pleasure. Extensive social-science research on sexual practices was driven by the HIV crisis, much of it funded by prevention campaigns. Tensions developed between positivist, ethnographic, and queer perspectives on sexuality, which are still unresolved. At much the same time, feminist activism sparked interest in sexual violence. In her chapter, Stevi Jackson argues for a full-scale sociological approach to sexual desire, object-choice, and practice. Critiques of heteronormativity have left only a shadowy idea of what lies behind the norm. In fact, heterosexuality is a complex and multileveled social reality. I'm convinced Stevi's argument is right; and to the reasons for paying attention, I'd add the social significance of that common consequence of heterosexual conduct, children. More on this, later.

Christine Williams and Megan Tobias Neely bring economic change sharply into focus. Anglophone gender theory in the 1980s presumed economic stability, but the "new economy" has disposed of that. Paradoxes abound: gender inequalities take different trajectories in different social classes; the domestic division of labor remains but the reasons for it change; corporations parade gender diversity but maintain gender hierarchy. Christine and Megan welcome us to the brave new world of neoliberal capitalism.

Though economic justice has always been a goal of feminist activism, the most influential feminist theories in the last generation have had a quite different focus. Poststructuralist thought began to have an impact in the 1980s (Foucault, I notice, scored nine mentions in *Gender and Power*). From the 1990s onward, investigations of gender discourses, gendered subject positions, normativity, gender identity, and gender subversion and deconstruction, multiplied on a grand scale. Some poststructuralist influence is threaded through most of the newer fields of gender sociology.

So powerful was this movement that many students and journalists came to understand "gender" as meaning "mutable gender identity" and not much more. In a recent photograph of a right-wing political demonstration in France, stern-faced demonstrators are carrying a bright red banner reading "NO to the theory of gender!" They are part of an international fundamentalist campaign against the idea of gender fluidity.

But poststructuralism has never been the only approach to culture. Barbara Poggio demonstrates this in her chapter on the world of neoliberal universities, where gender inequalities should not exist, but do. Barbara delicately demolishes the conventional excuses, in favor of a little realism about the gendered character of neoliberal restructuring—the long-hours culture at the top, the precarious workforce at the bottom. She gives a very useful demonstration of how to do a multidimensional structural inventory of gender in the university system—gender equity officers, please copy!

Yvonne Benschop and Marieke van den Brink address gender in the form of organizational power—with a subtle twist. They ask about the politics of *knowledge about* organizational politics. Their study gives a neat explanation of why academics mostly produce articles that lack practical relevance, while corporate consultants produce reports that lack depth and bite. So organizations launch one inclusiveness program after another, which make their CEOs look gravely concerned, but which change nothing of substance. I have seen the same thing happen in an academic organization close to home, which shall remain nameless as I would like to keep my library card.

Social research on gender has thus been deepening in all the areas from which the theorists of the 1980s drew, but it has also been widening into new areas. These include intriguing studies of science, rather grim research on international relations, close-focus ethnographies of gender in schools, startling work on biotechnology, and more. Among the new knowledge projects in this period is social research on masculinities, which has expanded tremendously, gone international, found many practical applications, and diversified in method and theory. We invited some of the researchers who are currently reshaping this field to contribute to this book, and part IV is the result.

Kopano Ratele, starting with the tensions in Nelson Mandela's relationship to his abaThembu heritage, explores the idea of tradition in understandings of masculinity. He makes an important correction to the very common assumption that "traditional masculinity" is fixed, authoritarian, and patriarchal. Kopano shows that traditions, like contemporary masculinities, are plural, and that they are constantly questioned. They are especially problematized when parent-child relations are disrupted, which happens on a mass scale during colonialism and postcolonial transformations. Gul Ozyegin's chapter pursues the problem of change through a beautiful case study of the contradictions in a young man's construction of masculinity in neoliberal Turkey. Gul argues that we need a concept of patriarchy, not as a fixed universal, but as a tool for understanding the new forms of gendered power being created now—and for understanding the troubles encountered by "unpatriarchal desires" for intimacy and recognition.

Tristan Bridges and C. J. Pascoe return us to the global metropole and accounts of changing masculinities there. They show how the structural model of multiple masculinities can be reshaped by rethinking the logic of hegemony, developing an analysis of "hybrid masculinities" out of the multidimensional theory of gender. They show how the mechanisms they call discursive distancing, strategic borrowing, and the fortifying of social boundaries allow the recuperation of gender privilege (and other forms of privilege) despite a fine cultural rhetoric of progress. The argument is painful but convincing.

Through a generation of effort, the promise of women's and gay liberation that a whole new realm of knowledge could be opened up has been fulfilled. But the promise of revolutionary change in society has not. While gender research expanded, so did resistance to reform—from religious fundamentalism, neocon and alt-Right politics to masculinist gun culture and Internet trolling. The neoliberal regime has created new forms of gender inequality, weakened the old forms of social mobilization, and disrupted the public sector institutions through which most gender reforms had been attempted.

In rich countries the politics of gender has taken new forms: feminist NGOs, online activism, corporate inclusiveness programs, and campaigns for human rights. Queer politics has inherited some of the energy of the liberation movements, but follows a different logic: it tries to explode out of the gender order rather than contesting power by mobilizing within it. In changed intellectual, economic, and political circumstances, the framework of social-scientific theory about gender must come into question. The most serious challenge has come from outside the world region where most of the institutional development of gender studies occurred.

Changing the Episteme

Knowledge about gender not only has a politics, it also has a geopolitics; and this geopolitics has a history. Global North predominance in feminism was questioned at the first UN World Conference on Women, in Ciudad México, in 1975, and at all the following conferences. In the 1980s some expatriate feminists sharply criticized Northern feminism's image of "third world women" and feminist aid work that assumed development meant becoming more like the North.

In the United States this critique was at first understood as a critique of racism, parallel to Latina and Black women's critiques of White feminism. This interpretation located the problem within US political and intellectual life, and saw a solution in rejecting racism and adopting multiculturalism, border thinking, or intersectionality. A literature on these themes soon developed, and still continues.

But this was not a complete solution, because the problem was not internal to the global North. Feminist thought, and for that matter gay liberation and queer thought, are embedded in a global economy of knowledge. A worldwide division of labor treats the global periphery as a vast data mine, while the global metropole produces and imports information, processes it in institutions such as research universities, and exports the result in the form of sciences, technologies, and trained professionals. In this economy of knowledge the metropole is the privileged site of theory. There is a structural reason why Simone de Beauvoir, Christine Delphy, Michel Foucault, Joan Scott, Judith Butler, and friends are read all over the world, and concepts created out of Northern experience or needs, even very confused ones like "LGBT," are adopted globally.

It is deeply important, then, to recognize that the colonized and postcolonial world *does* produce theory—concepts, methods, interpretations—and does so from a social experience different from that of the metropole. Since colonization was a strongly gendered process, and colonial power remade gender orders in drastic and often violent ways (mass rape, seizing of land, forced migration, missionary control of culture), the intellectual response to colonialism includes many analyses of gender. Southern feminism has as long a history as Northern feminism. Its analyses will be closer to the experience of the majority of the world's population.

There is, now, increasing pressure to decolonize social science and gender studies. This book has contributors from six continents, and part II concerns how to understand gender dynamics in a postimperial world. Raka Ray directly addresses the problem, noting how mainstream gender theory (*Gender and Power* included) failed to recognize the relations between metropole and periphery, and so was limited by an inadequate framework for knowledge. She is right, and is able to show the long-term effects of imperial and colonial history—such as patriarchal policing of the gender order as an assertion of postcolonial difference. Raka is optimistic that gender analysis can change, and her account of the contrasting lives of Gauri and Jagdish provides a vivid illustration of how it can be done.

So does Mara Viveros Vigoya's account of social struggles in Colombia, and the way revolutionary strategies in Latin America were obliged to confront difference. Mara's narrative of the development of feminism in the region will be of interest on other continents, but I would urge readers to pay particular attention to her discussion of the political trajectories of indigenous women and Black women in Colombia. This is a striking demonstration of the way solidarity among women is shaped, not by an abstract category of "race," but by the specific, deeply embedded racial dynamics of colonization and the social violence of postcolonial regimes and economies.

The main way Anglophone feminist sociology has addressed race is by taking up the model of intersectionality, the subject of Joya Misra's chapter. I have been skeptical of this concept as an updated categoricalism, a static cross-classification of "race, class, and gender." Joya shows that there are multiple types of intersectional research, and that the approach does give a grip on questions of power and social change. Gender theory needs a concern with social justice, and this is a contemporary way of doing it.

Northern feminist thought in the last generation went far into the terrain of discourse, identity, and representation; feminism in the colonial and postcolonial South has been grittier. Confronting realities that include mass poverty, epidemics, population struggles, rapid urbanization, coercive labor systems, state violence, and femicide, Southern feminist movements have been obliged to think about embodiment on a society-wide scale. That includes issues about sexual reproduction. An important current of thought in Africa and the African diaspora has emphasized lines of descent, seniority, and motherhood in thinking about women's status. Questions can be raised about some of these formulations, but they do underline the point that conception, birth, and childrearing really matter for understanding gender.

Let me make a large claim. In an ontological sense, gender is the way human reproductive bodies enter history, and the way social process, unfolding through time, deals with biological continuity. To say this is not to fall into biological determinism; gender is a *social* process, a dynamic of change quite different from biological evolution. Nor is it to fall into heteronormativity; biological continuity on a societal scale in no sense requires that all women should be married mothers nor all men respectable fathers with mortgages and lawnmowers. Humans have an enormous range of possibilities in relationship and pleasure. What our biological continuity does require, above all, is social arrangements for child care. Children and history are the crux of gender analysis. When states bomb children, economies starve them, adults infect them, or power holders stunt their education, we can legitimately fear for the long-term future of humanity.

Ethnomethodology and poststructuralism made us familiar with the idea that gender is performative, brought into existence as people act in ways accountable in terms of gender norms. But the concept of performativity is one of citation and repetition, not creation; it contains no dynamic of change. Gender theory needs the dimension of history. It needs to understand the downstream, the *consequences* of gender-being-brought-into-existence.

Beyond the concept of performativity, then, we need theories that recognize the ontoformativity of gender—the way gender practices bring social reality into existence though time, transforming their starting-points in the historical process that we call society. The postcolonial research in this book is only one demonstration of this fundamental feature of gender. Life-history research, studies of institutional change, studies of social movements, and studies of violence and its effects provide others. They all require us to think about the future being brought into existence now.

Questions for the Near Future

Our revels are not ended. The real pageant of the world goes on; and if theory is to be more than a cloud-capped vision melting into thin air, it must help us to see paths forward.

Where sociological gender analysis and strategies for gender justice should be heading now is the question we all want answered. The chapters in part V address this question most directly. Barbara Risman, Kristen Myers, and Ray Sin argue that the turn to identity and performance in gender theory needs to be balanced with a return to structure. Otherwise we arrive at an individual-choice view of gender, which suits neoliberalism, and curiously produces a new essentialism—as illustrated by the trans/cis binary that has regrettably become popular in recent transgender activism.

Judith Lorber takes up the theme of the multiplication of gender identity categories, and similarly argues that this does not challenge structural inequalities. It does not even demolish the masculine-feminine polarity that persists in most such identities. Judith argues, as she long has, for degendering practices in everyday life as the reliable way to move toward the abolition of gender. Another strategy for degendering is suggested in Mimi Schippers's chapter on monogamy and polyamory. Mimi argues that gender analysis has paid too little attention to the monogamous couple as a hegemonic social form, which embeds an image of gender polarity. This hegemony can be deconstructed conceptually by intersectional research, and is contested practically by subcultures of polyamory, which experiment in new patterns of relationship.

I think it is illuminating to relate these ideas to the strategies of change examined earlier in the book: for instance, the grassroots movements considered by Mara Viveros Vigoya, the projects of personal change documented by Gul Ozyegin and Raka Ray, or the organizational change agendas explored by Yvonne Benschop and Marieke van den Brink.

Indeed, most of the chapters in this book have implications for strategies of change. It was something I tried to address in the final seven pages of *Gender and Power*—which, I will confess now that it can do no harm, were modeled on a memorable passage by John Maynard Keynes. I learnt then how difficult the job of strategist was, but how necessary. It still is. Before I breake my staffe and drowne my booke, deeper then did ever Plummet sound, I will add my thoughts about the future of gender theory as a project of change.

Much of the debate on strategy has concerned new forms of struggle and new agencies of change. Gender politics has mutated in the last generation, as it has before. For me, a poignant moment was the recent ending of the annual International Women's Day march through central Sydney. Instead of marching, we were invited to purchase a corporate table at a fundraising event run by an NGO. Sydney's Gay and Lesbian Mardi Gras parade still attracts very big crowds. But the arrests of gay activists at the first Sydney Mardi Gras are a distant memory; police now march *in* the parade, and the public is entertained rather than challenged. In Australia, a certain kind of embodied mobilization has lost its grip.

It seems that models of gender politics that anticipated a direct confrontation of broad social forces are not very helpful. That seems to be confirmed by studies in this book. Yet struggle goes on—*lotta continua*—and that also is shown in this book. In our Twitter and Facebook feeds we hear of strikes for equal pay, court cases over harassment, sexist trolling, elections won and lost, femicide, wars, attempts to destroy abortion rights (yet again!), campaigns for marriage equality, closure of gender studies programs, censorship, laws against transgender access to toilets (good grief!), police action against burqinis (good grief, in spades!), and more.

It's easier now to see gender and sexual politics in terms of multiple projects, both emancipatory and repressive, that often interweave and often go down separate tracks. Even concepts like "diversity" and "intersectionality" seem too limited for this. Postmodern incoherence? Chaos theory? Yet I can't help thinking it's the business of theory to find intelligible connections between diverse realities. As long as the Twitter feed includes equal pay struggles, femicide, and political homophobia, the concept of enduring structure, complex structure, in gender relations still has value—and this book shows ways it can be developed.

We urgently need to understand the new geographies of gender relations. That's not just a metaphor for social relations on the Web, or in sexual life. The creation of a world neoliberal economy with its constant movement of goods and capital has literally reshaped the geography of global power, and posed major problems for social theory.

The coloniality of power has continued, and global privilege still attaches to the metropole—Western Europe and North America—in the twenty-first century. But the institutions delivering that privilege have mutated, with the decline of state-centered imperial economies and the rise of transnational corporations. With the financialization of corporate structures and the weird merging of masculinized corporate management with computer systems, the global metropole-apparatus with its strongly marked gender order is moving gradually offshore, connecting up the accumulation processes around the world. Major wealth has moved into transnational spaces of a historically new kind—touching ground from time to time at Davos. To understand the pinnacles of social power we have to look in new places that do not even look like places, such as the intranets of transnational corporations.

The neoliberal economy and state system place more restrictions on the movement of labor than on movement of money and goods, but there are still huge migrations of people going on. There are rural-to-urban tides, the long-distance travel of domestic and oil workers, and the refugee flows creating so much political turbulence now. These movements are gendered and are reshaping gender orders continuously. Indeed, they call into question the paradigm of a singular gender order in a particular nation-state or region. We need new theoretical models for these transformations too.

States have always been important in gender politics; the rethinking of global change needs to pay attention to the international state. The United Nations has had a Commission on the Status of Women since 1947—an important legacy from an earlier generation of feminists. A number of UN agencies make interventions on gender and sexuality: UNESCO, WHO, UNAIDS, the organizations now grouped as UN Women, even the World Bank. The World Conferences on Women were a highlight of international policymaking for gender equality. But they ended with the Beijing Conference in 1995; in the following years more member governments turned against gender reform. As shown in sexual abuse by peacekeeping forces, and the role of the World Bank and the International Monetary Fund in structural adjustment, UN activities are not always on the side of sweetness and light.

New social actors have appeared, such as indigenous women's movements and men's groups campaigning against gender-based violence. Such actors appear in transnational spaces. DAWN, a well-known feminist network in development politics, dates from the 1980s. The MenEngage Alliance of NGOs, which currently has 600–700 member organizations, dates from 2004. The International Sociological Association has a research committee (RC 32) for Women in Society that circulates information and organizes conference sessions—please join!

Maintaining international connection is now easier through the Internet, skewed as the Internet is in social terms. Feminist and gay rights groups have created a considerable online presence; so have their opponents. Even the idea of a "social actor" with collective purposes comes into question, when we think of the complicated dispersal of ideas through electronic as well as flesh-and-blood pathways. There is great scope for bold theoretical work informing new forms of activism.

The social science of gender has come a long way in a short time. Theory will keep changing, as intellectuals and activists grapple with these new realities and use new tools. I can't predict what the long-term direction will be, though I've tried to point in some promising directions. Making knowledge is a complex, worldwide social process, which is far from automatic. Its trajectory is, as the statisticians say, nonmonotonic; it goes in surges and troughs. We make errors as well as breakthroughs; we can learn from both.

In this book we have reflected on major issues in building social-scientific theory about gender in the conditions we live in now. We believe that social theory is a powerful resource for social action—but only if it is constantly regenerated by debate, empirical research, and new construction. That's what books like this are for. We hope the thinking here provides good starting points for the coming surge of research and activism.

ABOUT THE CONTRIBUTORS

Yvonne Benschop is Professor of Organizational Behavior at the Institute for Management Research at Radboud University, the Netherlands. Inspired by feminist organization studies and critical management studies, she studies informal organization processes that produce gender inequalities and the ways to change these processes and inequalities. She is co-editor in chief of *Organization*.

Tristan Bridges is Assistant Professor of Sociology at the University of California at Santa Barbara. His research addresses contemporary transformations in masculinity and gender and sexual inequality. He has studied these dynamics among bodybuilders, bar regulars, profeminist men, fathers' rights activists, and couples with "man caves" in their homes. With C. J. Pascoe, Bridges co-edited *Exploring Masculinities: Identity, Inequality, Continuity, and Change.*

Raewyn Connell is a sociologist, now Professor Emerita at the University of Sydney and Life Member of the National Tertiary Education Union. Her books include *Southern Theory* and *Gender: In World Perspective.* She has worked for labor, peace, and women's movements, and for democracy in education.

Myra Marx Ferree is Alice H. Cook Professor of Sociology at the University of Wisconsin–Madison where she also serves as Joint Governance Professor of Gender and Women's Studies. Her work is focused on gender politics in families, organizations, and social movements. Her most recent book is *Varieties of Feminism: German Gender Politics in Global Perspective.*

Stevi Jackson is Professor of Women's Studies and Sociology at the University of York, UK. Her long-term research interests are in the fields of feminist theory, sexuality, and family and intimate relationships. She has authored or edited several books, including *East Asian Sexualities*, with Jieyu Liu and Juyhun Woo, and *Theorizing Sexuality*, with Sue Scott.

Judith Lorber is Professor Emerita of Sociology and Women's Studies at the Graduate Center and Brooklyn College of the City University of New York. She is the author of numerous publications on gender, including *Breaking the Bowls: Degendering and Feminist Change, Gender Inequality: Feminist Theories and Politics*, and *Paradoxes of Gender*. She was the founding editor of *Gender & Society*, official publication of Sociologists for Women in Society.

Patricia Yancey Martin is Professor Emerita of Sociology at Florida State University. Her interests are gender as practice, mobilizing masculinity/ies, feminist bureaucracies, and rape/sexual assault on college campuses. Publications include *Handbook of Gender, Work and Organization, Rape Work: Victims, Gender, and Emotions in Organizations and Community Context*, and *Feminist Organizations: Harvest of the New Women's Movement*.

James W. Messerschmidt is Professor of Sociology/Criminology at the University of Southern Maine. His research has covered such diverse areas as gender and crime/violence, genderqueers, intersectionality, and global political masculinities. Messerschmidt is the author of a number of books, including *Gender, Heterosexuality, and Youth Violence: The Struggle for Recognition*, and, most recently, *Masculinities in the Making: From the Local to the Global*.

Michael A. Messner is Professor of Sociology and Gender Studies at the University of Southern California. His research focuses on gender and sport, men and feminism, and war veterans' peace activism. Messner is the author of several books, most recently *Some Men: Feminist Allies and the Movement to End Violence against Women*, with Max Greenberg and Tal Peretz.

Joya Misra is Professor of Sociology and Public Policy at the University of Massachusetts, Amherst. Her recent research focuses primarily on labor market inequalities by race, gender, nationality, citizenship, education, and parenthood status. She has published dozens of articles in many of the top journals in sociology and is a former editor of *Gender & Society*.

Kristen Myers is Professor of Sociology and the Director of the Center for the Study of Women, Gender, & Sexuality at Northern Illinois University. She studies gender and heteronormativity among preadolescent children, breadwinning ideals in neotraditional families, and strategies for undoing gender.

Megan Tobias Neely is a doctoral candidate in the Department of Sociology at the University of Texas at Austin. Her research focuses on gender, race, and class inequality in the workplaces of political and economic elites.

Gul Ozyegin is Margaret L. Hamilton Professor of Sociology and Gender, Sexuality, and Women's Studies at the College of William and Mary. Her most recent books are *New Desires, New Selves: Sex, Love, and Piety among Turkish Youth* and *Gender and Sexuality in Muslim Cultures* (ed.). Her current research is on intersections of gender, generation, and (un)belonging among different generations of Turks in Germany.

C. J. Pascoe is Associate Professor of Sociology at the University of Oregon. Her research focuses on youth, masculinity, sexuality, and new media. The author of several books, Pascoe recently co-edited *Exploring Masculinities: Identity, Inequality, Continuity and Change* with Tristan Bridges.

Barbara Poggio is Vice Rector for Equality and Diversity at the University of Trento (Italy), where she coordinates the Center for Interdisciplinary Gender Studies. Her research interests include the social construction of gender in organizations, gender and science, and gender and entrepreneurship. She is the author of several articles and books, among them *Gendertelling in Organizations: Narratives from Male-Dominated Environments*.

Kopano Ratele is Professor at the University of South Africa (Unisa) and researcher at the South African Medical Research Council—Unisa's

Violence, Injury and Peace Research Unit. Ratele's research, teaching, social-political activism, and community mobilization focuses on the overlaps among violence, tradition, class, sexuality, race, and gender. His books include *There Was This Goat*, with Antjie Krog and Nosisi Mpolweni, and *Liberating Masculinities*.

Raka Ray is Professor of Sociology and South and Southeast Asia Studies at the University of California, Berkeley. Her areas of specialization are gender and feminist theory, postcolonial sociology, inequality, and the emerging middle classes. Publications include *Fields of Protest: Women's Movements in India, Cultures of Servitude: Modernity, Domesticity and Class in India* (with Seemin Qayum), and *The Handbook of Gender*.

Barbara J. Risman is Professor of Sociology at the University of Illinois at Chicago. Her writing has focused on developing a theory of gender as a social structure. Risman is President of the Board of Directors of the Council on Contemporary Families, a nonprofit whose mission is to bring social science research and clinical expertise to public conversation. She is the author of several books, most recently *Where Will the Millennials Take Us: Transforming the Gender Structure?*

Kristen Schilt is Associate Professor of Sociology at the University of Chicago. Her work focuses on the cultural processes that maintain gender and sexual inequalities. She is the author of *Just One of the Guys? Transgender Men and the Persistence of Gender Inequality*.

Mimi Schippers is Associate Professor of Sociology and Gender and Sexuality Studies at Tulane University. Her research focuses on the intersections of gender, sexuality, and race as they take shape in cultural practices and representations. She is author of *Beyond Monogamy: Polyamory and the Future of Polyqueer Sexualities* and *Rockin' Out of the Box: Gender Maneuvering in Alternative Hard Rock*.

Ray Sin straddles academia and industry. At Morningstar, Inc., he is an associate behavioral researcher who leverages big data and randomly controlled trials to better understand investing behavior. And he is a PhD candidate in Sociology at the University of Illinois at Chicago.

Marieke van den Brink is Professor of Gender and Diversity at the Radboud Institute for Social and Cultural Research, the Netherlands. Her research focuses on ways gender and other inequalities are produced and countered in organizations, especially in recruitment and selection. She is a member of the Young Academy of the Royal Academy of Arts and Sciences.

Mara Viveros Vigoya is Professor of Sociology and Gender Studies at the Universidad Nacional de Colombia. Her research focuses on the relationship between social differences and inequalities, and the intersections of gender, sexuality, class, race, and ethnicity in the social dynamics of Latin American societies. Viveros Vigoya is the author and co-author of several books.

Christine L. Williams is Professor of Sociology and the Elsie and Stanley E. Adams, Sr. Centennial Professor in Liberal Arts at the University of Texas at Austin, where she conducts research on gender discrimination and sexual harassment in a wide variety of workplace settings. Her publications include *Inside Toyland: Working, Shopping, and Social Inequality*.

INDEX

Acker, Joan, 196

action research, 205

Afghanistan, 80–81, 86–87

Africa, 211, 216. *See also* Côte d'Ivoire; Mozambique; Nigeria; South Africa

African masculinities, 218

African American: intersectionality and Black feminism/African American women, 17, 19, 25, 114, 122, 250; masculinity and, 120, 271, 320; sexual stereotypes, 319–320

Afro-Colombian women, politics and rights of, 99–105

agency. *See* structure/structures

agender identity, 283, 288, 297

Agnes (case study), 61

Altman, Dennis, 60, 68

Anzaldua, Gloria, 19, 300

apartheid, 137, 218, 226–227

Appadurai, Arjun, 84

Arroyo, Leyla Andrea, 100

Arxer, Steven, 265

aspiration, gendering of, 84–85, 87

Australia: Australian feminism, 2, 16, 19; context for *Gender and Power*, 2, 74, 156–157; gender identity, legal dimensions of, 297; global position of, 21; social movements and, 343–344; transgender and, 65; women and leadership in, 157, 201

Barber, Kristen, 48

Barnes, Riché J. Daniel, 119, 123

bathrooms, 298, 300, 303–304

Bauer, Robin, 317

Beachy, Robert, 305

Beasley, Christine, 35

Becker, Howard, 59

Beijing World Conference on Women, 18, 22, 93, 345

Bem, Sandra, 278, 290

Benschop, Yvonne, 8, 132, 338, 343

Bhambra, Gurminder, 76

bias training. *See* organizations

Billings, Dwight, 60

binary. *See* categories; gender binary

biological determinism: gender binary and, 305; gender identity and, 285, 287, 289–290; homosexuality and, 285, 287; monogamy and evolution, 318–319; reproduction of gender inequality and, 57, 65–66; persistence of, 333; political efficacy of, 285, 305; sex role theory in relation to, 57, 333; social embodiment as alternative to, 57; transgender and, 285, 287; women and, 305

Bird, Sharon R., 265

bodies. *See* embodiment

Bologna Declaration, 178

borderlands, 300–301

Bourdieu, Pierre, 16, 77

breadwinner, male, 85, 179

Bridges, Tristan, 7, 48–50, 212, 265, 338–339

Britain. *See* United Kingdom

bro, the, 255, 261, 268

Burchard, Ernst, 283

Bush, George W., 46

butch women. *See* women

Butler, Judith, 21, 118, 146, 340